'With *Mobility, Modernity and the Slum*, Tzanelli proves once again to be a compelling guide through the world of cinematic tourism, offering readers a richly detailed analysis of *Slumdog Millionaire* that draws our gaze beyond the screen to reveal the complex web of artistic communities, culture and heritage industries, transnational tourism, and charitable activism that surrounds the film. Brimming with theoretical insights and perceptive analyses, this stimulating book will transform the way we understand global circulations of film, art, and volunteer tourism.'

Associate Professor Jennie Germann Molz, *Sociology and Anthropology Department, College of the Holy Cross, USA*

'In this book, insightful research meets meticulous interpretation. Bringing together social theory and cinema, Tzanelli's is an extraordinarily masterful contribution to the understanding of contemporary world society.'

Dr Bulent Diken, *Department of Sociology, Lancaster University, UK*

Mobility, Modernity and the Slum

Only virtuous humans are supposed to move in time to meet their happy destiny or karma. The tale of Jamal in *Slumdog Millionaire* is such a case of serendipitous mobility towards riches and love – a 'journey' in which good heroes and urban communities respecting solidarity are successfully modernised. Unsurprisingly, the film became tangled in many controversies around India's destiny in the world: the film inserted Mumbai into various financial, political and artistic scenes, increased tourism in its filmed slums, and brought about charity projects in which celebrities and tourist businesses were involved. *Slumdog Millionaire* served as a global example of a 'developing' country's uneven but unique modernisation.

This book examines such mobilities of ideas, art, tourism and activism together. In doing so, it reveals the significance of Mumbai as a post-colonial city in discussions of modernity – a form of mobile adaptation to new world realities. Tzanelli examines the various agents involved in controversies through multiple virtual and real journeys to India's colonial history and present social complexity, with a view to actualise a post-colonial future, a 'destiny' as the country's serendipitous destination.

Addressed to interdisciplinary audiences, the book will be a useful text for students and scholars of globalisation, mobility, tourism, media and social movement theory.

Rodanthi Tzanelli is Associate Professor of Cultural Sociology at the University of Leeds, UK.

Routledge Advances in Sociology

1 **Virtual Globalization**
Virtual spaces/tourist spaces
Edited by David Holmes

2 **The Criminal Spectre in Law, Literature and Aesthetics**
Peter Hutchings

3 **Immigrants and National Identity in Europe**
Anna Triandafyllidou

4 **Constructing Risk and Safety in Technological Practice**
Edited by Jane Summerton and Boel Berner

5 **Europeanisation, National Identities and Migration**
Changes in boundary constructions between Western and Eastern Europe
Willfried Spohn and Anna Triandafyllidou

6 **Language, Identity and Conflict**
A comparative study of language in ethnic conflict in Europe and Eurasia
Diarmait Mac Giolla Chríost

7 **Immigrant Life in the U.S.**
Multi-disciplinary perspectives
Edited by Donna R. Gabaccia and Colin Wayne Leach

8 **Rave Culture and Religion**
Edited by Graham St. John

9 **Creation and Returns of Social Capital**
A new research program
Edited by Henk Flap and Beate Völker

10 **Self-Care**
Embodiment, personal autonomy and the shaping of health consciousness
Christopher Ziguras

11 **Mechanisms of Cooperation**
Werner Raub and Jeroen Weesie

12 **After the Bell**
Educational success, public policy and family background
Edited by Dalton Conley and Karen Albright

13 **Youth Crime and Youth Culture in the Inner City**
Bill Sanders

14 **Emotions and Social Movements**
Edited by Helena Flam and Debra King

15 **Globalization, Uncertainty and Youth in Society**
Edited by Hans-Peter Blossfeld, Erik Klijzing, Melinda Mills and Karin Kurz

16 **Love, Heterosexuality and Society**
Paul Johnson

17 **Agricultural Governance**
Globalization and the new politics of regulation
Edited by Vaughan Higgins and Geoffrey Lawrence

18 **Challenging Hegemonic Masculinity**
Richard Howson

19 **Social Isolation in Modern Society**
Roelof Hortulanus, Anja Machielse and Ludwien Meeuwesen

20 **Weber and the Persistence of Religion**
Social theory, capitalism and the sublime
Joseph W. H. Lough

21 **Globalization, Uncertainty and Late Careers in Society**
Edited by Hans-Peter Blossfeld, Sandra Buchholz and Dirk Hofäcker

22 **Bourdieu's Politics**
Problems and possibilities
Jeremy F. Lane

23 **Media Bias in Reporting Social Research?**
The case of reviewing ethnic inequalities in education
Martyn Hammersley

24 **A General Theory of Emotions and Social Life**
Warren D. TenHouten

25 **Sociology, Religion and Grace**
Arpad Szakolczai

26 **Youth Cultures**
Scenes, subcultures and tribes
Edited by Paul Hodkinson and Wolfgang Deicke

27 **The Obituary as Collective Memory**
Bridget Fowler

28 **Tocqueville's Virus**
Utopia and dystopia in Western social and political thought
Mark Featherstone

29 **Jewish Eating and Identity Through the Ages**
David Kraemer

30 **The Institutionalization of Social Welfare**
A study of medicalizing management
Mikael Holmqvist

31 **The Role of Religion in Modern Societies**
Edited by Detlef Pollack and Daniel V. A. Olson

32 **Sex Research and Sex Therapy**
A sociological analysis of Masters and Johnson
Ross Morrow

33 **A Crisis of Waste?**
Understanding the rubbish society
Martin O'Brien

34 **Globalization and Transformations of Local Socioeconomic Practices**
Edited by Ulrike Schuerkens

35 **The Culture of Welfare Markets**
The international recasting of pension and care systems
Ingo Bode

36 **Cohabitation, Family and Society**
Tiziana Nazio

37 **Latin America and Contemporary Modernity**
A sociological interpretation
José Maurízio Domingues

38 **Exploring the Networked Worlds of Popular Music**
Milieu cultures
Peter Webb

39 **The Cultural Significance of the Child Star**
Jane O'Connor

40 **European Integration as an Elite Process**
The failure of a dream?
Max Haller

41 **Queer Political Performance and Protest**
Benjamin Shepard

42 **Cosmopolitan Spaces**
Europe, globalization, theory
Chris Rumford

43 **Contexts of Social Capital**
Social networks in communities, markets and organizations
Edited by Ray-May Hsung, Nan Lin, and Ronald Breiger

44 **Feminism, Domesticity and Popular Culture**
Edited by Stacy Gillis and Joanne Hollows

45 **Changing Relationships**
Edited by Malcolm Brynin and John Ermisch

46 **Formal and Informal Work**
The hidden work regime in Europe
Edited by Birgit Pfau-Effinger, Lluis Flaquer, & Per H. Jensen

47 **Interpreting Human Rights**
Social science perspectives
Edited by Rhiannon Morgan and Bryan S. Turner

48 **Club Cultures**
Boundaries, identities and otherness
Silvia Rief

49 **Eastern European Immigrant Families**
Mihaela Robila

50 **People and Societies**
Rom Harré and designing the social sciences
Luk van Langenhove

51 **Legislating Creativity**
The intersections of art and politics
Dustin Kidd

52 **Youth in Contemporary Europe**
Edited by Jeremy Leaman and Martha Wörsching

53 **Globalization and Transformations of Social Inequality**
Edited by Ulrike Schuerkens

54 **Twentieth Century Music and the Question of Modernity**
Eduardo De La Fuente

55 **The American Surfer**
Radical culture and capitalism
Kristin Lawler

56 **Religion and Social Problems**
Edited by Titus Hjelm

57 **Play, Creativity, and Social Movements**
If I can't dance, it's not my revolution
Benjamin Shepard

58 **Undocumented Workers' Transitions**
Legal status, migration, and work in Europe
Sonia McKay, Eugenia Markova and Anna Paraskevopoulou

59 **The Marketing of War in the Age of Neo-Militarism**
Edited by Kostas Gouliamos and Christos Kassimeris

60 **Neoliberalism and the Global Restructuring of Knowledge and Education**
Steven C. Ward

61 **Social Theory in Contemporary Asia**
Ann Brooks

62 **Foundations of Critical Media and Information Studies**
Christian Fuchs

63 **A Companion to Life Course Studies**
The social and historical context of the British birth cohort studies
Michael Wadsworth and John Bynner

64 **Understanding Russianness**
Risto Alapuro, Arto Mustajoki and Pekka Pesonen

65 **Understanding Religious Ritual**
Theoretical approaches and innovations
John Hoffmann

66 **Online Gaming in Context**
The social and cultural significance of online games
Garry Crawford, Victoria K. Gosling and Ben Light

67 **Contested Citizenship in East Asia**
Developmental politics, national unity, and globalization
Kyung-Sup Chang and Bryan S. Turner

68 **Agency without Actors?**
New approaches to collective action
Edited by Jan-Hendrik Passoth, Birgit Peuker and Michael Schillmeier

69 **The Neighborhood in the Internet**
Design research projects in community informatics
John M. Carroll

70 **Managing Overflow in Affluent Societies**
Edited by Barbara Czarniawska and Orvar Löfgren

71 **Refugee Women**
Beyond gender versus culture
Leah Bassel

72 **Socioeconomic Outcomes of the Global Financial Crisis**
Theoretical discussion and empirical case studies
Edited by Ulrike Schuerkens

73 **Migration in the 21st Century**
Political economy and ethnography
Edited by Pauline Gardiner Barber and Winnie Lem

74 **Ulrich Beck**
An introduction to the theory of second modernity and the risk society
Mads P. Sørensen and Allan Christiansen

75 **The International Recording Industries**
Edited by Lee Marshall

76 **Ethnographic Research in the Construction Industry**
Edited by Sarah Pink, Dylan Tutt and Andrew Dainty

77 **Routledge Companion to Contemporary Japanese Social Theory**
From individualization to globalization in Japan today
Edited by Anthony Elliott, Masataka Katagiri and Atsushi Sawai

78 **Immigrant Adaptation in Multi-Ethnic Societies**
Canada, Taiwan, and the United States
Edited by Eric Fong, Lan-Hung Nora Chiang and Nancy Denton

79 **Cultural Capital, Identity, and Social Mobility**
The life course of working-class university graduates
Mick Matthys

80 **Speaking for Animals**
Animal autobiographical writing
Edited by Margo DeMello

81 **Healthy Aging in Sociocultural Context**
Edited by Andrew E. Scharlach and Kazumi Hoshino

82 **Touring Poverty**
Bianca Freire-Medeiros

83 **Life Course Perspectives on Military Service**
Edited by Janet M. Wilmoth and Andrew S. London

84 Innovation in Socio-Cultural Context
Edited by Frane Adam and Hans Westlund

85 Youth, Arts and Education
Reassembling subjectivity through affect
Anna Hickey-Moody

86 The Capitalist Personality
Face-to-face sociality and economic change in the post-communist World
Christopher S. Swader

87 The Culture of Enterprise in Neoliberalism
Specters of entrepreneurship
Tomas Marttila

88 Islamophobia in the West
Measuring and explaining individual attitudes
Marc Helbling

89 The Challenges of Being a Rural Gay Man
Coping with stigma
Deborah Bray Preston and Anthony R. D'Augelli

90 Global Justice Activism and Policy Reform in Europe
Understanding when change happens
Edited by Peter Utting, Mario Pianta and Anne Ellersiek

91 Sociology of the Visual Sphere
Edited by Regev Nathansohn and Dennis Zuev

92 Solidarity in Individualized Societies
Recognition, justice and good judgement
Søren Juul

93 Heritage in the Digital Era
Cinematic tourism and the activist cause
Rodanthi Tzanelli

94 Generation, Discourse, and Social Change
Karen R. Foster

95 Sustainable Practices
Social theory and climate change
Elizabeth Shove and Nicola Spurling

96 The Transformative Capacity of New Technologies
A theory of sociotechnical change
Ulrich Dolata

97 Consuming Families
Buying, making, producing family life in the 21st century
Jo Lindsay and JaneMaree Maher

98 Migrant Marginality
A transnational perspective
Edited by Philip Kretsedemas, Jorge Capetillo-Ponce and Glenn Jacobs

99 Changing Gay Male Identities
Andrew Cooper

100 Perspectives on Genetic Discrimination
Thomas Lemke

101 **Social Sustainability**
A multilevel approach to social inclusion
Edited by Veronica Dujon, Jesse Dillard, and Eileen M. Brennan

102 **Capitalism**
A companion to marx's economy critique
Johan Fornäs

103 **Understanding European Movements**
New social movements, global justice struggles, anti-austerity protest
Edited by Cristina Flesher Fominaya and Laurence Cox

104 **Applying Ibn Khaldūn**
The recovery of a lost tradition in sociology
Syed Farid Alatas

105 **Children in Crisis**
Ethnographic studies in international contexts
Edited by Manata Hashemi and Martín Sánchez-Jankowski

106 **The Digital Divide**
The internet and social inequality in international perspective
Edited by Massimo Ragnedda and Glenn W. Muschert

107 **Emotion and Social Structures**
The affective foundations of social order
Christian von Scheve

108 **Social Capital and Its Institutional Contingency**
A study of the United States, China and Taiwan
Edited by Nan Lin, Yang-chih Fu and Chih-jou Jay Chen

109 **The Longings and Limits of Global Citizenship Education**
The moral pedagogy of schooling in a cosmopolitan age
Jeffrey S. Dill

110 **Irish Insanity 1800–2000**
Damien Brennan

111 **Cities of Culture**
A global perspective
Deborah Stevenson

112 **Racism, Governance, and Public Policy**
Beyond human rights
Katy Sian, Ian Law and S. Sayyid

113 **Understanding Aging and Diversity**
Theories and concepts
Patricia Kolb

114 **Hybrid Media Culture**
Sensing place in a world of flows
Edited by Simon Lindgren

115 **Centers and Peripheries in Knowledge Production**
Leandro Rodriguez Medina

116 **Revisiting Institutionalism in Sociology**
Putting the "institution" back in institutional analysis
Seth Abrutyn

117 **National Policy-Making**
Domestication of
global trends
Pertti Alasuutari and Ali Qadir

118 **The Meanings of Europe**
Changes and exchanges of a
contested concept
*Edited by Claudia Wiesner and
Meike Schmidt-Gleim*

119 **Between Islam and the
American Dream**
An immigrant Muslim
community in post-9/11
America
Yuting Wang

120 **Call Centers and the Global
Division of Labor**
A political economy of
post-industrial employment
and union organizing
Andrew J.R. Stevens

121 **Academic Capitalism**
Universities in the global
struggle for excellence
Richard Münch

122 **Deconstructing Flexicurity
and Developing Alternative
Approaches**
Towards new concepts and
approaches for employment
and social policy
*Edited by Maarten Keune and
Amparo Serrano*

123 **From Corporate to Social Media**
Critical perspectives on
corporate social responsibility
in media and communication
industries
Marisol Sandoval

124 **Vision and Society**
Towards a sociology and
anthropology from art
John Clammer

125 **The Rise of Critical Animal
Studies**
From the margins to
the centre
Nik Taylor and Richard Twine

126 **Atoms, Bytes and Genes**
Public resistance and
techno-scientific responses
Martin W. Bauer

127 **Punk Rock and the Politics
of Place**
Building a better tomorrow
Jeffrey S. Debies-Carl

128 **Bourdieu's Theory of
Social Fields**
Concepts and applications
*Mathieu Hilgers and
Eric Mangez*

129 **Global Management, Local
Resistances**
Theoretical discussion and
empirical case studies
Edited by Ulrike Schuerkens

130 **Migrant Professionals in
the City**
Local encounters, identities
and inequalities
Edited by Lars Meier

131 **From Globalization to
World Society**
Neo-institutional and systems-
theoretical perspectives
*Edited by Boris Holzer, Fatima
Kastner and Tobias Werron*

132 **Political Inequality in an Age of Democracy**
Cross-national perspectives
Joshua Kjerulf Dubrow

133 **Social Networks and Music Worlds**
Edited by Nick Crossley, Siobhan McAndrew and Paul Widdop

134 **Gender Roles in Ireland**
Three decades of attitude change
Margret Fine-Davis

135 **(Sub) Urban Sexscapes**
Geographies and regulation of the sex industry
Edited by Paul Maginn and Christine Steinmetz

136 **Advances in Biographical Methods**
Creative applications
Edited by Maggie O'Neill, Brian Roberts and Andrew Sparkes

137 **Social Cohesion and Immigration in Europe and North America**
Mechanisms, conditions and causality
Edited by Ruud Koopmans, Bram Lancee and Merlin Schaeffer

138 **Digital Publics**
Cultural political economy, financialization and creative organizational politics
John Michael Roberts

139 **Ideology and the Fight Against Human Trafficking**
Reyhan Atasü-Topcuoğlu

140 **Rethinking Serial Murder, Spree Killing, and Atrocities**
Beyond the usual distinctions
Robert Shanafelt and Nathan W. Pino

141 **The Re-Use of Urban Ruins**
Atmospheric inquiries of the city
Hanna Katharina Göbel

142 **Reproductive Tourism in the United States**
Creating family in the mother country
Lauren Jade Martin

143 **The Bohemian Ethos**
Questioning work and making a scene on the Lower East Side
Judith R. Halasz

144 **Critical Theory and Social Media**
Between emancipation and commodification
Thomas Allmer

145 **Socio-Cultural Mobility and Mega-Events**
Ethics and aesthetics in Brazil's 2014 World Cup
Rodanthi Tzanelli

146 **Seeing Religion**
Toward a visual sociology of religion
Edited by Roman Williams

147 **European Citizenship and Social Integration in the EU**
Jürgen Gerhards and Holger Lengfeld

148 **International Migration and Ethnic Relations**
Critical perspectives
Edited by Magnus Dahlstedt and Anders Neergaard

149 **Stigma and the Shaping of the Pornography Industry**
Georgina Voss

150 **Religious Identity and Social Change**
Explaining Christian conversion in a Muslim world
David Radford

151 **God, Politics, Economy**
Social theory and the paradoxes of religion
Bülent Diken

152 **Lifestyles and Subcultures**
History and a new perspective
Luigi Berzano and Carlo Genova

153 **Comedy and Social Science**
Towards a methodology of funny
Cate Watson

154 **Sociology of Economic Innovation**
Francesco Ramella

155 **Mobility, Modernity and the Slum**
The real and virtual journeys of *Slumdog Millionaire*
Rodanthi Tzanelli

Mobility, Modernity and the Slum

The real and virtual journeys of *Slumdog Millionaire*

Rodanthi Tzanelli

LONDON AND NEW YORK

First published 2016
by Routledge
2 Park Square, Milton Park, Abingdon, Oxon OX14 4RN

and by Routledge
711 Third Avenue, New York, NY 10017

Routledge is an imprint of the Taylor & Francis Group, an informa business

© 2016 Rodanthi Tzanelli

The right of Rodanthi Tzanelli to be identified as author of this work has been asserted by her in accordance with sections 77 and 78 of the Copyright, Designs and Patents Act 1988.

All rights reserved. No part of this book may be reprinted or reproduced or utilised in any form or by any electronic, mechanical, or other means, now known or hereafter invented, including photocopying and recording, or in any information storage or retrieval system, without permission in writing from the publishers.

Trademark notice: Product or corporate names may be trademarks or registered trademarks, and are used only for identification and explanation without intent to infringe.

British Library Cataloguing in Publication Data
A catalogue record for this book is available from the British Library

Library of Congress Cataloging in Publication Data
Tzanelli, Rodanthi, 1974-
Mobility, modernity and the slum : the real and virtual journeys of Slumdog millionaire / Rodanthi Tzanelli.
pages cm. -- (Routledge advances in sociology ; 155)
ISBN 978-1-138-90935-9 (hardback) -- ISBN 978-1-315-69400-9 (e-book)
1. Social mobility--India--Mumbai. 2. Slumdog millionaire (Motion picture) 3. Motion pictures--India--Mumbai. I. Title.
HN690.B6T93 2016
305.5'130954792--dc23
2015005887

ISBN: 978-1-138-90935-9 (hbk)
ISBN: 978-1-315-69400-9 (ebk)

Typeset in Times New Roman
by Taylor & Francis Books

Printed and bound by CPI Group (UK) Ltd, Croydon, CR0 4YY

For Majid, as always

We tried to transform the world in diverse ways; now it is a matter of interpreting it.

           Karl Marx, *Theses on Feuerbach* (1888)

I once read a silly fairy tale, called *The Three Princes of Serendip*: as their Highnesses travelled, they were always making discoveries, by accidents and sagacity, of things which were not in quest of: for instance, one of them discovered that a *mule* blind on the right eye had travelled the same road lately, because the grass was eaten only on the left side, where it was worse than on the right – now do you understand *Serendipity*?

    Horace Walpole to Sir Horace Mann, CCLI, 28 January 1754 in
      R.K. Merton and E. Barber, *The Travels and Adventures
of Serendipity* ([1985] 2004)

Contents

List of figures	xx
Preface and acknowledgements	xxi
Abbreviations	xxiv

PART I
***Slumdog* metaphors of globalisation** — 1

1. Globalisation as serendipitous adaptation — 3
2. The nexus of theory and methodology — 22
3. A *Slumdog* industrial community — 36

PART II
Reading *Slumdog Millionaire* — 53

4. Staging *Slumdog*: from realist fiction to 'ethical' acting — 55
5. The cinematic text scene-by-scene — 70
6. The frail dialogics of pop participation — 115

PART III
A plural slumdog *kósmos* — 129

7. Tourist modernities: *Slumdog Millionaire's* multiple sites as fields — 131
8. The virtual journeys of *Slumdog Millionaire* — 148
9. Slumdog economies of modernity — 165
10. Conclusion — 180

Bibliography	185
Index	231

Figures

4.1 Latika as fusion of cultural horizons 66
5.1 Technologies of vision and control: Jamal's police interrogation 75
5.2 From media surveillance to celebrity systems: Jamal's quiz performance 76
5.3 Slum 'excrement' as moral discourse: young Jamal's celebration of obtaining an autograph from Amitabh Bachchan 81
5.4 The 'dream merchant' as Taj Mahal's 'front stage' 93
5.5 Young Latika as trained prostitute 98
5.6 SM's 'aerial vision': Jamal gazing at Mumbai's urban development 105
5.7 Crime does not pay: Salim's anti-heroic ending 113
6.1 Mobility romance: Latika and Jamal's unification in VT (Mumbai's central train station) 119

Preface and acknowledgements

As writers, ideas we think we can *apprehend* (understand and arrest like a criminal) might elude definition until a series of unexpected discoveries help us pull some hermeneutic strings together. The present monograph's theoretical 'apprehension' took place amongst data framing theories of travel, migration and fundamentalism. Anomaly, unanticipated discovery and strategic theorisation converged behind my developing new conceptual tools and building upon pre-existing theory. I thank the School of Sociology and Social Policy at Leeds for financing Part II's illustration; my former doctoral student, Jane Reas, whose passionate criticism of volunteer tourist cultures enriched my knowledge; Maximiliano Korstanje for comments on my work; the Photofest (New York) team for their help with film stills; Emily Briggs from Routledge for believing in this project; and Majid Yar for the warm meals and the stimulating conversations over ideas we did (or did not) share on the book. His and my family – an example of the ways national hauntologies transmogrify into ethnic cleansing and global migration or travel routes and roots – provided inspiration in the early stages of writing. The outcome of all these interactions is neither wholly dark and immobile nor exclusively bright and mobile, as it is such polarities I criticise here. Also inversely, the study is not solely about inequalities but also about *art*-work, the pleasures of travel, digital connectivity and various consumptions of image and sound.

The first chapter sets the scene by explaining how a film (*Slumdog Millionaire*, 2008 – hereafter SM) evolved in the study into a node of multiple mobilities: the emergence of a transnational artistic community spanning two continents and many countries; the production and dissemination of cinematic and musical narratives by this cultural industrial community as a form of cultural hybridisation; and the emergence of multiple activist mobilities with the release of the film (by resident and non-resident Indians, filmed slum localities, government spokespersons, Mumbai's new tourist industries and the film's artists). Though with different agendas and objectives, all these groups' social actions matched the film's plot as a narrative of India's uneven but unique path to (post)modernity, drafting a tale of globalisation as creative adaptation to new cultural and political challenges. This take on globalising creativity is explored through *pangosmiopoìesis*, a term denoting aesthetic globalisation. Though of ancient Greek origins, the word conforms to Indian narratives of globalisation and synchronisation. The equivalent Indian term takes this a step further, because it highlights how the country's adaptive modernity sought to use particular forms of tourist and vagabondage strangerhood in exclusive ways to achieve global prestige amongst developed nations. Contra absolutely differential suggestions (Sheller 2014a, 2014b), Indian *pangosmiopoiesis* (*Alamgiriat*) stands at the heart of the new 'mobilities paradigm' and the compromises the Indian state had to make to harmonise its own ethno-governance with global governmobilities (Bærenholdt 2013), or the governance of polities through mobility.

Chapter 2 outlines the study's methodological tools and framework by drawing from tourist, art, film, globalisation and mobility theory and urban studies. First, departing from previous research focusing on tourism-induced migration networks, it presents 'articulation' as artistic symbolisation of the social. Second, it stresses the importance of such articulations across different sites, virtual and terrestrial. Finally, it provides a detailed analysis of combined sensory perceptions of such articulations (by cinematic viewers, tourists and activists) in terms of 'synaesthetic performativity': perceiving the world through ways of doing and aesthetically reflecting on it. The chapter concludes with a debate on the ways in which, contra the fundamentalist prerogative, SM's artistic community and the more forward-looking groups in Mumbai's ethno-cultural communities produce culture through the use of old (narrative) and new (internet, cinema, press) technological tools – even though for the latter this might be an adaptive necessity, reminiscent of vagabondage mobilities in the developing world. Progressive modernity is anything but equal in this respect. The use of technology interpellates the modern human as a potent engineer, a *tornadóros*, whose empowering tools run the risk of valorising local modernities in sexist and racist ways.

Building on the preceding analysis, chapter 3 takes a closer look at the profiles and social backgrounds of lead SM artists: screenwriter Simon Beaufoy, directors Danny Boyle and Loveen Tandan, composer A.R. Rahman, singer M.I.A. and actors Freida Pinto (Latika), Dev Patel (Jamal) and Madhur Mittal (Salim). It shows how art is made out of plural understandings of technology as embodied and digital artistic creativity. Members of this cultural industrial community use art to re-imagine their cultural and social identity. SM's *technopoesis*, a marriage between new digital and old narrative technologies with human creativity (art, acting, filming) produces ideas of 'home' and belonging in a globalised world. Chapter 4 sets the scene for a textual analysis of SM (the film and its music). It cautions readers that SM's textual products were based on Mumbai's socio-cultural histories and future aspirations. As such, it attempts to redefine the ethical basis of SM's narrative as well as this study's reading of SM. 'Ethics' are defined as performed cultural custom and habit – what inspires everyday social performances and cinematic representations of Mumbai. The chapter also proffers observations on connections between SM and actually existing cultures of slum tourism and dark tourism, suggesting that such tourism mobilities inform SM's filmic reality. Chapter 5 is a thorough textual analysis of the film. Divided into 'segments', self-contained but interconnected parts of the cinematic narrative, it draws on interdisciplinary theory to situate the film in the Indian social and cultural context by which SM artists were inspired. It is suggested that the film moves from a grim vision of a ruinous Mumbai to a brighter one in which Mumbai emerges as a spectacular global city that can heal its wounds of migration, national partition and inequality. In this respect, SM interrogates how 'McWorld' (Barber 2003, 2010) utopias mobilise oblivion to enable global governmobilities. Chapter 6 concludes the work of connecting cinematic text to socio-cultural context with an investigation into the ways A.R. Rahman's concluding composition recapitulates this transition, allowing SM products to enter global popular culture.

Chapter 7 follows the development of SM-related tourism in India by taking as a starting point India's main filmed locales: the Taj Mahal and Mumbai's mega-slum, Dharavi. Commencing with the argument that such sites betray the ways Indian culture is plural in its lifestyles and self-presentations, it proceeds to explain why Agra (Taj Mahal) did not refashion its tourism on SM but Dharavi experienced a tourist boom after the film's release. At the heart of such 'serendipitous' selectivity in India's global marketing stands the power of mobility to govern place and culture through marriages of ethno-national exclusivity and fundamentalist belief. Independent markets struggle to establish themselves in such political landscapes, as Chapter 8 explains. The chapter investigates interactions between hosts (slum residents) and guests (global slum tourists) through mutual styles of gazing and performing. Of particular significance is the development of Mumbai's sole slum tour operator, Reality Tours, into a cultural mediator and translator of Indian slum life but also an activist force. The charitable activism of Reality Tours is examined together with other recent support by transnational artistic groups on the web. Emphasis is given to such actors' online performances to investigate how their propensity towards 'junktivism' (the support of disenfranchised groups considered mere refuse) calls into being a vagabondage version of *tornadóros* as a post-modern labourer that emerges from India's migration histories. Reifications of the *tornadóros* as worker are of immense market value in today's tourist and media mobilities and invite comparisons with the essence of the film's fictional heroes. The chapter concludes with an investigation into the ways foreign 'junktivism' and native entrepreneurial action contribute to the reproduction of some primeval communitarian tropes of *technopoetic* belonging, which threaten artistic flows in the country. The concluding chapter examines the uses of the past and India's global position and national self-narration through various reactions to the film and its artistic leadership. In particular, it looks into (a) social movements in India in the aftermath of SM's release, as well as reactions of prominent non-resident Indians, and (b) charitable undertakings by SM's artistic leaders – Danny Boyle and Christian Colson – and their consideration in a post-colonial frame as an instance of 'First World' patronising intervention. These actions are constitutive of the construction of reputable individual and collective identities. Mumbai's *pangosmiopoiesis* attends to surfaces so as to allow the country to enter global domains.

Abbreviations

AMPAS	Academy of Motion Picture Arts and Sciences
BJP	Bharatiya Janata Party
DMIC	Delhi-Mumbai Industrial Corridor
IMDB	Internet Movie Database
ITDC	Indian Tourism Development Corporation
NGO	Non-Governmental Organisation
NREGA	National Rural Employment Guarantee Act
SM	*Slumdog Millionaire*
UN	United Nations
UNESCO	United Nations Educational, Scientific and Cultural Organization
VT	Victoria Terminus
WHO	World Health Organization

Part I
Slumdog metaphors of globalisation

1 Globalisation as serendipitous adaptation

World's unbearable lightness: moralising serendipity

As the preface explains, my focus on SM facilitates an excursus on two interconnected types of strangerhood – one privileged (what Bauman 1998 calls 'tourists') and one disenfranchised ('vagabonds') – that provide the cinematic story's urban frame. SM tells the story of Jamal Malik (Dev Patel), an 18-year-old orphan from the slums of Mumbai, who is just one question away from winning a staggering 20 million rupees on India's *Kaun Banega Crorepati?* (*Who Wants To Be A Millionaire?*). But when the show breaks for the night, police arrest him on suspicion of cheating (for how could a street kid know so many correct answers?) Desperate to prove his innocence, Jamal tells the arresting officer (Irfan Khan) the story of his life in the slum where he and his brother, Salim (Madhur Mittal), grew up; of their adventures together on the road; their vicious encounters with religious fanatics, local gangs and Latika (Freida Pinto), the girl he loved and lost. As the narrative develops, we learn that each correct answer is connected to his life experiences of exclusion. As Fox Searchlight Pictures suggest on the Internet Movie Database (IMDB, Slumdog Millionaire), at the heart of SM's storytelling 'lies the question of how anyone comes to know the things they know about life and love'.

The plot is about serendipity (how we get to apprehend the things we know), but also the original etymology's connection to Orientalist corruption. The original conception of serendipity connects to 'Serendip', an exotic place (later Sri Lanka) visited by three Persian princes accused of cheating, hence of the legitimacy by which they acquired their knowledge (Merton and Barber 2004:170–1). The old question of meritocratic progress meets one's assumptions concerning status, knowledge and the benefit of luck in this tale, which matches SM's basic plot. Jamal the 'slumdog' from Mumbai certainly falls short of these requirements before the police learn that he is a hard-working youth with an inclination to technological creativity and a fast learner of global histories. As the present study's primary figurative 'engineer', he reflects the varieties of strangerhood circulating in the discourse of individual chapters. In a country ruled by ethno-religious fundamentalisms, coupling knowledge with technology opens up Pandora's Box: such 'engineering' connects to the

4   Slumdog *metaphors of globalisation*

primary exogenous-exotic strangeness India is asked to emulate: that of Western modernity.

There is no stranger outside urban life and no city outside national and global cultural articulations (Sassen 2001). Bauman explains that all societies produce their unique form of strangerhood in inimitable ways (Bauman 1997:17), so Mumbai's historical trajectory and profile play a role in the ways SM strangers are celebrated or obliterated – both within the filmic and in India's contemporary social realities. The present study, which examines a convoluted digital, musical and cinematic circuit of ethno-national hauntologies, fits into this pattern of celebration and obliteration. By 'hauntology', I refer to alleged encroachments of versions of the past into the present so as to determine the future (Derrida 1994). Derrida's term places so much emphasis on metaphysics that does not examine *who* is responsible for the colonisation of the future by the past – or *who actually manufactures this 'past' and then offshores it abroad*. The consequences of the cinematic heroes' travels, the various stakeholders' subsequent strategic decisions over the development of Indian tourism and media policies tied to SM and my interpretation of them are facets of the book's theory. The global circuits of Indian hauntologies still occupy a central place in theories of mobility I employ. Today, the (Indian) ghosts inhabiting this circuit have assumed the phenomenological mantle of new (global) audio-visual technologies and are manipulated in diverse ways by different groups. Concealed from public view, Jamal's story of loss and hardship embodies a technological miracle surely ridden with corruption or merit (depending on the deliberator's viewpoint), as if political mobilities are morally black or white, like Niebuhr's 'children' of darkness and light (Niebuhr 1960). The country's 'technological' innovation (via the 'Shining India' programme I analyse elsewhere) incorporates the cultural terrain too, including its new digitally mediated tourism and budding markets of labour migrants, whose fates might be concealed from public view (unlike the mobilities of celebrities who help India shine on the global stage). Strangeness is selectively celebrated and awarded the badge of cosmopolitan citizenships.

The suggestion that this is a book about India and not a global occurrence would be wrong. We should treat the SM contingent as exemplary of luck, originally *syngyrìa* (in ancient Greek) or the meeting of two separate times – a literal translation of technological synchronisation or *peproméno* (from *pèras* that denotes mobility), the cosmic outcome of fortunate distribution (of riches and misfortunes) across society. India's *peproméno* is to shine, according to its dominant political campaign. One may ask: how and with what sort of help? Therefore, this study exemplifies post-modernity's new complexities that cannot be contained in national terrains as they involve various cultural, economic and political flows across the world. The subtitle's conception of 'journeys' alludes both to physical human relocation and the inner conceptual and emotional journeys of the book's various mobile subjects, which include SM's international artistic community, the film's heroes, the global tourist clientele this film allegedly induced and the ways its digital marketing overdetermined the nature of this clientele. All these 'mobility constellations' (Cresswell 2001:3) inform 'geographically specific formations of...narratives about mobility and mobile practices' (Cresswell (2010:17) from a fictional stance. Yet, India is also a repository of ethno-nationalist memories; even mythical narratives of national formation survive primarily in realist contexts – for, 'it is always through [a] process of interpretation' that cultures 'are kept alive' (Bleicher 1980:225). On the realist, rather that figurative plane, SM's 'journeys' converge behind practices of offshoring embodied or symbolic capital across borders, but such movements do not always involve 'elaborate forms of secrecy' (Urry 2014:8). In fact, these multiple journeys are subject to various interpretations, changing their shade, hue and colour along the way. Without refuting the presence of corruption, I intend to show that the discourse itself needs careful examination as a moralising exercise.

Where there are journeys, there is cross-cultural exchange, welcome and unwanted 'visits'. Classical tourism theory acknowledges that host-guest interactions in tourist zones shape their future directions. This matters in SM's complex case, which coerced Mumbai into operating as a host to film crews and subsequently film tourists. Nothing develops without interpretation of the social facts into fragile 'truths'; nothing comes into fruition without some sort of mental and physical labour, individual and collective. Conceptions of work form the analytical basis of tourism theory to date, and in our particular case guide ethological discourse about travel, tourism and migrant mobilities involved in SM's industry. These 'mobilities' point outwards: their necessities pull human contributors away from their community's cosmological centre, they are what we call 'centrifugal'. I identify as centrifugal force par excellence the work of collective human interpretation on labour. 'Work', or more pertinently, the convergence of *téchne* (as work untainted by technological interventions) and *érgon* (as work 'afflicted' by social classifications supported by (hu)man-made technologies) is not a neutral concept but a conception that moralises the basis of any community, whether this is hyper-mobile (like that of SM artists and virtual technicians) or allegedly immobile (like that of the film's slum-dweller 'objects'). Moralisations of work underscore the nature of tourism and tourists as much as they define that of national communities: if 'work' fails to meet the agreed ethical standards, the group's character (hence its public appearance) is tainted. Such essentially – that is, essentialised – phenomenological agreements date back to the emergence of Western modernity and its various interpretations across the world. Delimiting those to an 'exceptionalist' study of particular national communities suggests sociological blindness to the fact that all social groups attend to appearances. The proponents of modernity originally confined such processes to the visual regime – a tendency eventually refuted both in the Western *belles artes* and in scientific research.

The moralisation of serendipitous progress tends to ignore both hard work and collective sacrifice, highlighting only happy external intervention instead. SM's cultural invention in the tourism business fits into this pattern: as the story goes, the West must have done this ('this' being both good and evil doing). In the context of film-making, production and offshoring of Indian landscapes, humans and values, this produces a discourse of secular theodicy that attributes India's socio-cultural progress (both in the slums and its administrative centres) to a corrupt *peproméno* that is an internal feature of the country's 'social system' and a product of its geographical essence, as if Indian space and time are primordial, natural occurrences (Herzfeld 1992:4, 74 on theodicy and bureaucratic corruption; Urry 2007:29 on complexity theory; Urry 2014:9, 20–4 on offshoring and scandal). SM is today a highly acclaimed film in global cinematic circles, with several of its lead artists (including director Danny Boyle, scriptwriter Simon Beaufoy and composer A.R. Rahman) awarded for their contribution to the finished product. There is a vast amount of information on the work of other SM artists, as well as internet sites advertising SM holidays in Mumbai. There was also a public outcry about the film upon its release. Accusations centred upon the audacity of using the harrowing experiences of real slum populations and selling them to all sorts of affluent clientele, are at the heart of this study's serendipitous discourse. But a serious examination of such neoliberal expansion demands a more nuanced apprehension of the ways societal power games work (Bourdieu et al. 1999), inviting us in SM's case to consider how governmobilities – governing through mobilities – work through technological and institutional forms of self-government, through objects and digitised relations (Bærenholdt 2013:29; Urry 2007). This is a more complex call than that on a localised/nationalised, networked or historical-colonial focus: the approach must integrate these aspects to assess global risks and urgencies that might begin in one city but affect humanity (Beck 1999, 2005).

The call to contextualisation prompts one to consider the film's messages, stories and the indecorous global accusations of exploitation both separately and in unison – i.e. within the culture the film represents, its represented human beings and voices and those who represent them (Banks 2001:3–7). From the funny images of the young brothers playing in Juhu's airfield and little Jamal diving into a pile of shit to secure an autograph from a Bollywood star, to the depiction of Muslim-Hindu massacres, Mumbai's mafia and sex work networks, to the rise and fall of its main heroes and heroines, one is forced into a journey of conflicting representations of goodness, evil and finally into the grey zones of practical action. Slum destitution and criminalisation, media and police corruption and Bollywood dancing are odd couples, but they fit into the same interpretation when one directs ideas to a singular end, a *telos* (Bal 2010). Bourdieu's employment of 'refraction' as a methodological metaphor tries to avoid the 'short-circuit fallacy' of 'passing directly from what is produced in the social world to what is produced in more specific field[s]' (Bourdieu 1996a:220, 248), but does not suggest concrete connections between global and local social phenomena. I contend that it is possible to use SM media as windows to a network of scholarly discourses that do not delimit art to frivolous pursuit, tourism and travel to consumerist greed and media theory to marketing strategy, but view all these as a unity, a circuit interconnecting other smaller or bigger circuits. Rather than narrowing the investigative field to tourism, media, mobility, art or globalisation studies, this book aspires to shed light on intrinsic connections between them.

The film's plot alone connects at least three disparate theses on adaptation: as 'translation'; as a form of tourist-like mobility endorsing slumming; and as cultural appropriation. These theses function as interpretative tools of globalisation's role in shaping or eliminating cultural boundaries and the politics behind the venture. For this reason the film's plot is connected to actual cultural industrial contexts in which it induced business, including the promotion of collaborations and exchanges between Western and Asian (Bollywood) media; the rise of new internet (Prideaux 2002) or e-tourist industries (Bouhalis 2003); a networked management and promotion of film and philanthropic slum travel; and the adjacent production of activist networks supporting or rejecting (*negating*) such bilateral global flows. Globalisation-as-adaptation can only be operationalised with the maintenance of mobility routes, maintaining a socio-cultural kinetics that impinges on physical borders and virtual/imaginary boundaries (Cresswell 2009; Sheller 2014a, 2014b).

The *problématique* of adaptation is an offshoot of utopian discourses of (post-)industrial (post-)modernity. Here we enter the sociological terrain of paradigm shifts, which are marked by movements between individualised innovation and collaborative creativity. Early modernities were consumed with the para-theological fear of a 'theft' or 'Fall' from Western European civilisation, which connected to the anxiety that one's heritage might be appropriated by strangers (Herzfeld 1982, 1987 and 2005; Bauman 1992a). New post-modernities place more emphasis on innovation within global aesthetic plurality, which builds on other innovations. There is no clear epochal rupture, only willing oblivion to traumatic histories: older tropes of 'conning' and 'cloning' other cultures survive in new tropes on aesthetic or cosmetic pleasure and uniqueness, reigniting reactions by those who consider themselves custodians of old traditions. The question is not who reproduces any more but if they are insiders or strangers. As aesthetic flows travel in multiple ways, amongst post-modernity's new scapegoats we can count those trading in 'original' (authentic) marketed products of aesthetic value. Cultural industrial artists, such as those implicated in the creation of SM figure as both dangerous nomads and welcome enhancers of national and regional profiles (Cronin 2003:105–7; Maffesoli 1996). Mindful of Wolff's (1983) and Garnham's (2000) argument that we should not reduce aesthetic judgment to ideology, I maintain that evaluating or creating aesthetics is part of a wider problem 'of creating viable communities for autonomous agents under the conditions of modernity' (Garnham 2000:162).

In line with Bauman's more locally applicable commentary on strangerhood (Bauman 1997), I argue that in SM's controversies and ideological circuits we deal with a phenomenon of 'stranger traffic' (*Fremdenverkern*). This involves a blend of post-industrial travellers whose art-work inadvertently induced tourism, activism or other mobilities. These new 'transnational imagined communities' (a modifying tribute to Anderson's original thesis on nations (Anderson 2006) and a direct reference to Appadurai's 'scapes' (Appadurai 1990) and Meethan's comment that cultures are progressively more diasporic and transnational (Meethan 2003) produce a utopian poetics that promotes relations of 'affiliation' rather than 'filiation' or 'association' (Latour 2005). Gouldner's early caution not to view the 'shattering of traditional [affiliative] structures' as dysfunctional in (post-)industrialised areas 'from the standpoint of their relationship with the exporting country' is still valid (Gouldner 1948:399). Such transnational communal bonds are based on 'guild consciousness, consensus, collegiality, professional respect', or even 'class and the hegemony of a dominate culture' (Said 2000:234–5). But even such hegemonic affiliations are inherently shifting and positional. Whereas conceptualisations of artistic nomads in terms of purposeful travellers for work counter what Cohen describes as the drifter's venturing 'furthest away from the beaten track and from the accustomed way of life of his home country... [with] no fixed itinerary or timetable and no well-defined goals of travel' (Cohen 1972:168), the propensity of professionals to roam internationally and live amongst the indigenous population (Adler and Adler 1999:54; Westerhausen 2002:6) so as to mobilise native knowledge in their work has often earned them the badge of post-colonial cultural appropriator.

Considerations of professional art-work as enabler of cultural trafficking and adaptation suggest a combined analysis of tourism, migration and technology. As travellers living and exploring contemporary lifestyles, these professionals' art-works project familiar patterns of post-industrial mobility through ambiguous intersections between migration, tourism, leisure and work (Shields 1992; Bianchi 2000; Benson and O'Reilly 2009). As actors operating in global artistic networks, these professionals share and mobilise the same characteristics against organised power structures, producing alternative authorial systems and new forms of resistance to modern industrial life (Melucci 1989). Alternatively, or in a peculiar structural combination, they may insert themselves into global markets, as global governmobilities are more powerful than individual will. At the same time, as social beings they carry locally situated experiences that make their way into artistic narratives. From the social profiles of its lead artists to the trajectories of their enterprise, SM's values, modes and sentiments are anchored in a blend of subaltern post-colonial spaces. To communicate this I purposely use a linguistic transliteration of globalisation, which draws upon the logic of new mobility theory to assess the pitfalls of 'adaptation' as coercive political force.

Aesthetic permutations of globalisation and the mobilities paradigm

My key word, *pangosmiopoiesis*, captures better the aesthetic innovations of the SM cultural industry without discarding its structural affinities to hybrid Eurasian art-work or its systemic origins in Eurasian politics. *Pangosmiopoiesis* refers to a making or genesis (*poìesis*) of beauty (*kósmos*) within (*en*) that embraces everything (*pan*). My application of a Kantian-like Greek term to Asian cultural domains connects to scholarly debates on offshoring and frames SM's cinematic text, its global artistic mobilities contexts and the reactionary argument in favour of banning the film. Therefore, there is a fundamentalist subtext here that connects the aesthetic dimensions of globalisation to the unequal nature of global mobilities. Greek *pangosmiopoiesis* retains a striking similarity to Urdu renditions of globalisation (*Alamgiriat*): it is said that in northern India, where the British adopted Urdu as a language of colonial affairs, Hindu writers retaliated by portraying it as the language 'of dancing girls and prostitutes' and promoted a stylised Sanskrit Hindi in its stead (Hopkins 2011:153). As Urry notes, places of fun and consumption, including tourism, can also be places of work 'for the service providers, with many migrants travelling to build the attractions and to "service" consumers' (Urry 2014:82). Global sex industries thrive today on criminal networks that traffic women to offshore zones, where they can be consumed as pretty, sexualised objects. The virulent sexist content of the Hindu story merely replaces the ethno-racial context in which real class-based – rather than religious – relations are enacted today (Gupta 2003:ix). Like *pangosmiopoiesis*, it is underscored by a cosmetic sentiment crafting totalising views of Indian polyvocality. Such anecdotal anchoring of globalisation resonates with some actual uses of religious identities as reductive understandings of social identity and ultimately as racist stereotyping. In line with a critical mobilities agenda, the anecdote interrogates who and what is successfully demobilised and remobilised across many different scales to put the cogs of globalisation in motion (e.g. Hannam et al. 2006; Sheller 2003, 2004, 2014b). The anecdote's racist-sexist extension spills poison into Indian politics, if we consider domesticated understandings of the terrorist as the other (Pakistani) 'penetrating' post-partition borders. Such selective (global-local) phantasms of the notorious 'War on Terror' render politics with a racist-Christological arc, which by turn encourages Islamist or other religious distortions of bloody redemption (Sayyid 2003; Kahn 2008:27–8; Tzanelli 2008b: ch. 6; Tzanelli 2011: ch.6).

A different complaint in globalisation theory emphasises institutional convergence but runs the risk of conflating cultural and political models to legitimate their universal applicability (Meyer et al. 1997). The metaphor of 'flatness', for example, once consolidated a view on globalisation as a potentially equalising and democratising process (Friedman 2005), rendering cultural heterogeneity (Friedman 1994) or the coexistence of globalising and de-democratising forces invisible. The thesis is applicable to our study of SM as a suspect path to Mumbai's new tourist-media mobilities: it sprang from Thomas Friedman's fleeting travels to Bangalore in India, where he concluded that 'flattening' is a product of a convergence of personal computers with fibre-optic microcables with the rise of workflow software that led to 'Globalization 3.0'. I revisit this in Chapter 8, where I examine the role of technological communication in producing tourist-activist channels. Here it is pertinent to stress that Urry's latest revision of the 'tourist gaze' (Urry and Larsen 2011) is titled *The Tourist Gaze 3.0*. Mindful of our world's hypermobility futures, the authors prioritise in the concluding chapter the role of machine-based fast mobilities, leaving open the question of whether tourism has homogenised (and forcefully localised) rather than merely connected the world more. In

10 Slumdog *metaphors of globalisation*

Offshoring (2014) Urry concludes that the role of travel circuits and virtual systems in producing or maintaining global inequalities is definitely detrimental for the future of global democracies. Has tourism and digital connectivity eroded our humanity? Barber, who rejects Huntington's 'clash of civilisations' thesis, replaces such clear political fundamentalist vision with a constellation of mobilities supported by an originally *cultural-economic* encounter between 'Jihad' and 'McWorld' (Barber 2003:xvi; Huntington 1993, 2002). Her blaming of 'McWorld' for this 'dialectical expression of tensions built into a single global civilization' (ibid.) is relocated in the latter's 'infotainment industries and technological innovations' (ibid.) – yet another identification of de-democratisation with the 'cultural industry' (Adorno and Horkheimer 1991). SM interrogates this thesis in a surprisingly subversive way, setting its problems against some grander global risks, vaguely and yet successfully connected to today's discursive phantasm no. 1: political McJihadism.

Such periodisations (Globalization 2.0 being the era in which multi-national companies led the way in driving global integration, and Globalization 1.0 one in which countries and governments were the main protagonists) beg justification *in context* (note also Büscher and Urry's methodological caution on mobility research (Büscher and Urry 2009)). Indeed, the intimacy and agential flair of Western encounters with other forms of synchronisation applies to the experience of Asian cultural adaptation (Nederveen Pieterse 1998:79). My use of transliterated words from Greek aims to communicate the irreducibility of foreign linguistic universes to fixed translations: if academics also 'offshore' terms, they must be prepared to explain how contextual movement changes or amplifies the original concept's meanings. This has been the basis of comparative, global sociology (and more recent the sociology of globalisation and mobility) since the birth of industrial modernity and the discovery of alien cultural worlds outside Europe. There are echoes of colonial legacies in the thesis: *Haunted by Empire* (Stoler 2006) focuses attention on the politics of comparison – on how colonizers differentiated one group or set of behaviours from another – and on the circulation of knowledge and ideologies within and between imperial projects. *Mobility, Modernity and the Slum* proffers an archaeology of such domestications, partly alongside Urry's 'offshoring' and partly in memoriam of Beck's 'risk society'. In SM's case the very totalising force of domesticating cultural (con)texts is also interrogated by the blended ethnocultural profile of its artists, who nevertheless might represent majoritarian views on the global post-colonial plateau (Spivak 2000:406). The book nods in agreement with this ambivalence, as most of its transliterated master terms, including *pangosmiopoiesis*, produce polemics on the fringes of hegemony.

Some defenders of sociological empiricism and positivism are infuriated by the use of metaphors in scholarly writing. However, metaphors are rarely constructs *of* themselves, as their function is to move and shift realities – both literarily and literally (the Greek *metaféro* from post [*meta*] and carry or transfer [*fero*] means to move (Sontag 1991)). Much like the ancient *peproméno*, metaphor denotes the mental passage from enunciation to its phenomenal actualisation. The word's colloquial modern Greek use 'metaphysicalises' social events (It is apparently one's *peproméno* to experience good or bad things in life). The emphasis on fate and destiny retains a normative dimension across Eastern and Western cultures, here displacing free will and the acts of otherworldly spirits and God, there attributing blame to humans (Merton and Barber 2004: 153 on moral policy-makers). Such anecdotes sell well in cross-cultural consumption, as they move across cultural boundaries, especially in the tourist trade in the form of fortune-telling and other such 'Orientalia' conforming to inner experiential travel. As tourism scholars Urry and Dann stress, our social understanding is mostly based on metaphors, and combinations of physical with inner movement with a purpose are such metaphors (Urry 2000; Urry 2002).

Much of early sociological theorising was based on metaphors such as that of the body (Urry 2000:23) – a clear connection to the (meta-)physicalisation of terms such as *peproméno* and *pangosmiopoiesis*. Speaking of gift economies in the tradition of Harré's realism (Harré 1986), Zeitlyn prompts us to think of interconnections between metaphor and model, with the former as a device of comprehension and the latter as partial or incomplete representation enclosing claims about reality (Zeitlyn 2003). The very idea of transfer is constitutive of globalisation and its local permutations – we always reference some specific entity as implicit in holism (Thornton 1988:287 in Moore 2004:73). Art-work, I contend, bridges the two conceptions of globalisation because it is based on aesthetic (sensory and beautifying) principles. Art-*work* as *aesthetic labour* becomes inserted into such totalising structures to inject their moribund sites with new utopian possibilities. Art and aesthetic value (as in *pangosmiopoiesis*) produce the post-modern parameters of cosmetic globalisation, which mobilises, demobilises and remobilises as it pleases and with the help of disorganised global actors, who are often not involved in the original product or its labour. Any product of utopian art never emerges outside these systemic structures or pressures but always aspires to act as agent of change. Thus the auxiliary thesis on global artistic mobilities does not ignore the deontological dimensions of global art commerce but does not elevate them to an overt normative predicament, as it sits on unpredictable mobility constellations and routes.

The utopian predicament of *pangosmiopoiesis* can also feed into local self-presentations, performances and social action(s), thus proving that metaphors have no adequate a priori referent and are defined only in context, but there is always part of them that exceeds representation (Moore 1997:140–2; Moore 2004:73–4). 'Slumdog' itself – a word that, according to SM director Danny Boyle, is common, but according to his critics is opportunistically invented to commoditise slum culture – is such a slippery concept-metaphor: not only does it talk about global(ised) perceptions of (subaltern) localities, it becomes implicated in the biographical records of lead SM artists and mobilises slum-dwellers without their full consent in different domains. 'Slumdog' is by turn the marginal, the vagabond-migrant, the kitsch, the ethno-racial or gendered lowermost and the crafty artistic pilgrim to foreign lands. Each of these

12 Slumdog *metaphors of globalisation*

nominations appear in cinematic narrative, in virtual representations and political discourse to invigorate polemics from all social actors – artists, politicians, journalists, virtual businessmen and women and local artisans. Each of these perspectives proves how privileged and unprivileged voices remain partial and a mere sum of them does not provide the whole but certainly provides enough fragments of it to theorise globalisation (Strathern 1983, 1988, 1991; Appadurai 1996: ch. 4; Marcus 1998:62–3).

Metaphors are not allegories but communicate with them. Frederic Jameson's claim that 'all third-world cultural productions…are necessarily allegorical, and in a very specific way: they are to be read as…*national allegories*, even when…their forms develop out of predominantly western machineries of representation' (Jameson 1986:67) is contentious. The thesis fails to examine how any national worldview is relational and hybridised at both ends – that of the recipient and the 'maker' – and rejects the role of industrial (media and tourist) exchange as *de facto* damaging. Of course one must account for the ways various interest groups and agencies, including cultural corporations, may 'manipulate, channel (close or open) the cultural boundaries of others to the flows with varying degrees of success in relation to their…power resources' (Featherstone 1990:7; Held and McGrew 2007). Although market imperatives in cultural industries may exercise pressures in self-presentational terms, cultural markets also provide a safe(r) space for the articulations of values held dear by indigenous industries, but the practice underlines state-led expansion in hyper-neoliberal domains of post-modernity. Most of the criticisms levelled at SM's makers connect to this *problématique*, either by casting their art in terms of a Western mercenary outlook and a totalising (neo-colonial) practice, or by stressing its inaccurate depiction of alternative worldviews. To adapt presupposes a shift in the geographical, cosmological and aesthetic coordinates of the original thesis-product (in our case a film, its industry but also its makers' and audiences' belief systems) with a view to synthesising those anew.

Character, habitus and aesthetic markets: Bollywood scenes

Mumbai's slum socio-cultures, as well as the ways these are encoded in a film's hybrid production environment, betray the fluid processes in which a fictionally uniform *kósmos* wraps itself around diverse human communities to recreate them – just as any artistic adaptation. Deleuzean micro-sociology (Deleuze and Guattari 1988) invites attention to the significance of local idiom and 'linguistic' deviation or convergence in the grand scheme of things, where the 'multiplicity of often minor processes, of different origin and scattered location…overlap, repeat, or imitate one another; support one another; distinguish themselves from one another according to their domain of application; converge; and gradually produce the blueprint of a general method' (Foucault 1979:138). This general method of investigation of habitual reproduction is split into three distinctive but overlapping domains: that of art (the SM industry and its artist-activists), of tourism (controlled by multiple digital networks), of global intellectual communities (opposing SM art-work and activism as 'cultural imperialist' propaganda) and of slum communities (articulating their own social place in Mumbai's urbanity) (Tomlinson 1999:9). We might regard confrontational discourse or 'opposition' as a type of social relation thriving on every singular type of repetition, in which similar things are willing to destroy each other in virtue of their very similarity (Tarde 1989:70 in Tonkonoff 2013:272). A constant across these domains is the recognition of a valuable (for self-identification and marketing) 'character', which attracts the collector of exceptional trivia, the methodologist and the 'junkhunter' (Merton and Barber 2004:224). My emphasis on 'habitus' or ethno-national 'character' is anything but random in a book aspiring to transcend Durkheimian distinctions between organic and mechanical communities without discarding them. My understanding of habitus seeks to combine Bourdieu's understanding of class-culture based dispositions as ideal (hence fictional) ethno-national types with Tarde's (1901 in Tonkonoff 2013:268) micro-sociology of *dispositif* or social disposition. This allows for a study of ideoscapes or cosmological flows that claim patrilineages and moorings in a constantly mobile human universe (Cresswell 2001; Hannam et al. 2006). As we will see in Chapters 7 and 8, Mumbai's budding slum tourist industry hosts various such native and foreign 'junkhunters' with disparate agendas.

It has repeatedly been suggested that posing cultures in relation to each other ought to be based on accepting each other's right to be opaque (Cannella and Viruru 2004:38–9; Spivak 1999). But the very claim to Otherness does not acknowledge the Other's capacity to use opacity as strategy. Cloaking the fact that the notion of alterity is a product of European conceptions of 'suffering' can promote 'development work' at the expense of what the other truly wants to develop (Picard 2007; Tomaselli 2007:48; Tzanelli 2008b:149–50; Tzanelli 2011:ch. 2). But the difference between rendition of native worldviews and equivalence corresponds to differences between domestication or assimilation of foreign cultures and their promotion as a malleable, hybrid construct, bridging different worldviews in a Mannheimian fashion (Mannheim 1968, 2003). From SM's classroom lessons to its music's Babelic rhythm, lyrics and sound, domestic and global audio-visual recipients are immersed into the irreducibility of other cultures, whether these are of the slum or the Indian imagined community (Papastergiadis 2000:127; Spivak 2000, 2009). With about one third of dialogue in Hindi and a third of lyrics in blended English-Hindi, the SM enterprise neither wholly reduces differences into foreign domestic (con-)texts, nor does it smooth the realities in which the heroes operate (Venuti 2000). It may be argued that the trope of globalisation-as-adaptation thrives on the power of cultural translatability to cross physical and noetic boundaries. We deal with chains of translations and transliterations in SM: the book from which the film was adapted (*Q&A* was written in English by diplomat Vikas Swarup), the movie, its music and all the relevant cinematic products are united in economic terms under the same cluster of 'slumdog signs', granting the story with coherence (Lash and Urry 1994; Tzanelli 2010b). The observation carries more weight when applied to the translatability of the film's genre across cultural and politico-economic domains: SM's dubbed Hindi version, which was released in India under the title *Slumdog Crorepati*, pays tribute to the film's original title *Slumdog Millionaire: Kaun Banega Crorepati*. The title had to be shortened for legal reasons, as the subtitle copied the Indian version of *Who Wants to Be a Millionaire?* (Bollywood.com n.d.; India Forums 2009).

Much of the uproar about SM relates to the film's borrowing from Bollywood styles and its emergent tourist industry's connection to Western slumming. I reserve the latter for investigation below. For the moment, it is worth explaining that elitist condemnations of cheapness (of Bollywood art products) and public disorderliness (in slum tourism) match SM's cinematic take on deviance: any association of the indigenous industry with Western sites of production and consumption is bound to transmogrify or 'miscegenate' it – change both its surface and its depth in post-colonial nationalist terms (Herzfeld 2004:21; Johnson 1997, 1998). In Part II I argue that SM narrates shifts in the Indian industry from post-partition national allegories to the 1970s labour-induced social change and then the great NRI (Non-Resident Indian) imaginaries centring on pastiche, adaptation of Western form and the aesthetics of musical picturisations (Wright 2010:23). Although this imaginative journey is conveniently overlaid by a highly marketable love story, it retains its political-cultural potency. The power of this journey is drawn from national fixities and Western imperatives of synchronisation: the 1990s re-mapping of the mobile Indian subject, who struggled with essentialisations of his/her identity both at home and abroad, is replaced in SM with a struggle against globalised value hierarchies. Such hierarchies are based on externally validated aesthetics and while they parallel the trajectories of the new mobile Indian subject, they battle ambiguity as nuisance (Douglas 1993:125). Ultimately, SM's take on Mumbai's 'deviance' – told in the closing credits from a song created by a hybridising composer and through a Bollywood routine – is based on the metaphor of the Urdu courtesan, who aesthetically seduces viewers and deprives her homeland of its respectability. MacWorld apologises for Jihad, temporarily displacing risk society in favour of a beautiful, pure spectacle.

The discourse on Bollywood hybridity is crucial. As a portmanteau the term promotes a dialogue between two of the world's biggest cinemas, hinting at their inseparability and highlighting cinema's problematic relationship with cultural authenticity (Wright 2010:31). Presentations of the term as an empty signifier has fostered an ideological approach, whereby those invested in earlier models of Indian cinema resentfully propagate binary divisions between artistic (native) and popular (strange as populist) art-work (Prasad 2003). Bollywood musical picturisations are regarded as a non-native travelling culture, better promoting Western post-modern fragmentations of an Indian identity that will never return to its alleged ancestral roots (Kaur 2005:313; Hogan 2008). Reflecting the controlled mechanical vision of Bollywood cinema, text interacts with context to enhance the story's verisimilitude in the eyes of global audio-visual participants. Marketing strategies aside, SM industry's various products may also contribute to the (cyber-)stratification of languages, given that English is more endowed with electronic resources than Hindi, which, by turn, claims Bollywood victory over Urdu renditions of artistic text (Cronin 2013:60–1). This may globalise older divisions between 'public' and 'private culture', or alternatively contribute to the privatisation of the cyber-sphere by exposing conceptions of national intimacy to the global public (Bauman 2003a; Turkle 2010; Urry 2014:175, 190). I explore this through a combined discussion of specific soundtracks and cinematic segments, highlighting textual meanings alongside their (shadowy or not) contextual movement.

It is argued that the inclusion of Bollywood in 'the hallowed lexicon of the English language' (Govil 2007:77) was a tribute to the Indian film industry to which SM aesthetics appears to adhere linguistically and kinaesthetically. Prasad's (2003) Bollywood genealogy, which endorses blended forms of mobility (experiential travel, commercial tourism and mediated travel narrative), is based on American engineer Wilford E. Deming's journey (1932), and his claim to have produced India's first sound and talking picture. In his narrative he mentions how the word's first version (Tollywood) might be explained by the fact 'that our Calcutta studio was located in the suburb of Tollygung ... Tolly being a proper name and Gunge meaning locality'. Thus, he concludes, 'it was Hollywood itself ... that, with the confidence that comes from global supremacy, renamed a concentration of production facilities to make it look like its own baby'. Prasad then proceeds to relate this anecdote to local Calcuttan press long before satellite television and MTV, which referred to the Bengali film industry as Tollywood. 'Once Tollywood was made possible by the fortuitous availability of a half-rhyme, it was easy to clone new Hollywood babies by simply replacing the first letter. I suspect...that it was the trendy and smart young JS journalists who first adopted this way of slotting Hindi cinema into their otherwise largely Eurocentric cultural world' (ibid.). India's first spectacular engineers were strangers, endorsing this type of ambivalent attitude towards Western technology we will encounter in SM controversies.

His ambivalent take on Indian Westernisation aside, Prasad makes a significant observation on the word's genesis at the intersections of technological achievement, professional travel and cultural flows within and without India. I place my blended analytical discourse on contemporary Eurasian professional mobilities at such a crossroads, claiming that SM's artistic profiles present us with the image of a privileged *tornadóros*, a mechanic specialised in manufacturing social utopias based on conceptions of work and travel (Tzanelli 2013b: ch. 1). Again, the term's ancient Greek root prioritises European philosophical traditions intentionally, consolidating Prasad's commentary on Western European contributions to Indian culture and technology. It shows how urban paths to Indian modernity encountered Western discourses of progress, triggering an anxiety for the loss of man's connection with ideals of nature and 'naturalised' bonding (such as that within families and imagined communities). In short, the *tornadóros* is both the destroyer and creator of utopias, especially those focusing on travel. Again we have recourse to linguistic discourse, as there is indeed a language of consumption lifestyles such as those centring on tourist mobilities at the heart of this term (Dann 1996). Etymologically the word *tour* is derived from the Latin *tornare* and the Greek *tórnos*, meaning 'a lathe or circle; the movement around a central point or axis' (Theobald 1998:6). The suffix – ism used in 'tourism' is defined as 'action or process; typical behaviour or quality' while the suffix – ist denotes 'one that performs a given action' (ibid.). Even if we consider tourism as a commodity (Hiller 1976 in Dann and Cohen 1996:305) its essence appears to replicate the essentials of the industrial process Prasad so eloquently describes. The term also connects Jameson's criticism of 'slow' allegories (the slow and plodding man of 1970s Mumbai in SM's cinematic archetypes of migrant labour) to 'fast' postnational artistic innovations. On the realist plane, SM's diasporic artists also fall into the category of fast mobilities: symbolic 'distancing' from imagined and actual homelands in cinematic art-work is essential for the actualisation of symbolic creativity as imaginative 'touring', transforming subjects from members of an imagined community into strangers, migrants and tourists (Spode 2009). Desforges (2000) argues for a tourist Self that is relationally and reflexively produced through personal biography, McCabe (2005) highlights the normative significance of being called 'traveller' rather than 'tourist' and Williams (1965) attributes the uniqueness of creative workers to their dedication in transmitting their expressive journeys as 'experience'. At stake are connections of experiential uniqueness with authenticity and the authentication of the social reality in which the travellers/tourists find themselves during movement (Cohen 1996; Gottlieb 1982:168–73; McCabe 2005:88–96).

Hence, the art of *tornadóroi* points to forms of action implicated in articulations of modernity and post-modernity. Just like regular tourists, SM's *tornadóroi* are part of new 'neotribal' social formations that live beyond traditional kinship networks (Maffesoli 1996; Hannam 2008). As mechanical engineers and traditional labour, the old *tornadóroi* physically performed 'their turn' in industrial mobility complexes. But post-modern *tornadóroi* traverse in their narratives the world equipped with their senses and their prosthetic gadgets (cameras, ipads and mobile phones). Their imaginative travels are projected onto idealised humans in their art-work to actualise utopias of tourism-related migration (Garnham 2000 on the utopian possibility of art). As a result, post-modern *tornadóroi* perform a sort of pilgrimage to global cultures, which fuses spiritual and consumerist imperatives (Graburn 1977, 1983b, 2004) and even resurrects old renditions of the human mechanic. The word's masculine form conforms to old connections between manliness and civilisation (Bederman 1995) – a trend that feminist theories of spectatorship might connect to the domination of global film industries by male leaders (Bourdieu 1996a). Though not always applicable to the social profiling of contemporary cultural industries, as ideal types the *tornadóroi* contribute to selective valorisations of national cultures.

SM's camera-work also adopts a *tornadóros'* viewpoint through the protagonist's mobility from a migrant to a privileged consumer, a millionaire, and an audio-visual tourist. The story is a fine exposition of a progressively masculinised Indian *dispositif* through the emergence of aesthetically pleasing mobilities, when 'wasteful' aspects of one's image are *disposed of*. There is a Weberian twist in this reading of Marxist theory, in which the proletariat figures as 'waste' (O'Brien 2008:45–7; Tzanelli 2011:8–9). But SM also actualises a critical reversal of a conservative Indian narrative that sees in Bollywood-induced modernities the reduction of native cinema 'to a memory, a part of the nostalgia industry' (Rajadhyaksha 2003:38), replicating attacks upon touristifications of national heritage. If anything, SM proffers a contradictory panoramic view of Mumbai's great wastelands through its endless possibilities for audio-visual consumption, entrepreneurship and the good life. At this stage, we still inhabit the mental space of travel and act as 'junkhunters' or methodologists of character. As such, we stand between stereotyping and real understandings of cultural difference (Merton 1948:512). Forcing spectators to travel critically but comfortably and with repulsion or regret by turns, the film is unlike conventional adaptations of the black histories of European colonialism. Though partly appropriating the techniques of oral performance and enunciation by placing the hero-narrator at the forefront (Diawara 1992:190–2), SM does not project any specifically Indian 'language', but opts instead for complex symbolisations of socio-political anxieties we face in a 'global village'.

Cinematic pilgrimage, archplot and cosmological mobilities

Tornadóroi move, manipulate and rework *dispositif*. They manage to turn it from 'waste' into an absolutely necessary value-product for consumption by global audiences. These days, global audiences are audio-visual recipients and communicators of ideas but also kinaesthetically motivated like any tourist. Though Parts I and II focus on the cinematic *tornadóroi* (SM's lead artists), in the last part we encounter non-privileged, native groups acting as such, either voluntarily or through the global visitors' personal projects. For the moment, to comprehend how this is achieved in practice I highlight the interdependency of cinematic 'archplots' with anthropological renditions of 'cosmology'. Archplot is the central scenario of any cinematic plot (McKee 1999: 3–4, 41–2) But the stories scriptwriters narrate are unique hybrids of experience and knowledge rooted in collective pasts and individual endeavours, with intrinsic connections between the two always operating in the background. Real-life experiences communicate with cosmologies, the ways the social world is ordered at a collective level. Despite their structural ordering, archplots and cosmologies can also be used as interpretive vehicles of change (Herzfeld 2008; Alexander 2006). *Tornadóroi* accommodate both ends of Urry's original division of travellers-come-tourists into those attending to individualised, romantic gazing rituals and those 'succumbing' to the gaze's mass commoditisation (Urry 1995:137; Urry 2002; Urry and Larsen 2011:19–20, 203). Otherwise put, *tornadóroi* are connectors between structure and agency: they are romantic artists and mass producers, 'slow' makers of culture and fast industrial workers in post-modern urban networks.

It is in this respect that SM stands at a crossroads between world systems, structures and human agency (Archer 1995). My aim is to tease out of these systemic, structural and agential forces something more than a uniform Marxist critique of media or tourism capitalism. Rather than merely staying on the institutional surface of such an enterprise, I want to understand why both its infrastructural and superstructural components refer back to human progress and creative interpretation that Enlightenment traditions bestowed upon the 'liquid modernist' condition (Bauman 2000). As India is a post-colonial complex of cities, rural areas and disconnected socio-cultural outposts with diverse developmental needs, the book also responds to Jamal's and Hill's (2002:94–5) call to draw attention to the role of the post-colonial tourist in productions of space and authenticity. Dann (1996) and Edensor (1998) produced accounts of this phenomenon but spent less time on theorising intersections of travel, tourism and new/old media technologies – a gap Edensor (2005) began to fill later in European cinematic-tourist contexts. By the same token, Dann (1977) and Mowforth and Munt (1998) debated the ego-based, romantic motivations of tourists but were not interested in new technologies that Bell and Lyall (2002) first addressed in detail. Rather than exploring on-site, terrestrial tourism, I attempt an ambitious synthesis through conceptions of 'cinematic tourism' that will lead us to discussions of film archplots and cosmologies.

'Cinematic tourism' and the 'cinematic tourist' are not identical to 'film-induced tourism', which emphasises the importance of film in location marketing and tourism development (Beeton 2005; Croy 2010). As theoretical models, both concepts are internally differentiated by the moves and motions of travel through and after film-viewing, as well as the cinematic production of travel and tourism. Indeed, the original novel's cinematic adaptation produced a 'constellation of mobilities' that brought together practices of technological movement (film-making), professional migration (successive relocations of artistic and technical communities to filmed sites), virtual travel (setting up Internet sites) and embodied (film-induced) tourism. My consideration of these phenomena as aspects of a singular 'cinematic tourism', following the moves enacted from within and around films (Tzanelli 2010b, 2013a), matches Cresswell's (2001) emphasis on 'mobility constellations' (also Croy and Heitmann 2011:190).

SM's cinematic narrative is anchored on issues that haunted India's relationship with its colonizer-Others but also its internal peripheries: *dalits*, slum residents, women and children. The overarching themes of corruption and uncleanliness 'dress' these peripheral identities in dirt, passivity, disempowerment or innocence in various combinations, reiterating Marxian convictions that subaltern beings comprise a sort of 'refuse'. At the same time, the film, its music and also its overall activist culture suggest agential alternatives, however small in the grand scheme of global politics. SM capitalises on the protagonist's social rejection as an illiterate 'cheat' or on his younger version's ambiguous positioning between innocence and cunning intelligence that defines old colonial legacies (Cannella and Viruru 2004:88–9). The eco-feminist basis of such connections can be criticised – if anything SM turned such global sensibilities to vulnerability on their head. Notably, the idea that humankind and nature should be treated as unity, that we all have a duty to protect it as our very own 'sustainable garden' (Argyrou 2005:75), appeals to a particular brand of environmentalist discourse stemming from Western European post-colonial debts and duties. As the preferred cosmology, eco-feminism sketches the movement from biological determinism to Western technological manipulation as the sole (bad) path to civilisation, ignoring how we arrived at where we stand today thanks to technological progress – or that tourism necessitates and facilitates world connectivities and development thanks to technology. This ambivalence, which stands at the heart of cultural, economic and political globalisation, also connects to diachronic fears that a biologically determined 'character' of *hoi polloi* might corrupt Western civilisation. SM and its Bollywood contingent are systemically linked to such fallacies via cinematic adaptation, which began its cinematic career as a disreputable trend, originally regarded as impure art-work. Champions of film resented the dependency of film on literature, thus contributing to its widespread discussion in artistic circles as crude usurpation of literary masterpieces (Cartmell et al. 2008:1). The fear that cinematic adaptation would lead to the demotion of fine art-work to cheap reproduction befit only for the 'lower social orders' is connected to nationalist industrialism (Gellner 1998) and one of Europe's darkest moments, with the ascension of fascist populism and the coerced migration of Marxist intellectuals to the United States (Tzanelli 2011: ch. 6).

Notably, the publication of Adorno and Horkheimer's *Dialectic of Enlightenment* almost coincided with Hunter's interrogations into the class basis of film cultures; his article, 'The Art-Form of Democracy?' (1932) in *Scrutiny* was banned from literary studies. This conflation of new emergent tastes in popular cultures across two continents that ruled the globe for centuries with the populist politics of the Third Reich and later post-war trends in the American *Raum* provides the geopolitical coordinates of twentieth-century cultural globalisation and its coerced human mobilities (migrations). In SM's case, this old debate sheds additional light on aggressive responses to Boyle's and scriptwriter Simon Beaufoy's representations of Mumbai's urban underbelly and the film's oft cheerful – hence subversive – construction of a vantage viewpoint through 'slumdog eyes'. Beaufoy's adaptation *recreates* Swarup's story, better highlighting contact points between Western literary *ethographic* tropes and cosmological priorities steeped in post-colonial ethnographies of the former 'centre' (Wallerstein 1974, 1980). But the product itself is an example of the fragmentation of such world-systems and yesteryear's coloniser-subjects, who can be more reflexive in their actions. Part of the 'mobile multitude' (Hardt and Negri 2000:212) of elite creative worker nomadism, Beaufoy and his inspiration, *Q & A* author Vikas Swarup, redeem within systems of power the utopian search for liberation.

The product of a chain of adaptations, SM bears witness to a civilisational meeting point articulated through Western artistic eyes and hearts after a pilgrimage to the lands of inspiration. To remember Coleman and Eade (2004), the very notion of 'pilgrimage' is nuanced: it may comprise embodied, performative or symbolic movement in a semantic field traversed by the pilgrim. Indeed, the pilgrim's movement can be included in this book's metaphors of globalisation as a sort of meta-movement of no particular religious content or sacralised rationale (Eade and Sallnow 1991). As products of European histories, all three forms point to interlinks between travel, subjections and reinventions of the 'other', philanthropy and edu-tourism, tourism for personal education (Holdnak and Holland 1996). For example, a striking difference between Beaufoy's and Swarup's scripts is the protagonist's ethno-cultural profile. His very name in *Q&A*, Ram Mohammad Thomas, sneered at by the police inspector (Swarup 2006:14), suggests a pan-religious message lost in SM, where Jamal is a Muslim. Indian reactions to the film's use of 'slumdog' easily clash with its audio-visual take on Mumbai's social splintering and social inequalities (Graham and Marvin 2001). What no analysis seems to cover is an integrated understanding of the dynamic of the cinematic text, the background of media imperatives and the overarching discourse of cultural (re-)production that is managed by a group of Western(ised) artists. As a result the film has been read by critics and analysts from left and right in equally partial ways.

SM's aesthetic and cosmological connectivity to Bollywood musical melodrama via its use of 'good' and 'evil' oppositions sits on childhood and family tropes. There we detect another link between Hindi cinematic production, the new hybridities of Bollywood cinema and Mumbai's budding 'slumdog' tourism. Recent UNESCO statistics (2009) rank the Bollywood film industry and its regional variants as the largest in the world in terms of film production per annum and audience numbers (Ray 2012:1). Yet, whereas audience capacity can be attributed to the growing domestic viewers from all classes and castes and the combined consumption of Bollywood products by South Asian diasporas, slum tourism is a phenomenon overwhelmingly addressed to Western or generally affluent consumers (Basu 2012:68–9). Global SM tourists may in fact treat the film as less than an honourable or relevant motivation to visit Mumbai's slums – a tendency comparable with that of other sub-trends in 'cinematic' or 'film-induced' tourism (Macionis and Sparks 2009; Croy 2010; Croy and Heitmann 2011). Such global 'audiences' are more likely to incorporate visits to slums into personal agendas for self-betterment or humanitarian prerogatives. The film speaks a language of adaptation that can be perceived as conformist, whereas the project of 'being there' endorses ennobling action – a 'mission'. Significantly, despite their popularity in South Asia, India, Arab, African and Caribbean countries, Bollywood films are often criticized by intellectuals or even film-makers for their repetitive or 'un-realistic' plots and their extreme melodramatic habitus (Ray 2012).

We do indeed deal in this instance not just with what Appadurai (1990) depicts as clashes of various scapes, but with a hermeneutic conflict within media spaces that re-writes artistic styles as straightforward political statements, when nuances within the scripts suggest a more flexible approach. By this I do not mean that SM is an apolitical product; nor do I aim to exonerate its makers from any slides of conscience. But it seems that this normative agenda may obscure some analytical nuances and revert the project to fundamentalist discourse. My aim is to attack anti-adaptation arguments that form an unequivocal alliance with established Western (originally European, later also transatlantic) takes on popular cultures (Urry 1995 on tourist consumption and Jay 1988 on the gaze). In this spirit the following section explains how SM anchors its narrative on tropes of authenticity in overlapping discourses of art and tourism, attacking post-colonial themes from within, through their mocking reproduction (Hutcheon 2006). SM's interrogation of Indian subaltern cultures is not divorced from cultural or developmental ethics but examines the origins of this ethics in Western European discourses of development. Western European 'developmentalism' consigns knowledge and its economies to the domain of law, debating how ethics is diachronically rooted in conceptions of *ethos* as habit, from which performance and art theory were born as projects of comprehending cultural difference (Tzanelli 2013b: ch. 2).

The juxtaposition of the 'slow' mobilities of (colonial) history and justice with the 'fast' mobilities of cinema and tourism complies with Heideggerian (Heidegger 1967) juxtapositions of sacred time (*kairós*) as the site of myth in which spatio-temporal constrictions cease to define the subject's experience with *chrónos* as the mechanical and quantifiable time we read in clocks, the time of everyday life (Tzanelli 2011: ch. 3; Howard 2012:11–12). In a parallel analysis applying to tourist flows, Kirshenblatt-Gimblett (1997) debates three different dimensions of time in heritage tourism: the fixed, official historic time; heritage time as a move-the-clock-back time to provide authentic tourist experience; and personal time or that of the individualised experience of the place. This tripartite schema interacts with Heidegger's *chronic* and *kairotic* imperatives, and applies to cinematic tourism as an experiential, existential and cosmological journey via filmic myths. The alleged SM 'economic miracle' in Mumbai bore the possibility to bridge the two different times though a globalised *syngyrìa* or meeting of times. Yet, capitalisations on SM's *ethological* arc by new knowledge economies (tourism) endorsed the proliferation of normative discourses with various consequences. I return to these two formulas in Chapter 9, where I investigate global criticisms of SM-related humanitarian projects. Here it is imperative to stress that although fast or popular mobilities might not resonate similarly with all members of SM's artistic contingent, the very production of the film and its tourist networks contributed to Mumbai's global articulation as a community.

2 The nexus of theory and methodology

The multi-site as methodology

Examining the impact of media, tourist and local industrial collaborations, the book employs mobile methodologies so as to analyse contemporary phenomena of socio-cultural dis-embeddedness and de-territorialisation (Hannam 2008; Hall 2008). It first reconsiders the epistemological suggestion that the dominant visitor's gaze and ear that connect media to tourist consumption can be strategically manipulated by all parties, including the subaltern. The statement's original feminist underpinnings (Mulvey 2006; Spivak 1988) give way in this particular instance to other variables (class, status, race) defining subaltern group performance. We must acknowledge that even local performances are embedded in power structures (in fact, alignments of subaltern Indian communities with dominant cultural systems [English language] can be a liberating choice relative to individual circumstances (Rege 2011)).

The global public spheres in which such identities emerge are 'staged' with the help of new media technologies (Tzanelli 2010b:17), but the ways tourist formations emerge through connections between such spheres or sites deserves additional examination (Nederveen Pieterse 1998:79–80). We do indeed deal with multiple spheres and agents, including the media industries, the national centre and the community from which the media draw inspiration. The word 'local' or 'community' may distract from 'the intense complexity or micro-politics that all sides are inevitably imbricated within and shaped by' (Meethan 2001:61). Indeed, it is often easier to focus on the cinematic Juhu slum than on Dharavi's (the biggest slum in Mumbia) activism when evaluating SM's impact on tourism and identity. However, there are intersections and disjunctions between the sub-scenes and imaginaries of these sites (virtual, fictional and real) we may explore as discursive tropes – or rather, the ways such discourses are interpreted by various human agents (D'Andrea 2006:114–15). Interpretation becomes here coterminous with social representations that are promoted by global media communities (journalists, leaders and workers in film and digital tourist industries), involved state agents and localities.

Consequently, my sources are drawn from multiple actual and virtual sites in the West and the East. Treating the web as a multi-site in which SM debates acquire various meanings entails consideration of the ways in which the internet as a medium absorbs and recreates itself through hyperlinked content, breaking this up into 'searchable chunks' while also surrounding itself 'with various other media it has absorbed' (Carr 2010:91; Anastasiou and Schäler 2010). As SM is my starting point, I consulted reports primarily collected between 2008 and 2013 in multiple Eastern and Western virtual sites of newspapers, digital repositories and tourism websites drawing on the film industry's narrative. Peculiarly, SM never acquired its own website. For any press materials and information relevant to the film's making I consulted the extras from its official DVD (Blue-ray) release. Of help have been the well-developed Wikipedia entry on the film, which stores Eurasian reports on it and its industrial community, and the relevant Internet Movie Database (IMDB) entry, which links to various individual biographies of directors, producers and actors. The content of such sites is fluid and ephemeral, user (as co-producer) friendly, anonymous and, according to most people, inherently unreliable. But their academic use as information databases with links to various newspapers and online sites and businesses is still valid. When released into multiple socio-cultural sites, these digital narratives may transform into localised perceptions of identity or merge into official national memories. Web sphere analysis is a strategy including the analysis of the relations between producers and users of web materials, as potentiated and mediated by the structural and feature elements of web sites, hypertexts and the links between them (Schneider and Foot 2004, 2005). Hence, though methodologically I do not research through physical sites, I do consider contextual productions of meaning (Büscher and Urry 2009; Büscher et al. 2011). We deal with a multiple, rather than neat 'double hermeneutics' (Giddens 1987) of subalterns, artists, tourist business and authorities, to which one must add that propagated by the researcher.

SM's sites (the slum, the Taj Mahal, the brothel, the airport and Mumbai's main train station) acquire an excess of market meaning when used by various constituencies to bolster media business or urban tourism. As Part II endeavours to show, the sites provided the industry with iconic and aural referents from a repository of resources that is geographically located in the national periphery. The (however loose) social relationship between SM and these sites suggests that we consider causal connections in media-tourism growth as contingent linkages in global network systems (Schulman 2004:xxiiii) – a phenomenon conducive to the ways the local becomes inserted into the global to produce an often challenging – if at times conflicting – symbiosis (Robertson 1992; Urry 2014:189). Instead of considering 'glocalisation' as a phenomenon in which one particular locality interacts with globality in one particular interpretative contingent, it is suggested that many localities can partake in the same interpretative instance (Therborn 1995; Nederveen Pieterse 2009). The different responses that SM's iconography induced in different sites can only be examined in relation to the economic, political and cultural horizons and possibilities of their respective regions.

Synaesthesia or methodologies of audio-vision

Investigations into the cinematic tourist gaze and ear commence in this study with an extensive analysis of the film and its music, before interrogating how SM's audio-visual stimuli are received or rejected in Mumbai's (virtual and actual) sites. Music has always been a mobile cultural expression, with 'world music' networks being especially global 'through transnational spread of instruments, scales and styles through trading routes' (Connell and Gibson 2004:345). Music induces an aesthetic experience that provides us with a way of being in the world, and making sense of it is important; it is not merely traded by business travellers; it is created by mobile artists with aesthetic sensibilities and consumed by audiences who bring their own interpretations to it (Frith 1996:272). SM (world) music bears the mark of a mobility commonly associated with the irreducible image of the traveller. Unpacking some of the meanings of SM music's master signs in networks of producers, consumers and their technologies (Dwyer and Crang 2002; Tzanelli 2010b:ch.1) allows me to examine the circulation of soundscapes-as-artscapes in sub-cultural terms (i.e. beyond the routes and roots of music and lyrics (Hebdige 1979)), in terms of art-*world* and art-*work* context (i.e. their use in the cinematic narrative) (Becker 1982) and in terms of political mobilisation (Cohen 1997; Beck 2005). The term 'soundscapes' considers sound as a publicly circulated entity reflecting and implicated in social practices and the material spaces of performance (Schafer 1994). Although, just like landscape, soundscape encloses the 'contradictory forces of the natural and the cultural, the fortuitous and the composed, the improvised and the deliberately produced' (Samuels et al. 2010:330) that define SM's cinematic story of mobile 'human refuse', the transnational production of SM's soundscape interconnects to the significance of sound on tourist and digital sites. DeNora's (2000, 2003) call for the production of 'music ethnographies' *in situ* counters the claim that fusion music genres should be viewed as trivial entertainment (Kong 1995), introducing instead combined mobilities (global professional migrations, electronic media flows and slum tourism sensibilities), 'an implosion of peripheries into centres' (Kearney 1995:550). Clifford's (1986) and Erlmann's (2004) suggestion that we make space in social analysis for the 'ethnographic ear' resonates with urban and art sociologists, and complements sociologies of the 'tourist gaze' (Urry 2002; Urry and Larsen 2011). If silence is a 'vacant niche' and sounds of nature are popular with sophisticated ecotourists (Bell and Lyall 2002:44–5, 58–9), cinema's soundscapes are at least compatible with slum tourists' search for sublimation in the 'dirt and danger' of Mumbai's industrialised ecosystems.

To analyse music soundtracks one needs to examine how non-representational signs serve to induce feelings in audiences, generating a fan base, but also to automatise capitalist systems (Guattari 1995; Genosko 2008:14). SM music is primarily treated as constitutive of the film's aesthetic and political messages, which are communicated as audio-visual pastiche. Different tracks might adhere to the principles and values of different genres, complexifying conceptions of their geographical situatedness and prompting us to consider practices of 'social framing' of their meanings. The epistemological rationale of such 'deep listening' is a corrective to the deep cosmopolitan model that often proves to be 'hard of hearing' when it comes to cultural nuances (Becker 2004; Oliveros 2005). Deep listening invites deep travel to urban soundscapes, as SM's auditory landscapes are part of the sonic aesthetics of a phantasmagoric mega-city (Mumbai). There is extensive literature on world cities as 'products of voyages and circulation of daily movements' but also as audio-visual articulations of nostalgia (Samuels et al. 2010:336; Gray 2007; Solomon 2009; Sakakeeny 2010). This also prompts considerations of the (non-)diegetic nature of film music or the use of soundtracks as more than scores that accompany the film's narrative arc (Chion 1994; Kassabian 2000; Sider 2003; Buhler et al. 2009). Certain music scores from SM can be analysed in terms of corporate strategies to share or attune to popular fashion and music trends, but an examination of their flows in popular channels merits a separate note in terms of global popular creativity (Negus 1999; Hesmondhalgh 1996, 2007).

Research into SM's music is integrated into the study of the cinematic text with the help of scene theory. 'Scenes' are enablers of 'a particular state of relations between various populations and social groups as [they] coalesce around specific coalitions of musical style' (Straw 1991:379). As both local and translocal instances, scenes refer both to musical styles and human interaction in domains in which these styles circulate. The concept resonates with subcultural analysis and well-established neotribal theory because both enable us to examine networks of cultural flows (Maffesoli 1996; Bennett 1999, 2005; Malbon 1999). Although the concept of 'scene' is used primarily by academic researchers of music, it is compatible with sociological and anthropological understandings of theatre 'technologies', including staging terrestrial and digital venues for social performances (Bennett 2004:230; Peterson and Bennett 2004). The global professionalisation of the stager of theatre plays (Braidotti 2011:66; Tzanelli 2012b:14) communicates with an elaborate division of social performance into 'front' and 'back regions' (as in Goffman 1987). Associations between sites define the ethnographic object through a continuous translation, so that the researcher can uncover the significance and effects of various phenomena of mobility (Marcus 1998:84). The fluidity of scene-making (from local to regional, national and global) mirrors the use of theatre techniques in cinema (e.g. the reproduction of accent and paralinguistic gesture or cultural sensibilities) as a source of intercultural knowledge (Fabian 1999:28). The complex communication of art-scenes in the film, the digital terrain (as in You Tube videos or relevant websites) and its music products (CDs, MP3s, mobile telephone and internet track downloads) finds extensions even in the global debate upon SM's audio-visual node by academics, literati, journalists and audiences.

Latour (1993) has explained that the rise of sound machinery partook in epistemological purifications of sound that sought to abstract it from its immediate surroundings while noting its connectivity to place. Just like the process of touristification, film-making displays a technological propensity to 'drown out the human scale of the natural landscape' (Samuels et al. 2010:331), turning 'noise' into the binary opposite of 'sound'. Yet, the music of principal SM composer, A.R. Rahman, allows technologically manipulated soundscapes to communicate multiple urban histories and experiences: his primeval 'sound pollution' encroaches into SM's holistic concern with an alleged 'urban pollution' (by slum cultures, political corruption and the corruption of the human psyche) (Atkinson 2007 on urban theory; Truax 2008 on composition). What the film's script, camera-work and directorship add to visual refinement, Rahman's musical composure complements in tune, beat and vocal synergies. I consider each musical segment, fragment, or soundtrack article in context, as Rahman's music-work often replaces Beaufoy's dialogue or adds to the camera's visual narrative and the director's viewpoint to such an extent that they become essential to the wholeness of the finished product. The spectators' gaze and auditory engagement blend in an aesthetic orchestration that enables total identification with the cinematic object. Prioritising new digital technologies, SM's industry industrialises the city's passage to modernity primarily through vision and sound – what Bauman (2000:111) sees as the transition from 'wetware' to 'hardware'. My own analytical focus on SM's technologies would appear to decentre human actors in the enterprise by replacing the question of who creates and speaks with a focus on the techno-cultural assemblages that enable the transmission of audio-visual messages. In the case of SM's music my 'semiotechnological' exercise (Kittler 1997) prioritises the movement of music texts at the interface level, in social media channels where meaning *per se* (e.g. sharing video clips with others) is used to extract value (Deleuze and Guattari 1988:242; Langlois 2012:6). But similar strategies are implemented in determining whether such SM products do have value for localities. This enacts an investigation into the power relations through which practices of meaning production take place, once texts become completely detached from their creator.

My deployment of the term 'syn(a)esthesia' (heretofore synaesthesia) problematises the discourse of competing modernities from an artistic and aesthetic stance. The term was used in informatics (Gammack 1999) and urban tourist studies (Donald and Gammack 2007) with little theoretical elaboration as to its true origins in philosophies of mind and neurophilosophy (on which see Sacks (2013) for a sophisticated interdisciplinary analysis). Its medical associations with a true sensory disorder (the replacement of one sense (*aesthesis*) with another as a compensatory mechanism) were philosophically and empirically explored only very recently. I do not subscribe to positivist discourse, which reifies 'facts' through apprehension in immediate atomistic sensory experience (Bhaskar 1989:52–4; McCreery 1995:145). As interpretative artistic action, synaesthesia captures the mind-body complex of performativity, which in the case of cinematic viewing is limited to gazing and listening. The term considers Western European renditions of 'aesthetic cosmopolitanism' as a disorientating combination of corporeal movement and cultural *praxis* (Urry 1995:145–7; Hannerz 2002; Edensor 2011, 2014) only to deconstruct them in Mumbai from the localities' viewpoint. We can speak of 'performative synaesthetics' to explore the mind-body complex of tourist performativity, pointing to a productive reordering of visitor and host narrative pathways through combinations of image, movement, touch, smell and sound. As Bærenholdt et al. (2004) have pointed out in a similar vein, places are today 'staged' and performed by visitors via tourist networks (Lash and Urry 1994:ch.10; Urry 1995:17). Performative synaesthetics communicates with Judith Butler's 'performativity' as repetitive enactment of identity in public that originates in discourse (on performativity and embodied performance see Butler 1993; on synaesthesia Tzanelli 2013a). These synesthetic organisations induce pilgrimages that combine the monetary capital of arts (the generation of tourism or other consumption styles from movies) with the emotional and spiritual investment of audiences in values that exceed this capital (Thrift 2006).

Synaesthesia replaces Western 'scopophilia' (Mulvey 2006) or love of gazing: as cinematic art-work, SM is influenced by Bollywood plots rooted in Indian myths but updated with the help of musical and textual pastiche. Western scopophilic custom is happily adopted by Indian viewers and listeners claiming good taste but its implementation on hybridised Bollywood art-work may be rejected (Thomas 1985:116–17; Wright 2010:37–8; Tzanelli 2011:ch.6). In such cases, Bollywood is conceptualised as a cheap version of Hollywood, characterised by convoluted plots and further fragmented by hybridised music and dance scenes. Although SM borrows from Bollywood tropes, it is decisively Western in style. Thomas' (1985) argument that the concept of genre appeals to Western structuring principles of expectation and convention that do not correspond to 'intolerable' Bollywood hybridity is useful. There is ample space to discuss SM as an adaptation conducive to fusions of comedy, melodrama, musical and emotional eruptions – all distinctive Bollywood traits, according to Thomas (1985:120–1). However, with the determination of SM artists to eliminate stylistic repetitions, provide their art-work with clear beginnings, narrative threads and ends and to attack traditional values venerated by Bollywood fans we hit an impasse. Boyle and colleagues attack religion and patriotism, whereas SM's music opens its arms to all cultures or celebrates consumerism and mocks the state. SM's realism comes closer to anti-Bollywood structures of the epic story and does not sacrifice emotional content to subplots and gags (ibid. 123). The film's distinctive 'travelling flavours' come close to the vilified *masala* films of the Bollywood turn but part ways in terms of linear narrative development. The term *masala* involves a third absent sense in Indian cinematic pleasure (taste), suggesting that non-European audiences may be more synaesthetic than their Western European counterparts. SM's opening focus on destiny mirrors Western interpretations of Indian *karma*, whereas its discussion of the principles of respect, measure and inner harmony via its main characters resembles some Aristotelian views on tragedy and *hubris*. The film's serendipity needs to be explored by both Bollywood and Western synesthetic means, and their differences must be considered in Mumbai's touristified sites.

Thomas' (1985:130) categorical argument that Indian, especially Bollywood cinema 'bears no relation to Aristotelian aesthetics' as it rejects the unities of time and place and the dramatic development of narrative is valid up to a point. We must consider the development of Bollywood since 1985 and the intensification of global artistic synergies that further hybridised Indian plots. In addition we should examine the place of the theory of flavours/moods, which is concerned with moving the spectator through the text (or its corresponding touristic contexts) in an ordered succession of modes of affect (*rasa*), by means of highly stylised devices (ibid.) in Western art sites such as those of film music. Thomas' analysis promotes discourses of difference that may valorise racialised divides. It must be borne in mind that where SM initiates such Bollywood-centred Eurasian contact it also ignites criticism by Western and Westernised migrant subjects. SM's synaesthetic engagement retains a sense of ethnographic voyeurism in line with the politics of televised compassion (Tester 1994) – a point that brings it closer to Bollywood emotionalism. Occasionally, the film activates a sort of compassionate guilt we associate with volunteer tourism, destroying the subject's pleasure. Sprinkled with laughter and jokes in rather uncomfortable moments, SM turns audio-visual subjects into the primary object of criticism.

SM's music generated a separate controversy that communicated with the general intellectual and political criticism the film received in India and abroad. In line with the post-1980s world music project that emphasised the impossibility of tracing stylistic authenticity, Rahman's scores and lyrical matrix were so hybrid that were deemed to be neither 'in line' with the story's slumdog heart nor in agreement with Rahman's previous creations. Behind these criticisms, one discerns another that focuses on offshoring his creative products and Rahman himself, who appears in video clips of his most successful SM score by an American music band. But this leisurely consumption of the slum 'elsewhere', in the developed urban hubs of the global North or the affluent enclaves of the global South (see Urry 2014:76–7 on media offshoring), was based on Rahman's propensity to foster a political 'nowhere', a utopia. Also, there was not enough appreciation among critics for the soundtrack's actual synaesthetic innovation (as part of the cinematic narrative). Looking past any observations on the marketisation of 'strategic authenticity' or the fetishisation of ethnic marginality in music markets, Rahman spoke a language akin to that of Beaufoy's and Boyle's cinematic adaptation as a counter-polemic to the purist dialogues in contemporary artscenes. Just like cinematic adaptation, 'world music' was never accepted as a genre but demoted to a marketing category distinct only for its blend of multiple genres from the 'developing world' (Frith 2000; see Hesmondhalgh 2007:513–15 for a critique of Frith). We may speak of such professional synergies as a noetic form of activist 'music tourism' or 'aural tourism' (Cosgrove 1988 in Connell and Gibson 2004:352; Goodwin and Gore 1990). This tourism is constitutive of an expressive project fusing local, regional and global concerns while standing independent of the commercial enterprise of the soundtrack – its market routes and sign appropriations. It has been suggested that musical 'texts' both reflect and debate structures of tourism, especially because their lyrics become a site of contested meanings and changing community ideals (Mitchell 1996; Malbon 1999; Duffy 2000; Tzanelli 2010b:131). By dissolving hybrid music genres that even in Bollywood films complement hybrid cinematic stories, Rahman further promoted a de-territorialised ethics that spoke about exploitation, poverty, crime and the like.

Just like world music, cinematic adaptations of political content stir national consciousness or contribute to transnational political movements (Connell and Gibson 2004:343; Tzanelli 2013a:4, 6). It is in this respect that cinema is treated in this book as a place 'of intrinsic indiscernibility between art and non-art' (Diken and Laustsen 2007:6). Although guided by testimonies and interviews of artists and communities, my own reading of SM is a sociological monologue, where films proffer plural interpretations. Therefore, rather than treating Part II as cinema theory it should be seen as an *exposé* of social theory: a sociology of film. Whereas I adopt a particular reading of SM, in latter chapters I open up the interpretation to other constituencies, examining the rationale of their claims over meaning. In transitory spaces of 'combative cultural politics', film-making is streamlined through three distinctive modes of acceptance: resistance, habituation and interference (Baker 1995). Films of resistance produce alternative social paradigms, whereas films of habituation attune to existing networks of power and reinforce them. Films of interference disrupt institutional arrangements but do not necessarily proffer viable alternatives. This neat classification translates social movement theory in artistic terms, tapping on varied conceptions of citizenship and belonging in conservative and deliberative spheres of human action. Programmatic statements on the demise of alternative social visions in neoliberal spaces do harm as they reiterate the triumph of artistic instrumentality, the artist's blind submission to market imperatives and the eradication of critical aesthetic creativity. It is possible to appreciate and analyse aesthetic nodes such as that of SM – the film, the music and all its products – for their utopian messages that elude such monologic classification as sole capitalist tools. This excursus rests at the heart of the enterprise of cinematic tourist mobility, both enhancing and problematising it from within. If anything, the film's 'modified' Bollywood magical realism attacks convenient views on organised 'reality tours' we find in every part of the so-called 'Developing World', but especially in places such as Calcutta, Mumbai or Rio (Hutnyk 1996:207).

At the same time, the distant cinematic gaze makes what 'is unacceptable at home become acceptable when transgressing imaginary, mental, cultural borders' (Salazar 2004:92). Where 'on site', proximate sensory faculties may introduce ethical dilemmas and aesthetic distractions, audio-visual technology's distance allows the cinematic tourist first to encounter and later to process social phenomena. Mass spectatorship and mass tourism should not be examined in SM as causally related phenomena, but as part of a technological revolution that might support critical or uncritical processing of the world (Löfgren

1999; Franklin and Crang 2001; Meethan 2001; de Botton 2002; Beeton 2005). By moving between artistic utopian possibilities on the one hand and realist policies of gazing, touring and performing on the other, we observe moves from the aspiration to build a better world to actually making society work in actually existing conditions (Polanyi 1963; Kuhn 1970; Kracauer 2004:218; Diken and Laustsen 2007:1–2). SM's cinematic narrative is a slippery enterprise, here resisting or habituating and there interfering with institutional norms and cultural values.

One might claim that place or even time-space (*chronotope*) of production and consumption acts as an overriding discourse in SM's artistic products, an activist node. The word for cinema, *kinimatográfos* (κινηματογράφος), refers to the inscription (*grafi* from *gráfō*=to write) of movement (*kinima*). Following Bourdieu's (1984) theory of practice, Crossley (2003) suggests that activist and artistic movements overlap significantly. Artists and activists are socio-culturally disposed towards a particular type of social action that questions social norms and values and grants them with a form of pedagogical agency constitutive of bourgeois radicalism. Crossley views this 'radical habitus' as a manifestation of the 'submerged networks' and 'abeyance structures' that keep radicalism in constant flow through various mobility channels (ibid:45; Crossley 2002). But within the artist's art-work we also observe another type of cognitive and emotional movement: artistic activism resurrects the past in creative ways to remind us of our obligation to bring *doxic* (of collective belief) imperatives to the sphere of discourse (Bourdieu 1998:56; Tzanelli 2007:254; Habermas 1996; Tzanelli, 2013b:ch.6). Both art and social/tourism theory are viewpoints produced by 'communities of practice' (Grugulis and Stoyanova 2011:342). If, in addition to artistic representation, we consider the production and contestation of SM tourist networks, debates around the death and cultural reinvention of Mumbai slums as a 'place in time' come to the fore. Urry's discussion of 'places that die' (2004:208) provides a sociological *explanandum* for contemporary shifts from land (tangible forms of *Heimat*) to landscape (its transformation into an ideal based on novel technologies of the eye). The shift marks a replacement of concerns with representations as such with the ways these representations are produced, conserved or modified – otherwise put, how they are articulated (Mitchell 1994; Tarde 1903).

Articulation and new mobilities

The term 'articulation' is part of the book's mobility discourse. I borrow the term from the lexicon of music to convey the formulation of transitions and continuities between multiple notes or sounds. Like Said's (1993) post-colonial 'contrapuntalism', 'articulation' promises to transform the mediation of different viewpoints into a methodology of knowledge (Chowdry 2007:103), ingesting different ethnic idioms into the technological machine that institutes dominant forms of artistic idioms. As already highlighted, while music can be mobile, it can also induce embedded sentiment – a point connecting to modernist contradictions between Enlightenment belief in modern, universal progress and the Romantic spirit's rootedness in land and ideals that draw from the past to critique liquid modernity (Löwy and Sayre 2001:10). Music's connection to manipulated but de-mediated environments (Strain 2003) reinstates the power of nature in representations of the social. Notably, articulation's allusion to the act of bending one's joints (Latin *articulatio* from *artus*, Greek *árthosis*=connection, joint, from *arthrōnō*=verbally articulate) also extends to embodied understandings of nationhood via visions of human maturity and subjectivity (Tzanelli 2011:ch.5). Today, this 'physicalisation' of power is constantly countered by the polygenesis of sociality, which manifests in the form of assemblages or multiple competing social compositions such as those of the mobile artists (Tonkonoff 2013:277). Given the focus on temporary artistic relocations to Mumbai for the making of SM, O'Reilly's (2003:302) use of the term 'articulation' to explore migration and tourism's moves both separately and together, 'sometimes smoothly and sometimes causing friction' is pertinent. Let us not forget that 'articulation' is also an audio-visual manifestation of literacy: the term's Indo-European roots (*arta*) speak of organisation akin to that of the African-inspired ancient Greek *kósmos*, 'an iconic expression for "good order"' (Sandywell 2011:152). In the age of nations the paradox of literacy, in its print and audio-visual forms, was that it democratised knowledge while making it complicit to the emergence and preservation of political centres (McLuhan 1962, 1964; Anderson 2006). Rooted-national and mobile-artistic articulations share in method but differ in purpose: processes of nationalisation as political mobilisation change from complex to more stereotypical so as to articulate ideal types of citizenry (Gellner 1983), but transnational art-work tends to create 'human types' as symbols of intercultural communication. Art systems can be open-ended assemblages that negotiate anti-national and anti-statist forms of thinking, doing and feeling thus countering what Goldmann (1964, 1980) termed human societies tragic 'cosmovision' (*vision du monde*), a dystopian verdict that nothing and nobody escapes socio-cultural constrictions and rules.

The aesthetic aspects of Asian modernities such as those of India are often flagged – contra the rationalised aspects of their underlining policies (Vattimo 1988) – as imported or 'cloned' (Nederveen Pieterse 1998:78). In this context, articulation can be considered through India's glocalised transition to a haphazard program of national industrial modernisation and, more recently, translocal and transnational post-modernisation. India's story acts as model critique of Western conceptions of modernity 'as a modernity-without-windows, in which – as usual in Western conceptions – South-North and South-South (or East-West and East-East) flows and influences are either ignored or underestimated' (Nederveen Pieterse 1998:75). Although the country's most prominent leaders (Ghandi, Nehru) understood that they would have to address the nature of Indian modernity, they did not consider how localised cultural models produce multiple social realities even within the same nation.

Even the twentieth-century national scene suggested to Nehru a safe equation of individual and national growth, a conservative 'articulation'. The paradigm was as old as Herder's views on the socio-cultural formation of humanity and its linguistic articulation – a Western European suggestion that every national *Geist* (spirit) has unique, human-like, qualities and a special mission to carry out in the world (Bhatt 2000). The state's linguistic organisation – at the time, peculiarly resisted by Nehru in older states such as Mumbai (Parekh 1991:36) – affects Indian post-modernity in so far as its external recognition via (cultural) industrial growth relies on urban 'global financial articulations' (Sassen 2001) such as those of the city, which enable the commercialisation of the arts. Though often encouraging cultural production in other dialects, Bollywood is still dominated by the Hindu ethno-linguistic tradition – a contradiction in line with the structural 'heterogeny' and 'dis-articulation' characterising other multi-industrial conglomerates that constantly expand into new areas (Hesmondhalgh 2007; Tzanelli 2010b). Technological (linguistic and mechanical) calibrations of Indian modernity aestheticise its multiple realities (Dean 2007) so as to articulate the utopian parable of an 'Edenic futural history'. My oscillation between real and utopian discourse borrows from Schutz's systematic examination of stratifications of the lifeworld as 'multiple realities', finite provinces of meaning or 'sub-universes' (Henning 2002:170). There is a homology between institutionalised cinematic dreaming and tourist mythologisations of the slum I scrutinise in Part III.

Provinces of meaning are always conditioned by conceptions of self-worth and (in-)equality. We cannot avoid considering how even electronically mediated environments might produce zones of privilege and exclusion, as new professional communities and their infrastructural support systems reside in separate physical domains from those of the represented populations (Cronin 2003:107; Dredge and Jamal 2013:561). Considering the work of leading human actors in the SM industry in conjunction with network theory highlights the twin political and cultural nature of creativity. As a 'globally integrated network' (Urry 2003:12), the SM industry represents a macro-system with predictable connections that counter space-time constraints (e.g. uses of digital and cinematic technologies in international movie markets). Yet, as a fluid cultural formation, the enterprise comprised various media forms (film, music, photography and print materials such as the book) that produced ideas and aesthetic codes with plural meanings, uses, creative implementations and political applications. Of significance in hostile reactions has been a problematic post-colonial heritage that dictates mergers of contemporary development zones (Indian slums) and hired young actors (children from the Juhu slum) into a discourse of 'exploitation'. The discourse connects to the ways Western cultures were granted by colonial anthropology an aura of universality, which was conditioned by innovative combinations of the art of travel and the art of government (Pers and Salemink 1999:3–4; Cannella and Viruru 2004:51; Tribe 2008:20). This controversy necessitates a separate debate on image management through projects with which celebrities choose to associate themselves.

The problem with such reactions resides in the ways India's layered connectivities or articulations (local, national, global) are informed by memories (of colonialism, civil war, migration and diaspora). Remembrance mechanisms are responsible for the rise of 'heritage' and 'legacy' discourses in national sites. These regulate communal narratives of cultural and intellectual property in contemporary industrial settings, where transnational, national or regional agents have to agree on the use and consumption of tangible and intangible heritage. The functionalist dilemma is a clandestine structural question that collapses into biological discourse: as Gellner (1983), Smith (1995:98) and Habermas (1996:495) warn us, the 'nature' of culture is not a metaphor but a political model of belonging. In line with strategic oscillations between ethnoracial and civic understandings of citizenship, conceptions of 'legacy' and 'heritage' guide identity battles in the era of global digital reproduction. Legacy is a gift of a chattel or an item of personal property by will (Tzanelli 2013a:2). This presents the act of transaction as intergenerational reciprocity, forming a continuation with heritage as the process of inheriting, whereby the beneficiary (heir) is legitimated as an actor in transactions by kinship affiliation. In-heriting refers to pure exchange (Mauss 1954): the 'gift' of will becomes magically inseparable from the donor who transfers it only to those with whom (s)he shares in bloodline (Shohat 1992:109). Heritage and its intercultural communications – including those associated with heritage tourism – produce utopian parables of (family-like) belonging and pride in what 'we are' in public domains. But what happens when there are disreputable forms of heritage such as those of the slum that make as much money as Taj Mahal's beautiful temples? Does the national centre or its imagined community begin to treat varieties of heritage in different ways – and how does this change inform the country's place in global cultural circuits and cross-cultural reciprocities? A trope of debt, in which Indian landscapes and characters function as 'gifts' conditionally lent to foreign 'pilgrims', will guide our exploration of reactions to SM.

Types of technopoiesis

After exploring such activist-artistic synergies, it is pertinent to revisit my initial reference to 'affiliative networks' in globalised artworlds. Filiation and affiliation refer to modes of belonging, which organise individual and collective perception of the world around us. When Mulvey suggested that Hollywood's technological advances changed not only the economic conditions of cinematic production but also the nature of artistic socialities, with fusions of artisanal and capitalist initiatives now further glocalising artistic creativity (Mulvey 2006:343), she could not anticipate the scope of contemporary industrial fusions. Even Putnam's (1993) social network theory is transformed via new media routes,as artistic communities operating in new digital contexts are not always bound by regional or national belonging, but by shared interests and commercial infrastructures (Averill 1996:218; Gauntlett 2011:138; Grugulis and Stoyanova 2011; Manning and Sydow 2011). Capitalist structuration and neoliberal ideology seem to have won, according to some radical critics, sucking into their vortex people, technologies and musical practices and crafting complicity through global interdependencies (Erlmann 1999; Albertsen and Diken 2003:11). A.R. Rahman's art-work exemplifies the dilemmas creative workers encounter in global neoliberal settings, where 'speaking truth to power' enables market forces to use symbolic creativity in othering other cultures (Said 1994:14; Huss 2000; Born and Hesmondhalgh 2000).

But what sort of sociality is this? I approach the question through conceptions of *technopoesis*, 'the totality of practices and processes of "self-making" available to a community and embodied in the artefacts, techniques and technologies available to a culture' (Hand and Sandywell 2002:208; Cronin 2013:11). Tools and practices can of course be mobilised by various social groups for the promotion of disparate causes. Couldry's (2006) suggestion that some notion of commonality – hence the defence of possibility of any shared site – is essential for an emergent democratic politics is pertinent. But my *technopoesis* takes the uses of new technologies to a new level, arguing that democratic dialogues are now articulated by individuals living in different sites and are being connected with the help of new technologies because of shared interests rather than exclusively by blood bonds. The difference between the two forms of *technopoesis* (kinship and interest-based) is encapsulated in Ingold's (2000:142) differentiation between 'genealogy' and 'relation' – or the production of the social via ready-made attributes received from predecessors, and 'progeneration' or production of the social field through shared capacities and dispositions. National *technopoesis* looks to the past to replenish its creative repository (Coleman 1988:102–3), whereas transnational (network) *technopoesis* produces ways of being and knowing in society via contemporary experiences and shared interests.

The dialectic of Enlightenment appears to constantly reinstate the battle between the alleged originality of culturally specific pasts against a 'predatory' reproduction of the homeless human on the one hand, and the restrictive racism of national exclusivity against the idealism of free sharing, knowledge circulation and adaptation, on the other. The issue in this book is not whether social research needs to eliminate the human (f)actor in the production of semiotechnological assemblages but at what stage we should launch an investigation into the (filiative or affiliative) nature of human agency. The focus on semiotechnological organisations of the social world is necessary when we shift focus from individual artistic creativity and (imaginative) travel to power formations controlled by actors who overdetermine interpretative horizons. Semiotechnologies combine human hermeneutics with collective structural production and post-human systemic management of meaning at the level of new technologies (Gardiner 1992:12, 26; Archer 2003; Alexander 2006; Tzanelli 2013a:1–10). Ultimately, we must bear in mind at all times that language (verbal and visual) is also a technology, 'an artificial construct that stands between persons yet makes the connection between them possible' (Yar 2014:77). In contradistinction to technophobic takes on 'technique'

(Ellul 1964), a view of technology as an autopoetic force that shapes society in its own image, my understanding of *technopoesis* examines the creative potential of proximate and distant (technology-mediated) communication as an extension of each other.

SM's *technopoesis* suggests that we do not isolate one form of mobility (travel, virtual and/or terrestrial) from other technological complexes of movement (including the digitised dancing in new social media environments) or its equivalent activist movement and marketable products (the dancer's body, relevant music and paraphernalia). This hides a hypothesis: that there is such a thing as a 'technology of action', involving a combination of physical/ embodied and digital movement of people who aspire to present themselves as travellers, activists, artists (masters of dance styles) but also masters of technology (Archer 1996; Herzfeld 2009). As societies move towards more integrated mobility systems that combine digital and mechanical movement of ideas, highlighting the importance of some human variables (gender, ethnicity or sexuality) is enmeshed into new socio-cultural considerations, including the significance of mediated interaction in contemporary everyday life (Adler 1992; Shilling 1999; Uteng and Cresswell 2008; Kaufmann and Mantulet 2008). In the following chapter we explore the SM artistic community as one such example of new mobility systems.

3 A *Slumdog* industrial community

Art(iculations): the world as home

The chapter is concerned with the socio-cultural identity of SM's leading creative workers. With the exception of the Taj Mahal scenes (shot in Agra), SM was filmed mostly in Mumbai, so SM's creative workers had to temporarily relocate to Indian sites. In addition to the shots in Dharavi, Maharashtra studios and Agra, the creative assemblage took place in multiple Western and Eastern industrial hubs (including India, Britain and the United States) and was consolidated through virtual collaboration between multi-ethnic artists. We deal with questions of continuity and disruption in terrestrial and digital forms of authorship and need to address the complexity of this post-national enterprise. Unless I glorify tropes of mobility and nomadism – themselves offspring of European colonial stillness and prejudice – I do not contend that these artists operated exclusively outside homeland imaginaries (Appadurai 1990, 1996; Hannerz 1990, 1996). The suggestion that transnationalism can also be considered as an individualised project, whereby we deal with multiple or hybrid selves and 'an abstract awareness of one's self, diaspora and multiple belonging' (Gosh and Wang 2003:278), is taken seriously. Any emerging world culture 'is bound to be refracted…by the prisms of specific groups…and that diversity is bound to flourish' (Ritzer and Atalay 2010:416) even within one community. The call to create and diversify was answered with various degrees of enthusiasm, commitment or urgency by individual artists in SM's creative circuit, but one can safely assume it was everybody's minimum involvement in it that led to the production of a loose community of interest.

The new lifestyle mobilities paradigm crosses paths with the activities of the SM community and functions as a theoretical lens that magnifies intersections of travel, migration, work and leisure representations (McIntyre 2009; Cohen et al. 2013). Tourism theorists such as Graburn (1983a), Jafari (1987), Urry (2002), Urry and Larsen (2011) and Dann (2002) have already drawn attention to the ways work and home on the one hand, and leisure and travel on the other, are pivotal in conceptualisations of contemporary social life. It has also been argued that changes in tourist styles are geared towards the socio-environmental context in which travel takes place. This humanises such mobilities through ideas of cultural exchange, when at stake is a hierarchy of prestige and class (Krippendorf 1987; Salazar 2004:99; Hall 2008; Page 1991, 2009). The search for self-identity during such experiential journeys translates into a shift from (mass) tourism to (individualised) travel with a mission to transform the world rather than conform in it – to be an 'anti-tourist' (Löfgren 1999:266) or a 'negative sightseer' (MacCannell 1989:40) rather than a 'post-tourist' (Rojek 1993:177; Ritzer and Liska 1997:107). Although a conceptual paradox, which both excises and glorifies the systemic organisation of imaginative travel, SM's audio-visual anti-tourism generates competing conceptions of cosmopolitanism as a mode of meaning-management (Braidotti 1994; Hannerz 1996) and as a political project (Melucci 1995).

I do not scrutinise professionalism in line with the bourgeois bohemian *ethos* or the liquid individualist project as such (Brooks 2000; D'Andrea 2006), but borrow from these to examine ways in which such projects contribute to the reconstitution of collective belonging through the employment of old memories in new contexts (Pratt 1992; Hannerz and Löfgren 1994; Kearney 1995; Cronin 2013:47). I view SM art-work as a hybrid symbolisation of identities in flux, even where conversations on origins and beginnings cannot be avoided. Just as place is not defined by bounded areas as by 'open and porous networks of social relations' (Massey 1994:121, Dredge and Jamal 2013:560-1), so SM's artistic community is not so much defined by a consensually produced project of activism or activist art-work but by open-ended possibilities for contribution to globalised sets of relations and transnational political agendas (Gouldner 1948:398).

SM's core narrative adheres to a cosmological theme, which incorporates ideas of socio-cultural inequality or marginality. We cannot avoid mention of Pierre Nora's *lieux de mémoire* in the labour of such artistic *tonadóroi* as a repository 'where memory crystallises and secretes itself' (Nora 1989:7) only to be de-crystallised, liquidated and mixed with other *lieux* in art-work. Cinematic *tonadóroi* blend official and personal memories and histories, housing art-work that becomes by turn a *lieux* within a broader *lieux*. This mobility crux points to a larger memory web held together by 'an invisible thread, linking apparently unconnected objects' and ideas in which all of these separate identities belong, 'an unconscious organisation of collective memory that is our responsibility to bring to consciousness' (Gibbons 2007:71). Slow temporalities meet with fast in this crux, revealing how SM's memory art-*work* is conditioned by the 'ecumenical analytic' of cosmopolitanism (Ricoeur 1999; Inglis and Robertson 2005) and the adjacent question of who is included in urban ecumenes and under what conditions. Unfolding this analytic in Mumbai's post-colonial 'border zones' *par excellence* (the slum) constructs a space in which worldviews collide, collude or even merge.

These encounters are constitutive of the ways in which artists experience shifts from conceptions of the 'vagabond' to those of 'tourist', and of how mobility scholars can use them to explore artistic mobility as a new form of pilgrimage. Bauman's (1998) original differentiation between Southern 'vagabonds' and Northern 'tourists' provides a rudimentary division of human types on status (destitute migrants vs rich professionals), but pays less attention to the inner, experiential dimensions of travel – especially if this is enhanced by hallucinatory practices of daydreaming as is the case with Boyle's mobile hero. Hallucination is etymologically connected to the act of wandering and the need to satisfy one's need for purpose in life. Boyle's travelling hero is a hallucinating vagabond, an *alítis* (from *aláomai*= to wander (Vardiabasis 2002)), a Simmelian peripatetic stranger through urban and rural lifeworlds in search of an elusive, ultimate 'truth' through 'photographic' elicitations of memory (Wolff/Simmel 1959). The emphasis on anomie connects this typical (anti-)hero to contemporary privileged professionals in cultural industries, who manufacture visions of the original *alites* in their films while also acting as ego-enhancing cinematic tourist themselves (Dann 1977) or theoreticians who conceptualise the world via a cinematic vision. The final chapter questions whether artistic representatives of global film industries should also be conceptualised as *alites* in various activist fields, privileged tramps (original meaning of word) challenging organised governance in the foreign polities they visit. One could opt instead for understandings of their identity through Bauman's (1998, 2000) and Clifford's (1997) post-modern pilgrim, who is defined by endless inner and physical mobility. Such inner journeys would prompt us to move from artistic identity to artistic creativity – or from exploring the artistic tourist to investigating SM's fictional hero. SM's cinematic heroes are after all, like their artistic creators, pilgrims: first they enable distant enactments of historical archetypes (what Seaton (2002:237–8) calls tourist 'metempsychosis') and finally proximate engagement with the plurality of Indian culture (Seaton's (2002:150–4) 'tourist metensomatosis'. This move from imaginative to actual travel produces the cinematic tourist – the artist, film fan and common tourist, who perform synaesthetic mobilities.

SM's post-colonial human complex involved professional mobilisation of technology, which fed into the maintenance of a cumulative civilisational 'debt', including informational and aesthetic goods distributed across post-national spaces. SM's artistic community was made to be the bearer of this debt the privileged virtual and actual tourist discharges every time (s)he commences a new journey. The talents of renowned SM artists are recognised as 'gifts of European' (Argyrou 2013), or, even better, Eurasian thought – a 'thought' always dependent on serendipitous discoveries disenfranchised cultures attribute to powerful usurpers (Merton and Barber 2004:294). For similar reasons art, technology and embodied habitus cover different aspects of 'affordances', the possible choices available to us in the social field we inhabit to express our personal talents, or subjective experiences of the social environment (Michael 1996:149; Urry 2007:51). As much as we evolve or are defined by the artefacts and tools we use, prioritising them in the analysis of the SM creative contingent would trap us into a techno-determinism that ignores the social nature of human interaction (paying the bill or debt for the gift of such goods as it were). Emotional triggers and individual manipulations of cultural capital provide useful insight into epistemologies of production of audio-visual art by various actors in the field. Yet, by confusing the uneven distribution of capacities and competences that regulate physical, social, and political movement with the legal structures regulating who or what can or cannot move across time and space (colonial, post-colonial, East and West, urban zones) we do not effectively examine SM's artwork or the artists themselves.

The origins of travel in the pedagogical and administrative milieus of the colonial era provide a limited starting point. Cohen's (1973) identification of 'diversionary' tourist interest in advertising that promotes 'authentic reproductions' suggests that such contemporary professional mobilities are based on simulations. The claim that guidebooks and brochures depicting the developing world confirm 'what Westerners have historically imagined the other to be like' (Silver 1993:303) is banal in today's digital environments (Hand 2012:35). But as much as technology is a process of 'social and cultural instantiations of ideational innovation' (Fischer 2004; Fischer et al. 2008:521), it is part and parcel of our ongoing mastering of natural resources and symbolisations of nature and culture. Following the invention of the press, digitisations of image and sound enabled large-scale reconstructions of transnational communities of interest, assent and emotion but also the emergence of new forms of leadership not limited to charismatic nation-state personalities (Zeitlyn 2001). Below I reiterate that post-modern *technopoesis* is articulated in the interstices of national and cosmopolitan identities through distant communications and in disembodied forms that revise leadership paradigms. Mannheim's 'collective mentality' or state of mind that remains incongruous with the state of reality in which it occurs (Yar 2014:5) is synchronised with the possibilities offered by the state of the real through new, non-filiative forms of togetherness, which are now also enabled by new technologies. This advocates an analysis of human networks in the new technological environments (Thrift 2007), but also their continuities with older frames and modes of belonging (Herzfeld 2007). Once more, we draw on the nature of social organisation as nature (Tzanelli 2013a:8–9); once more, this connects the tools we use to their function, and the ways this human-mechanic complex (of *tornadóroi*) reproduces 'simulacra of sociality' (Herzfeld 2005:6–8, 12).

Beyond biology: new *technopoesis*

Digital *technopoesis* has auratic potential and transforms artistic professionals into 'staged celebrities' through calculated presentational strategies that bestow 'pop monumentality' upon them (Rojek 2001:121). Such professionals also form the human potential of transnational 'epistemic communities', groups or networks of experts whose shared beliefs or ideas are, voluntarily or not, mobilised in national or regional policies (Haas 1992). In anthropological theory there have been suggestions that we look to the 'axiom of amity' (Fortes 1969) or kinship-like connections to examine the social production of leadership. Although such human exchanges can become monetary, the primary value in the digital field is that of 'purified' reciprocity: I give and you give back, and our respective debt is organised in a concise time frame (de Certeau 1985:193; Zeitlyn 2003:8). Honourable transactions secure long-lasting friendships in the interest of all parties. Consequently, I argue that works of art such as SM are not mere 'things' used in struggles for domination but constitutive of re-imagining the social, even in commercial contexts (Albertsen and Diken 2003:2). Both a 'natural artefact' and a cultural prosthesis, the technological body of Baumanesque media tourists (Parrinello 2001) asserts its social nature when it becomes subjected to the rules of reciprocity.

Digital *technopoesis* is exemplified in Rahman's and M.I.A.'s multi-site creation of music. But it also applies to on-site use of SI-2K digital cameras by Boyle to achieve flexibility of movement and vivid visuals (*Slumdog Dreams* 2009). To capture the city's dynamism Boyle filmed with three different types of camera, including a Canon still camera that can shoot eleven frames per second and deliver incredibly high-resolution pictures blending into the film (Horn, 9 November 2009). India's extreme heat affected the small digital cameras that needed cooling off many times a day. The director tested 35mm cameras only to conclude that they create a feel of voyeuristic distance. 'I wanted to tell [the story] from the inside as much as possible', he admitted (Roston, 4 November 2008). His discomfort with voyeurism and his search for visual intimacy might suggest attempts at recreating ideas of home abroad, merging rootless mobilities with emotional rootedness (Jamal and Hill 2002:92). As the film was about memory, 'recalling things, the way images are burned on your mind' (Horn, 9 November 2009), technology was integral to SM's *technopoetic* parable. Much can be said about the ways new technologies fuse experiences and practices of being at home 'while being away' or vice versa (Bell and Lyall 2002; Germann Molz 2012). Yet, post-modernity's ubiquitous shift from 'orality' as oral transmission (Ong 1982) to 'digitality' is part of technological transformations that render camera-work an interlocutor in film-making.

As much as Mumbai is a city of slums, it is also a 'city of bits' in which combined physical structures and electronic spaces or telematics produce an architectural complex for new professionalised art and tourism (Mitchell 1995, 2003). Here one may highlight some well-established connections between different forms of mobility (incorporating both professional and educational projects) and critical nomadology studies that extend to neo-colonial paradigms (Cresswell 2009; Hannam 2008). Building on Hutnyk's (1996) 'rumour of Calcutta' as elusive Western representation allows sociologists to speculate on the ways the 'e-motion of Mumbai' is mediated by those fleeting travellers of its cityscape – not as mere feeling (the artist's unprocessed human encounter with the world) or pure affect (the artist's expressive articulation) but as a fully worked narrative offered to recipients though technology (Peirce 1998 on phaneroscopy). The fact that principal photography commenced in early November 2008 in Mumbai's megaslum and 'on the giant piles of garbage in Juhu, a shantytown near the airport' (Roston, 4 November 2008) already suggests that before passing the story through refined technological sieves, film artists savoured the feel of a lifeworld very different from the glamorous surfaces of Bollywoodland (Mazumdar 2007:173). Spatial perceptions of Mumbai and emotional responses to its polyphonic cityscape cannot be separated from the geopolitical coordinates within which the artists are invited to 'create' and act (Cresswell 2010; Hall 2008:28). As we will see in Part II, this issue extends to the experiences of SM collaborators such as M.I.A., whose work articulates Mumbai's slum life through personal experiences of migration, self-exile and political control. Musings over lifestyle comforts might be marginalised, as research shifts focus on intersections of (personally fostered) mobilities and (state-calibrated) immobilities affecting 'working life and individual life cycles, jobs and careers' (Veijola 2009:83–4). At the other end of SM's mobility matrix we can place Boyle and his mediated reflections (included in the movie's extras) on the spirit of 'bright Mumbai' as a living universe comprising different microcosms. These two examples showcase corporeal mobility as a more privileged specimen of movement: conceptions of space and time become necessary in (re-)interrogations of the limits of corporeality because any understanding of bodies requires a spatial framework (Grosz 2001:32): for some 'becoming nomad' is not necessarily a positive experience.

It has been repeatedly suggested that core project teams engage in collaborative practices that are compatible and evolve over time into creative networks based on trust (Faulkner and Anderson 1987; Manning and Sydow 2011:1380). Just as Beaufoy's task of transliterating Swarup's plot necessitated both actual journeys to India and the uses of technology, Boyle's directorship involved a variety of 'miniature electronic prostheses' to facilitate the production of good shots, and of face-to-face instructions to his film crew in alien sites (Hennion and Latour 1993:21; Castells 2004:7; Urry and Larsen 2011:141–3). As privileged artistic nomads, both Beaufoy and Boyle were allowed to wander and work outside Mumbai's mediapolis and into slums otherwise less accessible to Western outsiders (Linklater, 4 January 2009). But the process of any 'translation/transliteration' of difference involves the portability of the 'text', which must be able to survive the 'journey'. Inevitably, as intercultural mediators SM artists perform their own synaesthetic pilgrimages to the literal and real lands of their art-work (Cronin 2003:125). But if textual portability is possible, then imaginaries and feelings that enclose ideas of 'home' are also mobile. Burns and O'Regan suggest that budget travellers use various mobile devices such as iPods in everyday travel, ultimately 'bringing home with them' instead of 'escap[ing] their habits of mind' (2008:177). The relationship between the traveller and the world is neither only fluid nor just solid but blends mobility with immobility.

Cresswell's (2010:18) conceptualisation of slow mobilities in travel experience as the unity of representations of movement and ways of practicing them is useful: if being-in-the-world as a traveller means a broadening of the cultural horizons for the Self and Others, then new and old technologies subjected to personal or professional uses bind 'home' and 'away' in novel dialogical patterns (Germann Molz 2004, 2009). These two sites are always-already multi-sites encompassing imagined spaces, actual places and visited territories that artistic travellers modify technologically. We are back to understandings of *technopoesis* as method and practice – for, it would be naïve to speak of members of the SM artistic community as subjects totally devoid of roots from which they can differentiate their routes. For better or worse, art-work can communicate the novelty of experience with intense emotions only when something is left behind. I disagree with Bauman's pessimist polemics on the eroding rise of individualism by stressing that past experiences, hence ideas of home, contribute in multiple ways to the emergence of causes that might bind artists to one symbolic communal space and cause. Such simulacra of sociality are challenged outside the network's privileged sphere by various groups – including those the network represents in its art-work and their various global advocates. During these socio-cultural encounters the idea of 'adapting' someone else's lifeworld woes transforms into an accusation akin to old Indian conceptions of globalisation as effeminised human trafficking.

In this contingent SM's narrative works as a moral compass, reminding us of Murray's (2008) discussion of the 'phantom of adaptation' and Danto's (1964) institutional theory of art. Murray explains that like other works of art, the emergence of cinematic adaptations from novels might reflect the ways power structure overdetermines taste and hence selection – a point inherent in Danto's institutional embeddedness of art-work (Danto 1999:215; Harrington 2004:22–4). The fact that SM has been discussed as a 'sleeper hit' looks to Boyle's and Beaufoy's previous successful collaborations and their propensity to question norms and expectations. By walking a very thin line between accepted forms and contested content in context, they generated a controversy that spoke the language of development, leading to various conflations of aesthetic preference, cinematic creativity and social inequality (Banks 2001:51–4 on content).

The controversy was superimposed on old Orientalist debates upon the theft of history, which was intertwined with the Western racist tradition – the primary 'debt' in the SM controversies (Goody 2006; Tzanelli 2011). The enterprise's underlining idea of Indian phantoms as phantasmagorias, aesthetic (*phántasma* from *phaínō* or reveal) renditions of the market (*agorá*) in which human 'types' are processed, supersedes conventional understandings of colonialism's phantasmic presence. The verb 'processed' stresses that art-work becomes exceptional for the place in which it represents, the artistic community or 'school' to which it adheres and the epistemic environment in which it is classified in serendipitous ways – a posteriori as the SM miracle betrays (Merton and Barber 2004:262). Cinema is a phenomenological machine that partakes in adaptations of the human psyche and body into a set of practical laws, an 'east-oriented geo-poetics' (Italiano 2012:14–15) that fabricates proximate engagement with poverty because of its exotic flair. Camera-work's ubiquitous problem connects to the impossibility of representing racism without mobilising concrete representations – a conundrum also connecting to art's cosmological games with gender, sexuality and more generic understandings of human nature. Such unfortunate by-products of artistic and activist engagement with Mumbai's multi-sites are constitutive of SM's social scenes: not only did they 'stage' them in media environments; they also solidified a highly unstable community that, artistic utopian pursuits aside, probably never had a single cause (Habermas 1989; Thompson 1995).

Personal profiles as artistic roots/routes

Any presentation of SM's 'cinematic tourists' is haunted by customary associations of 'cultural industry' with old ideas of mindless commodification or mass deception *and* Western traveller-artists as neo-colonists (Castells 2009). We cannot avoid explorations of the 'post-colonial tourist' as a professional 'cinematic tourist' – bearing in mind that 'the roles of the post-colonial tourist and the post-colonial local (subaltern) are highly complex and involve discursive power relations, as well as performative resistance i.e. an intricate micro-relationship of structure and agency' (Jamal and Hill 2002:95). Having a quick look at the socio-cultural make up of SM's creative labour might prepare us for the accusatory shower we will encounter in Part III. Suffice it to mention in advance that the individuals who made up the SM community were reflexive enough to anticipate such reactions to their film-making. 'We didn't want to go down there like a bunch of colonialists', explained main SM's producer Christian Colson, who helped fill out the team with locals (Roston, 4 November 2008).

It is questionable if such a diverse industrial contingent can be neatly classified as a 'bunch of colonialists'. SM scriptwriter Simon Beaufoy is a product of the periphery: born in Bradford, which was repeatedly shaken by racism-induced riots in more recent decades, he has a (however flimsy) connection to Britain's turbulent multicultural(ising) project. Originating in migration hubs of England's 'blackened north', he brought some intimate experiences into SM's script: in this, the *Q&A* multi-religiously brought up Salim becomes a persecuted Muslim Jamal. A self-taught writer, Beaufoy attributes the effectiveness of his craft to his instinct: 'from the first principle of my process (and life) that plot comes from character.... Your main character needs to be active', he explains (Reeves, 12 April 2012). All the same, Beaufoy is a middle-class white professional, apparently fascinated by India and Mumbai like any tourist and who is determined to turn his experience into art – 'an operatic [...] sentimental, romantic love story' (ReetzChannel, 2008). Described as a blunt but self-deprecating Yorkshireman, Beaufoy lives today on the Thames in Wandsworth with his archaeologist wife and their two young children. He made little money from his earlier successful scripts (*The Full Monty*, dir. Peter Cattaneo, 1997) because he was unknown at the time (Rose, 13 February 2009). His decisive turn towards social realism brought him close to Boyle's pursuit of active characters. His thoughts about Boyle's film-making emphasise his ability to 'embody' the potential of the camera 'to move around subjects, time, characteristics [and] places' (Reeves, 12 April 2012). Indicative of

Beaufoy's identity as a Mertonian 'junkhunter' is the reflection on his three research trips to India to talk to street beggars: 'It is absolutely inappropriate to feel sorry for these people...I wanted to get (across) the sense of this huge amount of fun, laughter, chat and sense of community that is in the slums. What you pick up on is this mass of energy' (Roston, 4 November 2008).

Beaufoy's work has been the outcome of a reflexive journey through Mumbai's slum-world, from which he also published a short account in *The Guardian* newspaper. There we find references to Juhu's private airfield and slum toilets, on which some of SM's iconic scenes are based, but also to non-representational aspects of slum life ('an avalanche of the senses – an excess of smell, noise and colour'). And there the writer depicts India as 'desperately romantic, utterly unashamed of sentimentality, its generosity, its fierce pride and massive heart' (Beaufoy, 12 December 2008). A modern Grand Tourist in search of sublimation in real(ist) situations (Bell and Lyall 2002:11), Beaufoy elsewhere explains that 'any authenticity in the film is due to the people we met there.... It was they...who told us about the big gangster problem in the slums' (Rose, 13 February 2009). In the same interview Beaufoy outlines the parameters of the controversy surrounding SM's concluding Bollywood scene, highlighting how the stark realism upset the status quo, sparking an argument not just about whether outsiders should make a film about slum-dwellers 'but whether a film should show slums at all' (ibid.). Should this piece of information be spatially contained to Mumbai or does it become enmeshed into a post-colonial chronotope, in which silences kept at home explode in foreign spaces? Producing the script on the eve of the crippling economic recession (2008–) to hit the world – but hit national peripheries in developed countries even harder – shows how art-work can be culturally metaphorical and politically allegorical.

Cronin (2003:112) perceives the role of a translator as a 'third person', a 'third culture' practitioner, which includes 'not only the classic polarities of humanities and the sciences but many other areas of human enquiry'. Boyle's and Beaufoy's engagement with India's new spaces of (slum) exception, at once abject and enticing to the modern tourist, communicates fragments of 'home' (Germann Molz 2008). As an allegory of post-industrial alienation, SM provides escape from a disenchanted British landscape and encourages the adoption of a sort of 'tourist anomie' (Dann 1977). This should not make us lose track of Beaufoy's tip-toeing commentary around a very sensitive discourse on destitution and inequality, or his self-positioning as a dumpster journalist-artist collecting stories from zones of exception (Seaton 2012). His published travel account is marked by a sense of guilt for the writer's privileged status ('what does a middle-class white Englishman know of a Mumbai slum-dweller's life?' (Beaufoy, 12 December 2008)) that prompts him to return to his documentary roots. A meaningful Benjaminian metaphor *àla Angelus Novus* frames his sentimental interpretation of the city's history: 'People are not looking for pity', he insists; 'in this city of 19 million people hurtling into the future, there is still, very present, an ancient sense of destiny, a word hard to define' (ibid.). The comment is rife with meaning – natives possess knowledge of their future, a sense of movement towards a *telos* that should be admired for its mystical, nearascetic sagacity (Merton and Barber 2004:261). Much like Boyle's, Beaufoy's communications of dignity are marked by a distinctive understanding of his status, which is not matched by local knowledge. Much like Boyle, he seems to have an understanding of the childhood roots of his preference for realism but no deep knowledge of the imagined mysticism of the Indian poor. And much like Boyle's preference to front (melo-)drama with dance, comedy and action, he concludes: 'the tone of Slumdog Millionaire wasn't in the end created by us film-makers but by the city itself' (Beaufoy, 12 December 2008). The observation certainly related to the making of distinctive urban brands, which provide a meaning to which consumers can relate emotionally. Donald and Gammack (2007:48) warn us that 'cities lend themselves to anthropomorphic identification', which Beaufoy's discourse exoticises. The ubiquitous global discourse of humour as sure facet of hospitality (Tzanelli 2010b:ch.5) dresses the writer's journey into the clothes of the touristified spectacle. The script is a projection of synaesthetic performances by locals, but their *rasas* are mediated at least once, by Beaufoy, and then again through Boyle's camera-work.

Born in 1956 in Radcliffe, Lancashire, into an Irish Catholic family, Danny Boyle rejected priesthood for a career in drama. Years later he noted a 'real connection' between film directorship and religiosity because 'there's something very theatrical about it. It's basically the same job – poncing around, telling people what to think' (Leach, 14 January 2009). He was employed as a director at the Royal Court Theatre, with the Royal Shakespeare Company and with BBC Northern Ireland, but progressively moved from a kinship-orientated to post-traditional professional connections that today extend to Hollywood. Becoming known in the mid-1990s as director of films such as *Shallow Grave* (1995) and *Trainspotting* (1996), in the first decade of the twenty-first century he proceeded to direct commercial successes. These later landmarks betray an interest in the experiential dimensions of travel. In particular, they betray an interest in the liminality and insularity of backpack travellers in the 'Orient'; the phenomenon of adventurous travel as a root to self-discovery; and finally, westernised representations of poverty in the developing world as charitable attraction to repulsion (Stallybrass and White 1986; Tzanelli 2010b:ch.2). Boyle's art-work allows us to analyse tourist spaces as 'more than representational... simultaneously both visually engaged with but also embodied through the concept of performativity' (Adey 2010:146; Diekmann and Hannam 2012:1316).

Hence, Boyle's post-colonial art predates SM, as his other cinematic work engaged with 'twilight zones' in a liquid, undefined 'Orient' (Herzfeld 2002). His engagement with a hermeneutics of recovery and suspicion appears to be – unconsciously or not – connected to a personal battle against religion. Against a self-confessed loyalty to his own family as a personal constant (Linklater, 4 January 2009), Boyle's art-work betrays a fascination with mobility tropes. His direction of an adaptation of Alex Garland's novel *The Beach* (2000) in Thailand drew the attention of several global and local activist networks that saw an opportunity to promote disparate demands for 'justice' over the environmental protection of the film's locations. The question of the regulation of the collaboration of Thai authorities with international film companies such as 20th Century Fox, and also better organisation around the ensuing film-induced tourism in Thai film locations also raised attention at the time (Tzanelli 2010b:ch.2). Such instances suggest Boyle's interest in directing adaptations that cut pretty close to global sensibilities and invite equally problematic confusion between representational imperatives within the cinematic script stemming from marketing constrictions on the one hand, and various activist agendas on the other (e.g. political interpretations of his techniques of 'othering' the cinematic landscape and its people). SM followed in the steps of *The Beach* in terms of controversial form/content but diverged on marketing and target audiences. At the same time, it reiterated Boyle's focus on the experiential dimensions of travel and its extensions in sub-cultural frames and criminal networks.

SM's here-humorous-there-serious critique of slum politics and *The Beach*'s equally cutting visual engagement with Western tourist fantasies vs the harrowing local realities of drug and sex trafficking are embroiled in the controversies of de-colonisation. Boyle's narrative constantly hinges to the treble geographical, affective and cognitive journey of marginalised (anti-)heroes from national periphery to urban centres and from inner confusion to lucidity or vice versa. Travels through country landscapes (within Edinburgh's streets in *Shallow Grave*, from Edinburgh to a stereotypical replica of London in *Trainspotting* and from Bangkok to the Edenic Phi Phi Islands in *The Beach*) by public transport such as trains and boats (Page 1991; Diekmann and Hannam 2012) facilitates a form of mind-walking (Ingold 2010) usually amplified by the deleterious effects of drugs. And yet, this unlikely contrast between inner turmoil, self-destruction and criminogenic propensity on the one hand, and visits to tourist landmarks audio-visually organised for safe consumption on the other, produces a hybrid type of 'cinematic tourist' that in Bauman's (1998) terms is both a tourist and a vagabond. The notion of tourism has, after all, become 'a metaphor for conveying aspects of citizenship to public audiences and, in turn, has become a mechanism by which to regulate further short-term movements' (Coles 2008:69; Duval 2008).

The Eurasian tale of mobility is firmly embedded in SM's directorship, with Indian film and casting director Loveleen Tandan having considerable input in its making. In an interview she explained that she was approached by Tabrez Noorani, the line producer of SM from Los Angeles, who set up a meeting with Colson for casting the film. The Delhi-born sociology graduate was credited by Boyle as the film's 'Co-Director: India' and shared a New York Film Critics Online Award for Best Director with him. Tandan enjoyed a successful career before her involvement in SM: she served as casting director for several other films, including the Golden Lion winning and Golden Globe nominated *Monsoon Wedding* (dir. Mira Nair, 2001) and the BAFTA Award nominated *Brick Lane* (dir. Sarah Gavron, 2007). She was also the casting consultant for the Gotham Award and Independent Spirit Award nominated film *The Namesake* (dir. Mira Nair, 2007). Tandan's trajectory accommodates extensive experience in film-making steeped in cosmological permutations of migration, exile, uprooting, family values and human-made destiny. Boyle himself emphasised Tandan's contribution to the plot's transliteration (and comprehensible Hindi translation of about 20 per cent of the dialogue) for the benefit of child actors (CNN Entertainment, 12 January 2009). The casting involved a selection process in Mumbai, Bangalore, Delhi, Jaipur and Calcutta. Tandan explained that she had 'the best time' looking for the characters of Jamal, Salim and Latika in three age groups 'so 9 people play 3 parts and all with almost equal screen time'. Only two of the nine young actors were from Mumbai's slums (the eldest versions of Latika and Salim) and most of the others, were first timers in film (Hindustan Times, 1 January 2009).

Stating that SM strikes her as a 'totally Indian' film, with Javed and Salim as characters straight out of 1970s Indian productions, Tandan added: 'we did not want to cast middle-class children from English medium schools because they could not have matched the raw energy of the slum children' (DNA India, 13 January 2009). The discourse combines the familiar activist ethos of middle-class artists (Crossley 2003) with business imperatives regarding verisimilitude: a slum-dweller is working class or below, and not educated in private institutions. This *vision du monde* (Goldmann 1964) corroborates Boyle's realist focus on crime placed under the microscope discussed in Part II. Tandan was also involved to some extent in Dev Patel's casting as the tea worker Jamal Malik. During her search for the right person to dub Patel in Hindi she adopted the same social criteria that she applied to her selection of child actors. After long investigation, they found a boy from Chembur, Pradeep Motwani, to dub for the male lead. She said: 'I didn't want any exaggerated dubbing. I wanted an unspoilt voice' (India Forums, 10 January 2009). Her confession communicates the need for restorative utopian perfection and authenticity articulated by world travellers with emotional moorings (Ralph and Staeheli 2011; Cohen et al. 2013). There is a nomadic homeliness in Tandan's searches that matches Beaufoy's wandering in Juhu and Boyle's search for the perfect SM hero.

Having considered hundreds of young male actors, Boyle decided upon Patel with the help of his daughter, who suggested the young actor because of his role in the British Channel 4 television ensemble drama *Skins* (Dawtrey, 30 August 2007; Roston, 4 November 2008). Born in 1990 in Harrow, London, and with a GCSE in drama, Patel is an example of the socially mobile second-generation migrant. He appeared in *Skins Secret Party*, a one-off special available to view from the *Skins* website, as Anwar, a young pick-and-choose Pakistani Muslim, who is not serious or devout about his religion, uses drugs at parties, drinks, partakes in premarital sex, eats pork but still believes that homosexuality goes against his religion (IMDB, Dev Patel Biography, undated). In Chapter 5 we will explore how such ethical inconsistencies are transferred in SM onto Salim's persona. Patel's homely selection relates to his representativeness of routes and roots binding traditional post-colonial migration to contemporary work-related mobilities (Sheller and Urry 2006; Hannam et al. 2006). His SM casting returns him to imagined places of pilgrimage, where he can now act as an affluent traveller while acting the destitute slum subject of Indian histories of Partition and post-colonial industrial movement (Adler 1989, 1992; Kaufmann and Mantulet 2008).

Just as Patel reflects a British transnational ethos, so Freida Pinto's selection for Latika's role projects India's new cosmetic cosmopolitan ethos. Born in 1984 in Mumbai's Maharashtra to a middle-class family from Mangalore, Southern India (her father is a banker, her mother is high school principal, whereas her sister is an Indian news channel NDTV producer), Pinto traversed the modelling circuit in Mumbai before landing Latika's role. Between 2006 and 2007 she participated in *Full Circle*, a travel show telecast on Zee International Asia Pacific. She also went on assignments to Afghanistan, Thailand, Malaysia, Singapore, Indonesia and Fiji, amongst other countries. A late starter in acting (she did amateur theatre before she took acting classes after completing her debut film), she is known to be adept in Indian classical dance as well as salsa (IMDB, Freida Pinto Biography, undated) – skills that proved useful in her involvement in SM. Pinto auditioned for the role of Bond girl Camille in *Quantum of Solace* (dir. Marc Forster, 2008) and was considered to replace Emma Stone in *Sucker Punch* (dir. Zack Snyder, 2011) but lost both roles. Her Westernised career and her roots in a European colonial settlement (her surname is Portuguese and connects to the first colonisations of India in 1497) corroborate her cosmopolitan identity.

Matching Patel with Pinto (today also a real couple) in the film's adult part suggests a peculiar 'coming of age', an inner journey in SM also communicating with the public mobilities of its actors. The journey's beginning commences with the idea of 'contact zones' as domains of interaction between colonisers and colonised but concludes in post-national 'interspaces' (Urry 2007:274–7) in which work patterns, biographies and profiles produce global sociocultures. This medley of micro-social biographies and macro-social cultural habitus allows colonial and post-colonial modernities to engage in a dialogical *mélange*. As others have explained, hybridisation can safely be attributed to 'the new middle classes and their cultural and social practices arising in the context of migration and diaspora and the new modernities of the "emerging markets"' (Nederveen Pieterse 2004:88). Contact zones used to be 'the space in which peoples geographically and historically separated c[a]me into contact with each other [to] establish on-going relations, usually involving conditions of coercion, radical inequality, and intractable conflict' (Pratt 1992:4). But 'interspaces' are imaginary and virtually projected zones that different subjects can traverse and in which different worldviews may meet under the auspices of new permutations of a global service class. Normally such service classes claim specific technological professions as status symbol but professionals such as Patel and Pinto are a different type of class participating in aesthetic adaptation.

What is lost in this experience of *pangosmiopoiesis* is the military, racial and sexist contexts that brought such virtual spaces to life – what Urry (2007) would include in humanity's 'dark spaces and futures'. The young actors' casting as disenfranchised heroes capitalises on their established star-sign potential (Dyer 1982) to articulate a critique of contemporary inequalities. If Patel's sign potential evokes the derogatory and misleading ridicule of the dangerous 'Muslim Paki', Pinto's suggests the global circuit of a colonised beauty that auditions for a place in Western salons. Both signs sit at the back of SM's staging of mobilities as a Western complementary discourse: one that kills (the Muslim outsider who must be a terrorist) and another that enhances (a naturally beautiful model with inculcated acting skills). This unlikely combination also haunted the employment of Patel's, Pinto's and Mittal's younger likes.

Born in Agra in 1987, a north Indian city best known as the site of the Taj Mahal, Madhur Mittal won the Screen Actors Guild Award for Outstanding Performance by a Cast in SM. In 1997, he won *Boogie Woogie*, a popular reality-based dance show on Indian television, for his Michael Jackson impersonation and when soon after his family moved to Mumbai he forayed into acting and dancing in charity shows, cultural events and film-award ceremonies (Rediff News 2009). As a child actor he worked in well-known Hindi films, including *Say Salaam India* (dir. Subhash Kapoor, 2007) and as an adult he travelled the world performing in over 950 stage shows. In preparation for his role of Salim, he hung out with some gangsters in Mira Road 'to get into their heads' (Canton, 13 January 2009). Mittal's considerable contribution to SM's verisimilitude is not acknowledged as well as Patel's and Pinto's. SM's marketing as a love story left less space for an artist who conforms to – literally and symbolically – 'dark' roles (Mittal's childhood *Boogie Woogie* Jackson impersonation) challenging global codes of civility (*Say Salaam India* as the story of a group of boys with limited means who wish to harness their cricket skills). However, his profile connects to Pinto's and Patel's: not only is he a mobile cosmopolitan professional, he embodies the negation of the very cosmetic order to which his art-work conforms.

If Patel and Pinto represent socially uneventful examples of adaptation, lead SM composer A.R. Rahman's overall trajectory does not. Rahman's real life story matches SM's archplot of 'rags to riches' – a quintessential allegory of adaptation in which the hero turns from vagabond to tourist – and highlights how reciprocity in the form of philanthropic giving builds real Eurasian cosmological connections. Rahman is an Indian composer, singer-songwriter, music producer, musician, multi-instrumentalist and philanthropist (Humaa.com undated). Born A.S. Dileep Kumar in Chennai, Madras in 1966 and raised on Tamil movies and music, he converted to Sufism – a mystical form of Islam – in the late 1980s. His father, a film music composer and conductor for Tamil and Malaysian films, died when Rahman was nine. Thereafter, his family had to rent out his father's musical equipment as their source of income (Hindi Lyrics undated; Times of India, 30 September 2002). Described by the Asian media as the world's most prominent and prolific film composer, Rahman has won two Academy Awards and another two Grammy Awards, a BAFTA

Award, a Golden Globe, four National Film Awards, fifteen Filmfare Awards and thirteen Filmfare Awards South, as well as other awards and nominations (Corliss, 22 February 2011). His extensive body of work for film and the stage earned him the nickname 'the Mozart of Madras' while Tamil commentators and fans have coined him the nickname *Isai Puyal* (=music storm). Working with artists such as Andrew Lloyd Webber and with Shekhar Kapoor on *Elizabeth* (1998), he influenced directors such as Baz Luhrmann and managed to internationalise Indian music via film (Lakshmi, 30 April 2009).

Personal and professional circumstances found their way into the composer's art-work with intriguing results. His compositions are characterised by blends of Eastern classical and electronic musical sounds, world music genres and traditional orchestral arrangements. His training in Carnatic, Western classical, Hindustani music and the Qawwali style of Nusrat Fateh Ali Khan, in addition to numerous other styles, has been permeated with the Sufi mysticism he holds dear. But Rahman's compositional *mélange* – today constitutive of Eurasian narrative nodes marketed everywhere via the cultural industrial hubs of world cities (Tzanelli 2013a:ch.3) – also spills into his philanthropic activities. He continuously composes for charity media events and has set up the A.R. Rahman Foundation with a goal to eradicate poverty globally. The foundation is in partnership with educational institutions across India to provide education to children who do not have easy access to schools or funds. Appointed as Global Ambassador of the World Health Organization (WHO) 'Stop TB' Partnership (2004) and a supporter of Save the Children, India, he has also worked with Cat Stevens/Yusuf Islam for his song 'Indian Ocean', the proceeds of which contributed to helping orphans in Banda Aceh, one of the areas worst affected by the 2004 Indian Ocean Tsunami (Humaa. com n.d.). Rahman composed the theme music for the short film *The Banyan* (dir. Trilok Sharda) in 2006 to aid destitute women suffering from mental health problems in Chennai (Kamath, 31 January 2006; see also the project's website http://www.thebanyan.org). In 2008, together with the percussionist Sivamani he created a song titled 'Jiya Se Jiya', which was inspired by the 'Free Hugs' campaign and promoted it through a video shot in various cities in India (DNA India, 15 December 2008).

Rahman's personal investment in philanthropic projects bears the mark of a sort of empathy often criticised in development studies as a perverted form of racism. If not approached with caution, such criticisms (better addressed elsewhere) hinder assessments of his artistic contribution to the completion of SM. *The Banyan's* video clip with Rahman's haunting music theme – also uploaded on his You Tube channel (2006) – provides introductory reflections on this issue: the video adopts a familiar black-and-white visual narrative that in the context of slum-as-dark tourism raises equally familiar questions regarding political colouration. Such artistic content is better connected to Rahman's Sufi ethos that centres on pilgrimage as a form of esoteric, inner travel (Morini 1992:2 in Coleman and Eade 2004:19; Singh 2012). Sufism's outer law that is concerned with actions is complemented by an inner law concerned with the human heart: as surface (black-white) and content (purity-impurity) communicate in this version of artistic *pangosmiopoiesis* their audio-visual mediations have to communicate too. The example shows how political criticism, though generally important, can be based on misunderstandings of art-work's cultural resonance and political intentionality.

A more helpful observation on Rahman's contribution to industrial shifts from filiation to affiliation is provided by the involvement of another Tamil-born artist in SM. Born Mathangi (Maya) Arulpragasam in 1975, M.I.A. is a British-Sri Lankan Tamil songwriter, record producer, singer, rapper, fashion designer, visual artist, and political activist. In 2002 she received an Alternative Turner Prize nomination for her art. She has also been recognised for her work as a music video director, graphic and fashion designer (Starpulse, 'M.I.A. biography' undated). Her music features styles such as electro, reggae, rhythm and blues, alternative rock, hip hop, grime, rap ballads and Asian folk and makes references to musical influences such as Missy Elliott, Tamil film music, Lou Reed, Pixies, Timbaland, Beastie Boys and London Posse (Todd, 22 September 2008). Unlike Rahman, M.I.A.'s family was forced to relocate due to her father's political activities – something she also pursues in her art-work. But just like Rahman, she constructs amenable links between conceptions of the vagabond as a person in need and the tourist as the person that traverses the world, here collecting impressions, there offering a hand to those in need. The Tamil cosmological link articulates home imaginaries as world projects in not so dissimilar ways from those of Beaufoy's and Boyle's peripheral discourse of migratory ideas or ideoscapes (Appadurai 1990). Rahman's and M.I.A.'s contemporary social status as travellers with memories of vagabondage fused into Beaufoy's and Boyle's propensity to turn presents and pasts of global migrations (Irish-Catholic, South Asian) into core narratives of human mobility.

Evidently, whereas the 'artistic community's' routes supersede its particular roots through generalised discourses of charitable giving, they take a back seat when personal experience and knowledge is allegorised in art-work. The following part of the book is dedicated to unpacking how these ideoscapes of tourism and vagabondage become articulated and disarticulated within the SM community's ethnoscapes. This necessitates a thorough investigation of the film and its music as works of art, and also some key distribution and dissemination channels that produced more interpretations of SM.

Part II
Reading *Slumdog Millionaire*

4 Staging *Slumdog*
From realist fiction to 'ethical' acting

Redefining ethics

SM's text is not inconsequential to the study of Mumbai's socio-cultural profile, or irrelevant to the needs of contemporary India. Its rejection feeds into colonialism's sexist and racist structures via a discourse that pronounces certain *intangible* cultural products as authentic, while shunting aside those generated in everyday spheres of cultural consumption (Tzanelli 2011:ch.6). The elitist dimension such attitudes sustain propagates a particular public discourse of 'ethics' as contractual obligation between groups bound by blood affiliation – a phenomenon otherwise known as 'heritage'. It also injects this discourse into global domains the very moment transnational institutions such as the United Nations (UN) and the United Nations Educational, Scientific and Cultural Organization (UNESCO) strive to dispel mythical depictions of former colonised polities as 'underdeveloped' and therefore in need of 'instruction'.

Although the debate over what constitutes a respectable 'public face' for national polities and how this *strategically* borrows from dead or dying sexist and racist colonial structures is discussed in Part III, it is worth stressing here how it poisons academic analyses. With all its reductive representations (necessary for the creation of cohesive cinematic plots), SM challenges fixed conceptions of heritage that discard the development of post-colonial, industrial 'human refuse' into new consumption hubs. I refer to SM's audio-visual reproduction of mobilities, as the film appears to explore new ways of seeing and listening to Mumbai's and India's dissonant spaces of human sociality: the slum, the locally managed tour, the locally organised consumption of sexuality (the brothel) and the interpretation of Western popular culture in hybridised Bollywood forms. This extraordinary complex of production and consumption sits on broad understandings of what tourist theorists recognise as slum and dark tourism, and their representational interface. Much of what is discussed in this and some other chapters (5, 7 and 8), relates to what Bell and Lyall recognised as the 'inverted sublime' (2002:72, 92–3), which mediates both through natural planes (horizontal) and man-made industrial structures (vertical) through depth codes, ideas of (emotional) abyss or (moral) descent. Popular and specialised sociological imaginations constantly populate these depths with monsters and ideas of hell, visually coding sublimation into black or dark, like Niebuhr's (1960) theological divide of global ethics.

Although the transition from Hindu philosophy to Western camera-work in SM is conditioned by contemporary genre production needs, it also communicates an intermediary sentiment concerning present social inequalities in urban India. Ray (2012) argues that recent Bollywood movies appear to align with the UN's Millennium Development goals in terms of plots: their emphasis on gender equality, poverty, democracy and freedom, the right to non-violent protest, fair media, health, education and global partnership appeal to Indian multiculturalism and the call to eliminate socio-cultural discrimination. The country's statist interventionism in public life and disorganised capitalism in foreign business thrives on endemic administrative 'corruption'; it supports clientelism and an underworld mafia that Bollywood itself started debating from the 1970s in its cinematic plots. Again, we deal with questions of meritocracy and malicious rumour in consumption. At a basic cosmological level, SM toys with such Bollywood themes enough to resonate with domestic Indian audiences without alienating Western aesthetic sentiment. This aesthetic hybridisation can be partially attributed to pragmatic restrictions and needs: films have to be defined by the industry and recognised by audiences as such, as genres are not pure scientific categories but publicly constructed ones (Altman 1999:16). The globality of cinematic production as well as the internationalisation of the industry's human resources (Hesmondhalgh and Baker 2010), with actors figuring as a professional community of interests in media coverage, might also affect genre definitions. Even if adaptation is regarded as 'an invisible genre', film-goers usually recognise its distinctiveness, just as any literary genre that has been institutionalised so as to demarcate the audience's horizons of expectation and the author's writing models (Todorov 1990:17–18; Leitch 2008:106).

The fact that SM's protagonists were not famous as actors but could be instantly recognised as suitable for the role due to their psychosocial habitus further contributed to the story's genre classification (as a hybrid Bollywood-friendly movie). Artistic *technopoesis* depends on skill or gift – an embodied-acting knowledge that distinguishes serendipity from accident (Merton and Barber 2004:43–4). Suggestively, SM unfolds in Bollywood's non-European phantasmagoric heartland (Patke 2000) and the first half of the film preys on the power of global media to obscure or illuminate the lives of the social periphery. This immediately connects the movie to the diachronic development of slum tourism as a sort of need to relate with the underworld and the 'invisible' deprived human who deserves philanthropic support, including the right to earn while (s)he is being 'toured' and artistically represented (Low 1999; Koven 2004; et al. 2009; Meschkank 2011, 2012). There are also solid connections between the emergence of a digitally mediated romantic consumerist ethic (Coyne 1999; Campbell 2005) and charitable representations of deprived post-industrial communities that we cannot bypass. In a similar vein with Barlow's utopianism (1996) this new ethic acknowledges the role of

Staging Slumdog   57

materiality in progress but highlights this ideology's exhaustion. However, the proposed new utopian synthesis attempts to transcend ontological distinctions between the materiality of industrial society and the realm of virtuality. It does so by combining the scientific romanticism of Enlightenment progress with the Romantic critique of modernity into new possibilities to achieve material transformation, which lead to self-realisation and holism (Yar 2014:28–30).

These observations allow one to connect the 'high arts' to realist environments so as to re-examine 'ethics' as a pivotal concept in SM's multiple contexts (e.g. Kracauer 1997). The first conception of ethics is tied to slum and dark tourism as humanity's 'dissonant' forms of heritage (Dann 2001; Dann and Seaton 2001; Seaton 2012), whereas the second might both reinstate and challenge the first through audio-visual negotiations of slum *ethics as habit*. Both dark and slum tourism are rooted in European histories of exile, slavery, displacement or colonial genocide (Frenzel 2012); both can be viewed as responsible reactions to these histories via philanthropic intervention and privileged activism; both inform global aesthetic 'curricula' of edu-tourism or educational tourism (see also Spivak 2012). These forms of tourism are an example of Tardean *dispositif* (Tonkonoff 2013:268) – they enable a 'thick description' of transnational cosmological flows that claim patrilineages and moorings in a constantly mobile human universe (Cresswell 2001; Hannam et al. 2006). A deep and 'thick' description (Geertz 1973; Herzfeld 2008; Smith 2008:174) of the term *éthos* (literally repetitive character/custom) connects to Aristotelian *phronesis* as the prerequisite logical production of familiarity and respectability, but also to Tardean emulations of a social paradigm (Basic Lexicon of Ancient Greek Online 2013). To put theory in context: I argue that SM's art-work emulates Indian socio-cultural paradigms in the form of human characters (Barth 1981), but such perceptions are themselves also productive of the artistic community's ethos. Put otherwise, representations of Mumbai's slumscapes and its human characters in SM reflect the sort of ethics its makers propagate as part of a global socio-cultural contingent. Contra any elitist conceptions of 'deserving' academic investigation (an amusing equivalent of the political discourse on the 'deserving poor'), I argue that SM's cinematic ethos and its hybrid ethics of care for poorer communities should be treated as a unity.

Marketing necessities aside, from scriptwriting to directing and acting SM flags its makers' determination to break away from 'soft' melodrama by fusing social violence and new lifestyle rituals into a seamless discourse of everyday life in global cities. At the centre of all these remains the image of the stranger – a racialised, gendered and emotionally rich character that exposes the limitations and weaknesses of the familiar, the sedentary and the voyeuristic gazer (Wolff/Simmel 1959; Bauman 2003a). Both Beaufoy and Boyle stressed that the script acquires a dynamism precisely because its diegetic extremes reflect 'what is going on' in real India (Slumdog Dreams, 2009). Although the film takes the viewer for a journey into Mumbai's slum 'precariat' (urbanity's new social class suffering from job insecurity (Karin and Beck, 2010; Standing, 24 May 2011; Standing, 2011)) through its protagonist's (Jamal) memory flashbacks and his brother's (Salim) frustrations and criminal activities, it also allows the main heroes to enter other phantasmagoric realms of contemporary consumption distanced from gang violence and crime. This diversity does not foreclose hidden continuities between crime and glamour, Jihad-like violence and McWorld infotainment (Barber 2003): Jamal's appearance in a globally famous quiz show (Mumbai's version of *Who Wants to Be a Millionaire?*) foregrounds a safer cinematic 'reality' of show business; likewise, the young couple's (Jamal and Latika) concluding dance routines seem to stand miles apart from cinematic renditions of administrative violence, poverty and corruption. But the film's ultimate message is that nothing is as it seems in entertainment.

Slum tourism, dark tourism and filmic reality

Here we can unearth another connection between filmic reality and new philanthropic tourisms grounded in Europe's dissonant heritage. In terms of image and sound, the contrast between everyday rituals with crime blends form with content, in what can be likened to 'dark cinematic tourism'. Boyle acknowledged the influence of several Bollywood films set in Mumbai providing 'slick, often mesmerising portrayals of the Mumbai underworld' seasoned with 'brutality and urban violence' (Smith 2013:520), including *Satya* (1998) (screenplay co-written by Saurabh Shukla, who plays Constable Srinivas in SM) and *Company* (2002). The chase in one of SM's opening scenes that builds links between different mobilities – including slum and environmental tourist gazing and listening – was based on a 12-minute police chase through Dharavi slum in *Black Friday* (2004), an adaptation from S. Hussain Zaidi's book that discusses the 1993 bombings in Mumbai (Kumar, 23 December 2008). Insinuations of terrorist darkness creep into the scene in which Salim practices Islamic prayer while engaging in illegal activities. It would be equally accurate to attribute the origins of such connections to Beaufoy's preparatory writing travails in Mumbai, where he was able to gather a patchwork of stories that might, 'goodness knows how', knit together. 'A gangster trial is never off the front page of the *Times of India*. Hindu/Muslim tensions are bubbling up again and the gang of beggars at one of the road underpasses tell me as much as a Dickens novel ever could about the pay-scale of mutilation' (Beaufoy, 12 December 2008).

In terms of aesthetic practice SM projects a technological interchange of light with darkness, which establishes the hero's embodied, emotional and social journey (Campbell 2008) as a trope of labour akin to that we still associate with black slavery. And yet, it is debatable whether SM falls prey to the necropolitical aesthetics of colonial travel that ossified ethnic otherness (Mbembe 2001, 2003), subjecting it into the governmobile agendas of contemporary tourist industries. The film broadcasts a more ambivalent model of native propensity to self-fashioned civility through hard technological labour, forming an individualised *dispositif* supportive of Boyle's artwork and activism in academic circles (Pathasarathy 2009). Central to Jamal's story is a

Staging Slumdog 59

pedagogical process involving a progressively more refined manipulation of impressions: from cheating and swindling as a child, to serving tourist customers, to displaying personal knowledge in public as an adult, he is progressively cast as a Goffmanesque public performer and an Eliasian civilised human.

Dev Patel's and Freida Pinto's profiles in Chapter 3 are useful here: Jamal is an aesthetic version of *pangosmiopoiesis*, just as Salim and Latika are other versions of it in search of social recognition. SM's genre affiliations rely heavily on the – *cathartic*, if we adopt Aristotelian conceptions of social engagement (Aristotle 1996) – passage to social recognition of the protagonists: Jamal's recognition as an essentially good person rather than a 'dirty cheat', Salim as the misguided angry youth and Latika as a woman fighting sexist constraints. In terms of *ethographic* development, Jamal's distinctive Indian gesticulation articulates expressiveness in opposition to Salim's controlled, yet constant facial resentment and Latika's dreamy or sad glances. Paradoxically, Jamal's habitus is recognisably Indian, as opposed to Salim's confusing facial expressions that we find in characterisations of internal European 'others' such as the Germans (Tzanelli 2010a:102). In terms of genre theory, these observations culminate in the recognition of SM's adaptation as a story capitalising on certain textual markers through intertextual references to typified human character and action (Hutcheon 2006). Otherwise put, SM's text communicates ways of adapting and evolving to social change in an ecumene slowly losing its borders and rootedness and expanding as a map of generalised socio-cultural characters.

But SM's thanatourist (dark tourist) agenda also clashes with its slum tourist gaze: whereas the former more easily appeals to distant pasts of slavery and reworks them into de-politicised aesthetics, the latter can only revert to realist politics of labour and tourist mobilities (Freire-Madeiros 2009; Linke 2012). Nevertheless, this clash activates the film's politicised ambiguity, allowing space to articulate the ethics of 'doing' and 'recording' the realities behind the spectacle of slum tourism: contemporary 'world risk society' (Beck 2005) makes sense only through historicisations of the present. In another context Metz (2007:311) explained that although, just like cinematic adaptations, documentaries always allude to a missing whole, their methodological study rarely figures in examinations of documentary film and cinematic adaptations. Exchanging scenes of reality TV with Jamal's flashbacks (a recurring theme in SM's narrative) replaces traditional documentary techniques that preserve a false realist feel for the viewer (e.g. Bell and Lyall 2002:114, 117, 121) without reducing SM's memory-work to any of these genres. Even the snapshots of Jamal's past are not visually rendered in sepia colours (Johnson 2008:8–9) so as to be aesthetically united with the present (e.g. Jamal's participation in the quiz show). At the same time, both past and present inform SM's technologically mediated narrative, as they appear to be recorded and broadcast unedited in 'real' present time. Jamal's twin interrogation by different forms of authority – his live interview with *Who Wants to be a Millionaire?* presenter Prem Kumar (Anil Kapoor), and a police officer (Irfan Khan) – retain the visual palette of the present and are cinematically arranged as footage, ready to make sense as an organic extension of Jamal's biography.

Mobile characters, fixed archetypes

It could be suggested that shifts from a corporeal mobility, conventionally associated with tourist movement, 'to a virtual (im-)mobility via the cinema screen' (Gibson 2006:157) mediate between mind-walking and actual leisure regimes. Likewise, aesthetic renditions of travels 'down memory lane' could be viewed as a rejection of uncritical romanticisations of dark tourist tropes. Boyle's work did not follow the formulas of typical adaptation, which exaggerate the need for period settings, to avoid historical fetishisations of poverty. Jamal's agency moves between a remote and a proximate past, whereas events that shape the outcome of his actions (e.g. Salim's decision to help Latika escape slavery) develop in a parallel present. SM's cinematic and literary technique suggests interpretative complexity: whereas multiple readings can be generated to assess the socio-cultural context, our heroes stabilise the film's social hermeneutics as global modernity's archetypes (Pippin 1999). Beaufoy's writing style stays true to conceptions of *testimonio*, originally understood as novella-length (self-)narration of a life or a significant episode, including the experience of imprisonment and captivity. Boyle's documentary technique corroborates this: first-person esoteric self-narrations appear in his previous films, including *Sunshine* (2007). This apocalyptic sci-fi story unfolds on a spacecraft with a mission to reignite the sun and save the earth from death. Its stylistic claustrophobia – largely communicated through stark antithetical colours – matches earth's environmental 'endgame' with the crew's descent to insanity.

Testimonios are forms of writing that appropriate dominant discursive forms, involve editing of oral accounts by a significant interlocutor such as a writer or a journalist and call into being voices living at the social margins (Beverley and Zimmerman 1990). The consolidation of *testimonios* in Latin American contexts both coincided with their official Cuban recognition as a genre in the 1970s and the political turmoil that other South American countries experienced as post-colonial polities (Beverley 1989). First-person representations of Jamal's marginality from his childhood years and the centrality of Latika's vulnerability in them pose the question of one's power – or lack thereof – to speak and write for oneself (Vidal and Jara 1986). It is debatable whether Beaufoy or Boyle assumes the empowering role of the post-colonial speaker, given that both originate from the social-geographical margins of a former European empire. It may also be inaccurate to speak of the colonial condition in contemporary globalised settings, or conflate it with global economic structures. Suffice it to stress that the production of archetypal social stages and voices enables SM's viewers to acknowledge both the unattainable reality of Mumbai through its cinematic depiction and their own distance from the 'pro-filmic' reality only natives can experience on location (Peirce 1998; Vaughan 1999:79).

SM's text is an exercise in what Nederveen Pieterse (1997) recognises as cultural and structural hybridisation. Structural hybridisation refers to the ways in which forms become separated from existing practices and recombine with new forms in new practices (Rowe and Schelling 1991:231). This applies to SM's audio-visual apparatus, which guides the main heroes propensity to reinvent themselves as humans in different spaces. Yet, SM's cosmology suggests that we consider how mixing different civilisational models (Asian, European, African) produces a global *mélange* (Nederveen Pieterse 2004). This is the language of cultural hybridisation that SM promotes through the heroes' (auto-)biographical journeys. It is not coincidental that Boyle remained determined to grant music and dance a special place in the concluding part of the film. Contra the tendency of earlier adaptations, in which music becomes integrated into the background and 'is meant to be heard only unconsciously' (Gorbman 1987:73), SM's lead song ('Jai Ho!') foregrounds the plot through blends of traditional Indian and technologically modified vocals, lyrics in two languages and three different dialects and Bollywood choreography. Civilisational clashes need to be dressed in cultural garments to enter global markets.

The mythical structure of SM's main and auxiliary characters has regional and national roots in India stretching back to *Mahabharata* and the Upanishads. But as SM is a contemporary hybrid product, my reading focuses mainly on the ways these characters' roots project contemporary, intersecting mobilities. Individual characterisations in SM correspond to the logic of socio-cultural affordances, or the range of choices available to humans within their particular world and the subjective experience of their socio-cultural environment (Michael 1996:149; Urry 2007:51). In social and political theory affordances are mediated through citizenship discourse and the ways subjects respond to everyday exclusions and inclusions as individual agents, but also as part of imagined communities – localities, nations or nomad groups (Yuval-Davis 1997; Vertovec and Cohen 2002; Sassen 2002b:7; Vertovec 2010). The survival of original colonial *civilité* codes that once upon a time belonged to a distinctively European cultural heritage is one of the many affordance variants to which SM characters appeal (Mbembe 2001:37–9). But as Mumbai exceeds conceptions of the post-colony, it may be more correct to include in these affordances what transnationally manned cultural industries *perceive of* them (Hoesterey 2001 on post-modern art-work and hybrid characterisations). We are back to connections between ethnic characterisations of human populations in polities, and the ways these were immortalised, first in national and later in transnational art-work imaginaries (Leoussi 2004). But the association of Boyle's pastiche of cinematic characters with *la longue durée* of India was based on distant, rather than intimate professional knowledge of them, as was the case with his previous movies. Character and ethnic habitus (Bourdieu 1977) have practical and poetic qualities and hence partake in the production of a relativised humanity. A by-product of identity narratives, character appears as a stable referent in time, an instant identifier of individuals as parts of a cultural whole (Ricoeur 1993:119), even though these individuals are subjects in flux.

The application of such theorisation to SM's text-context nexus is crucial: note how the constant threat of prostituting Latika and her rape by Salim function as metaphors of what Robert Stam (2005) identified as a generalised 'hostility' to adaptation, which becomes associated with ideas of aesthetic violation, pop vulgarisation of 'literature proper' and an inability to preserve art's Platonic utopia intact. On a narrative level, in addition to romantic melodrama, SM alludes to the popular production of 'prestige films' in the 1930s that were based on books and plays by authors of known worth (Leitch 2008:110). Filtering a disreputable 'biography' of Mumbai through Jamal's hardship grants the story with historical depth. While not explored as such in the film, Mumbai's urban biography looms large, both like a vengeful post-colonial ghost and 'a strong distinctive brand personality...to which consumers can relate emotionally' (Donald and Gammack 2007:48). Though not a prestige film, SM questions the prestige of India's global 'network capital' (Larsen and Urry 2008), with its own version of exploitation, exclusion and corruption. Jamal's feeling of betrayal by his brother becomes in this re-modelling of the cinematic story constitutive of an archplot that declares eternal loyalty to fair development, unblemished by the prejudice of class, race and gender, and alert to the ways criminal entrepreneurship drains the spirit of those who stay morally pure against all odds.

This reading allows for further capitalisation on familiar cinematic representations based on social identity. Latika in particular operates as the story's self-sacrificial but calculative woman (she drives Jamal away to save him from his brother and a fight he is bound to lose), thus paving the ground for the ultimate clash between 'good' and 'evil' towards the end of the film. Everything is resolved at a utopian level, either as a tourist-consumer fantasy or through the cinematic city's anthropomorphic connections to a global politics of compassion (Thompson 2012). From chasing Bollywood stars through the public toilet to taking tourists 'for a ride' in Taj Mahal, to Jamal and Latika's dancing in the closing scenes, the film's utopia is steeped in what the literary purist would consider a copyist fantasy – the 'excrement' of an industrial modernity Marxian theorists identified in the 'Wallahs' or workers of the West (Berman 1981). A critical reading of the film's archplot through globalisation theory might identify in all three main heroes versions of impure reproduction (tricksters, gangsters and sex workers), blurring the once stark moral opposites and pushing the viewer to consider human action in specific spatial (dis-)continuums (slum, brothel, restaurants, telecommunication corporations, gangster haunts). An equally essential complementary reading via theories of 'mobile risk society' (Kesserling 2008) deconstructs polarisations of darkness-goodness, stressing instead the universality of human vulnerability.

The brotherly moral antithesis serves significant functional imperatives between SM's archplot and India's twentieth-century cosmological transformations; by extension, it manages to link both to changing textual narratives within Hindi cinema. The socio-economic crisis of the 1970s favoured the rise of certain cinematic stars to celebrity status within the nation, reinstating Nehruvian binaries in the illusion industry. Amitabh Bachchan and Raj

Kapoor's cases were cleverly adapted in SM to communicate this through a globally intelligible vocabulary. The two stars' pre-Bollywood status was in fact a prologue to Mumbai's cultural industrial change, especially its streamlining into global developmental frameworks centring on novel combinations of embodied and digital technologies. As much as the Bachchan cinematic persona, which in SM prologues Jamal's childhood trials, popularised the angry industrial man stereotype, Kapoor's Nehruvian idealist type provided a consumable counterpoint. Both men rose to Bollywood star status through such stereotypes that spoke to the common people's heart. Bachchan's resentful industrial character articulated national confrontations with the migrant, the often physically black-er labourer (Rollins 1996) with the inward-looking gaze, who could take it no more and asserted whatever individuality he could by illegal means, thus revealing a conflict within the country's industrial progress (Nandy 2001:21–6). The forever angry and always wronged man or *Karna* nicely reflects the vicissitudes of global migration theory by supplanting typical conceptions of the *Fremden(verker)* or mobile stranger (Wolff/Simmel 1959; Bauman 1991:56) with a psycholographic ambivalence rooted in gendered and racialised identities (Kristeva 1991:8; Tzanelli 2011:40). Bachchan mediated a realist vision of Indian urbanity that proved Nehru's optimistic planning wrong. As Kumar (2011:119) aptly proposes, in this socio-cultural context, 'Bombay brought back the mythical space of *Mahabharata*; but within the modern individual star standing for *Karna*, the metropolis could not redeem itself'. SM's Salim functions as such an anti-hero that, while recalling the middle cinema's realist portrayal of new human pathologies rooted in unattainable desires (to be reunited with the ideal woman or join the utopian community) (Prasad 2001:7), he is more representative of contemporary urban materialities and consumerist greed (Simmel 2004).

The protagonists' blended ethno-racial habitus matches Boyle's persistent focus on psychosocial types that do not 'fit into' their surrounding environment. Jamal reverses the controlled professionalism of David (Christopher Eccleston) and Alex (Ewan McGregor) in *Shallow Grave*, both of whom unravel under pressure, whereas Salim recalls the suicidal tendency of Mark in *Trainspotting*. There is symmetry between these (anti-)heroes and their experiential journeys that take place always in the psychological and geographical margins. Boyle's propensity to hinge camera-work on subordinate male types (abnormal, ethnically distinct, addicted or sensitive in stereotypically feminine ways) is part of his artistic signature. In interviews he stressed how his search for the ideal 18-year old Jamal was difficult, because young Asian men tend to work their bodies to a muscular-masculine ideal that conforms to Bollywood demands. Glamour is therefore associated with a healthy athletic appearance that slumdogs are not supposed to possess, as Jamal is supposed to communicate 'vulnerability' in a more realist fashion (Slumdog Dreams, 2009). The contrasting of Jamal's 'Ordinary Joe' ethos to Salim's worked-up black body is an aesthetic statement of post-colonial depth. Boyle's resonance is beautifully summarised in the angry protest of Mark Renton (Ewan McGregor,

Trainspotting), who articulates against Scotland's picturesque tourist countryside what it means to be a Scottish lowermost: 'shite...lowest of the low... wretched, miserable, servile, pathetic trash that was ever shat on civilisation' and subjected to the English 'wankers'. Here one may observe how cinematic *ethography* communicates with artistic idiosyncracy, making a note on Boyle's own origination from the British national periphery. The transposition of his films' damaged ethnic masculinities to Mumbai's cityscape bears witness to the ways artistic imaginaries are not rootless, only mobile.

Despite its makers' social astuteness, SM's core romance thrives on traditional gender complementarity: Jamal stands in this social framing for the skilful man's aspiration to social mobility, whereas Latika does not. This disengages her character from the destabilising forces in contemporary Indian society that have allowed predominantly middle-class women to become professionally and geographically mobile (Raghuram 2000). For the greatest part of the film, Latika occupies in the Indian 'gender order' (Connell 1987) the place of the working-class lowermost, a thoroughly subordinate type defined by the constraints of domestic abuse and antiquated social expectation. If Jamal serves in the film as a manifestation of blended literacy (from restaurant worker, chai waiter and call centre employee to genius millionaire), Latika succeeds only in SM's concluding scenes to transcend her designated cinematic role as *la femme attrapée* (Wager 1999:15). In Euro-American cinematic traditions this is the woman who, remaining trapped in social conventions, offers herself as a possibility for male redemption from the evil *femme fatale*, who mars family custom and conformist expectations.

Just like SM's allegory of 'technological redemption' (Pippin 1999; Bauman 2000), Latika is not an Indian character. Suffice to stress that her persona belongs to Beaufoy's pen, as she never appears in *Q&A*. Her hybrid, Eurasian habitus deliberately accentuates Mumbai's post-colonial trajectory: as the lead female hero, she shed the embodied attributes of Indian female 'coyness' in favour of predominantly European renditions of the tragic woman. By downplaying – rather than exaggerating, as the Bollywood norm dictates – emotional angst, resorting to whispers and low key expressions of sadness and pain, she too mediates the great civilising process (Elias 1982) that globalised Western etiquette displays in the public sphere, consigning human spontaneity to oblivion. One might even claim that the film's feminine, rather than feminist, dimension re-examines the spatio-temporal coordinates and origins of 'hybridity' as a post-colonial project rooted in the racist and sexist traditions of modernity. Processes of hybridisation reveal difference to be relative, encouraging also affirmation of similarity and points of contact/cooperation. However, on a *technopoetic* level ontological hybridity redrafts the category of the female human in global cosmological terms (Goldmann 1964; Bakhtin 1984:252; Tzanelli 2011:89–90). Instead of making hermeneutic recuperation their project *per se*, the makers of SM reverse hybridity's trajectory, asking what might happen if we take cultural-political forms out of their Western frame and place them in the India of Bollywood and global MTV collaborations. As a result, Latika *la femme* exceeds the cinematic story's meaning, because she succeeds to be(come) by turn trapped and mobile, romantic in the Western sense and joyous in the Indian sense, muted by sorrow and expressive through music, dance and tears.

Latika's oneiric persistence as Jamal's very own world(view) picture (Heidegger 1967) does not merely appeal to form but to an inner need to recuperate what has been lost in the turmoil of Indian (post-)modernisation: a connection to core narratives of identity and selfhood (Pippin 2005). As Beaufoy admitted, what Freida Pinto brought in the story was a 'startling beauty' that stays out of reach for the greatest part of the story but for which one 'would cross the world' (Slumdog Dreams, 2009). In this respect, the selection of a white-r face to embody this character is consistent with the tendency of the socially repressed to return symbolically as nostalgic apparitions in civilising processes: without them, we cannot move the world ahead, nor can we travel and apprehend it (Stallybrass and White 1986; Young 1995:115). The insertion and incremental fading of one of the film's key musical components, 'Latika's Theme' (music and lyrics by A.R. Rahman) in various scenes, complements Latika's visual 'apparition' and oneiric significance. Given that Boyle, who preferred to dress up SM in 'pulsey, edgy upfront styles that reflected modern urban India', emphatically asked Rahman to avoid romantic music composition (Broxton, 14 November 2008), the survival of the song's nostalgic tone in the final product is significant. The track sits in the released CD version between two blended themes – an electronic track ('Liquid Dance', music by A.R. Rahman) and a Bollywood adaptation ('Aaj Ki Raat', music by Shankar Ehsaan Loy, lyrics by Javed Akhtar). By intersecting two quite dissimilar auditory narratives (one post-modernist and techno-cultural and another late-modernist disco), the CD consolidates a specific artistic understanding of intersectional inequality.

There is a link between Latika's cinematic image and her potential *Q&A* inspiration, Nita, a young prostitute who becomes the literary protagonist's (Ram Mohammed) sweetheart. Although it is speculative whether Beaufoy drew on Nita's story to co-create Latika, it seems to be the best cosmologically rooted guess. The novel's protagonist muses over Urdu poetry under a moonlit Taj Mahal, unconsciously enmeshing his awe for India's architectural heritage with his love for this unfortunate girl, who was sold by her family into prostitution (Swarup 2006:312). *Q&A*'s affective potential and its visual dimensions (moonlight, darkness) were transformed in SM into bright, feminised, audio-visual poetics. Latika stands between stillness and hypermobility: the cold blueness of the televised stage in which events develop in real life time contrasts with the red and orange vibrancy of the station where Latika is recalled as a memory picture by Jamal (incidentally, also Mumbai's sepia tourist advertising). Wrapped in the fire of the sun, or in her shawl's yellow and gold glimmer, she is elevated to the status of a silent Virgin Mary. Such illuminations of suffering are also reminiscent of *Sunshine's* style, with the character Searle (Cliff Curtis) bathed in sun's sublime colours while its radiation slowly destroys the spacecraft (Icarus II) – a metaphor matching ancient Icarus' destruction by the sun.

Film critic Mark Cousins highlights a creative tension between Boyle's cultural Catholicism and his British inheritance, which communicates aspects of the puritanical social realism of John Grierson's documentary tradition. Unlike the bottomless pessimism of traditional Catholic cosmology, Boyle's art-work 'shows no sign of social pessimism' (Linklater, 4 January 2009). If Latika the violated Virgin enshrouds SM into melancholy and nostalgia, her intermediary cultural role in the film's concluding scenes as a Bollywood star showcases how the migration of a fictional figure (the Holy Mother) from the private domain of home to the public domain of fandom continues to condition the phenomenon of celebrity (Braudby 1986; Rojek 2001:11). Frow's (1998) suggestion that celebrity increasingly takes on the mantle of religion, or Schickel's (1985) claim that the public's relation to celebrity is founded on an 'illusion of intimacy', fuse in Boyle's visual-ethographic production of ideal feminine types that both communicate personal experience and contest the clash of civilisations from a Western viewpoint (Huntington 1993; Macmaster and Lewis 1998). A socio-cultural analysis of Latika's half-covered face can recall both Virgin Mary's facial enshrouding and the Hindu-Islamic use of *dupatta* (shawl) that accompanies female everyday and wedding attire.

These first glimpses at Boyle's visual technique mirror Kandinsky's (1977:28–30) observation that material forms (the scenes surrounding objects and human beings) cannot be neatly separated from colour, as both contribute to the production of inner meanings and a harmony that penetrates surfaces to reach the human soul. A real-life synaesthete, Kandinsky provides another useful observation in the present study's conception of *pangosmiopoiesis*. Visual

Figure 4.1 Latika as fusion of cultural horizons
Source: Warner Bros/Photofest.

contrast alludes to the normative structure of the cinematic story, re-introducing serendipity as an epistemological theme: are the lights of fame that erase everything else worth more than a smiling face? Should one go for money or love? If *ethographic* colouring is one of Boyle's signature techniques, Beaufoy's dialogue artistry – or its absence thereof – also contributes to SM's critical viewpoint. Just as the death of the mysterious travelling novelist (Hugo) is wrapped in red Carravagioesque sheets in *Shallow Grave*, Latika's image is wrapped in the warmth of coloured memory. SM's sole female hero is not only a de-hypostasised woman: through her embodied presence and redemptive power, she intersects between Jamal's (good, hard earned and self-taught) technological skills and Salim's (evil) criminal craftiness. But whereas Jamal succeeds in acquiring the ultimate reward, love, Salim redeems himself through self-sacrifice (he is murdered by the gang to save Latika). Latika is in the film an embodied form of middle-ground goodness, liberated and liberating by turns within Mumbai's ethno-cultural complexity.

SM's principal character triad personifies Mumbai's cityscape in organic motion. As indiscriminate childhood solidarity wanes in the story, the 'cinematic tourist' becomes more familiarised with various truths to which the triad is subjected as a group of socially vulnerable post-colonial subjects. The three young heroes' shared childhood fantasy as 'the three Musketeers' also draws on the logic of adaptation as precarious post-colonial globalisation. We may recall Luke and Freebody's (1997) remark that over the centuries reading has functioned as a means of determining who belonged to the colonial centre and who to the margins. The insertion of classical French literature in SM acts as a critical biopic that is absent from the original text (in *Q&A* the hero displays indifference to classroom lessons). Nevertheless, representations of classroom lessons in the film vary, and it may be worth resorting to contemporary realities instead to stress that with a literacy rate of 69 per cent, the slums in Mumbai are the most literate in India (Gosh, 27 February 2006). The gap between reality and representation resembles old Mertonian uses of Craftown literacy levels as an uncomfortable encounter with social anomaly (Merton 1948:507). In this instance, therefore, our movie taps into the exclusive logic of cultural translatability: as Graff (2001) has explained, literacy has diachronically been defined on the basis of civilisational attributes and virtues such as morality, democracy and progress in a variety of communicative fields across the science and technology spectrum. The insertion of a Western literary story into SM's script contributes to the film's cosmological ambivalence: on the one hand, it elevates literary archplots of the old colonising centre into a key moment in the story, but on the other it represents disenfranchised groups as interpreters of Western literary narratives.

Interpreting reality – or, an introduction to filmic phenomenology

In a different context Leitch (2008) used the Dumas family novels to provide some observations on the genre of adaptation. Identifying the characteristics of the genre in the writings of Dumas *fils*, Leitch presents the works of Dumas *pére* (including *The Three Musketeers*, 1844) as a sort of heritage background. He follows the analysis by Mireia Aragay and Gemma López, who claimed that post-feminist discourse has left notions of femininity and masculinity in Western romance almost unchallenged, allowing female viewers to both embrace the utopian promise of romance and acknowledge its imaginary nature. Leitch observes that 'just as the romances at the heart of the classic-novel and heritage genres emphasise female heroes and values, their swashbuckling counterparts, whose appeal Brian Taves has aptly described as "the romance of adventure", emphasise masculine heroes and values' (Leitch 2008:109). Boyle, Beaufoy and their associates worked towards merging both trends into an audio-visual adaptation, purposely fluctuating between heteronormative utopian fantasy and realist documentary. And whereas the former might well preserve and inspire 'an aura of middle-class respectability' (Leitch 2008:109), the latter remains incurably socialist in its rationale (Brecht 1964) and fit for 'hands-on' reporters and lovers of first-hand testimony, once associated with masculine positivism (Oakley 1998). It is through such alignments and collusions that the story's plot manages to win both Eastern and Western audiences of various social profiles. As Father Thomas becomes Ram's surrogate father that educates him to a blend of religious cultures, and as the city's 'lumpen' mob seeks to avenge his alleged harbouring of a Hindu (Swarup 2006:52–3), *Q&A's* story comes closer to SM's theme of social divisions – circumstantially presented as religious divides.

The endless pursuit of precision (what do we truly know about who Ram Mohammed Thomas and Jamal are?) produces globality's recurring confusion of surfaces for superficiality: the hero's profile has to be anchored to instantly recognisable socio-cultural traits, or he risks evading Western comprehension (and translatability). Communications theorists, such as Ananda Mitra, suggested that SM is reminiscent of other refractions of India through the Western lens, including classics such as *Gunga Din* (dir. George Stevens, 1939) and *City of Joy* (dir. Roland Joffé, 1992) – two films covering Boyle's riots and slumming narrative ends. There is little doubt as to SM's simultaneous accommodation of 1970s Bollywood productions such as *Yadon Ki Barat* (dir. Nasir Hussain, 1973) – a film using the 'siblings separated by fate' *motif* to 'acculturate' Indian masses that spoke virtually no Hindi but flocked in to watch the movie for its magical narrative (Tiruchi, 20 July 2012). The suggestion that SM's directors 'have updated the surface content' (Ani, 31 January 2013) to include half a century changes in Western cinematography suggests the recognition of all surfaces as gateways to social realities. Both the Indian and Western camera's visible worlds appear as an endless skein of surfaces and aspects, 'but upon reflection we find that there is no surface that does not reveal another surface beneath' (Sandywell 2011:561). If we are to read SM holistically, as a hybrid piece of art, we must penetrate what Peirce (1998) designated as 'firstness' or unprocessed encounter and Panofsky (1955) as 'iconography'. Just as in any great work of adaptation, reasoning out the meanings of its audio-visual scripts necessitates a constant shift across different interpretative planes, contemporary and historical contexts and even ethnoscapes, as every single layer remains dependent on the social biography of its makers.

As we will see in the following chapter, Jamal's emergence from the shadows of the studio alludes to a similar phaneroscopic question: is what/who we view and hear who they really are, or do we have to penetrate *a* surface to encapsulate their essence? Incidentally, Ram Mohammed's loss of Father during a homophobic altercation is both connected to one of the quiz's questions about religious hermeneutics (the meaning of INRI on the cross) (Swarup 2006:67) and the hero's answer to police questioning over his religious beliefs: 'Does one have to go to a temple or a church or mosque to pray? I believe what Kabir says. Hari is in the East, Allah is in the West. Look within your heart and there you will find both Ram and Karim' (ibid. 67). Considering Kabir's production of utterances (*bāṇīs*), short poems evoking *sākhī* (a lyrical way to witness the 'Truth' through ritual repetition as prerequisite for the calibration of good *dispositif*), may not be that disconnected from SM's social production. The use of camera techniques by Boyle and his associates as the 'truthful eye' reproduces some of the novel's rooted philosophical meanings while negotiating its hybrid aesthetic form as a worldview.

5 The cinematic text scene-by-scene

Segments and heterotopias

A book exploring the role of serendipity in global technological environments is incomplete without a detailed analysis of its primary text (SM) – an exercise in hermeneutics connected to the real controversies it generated as an artistic-touristic venture. Serendipity works on the logic of temporal layering, which was bequeathed to modernity by ancient civilisations (Mediterranean, African and Asian) (Alcock 2010:14, 18; Tzanelli 2011:30). Indian nation-building was based on two strikingly different brands of Ghandian and Nehruvian hermeneutics (the nation's essence in relation to its traditions and the West respectively). These 'brands' are constitutive of heritage tourism in the country. But simultaneously, Indian heritage tourism follows the global logic of rewinding the clock for the benefit of the tourist visitor so as to activate experiences from another age (Jamal and Hill 2002:85). Whereas, as a historical narrative SM abides to such techniques (to allow cinematic tourists to experience the slum as a diachronic *topos*), as a critique of Mumbai's 'truncated modernity' it prioritises the protagonist's individual hermeneutics. As is the case with any consumption of exoticism, Jamal is both the cinematic tourist object and the film's primary subject.

SM is a heterotopic (*héteron*: other, *tópos*: place) film: it builds individual biographies through intentional misplacement of time-levels, enabling human actors to rearrange experience and reconceptualise phenomena (Foucault 1986:16–17). The introductory scene in the setting of the fictional quiz show serves as the film's contemporaneous anchor. SM's televised present aside, we discern at least three epochal changes in the story. Rather than rearranging events in a neat chronological order, I organise the film's analysis by following the story's narrative flow. The restoration of Indian historical linearity would appeal to discursive arrangements of the state's archive (Foucault 1989; Nietzsche 1990:46, 49) and destroy SM's poetic fluidity as art-work. Staying true to Beaufoy's diegetic style, Rahman's technotronic influences and Boyle's experimentations with new digital technologies I divide the analysis into acts or 'segments'. Whereas 'act' corresponds to the inner (as in the hero's affective reactions) and physical (as in embodied performance) mobilities of theatre plays, 'segment' better encapsulates recent technological changes in the ways such mobilities are staged in film and documentary. Internet terminology has embraced 'segments' as sections of a network bounded by bridges, routers or switches. In virtual memory systems segments constitute 'a variable-sized portion of data that is swapped in and out of main memory', whereas in graphics they define a piece of a 'polyline' or continuous line composed of one or more line segments (Webopedia, 'Segment', 2013). Films have a hierarchical structure, with 'frames' and 'shots' (groups of frames), forming a scene, and all sets producing a film.

SM mobilises both Hollywood/Bollywood and documentary techniques. Whereas Bollywood films and Western films generally contain shot action within particular spaces, documentaries move the camera (hence the cinematic tourist) gaze from place to place even within a city. Mitrovìc et al. (undated:1) contend that the most important clue for scene segmentation in documentaries 'is the repeated appearance of visually similar shots and motives', but they limit their work to artistic archive documentaries. Combined with internet understandings of segmentation, their approach presents cinematic segments as components of memory nodes in the narrative (e.g. Latika's image as a diachronic urban symbol) and self-contained diaries of travel (e.g. where the heroes go and what they do). Segments also function as acts that better connect audio-visual participants (often conceived of as 'spectators' or comfortable 'slum/ dark tourists' enjoying gruesome stories from afar) to compassionate 'actors'. Such shifts communicate artistic variations of Arendt's (1973; Habermas 1983:171–2; Yar 2000:16–17) and Ranciére's (2011; Tzanelli 2013b) conceptions of spectatorship as action and are pivotal in the production of self-conscious and compassionate cosmopolitans. These shifts carried moral significance in earlier modernity, when middle-class *flâneurs* physically wandered deprived urban spaces, recorded their experiences in travel accounts and raised public consciousness about social destitution. Today, combinations of imaginative travels, lifestyle mobilities and tourist slumming stimulate the contemporary romantic ethic (O'Brien 2008; Williams 2008; Dürr 2012; Seaton 2012:43–4).

Mazumdar's (2007) suggestion that popular Bombay cinema first recorded fleeting but memorable forms of urban life, thus providing impressions of Indian modernity's texture, is useful for understanding SM's narrative flow and content. Bombay films produced a split imagery between the 'virtual city' and the 'city of ruins' – or the city of bazaars, dreams, lavish interiors and family utopias, where claustrophobia disappears on the one hand, and of crime, darkness, shabbiness, consumerism and brotherhood gangs, where claustrophobia returns, on the other. Mazumdar's Arcadian theoretical framing suggests oscillations between two ideal types of *flânerie* – one predominantly voyeuristic, violent and masculinised, and another mobile, refined and feminised. SM follows this stereotypical discourse up to a point, but also reverses gender roles and public rituals. Ironically, this experimentation leads to a predictable global reaction whereby the feminine gaze (in reality performed by male SM artists) is punished and destroyed for its propensity to glamour and aestheticised consumption (Kaplan 1983; Williams 1984:85; Mulvey 2006).

SM's self-contained acts or segments of Mumbai's urban profile are personalised through Jamal's cinematic autobiography. As a whole, the segments articulate uneven transitions to post-colonial modernity and a post-modern stage of artistic and criminal groups, disorganised or disconnected social action and network socialities. SM's audio-visual strategy produces at least two types of traveller through time (Mumbai's social history) and space (India's dissonant touring stages encompassing heritage and abandoned industrial-slum sites). Bearing in mind the mediatisation of this twin type through cultural industrial complexes (SM's industry and its budding tourist offshoot), I identify such 'travellers' as cinematic tourists. I consider 'cinematic tourism' and the 'cinematic tourist' as liquid modernity's travel apogee (*à la* Bauman 2000); as theoretical models internally differentiated by the moves and motions of travel through and after film (*à la* Macionis 2004; Diekmann and Hannam 2012); and as cinematic articulations of travel and tourism (Tzanelli 2013a:4). In what follows I proffer a detailed analysis of SM's cinematic text by reference to the socio-cultural contexts on which its artistic creators drew. In these contexts Mumbai's spatio-temporal coordinates serve as a tool for making realist fiction and romantic narrative within which a cinematic, audio-visual tourist emerges. I mobilise sociological understandings of such artistic constructs so as to highlight the text's significance as a script on globalisation (and glocalisation) connected to tourism, activism and nationalism.

Segment 1

SM's cinematic tourist is invited to share with SM's protagonist a personalised form of mind-walking. This inner journey is blended with artistic representations of Jamal's move through time and space and the subsequent production of 'outside' forms of knowledge only peripatetic tourists can attain (Adler 1989, 1992; Carruthers 1990, 1998; Ingold 2000:111–31; Ingold 2010:16; Cohen 2010, 2011). This should not be confused with conceptions of the global 'travelling nomad', who crosses physical and cultural barriers in search for difference and differentiation, thus standing in opposition to safe tourist itineraries (Richards and Wilson 2004). Whereas the film enables viewers to adopt a nomadic stance in a safe digital environment, Jamal experiences danger in Mumbai's memoryscapes. Jamal's memory-work as an inner journey is triggered by violent episodes through space and time, which do not necessarily conform to linear motion. His transpersonal memory transforms him into an active character who engages in performativity as a Butlerian creative repetition (Butler 1993, 1997) and a Tardean production of disposition. Bachelard has explained that humans 'only retain the memory of events that have created [them] at the decisive instants of their pasts' (Bachelard 2000:57); through such performative acts they succeed in tying these events in knots of significance. Ingold (2010:19) cautions us that by 'travelling from place to place one finds and recalls to memory particular ancestral beings and their stories'.

In order to tie characters to memory sites inhabited by SM's heroes, audiences are introduced to an array of images and e-motions through a generic question typed on the screen in fonts identical to those used in the quiz. This 'alternate reality' invites audiences to move in pace with SM's story but in a parallel plane, where challenges and queries are directly posed to them. As a carrier of developmental tourist messages, the introductory scene presses interrogations over the value of coevality or parallel timing planes in which victims are always less developed and therefore excluded from understandings of modernity (Lévi-Strauss 1971, 1972; Fabian 1983; Tzanelli 2008b:77–8). Hence, the scene articulates Mertonian serendipity as post-colonial *syngyria*. As we will see below, the cinematic script and the film draw upon intertextual repositories that necessitate familiarity with Bollywood's sign universe. These scenes highlight Boyle's inclination to use pastiche as a hybrid rather than a comical genre: hybrid pastiche subverts fixed attitudes to history and habitus (Hutcheon 1989:101) and sharpens the artistic subject's reflexivity (Hutcheon 1988:122). Comedy is erased from the violent scenes of Jamal's interrogation; these are replaced by our own indirect interrogation by a shadowy quiz-maker. The digital question on the screen takes us by surprise:

Jamal Malik is one question away from winning 20 million rupees. How did he do it?

1   He cheated
2   He's lucky
3   He's a genius
4   It is written

The selection of Prem Kumar ('that B-grade actor – not half as famous as Amitabh Bachchan' (Swarup 2006:16–17)) as a W3B host in the novel conforms to adaptation needs. The novel's show is presented as a cheaper replica of the globally successful *Who Wants to Be a Millionaire?*, thus adhering to stereotypical conceptions of India's phantasmagoria as the centre of artistic reproduction. Here the novel's core plot stands for Western cosmologies of globalisation, in which authenticity as originality sustains global value hierarchies rooted in national value systems. Otherwise put, *Q&A's* narrative structure reflects a globalised aesthetic system post-colonial polities happily adopt and reproduce for their own purposes (Jenks 1993:9). *Q&A's* and SM's renditions of this popular quiz show crack open a critical door to the ways mediascapes collaborate with financescapes to reify such global value hierarchies within nation-states and national cultures (e.g. first or second-rate entertainment of pedagogical value) (Appadurai 1990, 1996; Clifford 1997:17; Meyer and Geschiere 1999; Sheller and Urry 2006).

The claustrophobic ticking of a clock prompts the viewer to make a sensible but rushed choice. Yet, just as the quiz-maker is tricking us into following impressions and our fallible intuition, the opportunity to answer disappears and we are transferred back to the televised show's time. The fourth option in the digital question already introduces an ambivalence that is central to the cinematic resolution: whereas our hero remains convinced that it is his destiny to be with his loved one, we are led to believe that events will move towards his victory in love *or* money. Of course 'it' is written in the movie, but exactly what is written? Here the film mobilises Orientalist stereotypes on fatalism in a society where televised spectacles promote cultures of the gambling market (Debord 1995). The fatalist discourse is rationalised in the film less than in the novel, in which it takes two forms: one connects to Ram Mohammed's flipping of his lucky coin with two identical sides (heads but no tails). This piece of wizardry concludes the novel with the protagonist's confession to his solicitor: 'as I said, luck has got nothing to do with it' (Swarup 2006:361). A Weberian (1985; 2002:185) rendition of 'election', the novel's hero revises stereotypical conceptions of the 'Oriental human': he too makes his own choices and crafts his own destiny. Of primary importance here is Adorno's (2001) reading of astrology as a psychic desire for clarity in a world defined by the decline of individual autonomy and a rising 'independence of social institutions and arrangements' (Herzfeld 1992:ch.1; Tester 1994:50). Although two thirds of the movie deals with the structural constraints of India's 'totally administered society', SM's narrative arc follows Jamal's Odyssey to a personalised emotional 'Truth' no state apparatus can replace (Brittain 2010:85). In this respect, SM functions as a Bollywood structural innovation: it is both predictable in terms of thematic focus (destiny) and unpredictable in emotional depth and exaggeration (Thomas 1985:121).

The second rendition of fatalism concerns Salim's in SM (Ram Mohammed's in the novel) personal conviction that he is destined to become a famous Bollywood star. Thus, SM's representation of Jamal's tribulations via a popular Indian quiz show and the film's conclusion with a Bollywood dance routine pay tribute to the novel's particularities in indirect ways. Yet, unlike *Q&A*, SM prioritises the role of spectacular techniques (camera-work, film-making) in the production of coherent self-narration, where disorderly and threatening environments promote fragmentations of the self. 'Destiny' is translated into 'destination', a near-teleological narrative on which film-making thrives structurally as a marketable *téchne* that transcends fictional civilisational boundaries (the West and the Rest) (Herzfeld 1987:126; Carrier (ed.) 1995; Hall 1992, 1996; Tzanelli 2011:38, 95). This is not Boyle's first use of televised quiz shows as an allegory of human greed: Alex's fixation on *Lose a Million* in *Trainspotting,* a televised game in which one is invited to 'do badly' in order to win cash, points to a similar teleological structure. Likewise, the broadcasting of a generic quiz show while Mark Renton struggles to detox, his subsequent depressive state during a pub quiz and his escape from criminality with a bag of stolen money, liken such public game-making to human teleological machination.

The scenes of Jamal's interrogation and torture by police complement those of the live quiz show: both capitalise on a claustrophobic effect that enmeshes time levels and disorientates the hero's vision (and by extension ours). Here

The cinematic text scene-by-scene 75

Figure 5.1 Technologies of vision and control: Jamal's police interrogation
Source: Warner Bros/Photofest.

connections between frames and segment conform to the rules of 'official archiving' that define documentary technique. Scott (1998:11) explained that certain forms of knowledge and control, 'require a narrowing of vision'; a way of understanding that reduces everything to manageable proportions. This 'technology' characterises states or governments (Herzfeld 1992) but also large corporations with specific commercial interests that dictate tight control of resources. SM mobilises the technique whenever the hero is faced with the undefined powers that control his future. But as the 'state' as such is always absent in Mumbai's fragmented 'urban palimpsest' (Huyssen 2003), we are left with visual traces and fleeting violent characters that allude to it. Physical torture becomes in these introductory scenes almost synonymous with a statist tunnel-like vision and its criminogenic collaborators, who are ready to classify, discipline and control its subjects.

SM's televised show presents us in dim lighting two important dramatis personae seated in front of computer screens: a terrified Jamal and the confident *Who Wants to be a Millionaire?* host. Their paralinguistic display of status is complemented by the show's linguistic articulation in Hindi and English, framing the story in relation to individual status (Krutnik 1992). Externally, bodily display of fear and confidence is embellished with the actors' accented English that confuse habitus classifications, as both Dev Patel's and Anil Kapoor's metropolitan English allude to their true social identity. But the scene's paralinguistics replace mechanical technologies with embodied ones in more ways than one. Kumar's stylised performance is in

76 *Reading* Slumdog Millionaire

Figure 5.2 From media surveillance to celebrity systems: Jamal's quiz performance
Source: Warner Bros/Photofest.

fact based on improvised habitus: as Kapoor admits, in Bollywood 'we do not read scripts' (Slumdog Dreams, 2009). This habitus, which projects intimate Indian knowledge of Bollywood melodrama, is also constantly reproduced by SM's child actors:

> "Everyone is watching movies on pirated DVDs", explains Boyle, who would tell a street kid to look scared and the child would imitate scenes from other movies. "They do it through reference points". And you have to say "No, no, just do it. I don't want you to give me looks – just do it yourself.
> (Roston, 4 November 2008)

The quiz show defines the first segment as a whole and connects it to the rest of the film, as through Kumar's questioning we are immediately presented with another puzzle that will haunt the story till the end. This happens after Kumar's cheerful exclamation 'Let's play who wants to be a Millionaire!', which cuts to a close shot of Latika's face standing in the train platform and facing Mumbai's blasting sun.

Latika's image still, refracted through sun rays, might aim to return the spectator to the source of the story through the uses of a woman's constant, static presence – a theme Diawara (1992:164) connects to the originality of non-European oral traditions. Spivak (1999) reminds us that certain linear conceptions of time dominated Western thought, whereas Chakrabarty (2000:73) examined how time exists in European existential narratives as an independent presence. Fixed though Latika's presence might be, it is also emotionally destabilising and geographically mobile in the non-European traditions of travel as a sort of existentialist pilgrimage. Singh (2012:215–16) suggests that 'slow travel' or pilgrimage has always been laden with empathic and sympathetic values – a trend surviving to the date in international tourist networks (Singh 2009). In this segment Latika's image is mobilised through Jamal's individualised mind-walking through Mumbai's temporal and spatial corridors, binding slum to pilgrimage mobilities. This paradox of slowness (projection of national histories and traditions) in fastness (their temporal and spatial compression and innovative rearrangement in a person's cinematic life) is complemented by a cultural hybridisation of the cinematic narrative. In this schema the Heideggerian conception of *chrónos* is juxtaposed to *kairós*, the site of myth in which spatio-temporal constrictions cease to define the subject's experience. As much as SM's story is framed by conceptions of everyday, profane time (of petty theft, human clashes and death), its artistic hybridity borrows from the *kairotic* narratives of the city's life course and development. Latika's returning image in SM's time becomes a cultural code that enhances its audio-visual artistry and the real(ist) dimension of the movie that enhances its overall verisimilitude.

Flashbacks are a popular artistic device in films with melodramatic elements, especially where they accentuate clashes between good and evil; they also heighten the hero's emotional state by revisiting key biographical moments (Turim 1989:39). The technique was used in *Deewar* (1975) – a film that catapulted Bachchan to Bollywood fame – to merge or provide confrontations between versions of past and present. Proust highlighted first the creative role of memory in bridging past and present in ways that connect personal truths to wider audiences (Proust 2002; Gibbons 2007:ch.1). The near-oneiric positioning of Latika's face connects to Freud's (1991) 'dream-work' or the filtering and reorganisation of knowledge so as to sublimate or assimilate past experiences. As SM's story unfolds, in addition to her significance for Jamal's personal longing, Latika comes to represent the global city's passage to modernisation, and the traumatic experience of corruption sustained by a state machine struggling to cope with internal difference – to be both a good 'architect' and a fair arbitrator of conflict. Comprised of fragments of an individual's life trajectory and a community's path through rapid global transformations, the cinematic narrative develops in at least two time levels (past and present), two lifeworlds (a local steeped in religious feudalism and a glocal infused by moral and material contradictions) and at least three perspectives that cross and interact (Jamal's, the director's and the camera's). Latika's face is akin to the ways 'secondary revisions' of the past condition the self-narration of whole imagined communities – nations, cities and localities (Gourgouris 1996). Such revisions are filtered through SM's camera that contributes to the beautification of the individual-collective trauma: as has been suggested by Ricoeur (1970:520; 1974), the structural continuity between dream-work and artistic creativity involves practices of disguise and disclosure, 'but in inverse proportion'.

Boyle, who has never granted a woman the absolute protagonist's role in his movies, certainly populated SM with sublimated female icons. At the same time, given Swarup's and Beaufoy's art-work, it was only fitting for Boyle to connect the story's audio-visual memory fragments through Jamal's personal tragedy of losing his mother during the Hindu-Muslim riots. Freud saw in the substitution of an image for an idea the key to the method of the classical mnemonist. He called such substitutions 'screen memories', claiming that they should be seen as part of the linguistic apparatus of human experience. Their role is to foreclose traumatic experiences, which we prefer to keep at bay because we cannot bear their burden (Freud 1965:42–5). Though divided by generational difference, just like Latika's persisting face, the image and the value of Jamal and Salim's mother stands for the preservation of a fading ethno-cultural intimacy in SM – the recognition of those aspects of a cultural identity that 'are considered a source of external embarrassment but nevertheless provide insiders with their assurance of common sociality, the familiarity with the bases of power that may at one moment assure the disenfranchised a degree of creative irreverence and at the next moment reinforce the effectiveness of intimidation' (Herzfeld 2005:3). The shift from the mother's violent death to Latika's survival and personal victory through compromise reflects how personal stories often converge with formative national events to turn generations into models for worthy behaviour (Ben-Ze'ev and Lomsky-Feder 2009). The ability of Latika to function as a plural image is totally absent in that of the 'mother', who operates as the archetypical 'vagabond' in SM (Bauman 1992a).

The nameless mother is individual and collective childhood – which is why, before the introduction of a new question in the quiz's time bubble we are transposed to a past time-frame where young Jamal and Salim play cricket with a group of slum-children in Mumbai's airfield. The children, who are apprehended by Indian police for disturbing air traffic and placing themselves in danger, attempt to escape while mocking the officers; a chase commences through a wasteland and the narrow streets of Juhu's slum. Boyle singled out his shooting in slums, which he recognised as fluid 'mini metropoles' rather than domains of death (Slumdog Dreams, 2009). This betrays the willingness to separate slum from dark tourist tropes and the need to move away from their traditional static representations. McLuhan's (1964) argument that every medium encloses a message points to Boyle's decision to ditch static cameras so as to merge actors into the cityscape (Slumdog Dreams, 2009). Although these cameras made SM's shooting crew look 'like cumbersome tourists from Denmark', they allowed them to 'dodge around' the narrow slum alleyways (ibid.). Indeed, the chase through the slums was used by the director as a way to make Western audiences immediately involved in the heroes' tribulations. For similar reasons their police chase through the slums was singled out as Boyle's favourite scene.

Drawing on Sheller and Urry's (2004) theoretical excursus on mobilities, Diekmann and Hannam (2012:1325) note the use of 'archetypal mobilities scenes' in SM as enablers of the Western tourist gaze. However, there is an excess of meaning that they forgo in their observations: this is suggested by a visual transition from the runway of a global financial and cultural articulation

(Sassen 2002a), Maharashtra airport, to its littered landfield, a stereotypical 'zone of exception' (Diken and Laustsen 2005), where India's very own brand of 'lumpen proletariat' collects and recycles things no one else is willing to touch (O'Brien 2008). We discern a clash between two narratives and two social milieus: one recreates the 'residual city' (Mazumdar 2007:151) that SM replays through Jamal's personal memory traps and his individual journey though Mumbai's new underworld. The other narrative explores the city's phantasmagoric function and global connectivity (Patke 2000; Sassen 2001) and frames the movie's opening (quiz auditorium) and ending (dance routine) scenes. In between we watch Bombay itself developing into a star figure through the auratic potential of its lonely heroes, who constantly oscillate between a glorious 'destiny' and Juhu's 'aesthetic garbage' (Mazumdar 2007:173). When combined, the residual and the phantasmagoric reinvent the conventional romantic sublime, the moral and imaginative 'echo of greatness of spirit' that can induce paradoxical pleasure, astonishment, terror and dread in equal measure (Bell and Lyall 2002:5–7). The penetration of the slum's peasant-like life by the gaze of tourist urbanity ultimately disposes of its traditional features for the benefit of the phantasmagoric urban centre (Lefebvre 1996:119), just as tourist penetration of localities always claims to preserve local authenticity intact while changing them. Post-colonial theorists may claim that the scene activates for the cinematic tourist processes of 'worlding of the world on uninscribed earth' (Spivak 1985:128) – a sort of Heideggerian reconstitution of Mumbai's slum space as the domain of treachery or brutality (Heidegger 1975). But SM's worldliness is part of its social critique.

The wasteland's consumer democratisation is achieved through exclusion of senses other than vision: in line with critiques of the original 'tourist gaze' thesis (Veijola and Jokinen 1994; Veijola and Valtonen 2007), interpellations of cinematic slum tourism in SM aestheticise the 'runaway' spectacle thanks to olfactory omissions. The scenes happily blend the comic (an overweight police officer too slow to catch up with the young transgressors) with the tragic (the dissonance between Indian nation-building, urban regeneration and social harmonisation). But they simultaneously remind us that since the dawn of modernity, in Europe's largest urban centres representations of slum subjects in 'low-life travelogues' oscillated between compassion and *carnivalesque* comedy (Seaton 2012:36–7). This ambivalence attains auditory extensions in the scene's musical overlay: the chase through Juhu is conducted through A.R. Rahman's 'O...Saya' which is sung by a children's choir in the style of a game.

The speed with which the children run through the slum's alleyways resembles the opening scene in *Shallow Grave*, where the viewer is rushed through the iconic streets of Edinburgh against an auditory background of personal narrative and electronic music. Symbolically portrayed as India's budding 'social refuse' with its own social practices and rituals, Juhu's slum children can only appear to disrupt the city's civilising process with their makeshift cricket game in spaces demarcated for global business and consumer traffic ('street shops have made me shift', says the song). Here cinematic art ameliorates the schism in India's social fabric by having recourse to ambivalence: the stranger-enemy within the city is 'just' a group of kids. The utopian Juhu/Dharavi 'village' is thus incorporated into the city's 'superstructural consciousness' (Prasad 2001:3) as a mechanism orientated towards the spectacular display of 'vanishing characters' before they reach their adolescence. The spectacles of the city-state and the nation-state collude in the scene's critical discourse, exposing through an innocent and funny cinematic scene the nation's dirty laundry (James 2006; Tzanelli 2008b:66).

'O'Saya's' internal vocal arrangement emulates a children's group game, but endows it with hints of mocking. Here SM's artistic node borrows from old colonial tropes of domestication to indict through selective silences. Herzfeld (2002) speaks of an 'absent presence' as the ability of scientific frameworks that survived colonialism to retain the ghost of cultural otherness in interstitial political spaces, but we can update his thesis in Mumbai's post-colonial event. In contemporary Mumbai, cultural orders are not the sole property of liberated post-colonial nation-states, but fluid formations seeping through the ever-changing borders of world civilisations (Nederveen Pieterse 1997). This exchange of culture for civility leaves artworlds in an interstitial space to do the work policy makers constantly shunt aside. Slum-children are, in Rahman's and Boyle's art-work, the elusive essence of those exceptional urban zones that may attract or repulse tourist gazes or charity organisers.

Domestication and activism join forces in an unlikely combination: let us not forget that art that '"habituates" speaks the disciplinary truths of the established order; but art that "indicts" utters those things left unsaid and is silent about those things spoken too much' (Baker 1995:28). The audio-visual function of children in the scene resembles Radin's (1996) 'contested commodities' as painful controversies impregnated with some degree of personhood (body and soul alike). The song's lyrics speak of the experience of the lowest identities and their situational racialisation and exclusion, proceeding to mediate the realities of community introversion ('we live by the buck we get for the family') and concludes with dreams and ambitions of escape ('I wanna be a star so I get hang in a bar, I'll go to Vegas with the playas, just to forget my scars'). Comparable to the 'American dream' with 'Indo-British subtitles' (Liebes 2003), this admission proffers master interpretations of reality that conform to neoliberal tourist industrial imperatives: escape is possible only through combined mobilities promoting purchases of humans, their skills and dispositions (Turner 1994:21–2; SánchezTaylor 2000). The song also attacks SM's filiative utopia (family, descent and heritage) through an affiliative reading of the conditions under which slum-children 'make do' in a difficult world. By communicating their own sensibilities from a privileged stance, the makers of the song succeed in 'giv[ing] materiality back to the strands holding the [musical] text to society, author and culture' (Said 1983:175) in an activist ethic artistic travellers display.

The presence of police in the scene suggests a link to formalised mechanisms of urban surveillance in zones of exception that can generate tourism as new cultural capital. When the children's chorus states 'They can't touch me, we break off', we are left to wonder whether this aversion to touch refers to the police officers' inability to make an arrest, the tourist's ambivalent attraction to adventurous slum visitation or the cinematic viewer's truly safe distance from Mumbai's harsh realities of social exclusion. The mocking chorus that dominates the minimal electronic soundscape challenges interlocutors to physically connect to the 'gypsy' children. Though negatively compared to Jewish exiles in Europe, gypsies were historically linked to the Sind region that now belongs to Pakistan. From there, gypsies moved to Persia and then to Byzantium, fleeing Ottoman persecution. The Greek word *athínganos* (from which the modern 'gypsy' comes) is literally the 'untouchable' – a clear connection between race and civilisation that may even date back to the Hindu caste system. The term 'gypsy', however, has also been used by the Roma to generate plausible links with Egyptian civilisation. All these designations suggest implicit classificatory uses of Roma identity in Orientalist discourse across linguistic traditions, cultures and continents (Tzanelli 2010a). Not only is the journey of the puerile vagabond of the song connected to environmental scientism's recognition of the material value of balanced ecosystems for the future of humanity (Orr 2005), it is also an inextricable aspect of ecosystemic racism in environmental tourist destinations (Jamal et al. 2003; Blanton 2011). Human character and landscape blend in an allegorical discourse of 'signs', ready to be decoded by the viewers, but already hooked on (con)textual systems of artistic and social representation (Mitchell 1994; Bell and Lyall 2002:10).

Figure 5.3 Slum 'excrement' as moral discourse: young Jamal's celebration of obtaining an autograph from Amitabh Bachchan
Source: Warner Bros/Photofest.

Also an inextricable aspect of dark tourist heritage that commemorates sanctioned genocides (Korstanje 2011:425), such ecosystemic racism presents 'coloured' humans as what Mary Douglas (1993:125–6) discusses as 'matter out of place' and hence a threat to set conceptions of civilised mobilities (O'Brien 2008:ch.6). The clash between Mumbai's phantasmagoric miracle and its slum 'excrement' is thus purposely connected to the ensuing latrine event and the religious riots, in which angry Hindu mobs attempt to obliterate groups 'out of place'. The scene in which Jamal, who, trapped by Salim in an outdoor toilet, charges into Bachchan, who is visiting the slum, through the only available escape route (a pool of human excrement), turns shit into a transcultural allegory of social classification. The scene recalls Mark Renton's (Ewan McGregor) dive into the 'filthiest public toilet' in order to retrieve his last drug supplements. This humorous note includes in *Trainspotting* an image of the fading morning light that 'drowning' Renton watches from the bottom of the sewer. The same image of watching life fading from the bottom of a pit was also transferred by Boyle to iconic scenes in *The Beach*. It has been noted that Boyle's northern English childhood and attachment to the labour movement were streamlined into his film-making techniques – 'resolutely egalitarian in his treatment of crews, suspicious of the champagne socialism of his peers in the British movie business, yet determined to break with the bitter culture of the northern hard man' (Linklater, 4 January 2009). The background allows us to understand why the prologues to SM's thanatourism (the Hindu-Muslim riots) are filtered through the history of Bollywood celebrity fandom: not only is Jamal's urge to secure an autograph from Bachchan a rather unhygienic (but purified from clear religious traces) rendition of the 'hermeneutics of recovery', it is also sharp social criticism. Eleftheriotis (2001) discusses how 'cinephilia' in movies is mediated through little boys and audiences in films. Within it 'the presence of the audience in their messy interaction is a rich source of pleasure and as important as the film itself' (Eleftheriotis 2001:198). SM mediates this contact with celebrity both emotionally (the brothers' engagement with movie heroes) and analytically (Jamal's more purposeful coherent account to his police interrogator) – at once through 'a child's vision and an adult's understanding' (Ferrera-Regis 2002:7 in Demiray 2011:34; Everett 1996).

As (auto)biographical testimony, the communication of this particular flashback to police authority provides another important link between environmental danger and social risk as best conceived by social anthropologists and globalisation theorists (Douglas and Wildavsky 1982). Being at risk in modern jargon 'is not the equivalent but the reciprocal of being "in sin" or "under taboo"'. Sin belongs to the discourse of religious faith, according to which the community has to be defended against individual misbehaviour. Conversely, the modern world, which is dominated by individualism and regulated by secular modes of thought, is a world of risks: 'the neutral vocabulary of risk is all we have for making a bridge between the known facts of existence and the construction of a moral community' (Douglas 1992:26, 27–9). According to a conventionally agreed distinction, sickness, short life expectancies, wars and epidemics can easily fall under the ambit of 'threat', whereas risk is a modern concept presupposing human intervention in future decisions (Beck 1992, 1999). SM's cinematic tourist as a post-modern subject is allowed to slum Mumbai's public latrine at no risk, while also being subjected to menacing religious disagreements that lead to massacres. The transitional riot scene links 'risk' to 'danger', reducing Jamal's Bollywood autograph to autographic narrative. In Jamal's account, SM's religious wars are not an instrument for exploring the past, but what Walter Benjamin identified as the medium though which experience is processed, excavated *and reviewed* (Jennings et al. 2005:576). Jamal's testimony grants him the ability to recreate painful events for the benefit of audiences who are rather difficult to please: police officers and, by extension, film viewers.

Implicit connections to the identity of northern scriptwriter Beaufoy and director Boyle are hard to ignore, begging the question of Jamal's functional projection. The violent depiction of the riots in which Jamal's and Salim's mother is murdered, solidifies the connection between cinematic flashback, personal testimony and sociological conceptions of 'flashpoint' events, with mobs partaking in pivotal acts that spark social movements (Waddington 2010). Waddington's (1992:13–20) 'flashpoint model' of public disorder suggests that riots occur when certain events (flashpoints) prompt an outburst of anger amongst a group of people who are frustrated and resentful about the conditions in which they live. Power inequalities and uneven distribution of material resources culminate in a single, or multiple pivotal public events that may lead to hostile interactions between police and members of the aggrieved group. In SM the primary target is an 'enemy within', the poor slum-dwellers, who are wrongly identified with the Muslim other. Beaufoy's Bradford origins tie him to his birthplace's social movement culture and its South Asian connections (Bagguley and Hussain 2008).

Denzin (1989:22–3) shows how *epiphanies* as flashpoint events in one's life are deeply entrenched in Western thought and typically structure biographical texts. Art works from archetypes – often wrongly confused with social stereotyping (Turner 1999:155). At the same time, Dyer (1993:14) explains that representations are the product of hegemony, a term commonly used to convey the domination of a particular narrative of the world in society. This compares to sociological criticism concerning singular formulaic approaches to social movement theory: who starts riots, how and why. In SM's case, even artists need to appeal to a public consensus 'constantly constructed and produced inside the different fields of public representation and social life' (Chambers 1990:44). This means that in SM, which fuses history with documentary, the cinematic text draws its plausibility from agreed versions of social reality. SM's social reality is transnationally inspired but with archetypical undertones. The actual event to which SM's violent scenes were based was the 1992 anti-Muslim riots in Mumbai (Escavone and Srivastava, 21 February 2013). Influenced by Swarup's fixation on ethno-religious divides, but also possibly inspired by Bradford's turbulent multicultural life, Beaufoy shaped SM's riot subplot on a single collective purpose, bypassing the admission that rebellious group coherence often mutates, and their conceptions of injustice pluralise as events unfold (Bagguley and Hussain 2008:13). From a cinematic tourist perspective, SM's violent scene produces the adventure tourist, who peeps in a voyeuristic manner into someone else's (Jamal's) family chronicles, listens to his stories and collects impressions. Through Mumbai's riots, an imagined visit to the slum is literally performed, allowing 'place' to come to life as a dangerous tourist site (Bærenholdt et al. 2004). Through this scene we are introduced to ideas of a broken social contract that sustains neither the healthy function of a utopian (Indian) nation-family, nor the needs of real families in (Indian) shantytowns. It has been remarked that global social movements often adopted the garb of Islam to articulate their alienation (Prashad 2002:27; Spivak 2004:88–9; Tzanelli 2011:chs 5 and 6). The film follows this narrative throughout Jamal's childhood, so as to possibly allude that any such religious discourse reduces complex global social transformations to manageable political formulas (e.g. Huntington 1993). But the same reductive discourse reiterates Islam's non-representational nature as a destructive force. The injection of an array of destructive emotions in the scene is in itself iconoclastic, in that it destroys (*clásis*) icons, simultaneously countering the histories and futures of family sociality, kinship travel and their ritual immortalisation in photography (Chalfen 1999; Bell and Lyall 2002:15; Larsen 2005; Larsen et al. 2006; Tzanelli 2011).

Sontag recognised in photography a 'rite of family life, just when in the industrializing countries of Europe and America the very institution of the family starts undergoing radical surgery' (Sontag 1971:9). SM allows space for the creation of a similar global, comparative discourse through Jamal's articulation of such painful memories in the police department. The narrative assumes the nuance of public complaint or chagrin for the loss of solidarity, casting the protagonist as a collective interpreter of failures of justice. Incidentally, Salim and Jamal's escape from the mob in Juhu's streets is halted by the image of another child that operates in the story as depiction of God Rama – another religious symbolisation of community rifts through childhood imagery of magical realist quality (Slemon 1988). Children are 'origins' calling into question Western conceptions of developmental innocence, but SM's children become a 'world picture' (Heidegger 1967) that naturalises Indian nationhood for the benefit of the tourist-viewer (Bell and Lyall 2002:33). Reifying the origins of social conflict, the memory allows Jamal to express a collectivised chagrin to the police officer: 'If it wasn't for Rama and Allah, I would still have a mother'. Rama the blue child is a Heideggerian metaphor of the *Unheimlichkeit* – the identification of homelessness with uncanniness and the subsequent call to be culturally reinvented through language as an extension of culture (Rajan and Mohanram 1995). In fact, Jamal's response to his police interrogator is articulated in accented English and accompanied with relevant paralinguistic signs that connote indecisiveness, complexity or ambiguity: his head swinging and direct eye contact with his interrogator correspond epistemologically both to the hero's genuine turmoil and the actor's (Dev Patel) diasporic ambiguity. Swinging back and forth in time mediates causality in explanations of personal developmental 'corruption': the film will subsequently explain how innocence faded in Jamal and how it transformed into moral 'degeneracy' in Salim. This individualised formula of inner movement matches the programmatic statement of India's modernist architect, Jawaharlal Nehru, who strived to unite different ethno-religious communities through India's alignment with European industrial civility (Parekh 1991:35).

Proof of injustice is provided when, following the end of the riot episode, the two brothers find themselves for the first time homeless, occupying what will populate the film's landscape from now on: deserted train wagons. The abandoned carriage in which they spend their first motherless night matches the wreckage of India's multicultural urbanity. Notably, Jamal and Salim have been fatherless from the outset, offspring of what stereotypically figures in British conservative discourses of the 'underclass' as unproductive subjects, non-citizens. There is correspondence between cinematic 'technology' and everyday practices and discourses (de Lauretis 1987:2) in the scene that attacks crime causes as moralistic discourse. The fatherless underclass argument found significant support in populist social policy advisor Charles Murray (1990) and sociologist Amitai Etzioni (1995), who claimed that the weakening of community and its ideological pillar, the family, led to a decline in moral standards and the rise of criminal activity. Etzionian and Murrayian connections are pertinent, given Beaufoy's and Boyle's British identity and the discussions of the underclass thesis in British politics from the late 1980s. The global cinematic mythology of the 'nuclear family' ties heterosexual parenting to social normalisation (Williams 2004). The orphan siblings produce further associations of social disorder in inner city zones with the absent 'Name-of-the-Father', the first powerful 'Other' of adult life, the abstract 'Law' (Lacan 1994), ultimately endorsing understandings of fraught multiculturalism as part of India's 'problematic' post-colonial heritage. Latika's first appearance as a child in the downpour, following the brutal murder of the 'Mother', as well as the two brothers' initial disagreement on accepting her into their group, mediates the traumatic loss of family. As a result of iconoclastic acts, the loss of the utopian family consolidates the demise of mobile social networks – a realisation reflected in the brothers' subsequent self-employment as petty thieves and tricksters in India's tourist sites. The melancholy tones of the first part of 'Mausam and Escape' (composed by A.R. Rahman), which makes a brief appearance in the downpour, complement the scene's emotional depth: as soaking Latika is invited in the carriage, we become aware of her centrality in Jamal's autobiography. The scene amplifies her significance when it concludes with a close up of sleepless Jamal, who remains as shy and quiet as the scene's withdrawn musical ambience.

The mother figure in Indian cinema has acted as host of multiple meanings with that of the family role being the least important (Kumar 2011:117). Following closely the trajectory of colonial and post-colonial stereotyping, mothers in Hindi films developed into a sort of 'moral axis of the entire landscape of the story' (ibid.). Mothers as abstractions of family privacy, in contradistinction to the public domain, are rooted in India's uneven post-colonial social transformation

(Tzanelli 2008b:ch.7), and SM's artistic contingent capitalises on this phenomenon. The conflict between family and society was repressed in cinematic narratives until the 1970s, when the failure of Nehruvian transformation transposed it to public street fights and riots and turned it into an allegory of utopian rupture. Boyle's film-making places the beginning of Jamal and Salim's childhood memories at this particular rupture, when social harmony, largely represented in SM as 'slum community consensus', ceases to exist and religious bigotry mars what utopian potential this community rescued from rural times (Prasad 2004:98). Significantly, Jamal spends some of this first motherless night dreaming of his mother's image through a series of refracted mirrors warning the brothers to flee the mob, but the scene's muted sound suggests a symbolic sensory blockage. The burning image of the 'Mother' contrasts with Latika's young body in the rain. The scene translates an epochal transition into personal dream-work – another secondary revision of the fragmented nation-building.

Hence, if Latika is 'destined' in the film's own terms to become a representation of the city's 'cultural intimacy' (Herzfeld 2005), its slum-children assume the role of urbanity's repressed origins. An idea of vulnerability, a literary image that escapes precise articulation (the Third Musketeer's forgotten name), and a 'contested commodity' (Radin 1996), young Latika feminises the city's 'absent presence' (Herzfeld 2002) from the global chronicles of civility. Her forgotten literary alias (Aramis) becomes symmetrical to Kabir's forgotten name Jamal contingently retrieves during the quiz only because of its unsavoury connection to a childhood incident. Kabir's Eastern conception of good *dispositif* clashes in this memory with the marketing of maimed orphans to Mumbai's global visitors by criminal gangs. As the film's narrative moves to provide glimpses at the heroes' initiation into shadowy tricks at the expense of compassionate passers-by, even the soft feminine vocals of the previous scenes are interchanged with modern electronic sounds: modern 'professional' Mumbai is born rotten and exploitative. Perhaps this subplot's most evocative scene is aimed at deceiving the spectator into a romantic humorous vision of street swindling. It is the same humorous tones that will accompany the escape of Jamal and Salim from the gang's orphanage, albeit in a poignant style: Latika's inability to catch up with them results in their first separation in a musical crescendo that blends modern electronic background sound, anguished violin music and a sober male chorus straight out of Bollywood melodrama. Playing in the river-dance style with an electro background (Rathore, 25 February 2009), a sitar foregrounds the scene in a traditional Bollywood narrative (orphans escaping villainous abuse). Designated in the released CD as the second part of 'Mausam & Escape', the crescendo literarily and musically concludes young Latika's inclusion in the adventure.

Segment 2

Latika's excision from the action does not disturb the unity of the plot, which is still foregrounded by diachronically established views of the touring object (slum-dwellers) in relation to humour and petty theft (Stedman Jones 1971; Steinbrink 2012). Such archetypal conceptions of slum poverty communicate with images of East London deprivation following the 2012 Olympic Games, which planners claimed to combat through urban regeneration. Incidentally, Boyle's later direction of the opening ceremony of the 2012 Olympics encompassed on-stage performances of working-class labour steeped in soot as an Olympic allegory of post-modern social and spatial mobility (Tzanelli 2013b:49–50). Hence, the two brother's departure from the 'orphanage' provides space for further critical exploration of the moving slum subject, who continues to serve as someone else's viewing object.

Enacted in and on moving trains, we watch in the subsequent scene a gang of street children stealing food from train passengers while enjoying their precarious freedom. The mesmerising soundscape of the song 'Paper Planes' by M.I.A. complements the visual aspects of the story, embedding images with lyrical descriptions of playful hustling. The song's inspiration matches Swarup's caustic account of Mohammed Ram and Salim's day trip in Delhi with an international NGO during their time at a 'Juvenile Home' that maims and exploits homeless children. The excursion, which is narrated in *Q&A* as a visit to the city's tourist markers, culminates in the recovery of a ten-rupee note thanks to Mohammed's 'lucky coin' (*panditji*). The song also seems to be a reference to a class in literature during which students 'pass the[ir] time making paper planes' (Swarup 2006:100). The class comes to a premature end with the visit of criminal Sethji, a potential Mumbai step-parent, who allegedly introduces children to the glittering world of Bollywood. This intertextual background suggests a rigorous reading frame for 'Paper Planes' as an excursus into social corruption. The track proved to be M.I.A.'s breakthrough hit and was nominated for Record of the Year at the 51st Grammy Awards. The song, which appeared on the film's soundtrack album but not on an M.I.A. studio album, was released on M.I.A.'s own label N.E.E.T. and nominated for the Oscar for Best Original Song at the 81st Academy Awards. However, 'Paper Planes' is a parable on the fragility of child innocence and just as is the case with 'O'Saya', its music conflates collective play and a 'carousel feel' with swindling and theft. SM's accompanying scene, in which orphan children board a moving train and steal from passengers is perhaps a pivotal link to the film's archplot of adaptation as a sort of globalised deception (Westerhausen 2002:95; Tzanelli 2007:55). Not only do they situate the heroes into the familiar genre of the 'drifter tourist' (Vogt 1976), an alternative backpacker with no plan and no backpack to carry in his sojourns (Cohen 1973, 2003), they put the post-modern subject's aesthetic reflexivity to the test (Cohen 2010).

The children's mobile theft cannot be de-linked from the two brothers' subsequent stop at Agra and their enactment of the tour guide: the Agra scenes in Taj Mahal that follow the train scene make one realise that the 'native' remains an unattainable object, while the 'visitor' is tricked into believing that the aesthetic value of their lifestyle consumption somehow counteracts power structures – except that it does not (Binkley 2004; Maoz and Bekerman 2010;

Cohen 2011). Here the cinematic story's structural organisation conveys the essence of its agents' social action: just like the preindustrial 'hack' journalists' habit of making a living by using their alleged encounters with doxies and confidence tricksters (a.k.a. 'slum-dwellers') (Seaton 2012:22–3), the mobile orphans' propensity to steal the property of train passengers conveys an embodied labour narrative ridden with ambiguity and untruthfulness. On a cinematic meta-level, these scenes administer an antidote to those still 'buying into' conventional tourist myths of authenticity and 'pure' cultural exchange. Treating the scenes as an artistic rendition of the 'anti-tourist' experience (Welk 2004) via beaten mobility tracks (by train) or 'post-tourist' (Ritzer and Liska 1997) consumption of 'simulacra of sociality' (Herzfeld 2005:3–4) (playful cheating, theft by orphans tourists might be warned of in tourist guides) acts as corrective to the conventional naïveté of global consumers. On a social meta-level, the inclination to manipulate impressions will provide a gateway to social representations of SM artists as mercenary tricksters constantly revising global developmental 'Truths' (Denzin 1989:23).

The released CD's remix of 'Paper Planes' (lyrics Strummer, Jones, Simonon, Headon/Arulpragasam/Penz, Domino and Universal Music) capitalises on blended human and electronic repetition. This fronts the title of the CD's EP version 'Paper Planes – Homeland Security' that was released digitally in February 2008, becoming a triple-platinum seller in the United States and Canada and one of the most downloaded songs in the digital era (Thompson, 13 February 2008). The same electronic *motif* underscores the song in the film: repetition allows the hypnotic consumption of travelling slum-children through vocals. The singing children – the story's 'bona fide hustler(s)' – claim that they travel on fictional paper planes they 'make all day' and with visas 'in their name' to trick anyone who could catch them. As innocent as the first part of the lyrics is, its latter verses appear to allude to the pragmatics of drug trafficking ('one on the corner has swagger like us') and the role of telecommunication technologies in criminal mobilities ('my prepaid burner' allows for packing and delivery 'like UPS trucks') (Urry 2014:80). The cheerful conclusion that everyone can be a winner and make 'their fame' clashes with the conviction that such acts send exploitative humans 'to hell, just pumping that gas' (Metro Lyrics, 'Paper Planes' undated). But Graff's (2001) argument that literacy can play different 'harmonies' in the hands of different agents suggests that the song's lyrics merit additional 'thick description' grounded in their maker's experience of mobility – for, as I proceed to argue, the singer is the primary artistic trickster of the musical plot.

M.I.A.'s family had to move to Sri Lanka when she was six months old and reside for a decade in a village outside Jaffna in the North, and in Chennai in India. Her father's anti-government activism forced them to return to London in 1987, where they lived under strenuous conditions in bedsits, hostels and council flats. A passionate philanthropist and humanitarian activist, she took up various causes that instigated public uproar and criticism. When *New York Times* declared Sri Lanka its no. 1 tourist destination in 2010, she stressed that tourism is always connected to national politics, provoking authorities to label her a Tamil Tiger supporter. Sri Lanka's Foreign Secretary denied her accusation that the country perpetrated genocide, responding that M.I.A. was 'misinformed' and 'it's best she stays with what she's good at, which is music, not politics' (Baron, 19 February 2009). His pointed remark reiterated conventional splits between artistic and technological representations of nationhood as mirror images of a broader division of labour tasks, stereotypically demoting artistic work to unessential or peripheral labour performed by women or neurotic men (Molotch 2004) and reserving technological labour for those who conform to normative models of hegemonic masculinity (Connell 1987, 1995). State surveillance would figure in this hermeneutics as technology *par excellence* – a point matching M.I.A.'s art-work: her songs were banned from MTV and removed from You Tube for their violence, her pop videos were scrutinised for propaganda and she even entertained a brief presence on the US Homeland Security Risk List in 2006 due to her work's political content (Durham, 20 May 2009). Although she has distanced herself from her father's political activism (in Sri Lanka he set up Eelam Revolutionary Organisation for Students in peaceful support of Tamil minority rights), the Sri Lankan government launched an attack on her via the Internet, even contacting fans individually to 'present a clean image of their country' (Sawyer, 13 June 2010). In an interview with *Pitchfork*, she also claimed that American media are unable to credit her for her own music, asking 'why the fact that she is a brown woman makes it difficult…to see her as powerful, creative, and autonomous' (Kapadia-Bodi 2008:13).

M.I.A. proffers a textbook shift from 'vagabond' to 'tourist' and notably, even academic constituencies critiqued her of turning commercialising activist art (Vogt-William 2009:261–73). Her second studio album *Kala*, named after her mother, was recorded in multiple locations due to censorship and visa complications in the United States – including India, Trinidad, Liberia, Jamaica, Australia, Japan, and the UK (Breihan, 18 July 2007). A perfect *alìtissa* or theoretical mind-walker, M.I.A. conforms to arguments concerning the ability 'roaming' musical bands have to symbolise artistically the 'nation' as a transient entity, a symbolic being 'in motion' or an angelic transmitter of image, texture, sound and word, ever fluid and polyvocal in its spatial mutations (Serres 1995). Connecting 'Paper Planes' to M.I.A.'s double tourist/migration hermeneutics suggests the artist's performative return to childhood in Sri Lanka, when 'government soldiers kept turning up to find [her father]; they would sit her on their knee [and] ask her if her toy was a present from her dad' (Sawyer, 13 June 2010). If SM's train scene debates India's 1970s socio-political breakdown (Prasad 2001) by associating play with 'abnormal' experiences of child labour, M.I.A.'s own hermeneutics resets (repeats in a Tardean fashion) corruption in a different socio-cultural setting. Her memories excavate personal traumas and connect those to wider global political shifts in a recuperative ('healing') fashion: let us not forget that play as a psychological construct was promoted as an 'outlet for healing the emotions' (Cannella and Viruru

2004:105). However, the European toy is firmly connected to adult rituals and pleasure (Aries 1962) – a reminder that propels audio-visual participants to ask whether the scene's consumption object is in fact the children. SM's carousel feel ultimately questions Western corporate structures that in post-tourist spaces such as that of Disneyworld, visually focus on play and fun while obscuring the workers' labour (Hunt and Frankenberg 1990; Ritzer and Liska 1997:99). This essentially Western viewpoint can only be disrupted from outside viewers, as in other cultures and poorer social groups this neat distinction between play and labour does not apply at all (Bloch and Adler 1994).

Oscillations between past, present and the ambiguities of global futures propel us to consider 'Paper Planes' in relation to M.I.A.'s overall track record. Recuperations of one's threatening past through art-work that blends pain with pleasure and constitutes the artist as a fragmented rather than a complete being have been applied before in entries to the Turner Prize – an occasion in which convergences of anti-art and extreme artistic self-reference promise to dispel neat binary oppositions between private and public realms (Gupta 2005:61; Smith and Watson 2001). M.I.A.'s inclination to insert everyday sounds and noise into musical assemblages produces an alternative poetics of social identity or *echopoetics* (making through sound) – a technique inviting the listener or viewer to operate as synesthetic participant/spectator. M.I.A.'s *echopoetics* match what has been identified as the 'darker' aspects of the tourist gaze that we associate with contemporary photographic cultures of surveillance and phenotypical classification of dangerousness (Hollingshead 1992, 1999; Morgan and Pritchard 2005). 'Paper Planes' audio-visual text ties to the contemporary social context in which the song was produced, where the singer recites sentences that disrupt the melody: 'M.I.A. third-world democracy – we sold more records to the K.G.B.!' (Metro Lyrics, 'Paper Planes' undated). The artist's mocking tone matches the style in which earlier Hindi film soundtracks questioned India's fading socialist dream (Prasad 2001:4). But the lyrics also communicate what she perceives as Sri Lankan and American state paranoia when it comes to terrorist surveillance. M.I.A. was vocal about her experience as a transnational subject, laying out in interviews the background of her inspiration for 'Paper Planes':

[The sample of the gun reloading and then the cash register ringing] was a joke. I was having this stupid visa problem and I didn't know what it was, aside from them thinking that I might fly a plane into the Trade Center…. I actually recorded that in Brooklyn, in Bed-Stuy. I was thinking about living there, waking up every morning – it's such an African neighborhood. I was going to get patties at my local and just thinking that really the worst thing that anyone can say [to someone these days] is some shit like: 'What I wanna do is come and get your money.' People don't really feel like immigrants or refugees contribute to culture in any way. That they're just leeches that suck from whatever. So in the song I say 'All I wanna do is [sound of gun shooting and reloading, cash register opening] take your money'. I did it in sound effects. It's up to you how you want to interpret. America is so obsessed with money, I'm sure they'll get it.

(The Fader, 7 August 2007)

The artist depicts in bold strokes the ubiquitous statist obsession with cultural capital as precondition to any subject's official acceptance. Aware of her own status privilege, she interrogates the ways in which forms of *scholé* (as lifestyle, education and the ability to freely tour the world) contribute to the amplification of native encounters with a dual form of *Fremdenverkhr* (stranger traffic as tourism and as immigration) (Lanfant 2009). Her humorous self-fashioning as a terrorist also alludes to the power of digital networks to spread fear and information – on a symbolic level she exemplifies how viral dissemination of music online transforms a 'stranger' into a global icon. Forced and voluntary migration of intellectual and artistic communities is by no means an isolated example, so her fluid identity is nicely blended in her testimony into diverse social milieus of global cityscapes.

Back in the film, Jamal and Salim's mobile tricks literally throw them off the train and in front of another global image of India's modernity, the Taj Mahal. This abrupt change of landscape is deceptive, as the relevant scenes' content relies on covert incorporation of the train's audio-visual subplot (orphan stealing) into SM's overall archplot of adaptation by the 'hack tourist'. In tourism and cultural studies the Taj has been studied beyond the linearity of value guiding commercial promotion, as a vortex of signs upon which visitors and hosts confer meaning (Edensor 1998). The performative potential for understanding tourism is considerable, 'given the ways in which tourism can be presented and contextualized in terms of its potential for breaking free, and the exotic' (Crouch 2006:361). The tourist interacts with heritage sites such as the Taj by making sense of space, artefacts, or the location as a lifeworld produced through relevant economic and social networks. As a visitor, (s)he plays an active role in its constitution as meaning, knowledge, and value. But for SM's cinematic tourist, this change of landscape participates in the production of the slum as alternative rurality – a realisation constituted in the process of the host-brothers' encounters with gullible tourist-guests.

Cinema's Agra lifeworld is by necessity reduced to social glimpses proffered by Indian officialdom that manages internal difference through binary oppositions of rural versus urban, slum-as-impoverished versus privileged, uncivil versus civilised, and internal versus external (Williams 1974, 1999). This collusion of visions acts as 'wakeup call' for the spectator, who thought (s)he could forget to look inside and look around instead, admire and enjoy India's heritage Eden but confine pilgrimage to the monument (Graburn 1977; Mulvey 2006:344–7). SM's *scholé* replaces spectacular material sites with inner sites replete with human attrition conventional tourist journeys cannot restore. There is an ambiguity in the pleasure audiences extract from the Agra scenes: they *look at* world heritage sites melting in the background, when Beaufoy's pen and Boyle's camera-work coerce them *to see, hear and feel* the foreground of frail human socialities. In this respect, these scenes stay true to the spirit of tourist theory that highlights the significance of the everyday, the experiential and the transformative (Boorstin 1962; Gottlieb 1982; Cohen 1996; Urry and Larsen 2011:1–17).

A World Heritage tourist destination, the monument allows the brothers to hone their 'entrepreneurial activities', convincing foreign visitors to part with their money and show enough compassion for the working orphans' destitute condition. The cinematic narrative attains a critical stance when the children meet their nemesis in Indian law (a police officer catching them while they steal from tourists) or when they are coerced into acknowledging the regulatory function of social distance in host-guest exchanges (Bourdieu 1984, 1993; Bourdieu and Nice 1980). Watching 'Orpheus and Eurydice' in an open air theatre reminds the spectator that the world of tourism positions them as observers from 'afar' unable to comprehend the drama 'from within' but able to enjoy as 'comedy' from without (Ingold 2000; Szerszynski and Urry 2006). SM's scriptwriting inspiration must be associated with Ram Mohammed's arrival at Agra after his unfortunate implication in the murder of a train 'bandit-thief' (Swarup 2006:276–7). Agra is one of the few instances where the literary and the cinematic story overlap to debate globalisation-as-adaptation, because the cinematic and literary protagonists become enmeshed into marketable art as 'ideal types' of vagabond-come-tourist. Foregrounding this harmonisation of the literary script with its cinematic adaptation, with children acting as entrepreneurs/swindlers, further destabilises contemporary Western conceptions of childhood as the time of innocence. Both the novel (Swarup 2006:277–82) and the film present the young protagonists' short stay in Agra as a rite of initiation into styles and skills of labour that combine affect with reason.

Hochschild (1983) debates the bureaucratisation of labour in relation to service provision in an adjacent travel industry (air flight), where workers (flight attendants) learn to simultaneously employ emotion and distance themselves from it, and Ferguson (1984) compares work and personal life patterns to uncover how gender stereotypes run deep in the language of bureaucratic organisation and everyday life (Tzanelli 2008b:ch.7; Ferguson 1993). Similar insights are offered by Herzfeld's (2004:152–3) analysis of apprenticeship, not just as a 'social skill', but also as a form of social action. In the post-colonial tourist setting of *Q&A* and SM we note the employment of such feminine 'skills' by Indian children evading the radar of Western suspicion. This provides a fine example of what Bhabha (1994) debates as 'colonial mimicry', a sort of performative slippage, embodied and normative at the same time, which can discredit the coloniser's version of colonised otherness. Mimicry (mocking) and mimesis (of Western civility as in provision of tourist services) 'interact and cross continually', producing confusion and subverting roles in colonial discourse (Fuss 1994:24).

Ram Mohammed's constant reinvention of Taj Mahal histories for tourists and Jamal's photographing of visitors while the brothers steal their shoes, or use tourist empathy to evade police pursuit, project variations of reality onto formulaic artistic templates, providing renditions of what Bakhtin (1968) saw in the *carnivalesque*. Such stereotypes escape structural constrictions through their insertion into global networks of artistic representation (but see also Dyer 1993). Yet others noted how performativity has a reconfiguring or reconstitutive potential that helps to modulate life and discover the new and the unexpected, in ways that may reconfigure the Self (Grosz 1999). Ultimately, the *carnivalesque* of such apprenticeships in international power negotiations both broadens the horizons of the human spirit and lays the reproductive foundations of power (Clark and Holquist 1984:302): both Jamal-Ram Mohammed and Salim are boys on the path to maturity ascribing to norms that define a global 'poetics of manhood' (Herzfeld 1985; Ferguson 1993) as a rite of collective emancipation from 'slavery'. Their insertion into a global tourist system, where service provision interlocks guests and hosts into socio-economic interdependencies, reiterates the archplot of globalisation-as-adaptation: everyone has to adapt in style to achieve recognition, emancipation, economic independence or some of these ends in various combinations. Constantly reinventing the monument's story proclaims that Taj Mahal is a palimpsest, as malleable in the narratives of global visitors and crafty tricksters as in the hands of cinematic wizards (Carter 1987). As Boyle himself proclaims, 'we have a wonderful expression here, that film-makers are "dream merchants"' (Slumdog Dreams, 2009): their cinematic craft is always *stratigraphic* (layer recording), like that of an archaeologist, who strives to study human civilisations' temporal layering, chronological depth and change with constantly updated tools (Alcock 2010:120); but while updating those, (s)he builds archaeological palimpsests anew, like Walpole's serendipist.

Figure 5.4 The 'dream merchant' as Taj Mahal's 'front stage'

Ultimately, the Agra segment reintroduces questions regarding the nature of community in a global stage, where transitory human encounters allow little time for the development of meaningful solidarities beyond those rooted in kinship networks (Elliott 2002). Artistically, mimicry and the *carnivalesque* operate as a sort of 'safety valve' that replaces social breakdown and revolution with ritualised venting (de Certeau 1984; DaMatta 1991). In SM this is communicated through a dis-embedded sonar logic that transforms electronic noise into the sound of tourist nomadism (Levin 2006). This electronic intervention achieves a peculiar 'de-humanisation' (Schafer 1994) of Agra's heritage environs that matches the idolatry of things customers purchase in this context. As the Agra cinematic tour enables the spectator to assume the carefree gaze of the backpacker from Jamal's childhood stance, the omnipresence of monetary calculation and staged authenticity even young guides adopt dispels this illusion. SM's Agra scene proffers a here humorous, there incisive deconstruction of MacCannell's (1973) 'staged authenticity', asking viewers to consider that in globalised tourist settings there is little community to perform uniform stories of culture and identity; that tourists must be prepared to consume MacHeritage stories or be amused by guides who cannot build their own life-story; and that our tourist post-modernity is an adventure in its own right (Feifer 1985; MacCannell 2001; Urry and Larsen 2011:ch.1).

Segment 3

The camera's paradoxical narration of intimate worlds from afar, in auditoriums and on TV, is complemented with a vision of the new urban space in the film's third segment. The two brothers return to Mumbai and their subsequent con adventures are foregrounded by the admission that things have indeed changed 'at home'. This is communicated via adolescent Jamal's voice, stating that 'Bombay had turned into Mumbai'. The introductory scenes of the brothers' *nostos* are supported by a visual narrative of the changing cityscape. SM's distant shots of old slums in the process of reinvention retain an intimate musical tone of 'structural nostalgia', a call for the return of long-lost social solidarity both the state and its subjects invoke in the face of modern fragmentation (Herzfeld 2005:150; Gray 2007). SM borrows in this instance from audio-visual legacies of the chronotope, probing the relationship between place, time and personhood through socially situated voices (Fox 2004; Weidman 2006). The lost childhood *topos* is also communicated through Jamal's searches for Latika in street markets – another surviving culture in an ever-changing Indian lifeworld we will encounter again in global advertisings of slum tourism. Jamal's frustrating search for Latika in Mumbai's human bazaar reiterates the moral-cultural dimension of organised exchange in the dawn of late modernity, wedding market with moral economies (Appadurai 1986:11; Sayer 1999:65). In this new era, humans find themselves isolated from their original emotional source, and as true nomads of the globe, they depart on a haphazard journey of self-invention (Giddens 1991; Bauman 2001).

If the first segment attempts to recover early Indian films' attachment to what might resemble a biological family, the return of the adolescent migrant brothers to Mumbai in the third segment signals a decline of hometown, traditional community rhythms and the family as a secure hearth. The segment's introductory scenes contrast audio-visually feeling and morality to law and contract (Collier et al. 1982:34) to stress the irrevocable passage to this new uncertain era. Thereafter, Latika begins to function as 'place' in a placeless, mobile world, a fetishised marginality befitting the soundscapes of blended word and contemporary music – an aural and auratic object (Erlmann 1996; Mitchell 1994; Mitchell 1996). This socially intimate scene is succeeded by a stop at Mumbai's new fast food cultures, where for a short period Jamal earns a living. The camera only offers hints about the city's MacDonaldisation. All we are allowed is a glimpse into the 'back stage' of its food cultures: the kitchen (Goffman 1987). As others have suggested, not only are food and eating essential types of post-colonial acculturation (Obeyesekere 1992:630; hooks 1992; Sheller 2003:82; Loomba 2005:88), they are global metaphors of what it means to be human (Duruz 2004), a version of 'travelling cultures' (Clifford 1992; Tzanelli 2012a) and the foundation of new tourist economies (du Rand and Heath 2006). The same visual transition introduces adult Salim as an angry character, ready to espouse new ways to get what he wants by breaking from the brotherly bond and Latika's search. Through this double rendition of 'anthropophagy' as consumption of culture and destruction of solidarity (Tzanelli 2011:8–9), SM transforms from historical melodrama into a gangster film, 'marked by a loss of delicate familial emotions', homelessness, violence and 'subaltern excess' in opposition to what lies beyond its reach: the riches of consumer globalisation. The scene's clinical look isolates the two heroes' personal desires and longing for the good life, thus accentuating individual pathologies in new Mumbai's cityscapes (Prasad 2004:90).

True to this transition, the diegesis develops for a while through a montage of Mumbai's underground world – from Mumbai's fragrant kitchen to the begging of Arvind (the blinded street child that manages to recognise both Jamal and his $100 note with Benjamin Franklin's face), to the show's chiaroscuro shots in which Jamal is called to answer the relevant quiz question (a technological update of serendipitous discovery). Arvind will set Jamal and Salim on a trail leading directly into Pilla Street, where Latika is trained to act as 'Cherry' the prostitute. The introduction technically enhances visual revelation with sensory confusion: the two brothers find their way to the district through smog with no defined actual plan and no visible route for the spectator. The scene seems to originate in Ram Mohammed's (*Q&A*) engagement with a group of affluent young men in Agra and his first sexual encounter with Nita, a young sex worker with whom he falls in love (Swarup 2006:296–357). These two encounters seem to guide two key elements in SM's adaptation: the first connects to Jamal's and Salim's responses to status insecurity (poverty, class inequalities), and the second to Latika's invention as an all-embracing symbol-motivation. After the brothers' Pilla visit, the recovery and salvation of Latika becomes Jamal's personal project and is bound to a thematic much broader than that of criminality. Cornered into an uncomfortable urban *flânerie*, SM fits spectators into the clothes of male detective-like voyeurs, before allowing them to pluralise their 'illustrative seeing' (Benjamin 2002:419; Parkhurst Ferguson 1994; Mulvey 2006; Reijnders 2010).

If Salim's accidental murder of Maman during a macho grandstanding in Pilla, or his subsequent rape of Latika at gunpoint speaks the language of criminal resentment, Jamal's desperate hunt for his childhood love articulates a well-established controversy in which embodied arts figure as the binary crux of high and low culture. Otherwise put, who would want an amateur prostitute to dance in the stead of a Bollywood artist? The role of sentiment in this discourse, which also informs an intentional split within SM's creative enterprise (i.e. Boyle's aversion to emotionalism and Rahman's romantic musical masterpieces), becomes a driving force in the story's depictions of Mumbai's criminal underworld . Gangs turn girls into badly made-up and over-embellished whores, not glamorous professional artists – or, to turn a pun into meaningful social commentary, 'kitsch' is crime for the educated tourist who 'knows' how to consume the ornamented other (Binkley 2000). We could make more connections to world tourist economies of sex, pointing out that disreputable tourist sites such as Pilla are also a staging ground for 'banal' identities and cultural stories. As spectacular settings, they afford tourists with the performative spaces in which they can toy with or project quasi-colonial kitsch onto the other safely and away from home or family networks (Haldrup and Larsen 2003; Haldrup 2009). Jamal's search for his 'home' comes thus into yet another clash with the cinematic tourist's search for excitement.

As an original form of working-class stylistic reproduction, the scene's communication of feminine kitsch intentionally connects ethnicity to class and racialises both. SM achieves this by transforming Latika's future prostitution into an artistic narrative through music and dance. Young Latika's dance training in Pilla by her future pimp is foregrounded by 'Ringa Ringa' – a music track of value as an adaptation chain. The track was developed by Rahman (lyrics Raquib Alam) as a tribute to the famous Laxmikant-Pyarelal song 'Choli Ke Peeche' from the film *Khal Nayak* (dir. Subhash Ghai, 1993). Also known as LP or Laxmi-Pyare, Laxmikant-Pyarelal was a popular Indian composer duo consisting of Laxmikant Shantaram Kudalkar (1937–1998) and Pyarelal Ramprasad Sharma (b. 1940). Their involvement in the composition of 'Riga Ringa's' original inspiration opens up new intertextual avenues for SM, showcasing the song as a tale of global cultural adaptation.

An innovative Bollywood action thriller, *Khal Nayak* narrates the escape and attempted capture of terrorist-type gangster Ballu (Sanjay Dutt) by Inspector Ram (Jackie Shroff) and his girlfriend officer, Ganga (Madhuri Dixit). Box Office India declared the film a blockbuster (Box Office India, undated), and the dance and song 'Choli Ke Peeche' became an instant classic for its choreography and its sexually suggestive lyrics. Its female protagonist, Mumbai-born Madhuri Dixit, is one of India's great Bollywood actresses, with formal training in and great admiration for kathak dancing. As the legendary stage courtesan of a world acclaimed (Hindi) version of *Devdas* (dir. Sanjay Leela Bhansali, 2002), Dixit recovered stylistic elements from earlier styles that originated in India's biggest film industries, Hindi and Tamil. Classical dance forms were transposed directly from stage to screen in these industries before moving into select commercial Bollywood films, where the classical dance medium was thoroughly hybridised (Rajan, 4 March 2010; Bhattacharya, 26 February 2011). Dixit's famous role in the 2002 version of *Devdas* – one of the numerous cinematic adaptations of Sharat Chandra Chattopadhyay's novel *Devdas* (1917) – and her *Khal Nayak* impersonation of a female police officer instantiate in SM's Pilla scene a new version of feminised subjectivity that is both inspected by cinematic *flâneurs* and enables them to question global structures of inequality.

'Ringa Ringa's' lyrics and music echo kathak traditions. One of the eight forms of Indian classical dance, kathak traces its origins to the nomadic bards of ancient northern India, known as Kathakars or storytellers. When kathak was enmeshed in Sanskrit drama and theatre in the twentieth century, its dancers and teachers transformed into artistic nomads. The most famous of them moved to, and became educated in Europe that was already developing into a post-Orientalist laboratory of artistic modernity (Gassner 2002:453). The distinctive position of 'Ringa Ringa' in SM's text agrees with the argument that, although the original kathak narrators were not women, the genre was feminised in film when it was matched to particular dance routines. Comparable to the hybrid Eastern genealogies of belly dancing (subsequently known in European and American cities with buoyant art scenes as *dance Orientale* and *dance du vetre*), embodied kathak narratives highlighted particular female subjectivities with an emphasis on aurality – rather than physicality – as an honourable feminine poetics. In many Eastern contexts female singers were considered *awalim* (=learned women) in opposition to the *ghawazee*, female touring dancers, literally stigmatised as invaders, outsiders and prostitutes (*ghawa*=enamoured) (Buonaventura 2010:40–2, 50).

In the context of film-making others have noted the emergence of a 'cinema on cinema' trend, whereby films are using cinematic images of the past to construct their own discourse (Demiray 2011:31). The underlining mode of such 'meta-film' practice (Law 2003:7) is constitutive of Boyle's excursus on Mumbai's architectonic past through individual storytelling. Rahman complements this 'feel' and 'feeling' through further adaptations of old Bollywood tracks. Here we may recall Williams's 'structures of feeling', or the ways individuals constitute their everyday lives beyond the capitalist imperatives (Crouch 2009), and Bauman's (2010) acoustic dimensions of voice and its connection to the politics of time (Cavarero 2005). Because of its Bollywood background and its connection in SM to trading in human flesh, the song makes a bold statement on migration politics deliberately through its 'strategic inauthenticity' (Taylor 1997:126): in a corrupt world, songs portraying 'cheap women' are nothing other than copies of a long-lost original track – a perfect way to explain how 'Ringa Ringa' was conceived within Mumbai's pop illusion industry (Tzanelli 2012a).

Figure 5.5 Young Latika as trained prostitute
Source: Warner Bros/Photofest.

Again Latika's character stands for a form of structural nostalgia always-already modernised within regional and national artscenes, before joining the 'global bazaar' of cinema, the music market and the internet (Erlmann 1996:475; Dean 2007). This is so because the song's musical assemblage debates the relocation of sexual intimacy in the marketplace (Featherstone 1991; Giddens 1992; Beck and Beck-Gernshein 1995; Plummer 1995; Bernstein 2001; Bauman 2003b). Just like Jamal's service trajectory, musical renditions of Latika articulate the Western cinematic tourist's perverse longing for authenticity and its identification in a dispossessed working-classness. Mediascapes, ethnoscapes and artscapes converge behind this musical fetishisation that both reveals and conceals the global political economy of sex (Lee 2007; Purkayastha and Majumdar 2009). The song's sensual lyrics speak of a 'very clever bug (or might be cockroach)' that crawls under the sleeping narrator's scarf and touches her. They subsequently develop into a sexual innuendo ('doesn't know where he reached') that does not foreclose violence ('how much I squirmed and suffered' and 'my whole body was burning inside') and becomes rife with self-chastisement ('such was the trick of the faithless') (Hurricane, 26 April 2009). The boldness of the lyrics (today translated and digitally disseminated into English and Tamil) is matched with the song's instrumental ambience as a way of doing (*praxis*) through organised, repetitive sound (*échos*). This connects to kathak performance, in which 'each syllable is designed not merely to represent the sounds of feet and bells but also to be in harmony with the strokes of the accompanying percussion instruments' (Kippen and Bel 1996).

But 'Ringa Ringa' also seems to speak a global language of transliteration. In a different cultural context Olga Brumas invokes linguistic images of transliteration as *metaglotismós*, 'a kind of transport but through the body, and it's almost like a French kiss. You take the tongue and you put it in another mouth' (Van Dyck 2000:84). In 'Ringa Ringa' the listener-spectator is called upon to mediate their visual understanding (*gnosis*=knowledge) of the social context through rhythmic speech that represents certain kinds of action (*echopraxis*). Otherwise put, the song's melody depends on *echognosis* (=knowledge of the audio-visual semantics of sound), an assemblage of instrumental and digital sounds that are set against a foreground of human singing without words to allude to social action (*praxis*). In SM's Pilla scene the practical-poetic nexus signifies the art of trading in young female bodies by educating them to move, sing and behave in certain ways. Despite the immediacy of this audio-visual assault, the spectator is already trained to 'read' them in ways that transcend imaginary boundaries between East and West as these assemblages constantly inform the cultural politics of global mobilities.

Stoler (1997) suggests that gender inequalities partook in the consolidation of colonial logic as a form of sexual domination, whereas Morley (2000:56), Kristeva (1991) and Irigaray (1974) stress how the realities of literal and figurative movement between spaces can be gender-specific, with women forced into positions of servitude. 'Ringa, Ringa's' vocals produce an intergenerational female dialogue: the 'younger voice' and the 'mature', huskier voice of the song connote different forms of art-work just like two women's (sexual) 'labour'. Rahman retained in his musical update the original singers, Alka Yagnik and Ila Arun, to consolidate such intertextual continuities (Rathore, 25 February 2009). Female utterance is in this instance positioned as mediated orality and as a speech act that invites the listener to engage in questions of answerability or responsibility in situated events (Ong 1982; Bakhtin 1990:32; Landry and MacLean 1996; Inoue 2006). Pinpointing the audio-visual recipient of this multi-sensory spectacle might lead to an exploration of SM's bourgeois audiences that can easily engage with European civility codes steeped in associations of race with culture (Cohn 1987; Kaplan 1995; Mbembe 2001:37–9). Latika's young body evokes associations in the song's intergenerational dialogue that both exclude and invite the compassion of Western spectators and audiences.

As Mohanty (1991) and Doezema (2001) have suggested, Western feminisms served in many ways to reify the identity of 'Third World' women – especially those in sex work professions. The song examines the marketing of human beings by amplifying the subject's voice, while retaining other strategic silences: what is not articulated is the space of visual ambiguity, the cinematic recipient's eavesdropping power (Becker 2004). Via word and sound metaphor and metonymy it articulates terror, love and romance in various degrees, producing a post-colonial discourse in which personal tragedy, fear and desire respond to Western tourist consumption, sex trafficking and racist idealisation (Mbembe 2003; Oliveros 2005; Tate 2011). At the same time, the lyrics feminise embodied practice as expressive or a self-ascribed sort of 'embodied semiotics' (Game 1991) to provide a useful guide in relations between touch, gesture, haptic vision and their mobilisation in 'feelings of doing' or 'dwelling' as ontological knowledge of identity (Harré 1993; Ingold 2000; Crouch 2006:361). Whereas much earlier literature was dominated by a 'representational' paradigm, focusing the analytical gaze on the symbolic and discursive aspects of tourism, recent accounts of tourism in social and cultural studies sought to drive attention away from symbolic meanings and discourses to embodied, collaborative and technologised doings and enactments (Haldrup and Larsen 2006). The song's sonic environment, especially via the production of repetitive rhythm, emulates the sexual act and recalls how the institution of dance style (exoticised via cinematic routes) performatively moved from the torso (demarcated as the domain of male rationality) to the hips and belly button (demarcated as the domain of female emotion and reproduction) (Bakhtin 1968:26; Buonaventura 2010:114–17).

The same processes produced contemporary sub-cultural spaces, thus affording new spaces of belonging. Keft-Kennedy (2005:292) notes that belly dancers entered the public domain not just with performance, but also with the artifice of femininity: the cabaret costume, the veil, the cymbals and body jewels activate an audio-visual complex that is spectacular and excessive. Hyper-femininity is a 'dramaturgical, glamorised femininity' that dissociates women from family roles and is 'idle, or at least leisured', operating outside the practicalities of the heterosexual family (Paechter 2006:255). Young Latika 'the whore-to-be' conspires in SM with articulations of Bollywood's global brand – an industrial supra-trafficker of human *dispositif* for the eyes of global consumers. Perhaps 'Ringa Ringa's' artistic contingent articulates this paradox of India's new professional cinematic ethic as a sort of 'practical orientalism' that contests and reinstates Western ideologies of subjection (Herzfeld 1992; Haldrup et al. 2006; Tzanelli 20010b:ch.4). But beyond such speculations, we deal with an ever-expanding DIY digital culture that mobilises 'Ringa Ringa' video clips, creates personal *bricollages* from SM image stills or allows anonymous dancers to accommodate its music into their own choreography and gendered statement (Deagon, undated).

The same scene is tied to Salim's decision to join Javed's (Maman's archenemy) gang via a broader metaphorical discourse of art and popular culture. Salim's declaration of loyalty to Javed visually foregrounds an old wall poster that depicts Pran, a famous Bollywood villain, and reminds us of Bachchan's earlier appearance in the film. Bachchan and Pran belong to the same affiliative network: their long-standing relationship is documented in the support Pran provided to Bachchan in securing big roles in films such as *Zanjeer* (1973). Just like Bachchan, the 93-year-old veteran, who was recently honoured with the Swarna Kamal medal, changed the face of Bollywood villainy. The Delhi-born (1920) artist's acting verisimilitude was such that a whole generation of parents refused to name their newborn boys 'Pran' (Chakravorty, 13 April 2013). As an alternative to a montage of Mumbai's famed tourist spots and landmark sites, this residual reference to film posters recalls the use of similar techniques in twentieth-century popular Hindi cinema (Prasad 2001:3). At the same time, Pran, whose career began in the years before Partition (early 1940s) and encompassed at least two urban centres split into two states (Lahore, Mumbai), articulates the city's vagabond historical depth. This way Mumbai's background phantasmagoria merges into the realist foreground of its criminal networks to produce SM's artscape.

The track of the scene, 'Gangsta Blues' (A.R. Rahman, singers BlaaZe and Tanvi Shah), consolidates Salim's initiation into the criminal network. The song amplifies his angry machismo with predominantly male-delivered lyrics: 'Do you see me? Do you dare?' Framed with audacious phrases, the song invites spectators to come and find the criminal 'like a shadow in the dark', reiterating global moral binaries of light and darkness (SongLyrics, undated). The tourist gaze of the scene communicates iconological knowledge of Mumbai's social environs: seeing, listening and doing form deep synergies to produce Salim's new criminal ethos as a black masculine habitus created through histories and politics of oppression (Balaji 2009:21). The track's hip-hop *motif* also ties the Americanisation of 'subaltern' music genres to the origins of gangster film in 1930s American film production (Zumkawala-Cook 2008; Rathore, 25 February 2009). Therefore, Salim's rape of Latika and the subsequent display of his violent masculinity (to Jamal he says: 'I am the master now [...] Go now or Gunmaster will shoot you right between your eyes') accentuate this clash between the city's glamorous front stage (Bollywood) and its criminal underbelly. Latika is, after all, the dream cinema-makers constantly retrieve, the city's controversial autobiography and a vision always incomplete – a project in (e)motion. It is hardly surprising that at that particular moment the film returns us to the interrogation room, where the police officer exclaims how most mistakes in life are made because of money and women.

Segment 4

In terms of diegetic continuity this cynicism will preface Jamal's steady transition from Mumbai's kitchen spaces to its cultural industrial and telecommunication complexes. In these scenes Jamal serves tea to industrial workers while displaying knowledge of the technological apparatus they are supposed to use with exceptional humility. His initiation into this world of business as 'chai wallah' allows audiences to explore his developing technical skills, detecting a performative dissonance between his knowledge of the world of the spectacle as a lowly servant, and the moderate knowledge or ignorance of the college students or Arjun the technician. Jamal's sagacity – therefore the justification of his quiz fortune – is established at this early stage. As social commentary on the 'digital divide' – the 'differential access to and use of the internet according to gender, income, race and location' (Couldry 2007:386) – Jamal's voyage through Mumbai's budding telecommunication industries, and Latika's inconspicuous absence, suggest the globalisation of a battle of privilege, affordances and merit (Van Dijk 1999; Wellman et al. 2003; Uteng and Cresswell 2008). The scene also suggests that telephone call centres harbour social activities 'structured by values, norms, moral dispositions and the interconnectedness of social ties' (Bolton and Houlihan 2005:699). We watch Jamal speaking to clients on the phone in Arjun's stead and admire his good use of English (he communicates information in pre-authored English script while also speaking the local language). Such linguistic affordances bear the double mark of civility (speaking a foreign language while speaking in native tongue politely) and are essential for the maintenance of post-modern travelling cultures: information travels in every direction, connecting humanity as a whole.

Jamal's insertion into this call centre microcosm projects both the onset of automation and the process of rendering cultural nuances invisible in post-Fordist environments of liquid modernity (Cronin 2013:91–3). Call centres provide offshored services to international clientele, with those residing in India comprising about three-quarters of the sector (Urry 2014:38). In the film, the dichotomisation of humans and the automated apparatuses that govern social life (Agamben 1998) is symbolically 'intercepted' by the camera's persistent focus on social intimations (Jamal's telephone speech). When the fading of kinship ties in digital domains becomes a dead certainty, we are reminded that the emotional bonds of filiation (Jamal's love for his brother) can never replace affiliation (Jamal's new friends). The scene in which Jamal is tracking down his brother while 'doing a favour' to Arjun on XL5 call duty ('I am on millionaire duty today', he says to Jamal and leaves to try his luck on being selected for participation in *Who Wants to Be a Millionaire?*), articulates an irrevocable 'profanation' of governing apparatuses by traditional subjectivities (Agamben 2009:10). If the Taj Mahal and the brotherly train voyage salvage allegorically what little kinship consensus was possible to retrieve, the normative basis of professional difference between Jamal and Salim slowly transports us to the post-modern era, when Mumbai begins to harbour all sorts of business activity, including mafia networks.

Coupling Jamal's steady upward educational trajectory with Salim's downward criminal spiral conveys the failure of post-Nehruvian political idealism through Western eyes. SM's allegorical lens conveys this disappointment through artistic shifts from melodrama and history to an easily recognisable gangster genre – an intentional slip befit for experimental audio-visual adaptation (Prasad 2004). Only Latika's adult face survives these changes throughout the film, perhaps to rescue Nehru's dream-like approach to politics after the end of his career (Kumar 2011:118). The battle between 'good' technological knowledge, search for love and social solidarity on the one hand, and 'evil' criminal craft facilitating social mobility and the search for revenge on the other articulates a Mertonian thesis that underscored the 1930s American gangster films (Munby 1999). This Western binary will guide the cinematic narrative to the end, when Salim's self-sacrifice will collapse it into a grey moral discourse. Until then, SM's allegory borrows from binary modes of colonial representation to generate counter-discursive alternatives (Slemon 1987:11).

The Mertonian framework of the movie provides an essential link between realist perceptions of social deprivation and the importance of a social environment that stimulates and instils discovery and learning (Merton 1994). It is as if Jamal's cinematic biography reflects the intellectual mobility of Robert Merton from the South Philadelphia slum, where 'rows of dingy, decrepit houses sheltered first-generation immigrants from Italy, Ireland, and (Merton's parents among them) Eastern Europe' (Johnston 2007:2958). The absence of resentment from Jamal's *ethological* characterisation, in opposition to Salim's misplaced bravado and envious machismo, serve as the Mertonian basis for each brothers' positioning in global understandings of the 'wallah' or labourer (Merton and Sorokin 1937; Merton 1938a:415). As a global cultural icon, the wallah partook in nation-building's 'politics and poetics of transgression' (Stallybrass and White 1986), especially where labelling an action 'terrorism' would allow the state to control boundaries between legitimate and illegitimate camps in the national polity. It is not a coincidence that SM's audio-visual project recalls the category of 'terror' and 'terrorist' every time it debates forms of human mobility that upset the state's definitional apple cart: labour, migrant, sex worker and nomad.

Terrorism 'grew out of the failure of some national liberation movements to…achieve sufficient political potency' (Miller 1980:1) in opposition to 'state-sponsored' violence, which remained legitimate at all times (Tzanelli 2006). This Eliasian 'civilising process' (Elias 1982) allowed nation-states to assume the role of violence adjudicator (i.e. to kill in the name of order and peace, imprison and punish criminals for the nation's security). The global wallah is therefore a borderline figure: in Europe and the societies of the Eurasian border undergoing nation-building, wallahs were ethnic tribesmen nominated by authorities as 'criminal' due to their engagement in acts of banditry, kidnapping and border crime (Gallant 1999; Tzanelli 2008b:part I). This labelling carried an ambiguity that SM attempts to resolve in a contemporary modernising setting. In the eighteenth and the nineteenth centuries in the Mediterranean region, gangs of irregular troops partook in independence movements (Spain, Italy, Greece, Bulgaria and Serbia), but when nation-states consolidated their control, they were outlawed. Similar processes can be observed in the post-Partition borderland regions of Bengal, East Pakistan, Bangladesh, Burma and Northeast India, where *dakaitee* (Hindu-like dacoits-brigands) operated in liaison with state authorities while engaging in rural plundering (Gallant 1999:27; Van Schendel 2005:282). The universally applied divide between the *gendarme* (represented by the Indian police official in SM) and the thief-brigand (Salim) is artificial however, as even state governments used irregular gangs in the post-independence era to consolidate their power. Salim's *ethological* makeup introduces precisely this moral and institutional-come-definitional ambiguity as part of Mumbai's emergent gang networks that operate both beyond and within the law. Salim is a special type of wallah facilitating the city's white-collar criminal activities: drug trafficking, sex and gang violence (Woodwiss 1988; Chambliss 1978,

1989). As opposed to Jamal the tourist-to-be, he represents contemporary updates to the old vagabond model.

The ethnicity of these early outlaws determined their popular representations in literature and art, further enhancing their ambiguity as community status symbols. The makers of SM cast the two characters cleverly, presenting Jamal's as one tone lighter than Salim – a sure sign of evil in standard Western depictions of danger and criminality (Dyer 1997 and Denzin 2002 on race and civilising processes). In a realist manner SM's articulation turns colour into a programmatic statement of India's late-modern civility: whiteness moves up and abroad, as opposed to blackness that moves up but inwards. Just as his Bachchan childhood preference, Salim is merely propelled to (criminal) action to compensate for the civil peacefulness of his brother. The binarism between action and reflection stands for the appropriateness of educational affordances, downgrading angry (re-)action to lack of consciousness and problematic intellect (Todorov 1990:74). The 'dumb' action criminal can only be manipulated by the littèrateur, the cameraman or the 'knowing' scriptwriter, but never be himself the narrator. Salim says and sees little but does a lot in the film, leaving the main mind-walking tour to his educated brother. Jamal remembers for both and produces image-narratives for both and for Latika.

A blend of diachronic and synchronic observations adds depth to the cinematic analysis: when it comes to crime each culture has its own romantic heroes that stand on the fringes of social convention. What state law labels 'criminal', the folk imagination commemorates as the romantic 'deviant' in literature, painting and film (Ryan and Kellner 1990; Leoussi 2004; Hutchinson 2005; Tzanelli 2008b:ch.5). Salim's wallah identity as a criminal worker enabling all sorts of shadowy mobility in the city grants the story with a virtuous resolution: crime does not pay – at least not before the criminal exonerates himself in an alternative mission. The mission involves Salim's 'becoming' a virtuous 'technological God', who supplies Latika with a car and a mobile phone to escape Maman's claws. Salim's slippage from grace allows the plot to establish clear divides between him and Jamal's acquired social capital. Their reunification on the top of a new skyscraper overlooking Mumbai's old slums allows for some expression of bitterness from Jamal: 'I will never forgive you', he shouts in tears, suggesting a brotherly rift that equates the loss of Latika with that of their childhood utopia.

Segment 5

The reunification of the brothers introduces another turning point in the cinematic narrative. Although the communication of structural nostalgia for the fading slum paradise persists ('This used to be our slum', Jamal says to Salim on a newly erected building), their vantage point grants them a God's vision. A conventional, static representation of Mumbai's physical environment is substituted for a while with the equivalent of the liquid urban architecture of the global information network (Novak 2010), producing a sort of environmental telematics akin to Jamal's insertion into Mumbai's knowledge economies. Boyle and Beaufoy stated in wonder how the city is like a changing 'sea' that ebbs and flows, a mobile structure that does not allow visitors to fix its feel (Slumdog Dreams, 2009). The scene probably drew upon Ram Mohammed's stay in Mumbai's Dharavi in *Q&A*. The novel's hero describes the area as:

> A cancerous lump in the heart of the city it refuses to recognise. So it has outlawed it. All the houses in Dharavi are 'illegal construction', liable to be demolished .... But when the residents are simply struggling to survive, they don't care .... They work in Dharavi's numerous illegal factories and illegal shops, and even travel illegally ... on the local trains which pass directly though the colony.
>
> (Swarup 2006:157)

In the novel's tale a corrupt network of labour mobilities resurrects colonial ghosts through practices of seclusion and ghettoisation – a 'state of exception' that reveals the real conditions of 'bare life' (Agamben 1998:15; Diken and Lauststen 2005). Bareness communicates exposure, just as SM's skyscraper skeleton communicates the superimposition of material structure on urban lifeworlds (Bell and Lyall 2002:98). This process of 'solitary amnesia' (Tzanelli 2011: ch. 2) is criminalised, stripped-off of its dignified veneer and rendered harrowing rather than welcome. Jamal the tourist-to-be gazes from above but longs for what will be lost below: the social architecture of India's slum childhood.

Figure 5.6 SM's 'aerial vision': Jamal gazing at Mumbai's urban development
Source: Warner Bros/Photofest.

Following Lefebvre's (1996) conception of the city as an expansionist force and de Certeau's (1984) dual city of abstraction and experience, Prasad (2001) identifies the rise of two literary-cinematic figures in post-1950s Indian cinema. These correspond to the vertical, controlling and organising gaze of governance on the one hand, and the horizontal *flânerie* of those residing on the plane of everyday life (ideal types that correspond to Bell and Lyall's (2002) horizontal and vertical tourist gaze). In this particular scene SM's visual poetics match the social production of new neoliberal enclaves controlled by global capitalism (Lefebvre 1991; Harvey 2006). At the same time, the scene's vision is that of the expansionist nation state. 'Can you believe that, huh?', says an optimistic Salim to a nostalgic Jamal. 'We used to live right there, man, now it's all business. India is at the centre of the world's hub, aye! And I...am at the centre of the centre. This is all Javed's'. Moving away from the humorous travel utopia of earlier segments, the narrative begins to outline the contours of a modernising machine, in which architectural structure and spatial cleanliness become articulated through criminal machismo (Massey 2005).

Rajadhyaksha (1998) has explained how orthodox periodicisations of Indian cinema parallel the biography of the nation-state, with film histories having as starting point state policies on Indian cinema after 1947 and with a focus on realism, political usefulness and respectability. SM's art-*work* assumes what global sociology defines as structural violence – a sort of state-controlled 'gardening' (Bauman 1992a), 'cleansing' (Herzfeld 2006) or 'building' (Tzanelli 2008b) glorifying manual labour as metaphor for order and regulation. The politics of masculine self-presentation in the scene visually foreground the fading feminine vocals ('Latika's Theme') once more, supporting Massey's (1993, 1994) observation that power geometries define place through variables such as gender and class. Here, the camera says, Mumbai emerges as an Indian phantasmagoria and a global financial articulation at the expense of social and ethnic difference, setting one type of wallah (the criminal gangster) against another (the new technologically equipped service class) (Lash and Urry 1994:ch.6).

SM further problematises the sedentary logic of the state, science and civilisation through Jamal's visit to his brother's apartment. In this cinematic segment Jamal adopts the role of the 'dweller' with roots despite his many routes, whereas Salim is positioned as the menacing wanderer (Clifford 1997; Deleuze and Guattari 1988). Notably, in *Q&A* Salim is depicted as the Cherubic-looking, good-mannered child of a poor Muslim family Ram Mohammed befriends (Swarup 2006:94–5). Even murder as a driving cause for residential mobility is not attributed to Salim but to Ram Mohammed in one of his train journeys (ibid. 173, 188). The ethological transformation of this character through cinematic adaptation appears to follow post-9/11 adaptations of older colonial *ethographic* norms. We need to account for genre and wider marketing necessities, as well as the critical commentary of SM's makers on the ways such contemporary events affect global cultural and political landscapes. It is the family of Swarup's Salim that is burned alive during the ethno-religious riots that foreground SM's plot. And whereas Ram Mohammed struggles through associations with Pakistani Islamists in the aftermath of terrorist attacks (ibid. 195), as a handsome would-be actor Salim also experiences similar Hindu retaliations during a bus journey (ibid. 224–33).

The *ethological* reversal has an adaptive rationale that further problematises traditional, old definitions of 'traveller', 'tourist' and 'vagabond'. In the film Salim's nomadic movement is defined by rational calculation and intention, much like that of New Age travellers, who promote mobility into a learning tool that can be converted into professional advantage (D'Andrea 2004). Salim's character is a far cry from the sedentary mobility of Jamal, who nevertheless appears to be more committed to self-improvement than his brother. Salim's 'professional' identity – a once innocent dream he upheld as a child in the hands of Maman – is revealed to Jamal by suspicious evening alerts on his brother's mobile phone. The scene dissolves the usual 'compulsion of proximity' through which humans define 'thick interaction' (Boden and Molotch 1994) into a voyeuristic parable of public inspection (Turkle 2010). We are presented with at least two 'parallel front stages' that render old divisions between the public and the private redundant (Ling 1997; Cooper 2001). The mobile's ringtone is also music from the film, a 'Liquid Dance' (music A.R. Rahman) at once articulating the coming of post-modern age and post-modern anti-law.

The track proffers a mixture of classical Indian and contemporary sounds to remind us that, just as 'Mausam & Escape', the scene blends an Indian mythical plot into new Western artscapes (Rathore, 25 February 2009). Audio-visual participants experience a space-time distantiation (Giddens 1984) relative to Salim's telephonic dialogue, as they are not allowed to partake in it. This 'asynchronous mediated communication' (Rettie 2009:425) is supposed to emulate 'true' concurrent and mutual monitoring of the subject's mediated performance that should expose the true 'self' behind it (ibid: 434). In 'Liquid Dance', Bakhtinian notions of dialogism, polyphony and the chronotope (Bakhtin 1981:84) are gendered and racialised in choral *motifs*: the song thus re-presents voices as utterance that is shaped in relation to other voices in the lyrics but also in relation to an electronically mastered sonic background. This is connected to the segment's situated events so as to articulate a sort of 'environmental racism' (Blanton 2011). In such a risky context, a cinematic touring of the slum and its sonic ambience cease to be innocent consumption rituals; instead they enmesh the audio-visual politics of space-time distantiation to Mumbai's ideoscapes (Lash and Urry 1994; Giddens 1990; Giddens and Pierson 1998). At the same time, the song gestures towards a digital-linguistic transformation of 'speech acts' in new media environments, where specific music trends (gangsta) decentre old understandings of the subaltern subject (Shohat and Stam 2003; Bauman 2010).

Accordingly, Palakkad Sriram's and Madhumitha's electronic vocals – a confusing repetition of 'daka da dees' and 'doom dede daas' (MP3 Lyrics, undated) – signal a double awakening in Salim, who is on his way to do Javed's 'dirty business'- but not before doing his morning prayer. The imagology and performance of the wallah as a Muslim is matched with electronic melody while Salim begs Allah to forgive his sins. Salim is the product of a vengeful Allah and provides a distorted vision of solidarity and empathy – just as SM's proximate the Mumbai bombings and 7/7 experience that revised terrorist profiling and coerced UK authorities to accept that even tertiary education students blow up trains (Race 2008:2–3). As allegorical imperatives make their way into cinematic art-work, the slum appears to harbour more and more global risk – wrongly be perceived as mere domestic business, when its consequences are universal (Beck 2000, 2002b). It is precisely the Cherubic image of Salim in the novel that alerts us to the role of such angelic transmissions in infelicitous mergers of travel, media, art and terrorist mobilities (Serres and Latour 1995; Žižek 2002; Tzanelli 2011). The music complements an overarching discourse on 'racial education', whereby 'environmental' (as in social context) recording is mediated by technologically distorted human vocals to such an extent that we are left with an automated version of humanity (Samuels et al. 2010:335). Broken articulation seems to produce a new subcultural theme, in which human circumstances match human types neglected by the powers that be. The music theme deliberately confirms the omnipresence of terror, reminding audiences that there is always an 'internal line of cultural difference within "the same culture"' relentlessly commoditised in global markets (Tzanelli 2002; Spivak 2004:85).

The electronic beat of the scene is also in agreement with Salim's underhand dealings for Javed. Following the *motif* of vertical travel-mobility embraced by New Age and techno travellers (D'Andrea 2006:106), its musical aspects encourage a wandering hallucinogenic vision. Akin to a nomad figure that has been terrifying and fascinating the West 'as a contemptuous case of pre-civilizational barbarism or as romanticised icon of holistic freedom' (ibid. 106), Salim the motorbike rider and smuggler embodies post-modernity's hyper-mobile, techno-fetishistic sentiment (Korstanje 2008:170). As Bauman argues (2008:10), 'the fear is more terrible when it is diffuse, dispersed, not very clear; when it floats freely elsewhere, without bonds, anchors, home or a clear cause'. The absence of dialogue in the scene amplifies the practice of sound inscription, which is as fleeting and impermanent as liquid modernity's dis-embedded nature. The intangibility of sound introduces a sonar dialogue with the past as a sort of trans-disciplinary 'archaeology' of contemporary urbanity (Witmore 2006). One may even argue that 'Liquid Dance's' audio-visual assemblage reinforces a rather familiar trope in Hindi film that endorses the supremacy of 'village communitarianism' over the city's 'capitalist incursions' (Prasad 2001:10). If linked to Jamal's toiling in India's cultural industrial machine, this mobile call-come-melody signals the demise of all-encompassing, socially controlling communities and the rise of 'individualised, fragmented personal communities' (Haythornthwaite and Wellman 2002:32) – a 'call' to revise traditional Nehruvian conceptions of communal-technological development so that all subjects can effectively participate in national culture (Parekh 1991:36–7; Stevenson 1997:42; Turner 2001:12). 'Liquid Dance's audio-visual trope is not mere diegesis of the realist cinematic city, but a diversionary path to the protagonists' redemption through selective amnesia. Significantly, rather than begging for forgiveness, Jamal and Latika depart on an alternative liquid dance at the end of the film, when Salim the terrorist is no more.

Jamal's decision to follow Salim's trail is an important moment, as this leads him to the newly built gated communities of Mumbai and to Latika, who now lives with Javed. The camera grants Jamal a first look at his childhood love through gate bars, creating connotations with imprisonment and privileged protection. Atkinson (2006) discusses such ghettoisation as a process beginning with the expression of residential and neighbourhood preferences to secure 'relative immunity from the negative externalities of such problems as crime, disorder and anti-social behaviour' (insulation) and proceeding with the establishment of connections with other key elements of social reproduction such as work, schools and leisure facilities. But Marcuse's (1996:198) 'quartered' or 'segmented' urbanity directs attention to post-Fordist transformations of the city, 'from a manufacturing to a service economy, a national to a global organization of production, distribution and services, a welfare to a post-welfare state, and from modern to post-modern structures'. Latika *la femme attrapée* is granted with a twin symbolism as Mumbai's surviving intimacy, steeped in romantic vocals and ethereal colours ('Latika's Theme' returns in this scene) but characterised by submission. The scene suggests that Jamal's utopian return to 'home' has been overtaken by a 'privatopia' (McKenzie 2005) that supports the symbolic enclosure of commons into new legal frameworks and assemblages of material gates (Atkinson and Blandy 2005; Levi 2009; Jeffrey et al. 2012). Just as Salim's aerial vision on the top of a skyscraper communicates the triumph of state surveillance, Latika's material enclosure outlines the contours of 'gating machines' as a novel emotional defensive reaction to the imagined terror of poverty (Bauman 2005b; Vesselinov et al. 2007) Latika's decision to stay with Javed is communicated by various paralinguistic signs in her first encounter with Jamal in the house – silent terror and wide looks shoo him away, to no avail. The encounter is sealed by the young couple's whispers against a conspicuous clash between televised episodes of *Who Wants to Be a Millionaire?* ('A chance to escape, walk into another life', Latika says to an increasingly agitated Jamal preparing a meal for Javed), a cricket match and Javed's temperamental outbursts.

This domestic scene in Mumbai's new gated communities also amplifies Javed's middle-aged criminal machismo. Such machismo is mediated in Boyle's cinematography through masculine bonding rituals of football watching, from which women are conspicuously excluded (i.e. Alex in *Shallow Grave* and Mark in *Trainspotting*). Domestic abuse haunts the scene through the display of Latika's bruised face and her announcement that soon 'they'll be getting out of Bombay'. The news fits nicely into a broader analysis regarding the fluid nature of criminal networks in a 'gardening state' that has embraced disorganised capitalist rules (Lash and Urry 1987; Bauman 1992a). In this sense, Latika's cold instrumentalism ('And live on what?' she retorts to Jamal, who begs her to escape with him) is a critical take on old Indian female mores: it seals the pact of submission as a strategic alternative to Jamal's suicidal escape (Basu 2000). Mediating between the failures of Mumbai's bureaucratic machine to resolve everyday problems and antiquated patriarchal rejections of female social citizenship, Latika is a sure identifier of social difference never completely resolved (Haraway 1988). As a powerful complex of image and words that 'stutter rather than speak' (Baker 1995:33), Latika humanises 'Liquid Dance's' techno-lyrics.

Crime scores high then in the history of global civility, by turning yesteryear's vagabonds into disreputable tourists in ever-expanding cityscapes. Boyle delivers a masterful piece of directing by cutting from the story to a question in the televised quiz show on the identity of the cricketer who scored the most first-class centuries in history. Cricket assumes new meanings as a strategic game of winners and losers. Becoming a way to highlight the country's social disarticulations, cricket allows a Freudian understanding of social learning through carefully organised behaviour in public (Wenning 2009; Campbell 1964:66, 312–14). Javed the former Juhu warlord and current estates owner might not be master of such embodied skills, but he controls a combination of legitimate (connections with authorities) and illegitimate (his own gang network) means of violence.

This explains why, as Prem Kumar completes another quiz question, the film cuts again to Jamal's first meeting with Latika at Mumbai's station and their failed escape attempt that leads to her kidnapping and scarring by Salim and Javed's gang. Permanently marked by crime, Latika, the utopian vision of Mumbai, is suddenly overridden by a commercial break in the TV studio. Everything has its price, Kumar suggests to Jamal; and when tricking his guest into accepting the wrong answer fails, he reveals his resentment by having him arrested by police. This way, SM reveals Kumar as Javed's polished alter ego: himself a case of a contestant moving 'from rags to raja', Kumar tries to manipulate Jamal's 'destiny', like a common confidence trickster. It is as if the scene replays 'Paper Planes' visually, turning Mumbai's spectacular machine into an accomplice of its criminal underbelly. Here the cinematic narrative runs full circle: from childhood cricket play to the regulation of behaviour by the cultural industrial machine, humans are only what they *appear* to be on camera.

Segment 6

We observe then that, scene-by-scene the heroes' fragile innocence is replaced by deception and a futile pursuit for stabilisations of meaning in post-modernity's hall of mirrors. As a paradoxical counter-narrative of museum elitism, the presence of SM's 'menageries' suggests that associations between realism and 'authentic' human types is a bad joke at the expense of the subaltern (Bal 2003:21). It is befitting for such a film to conclude with a double audio-visual climax: both 'Aaj Ki Raat' and 'Jai Ho!' (music A.R. Rahman, featuring Sakhuvinder Singh, Mahalakshmi (Mahalaxmi) Iyer and Vijay Prakash) transpose viewers from the slow mobilities of history to the speedy cultures of the automobile, human-mobile interaction and transnational cultural industrial networks (Castells 1996). The statist vision of the previous segments is about to be replaced with cultural flows defying nationalist spectatorial narrative-as-practice (Rajadhyaksha 2003:33). Once more, Western technology activates discursive teleology, virtually displacing human actors from the centre of the universe. Techno-teleological speed connects different cinematic shots into SM's concluding segment: while Latika, liberated by a repentant Salim, drives through the city to find Jamal, who is still in the live show, the whole nation watches at home the slumdog hero struggling to answer the final question. Dressing these stressful moments in a Bollywood adaptation is appropriate: 'Aaj Ki Raat's' disco combination of male and female vocals culminates in a technological climax.

The song is from a Bollywood film soundtrack for *Don: The Chase Begins Again* (dir. Farhan Akhtar, 2006), a Bollywood remake of the 1978 film *Don* (dir. Chandra Barot) starring Bachchan. Reminiscent of 1980s retro-disco, *Don's* 'Aaj Ki Raat' presents the movie as a modernised retro story. The song appeared in SM's climax, when the gangsters and Javed dance to the tune of 'Aaj Ki Raat' played on the TV, on which we nevertheless watch a video clip from another movie, *Fanaa* (2006) (Oxy, 20 January 2009). The addictive ambience of the lyrics communicates modernity's liquidity ('body and heart are molten') and 'restlessness'. While Javed prompts his female 'harem' to dance, the song's heterosexual duo proclaims that 'the crazy lover has no idea as yet [of] what will be gained [and] what will be lost .... Who is in whose heart will be decided tonight. It's decided, I will be the winner' (Hindi Lyrics, undated). As the song warns viewers that Latika will be 'take[n ...] away secretly', we come closer to SM's happy resolution. At the same time, however, the presence of so many young women in the scene, who act a Javed's 'property', parallels the role of women in the music business as embodied commodities. Their muted hyperactive presence resembles that of 'vixens' or 'hos' in video clips that enhance sexist and racist stereotypes (Sharpley-Whiting 2007). In an equally stereotypical ambivalence, the scarred Latika retreats to another quiet room, a 'safer space' akin to that of the 'kitchen' that, according to Hill-Collins, kept black women away from negative stereotypes (Reid-Brinkley 2008:240). This exquisite double contradiction, which corresponds to the ways cinematic narratives can both amplify and neutralise stereotypical views in the same space (Ryan and Kellner 1990), better connects SM to the histories of Indian cinema.

In *Don* the song included Priyanka Chopra and Isha Koppikar dancing at a private underworld party, while famous Bollywood actor Shah Rukh Khan watches in the background. Khan, who is a moderate Muslim married to a Hindu woman, and who repeatedly starred in films depicting women in revealing clothing, has also declared in an India magazine that he feels discriminated against in a constitutionally secular India for his Muslim identity (Imam, 30 June 2013). Therefore the pop-gangster theme of SM's scene provides only 'surface reading' of what emerges as India's and the world's 'terrorist palimpsest': *Fanaa* was released in India on 26 May 2006, but subsequently banned in the state of Gujarat due to protests against lead Muslim actor Aamir Khan, who, while promoting his film there, made critical comments regarding the Chief Minister's (Narendra Modi) handling of the Narmada Dam and the necessity to rehabilitate the displaced villagers in the region. His comments were met with outrage from political parties such as the BJP (Bharatiya Janata Party) and the Indian National Congress, and the government of Gujarat demanded an apology. Khan refused to apologise and his remarks evoked violent protests in Gujarat, prompting Prime Minister Dr Manmohan Singh to endorse non-violent protest (Singh, 25 May 2013).

The protests were directed against the actor and involved the burning of film posters depicting him, coercing several multiplex owners to admit that they could not provide security to customers. As a result, most theatre owners in Gujarat refused to screen the movie (*The Times of India,* 27 May 2006). Producer Aditya Chopra moved a petition to the Supreme Court of India, asking them to direct the Gujarat government to provide protection to all cinema halls that wanted to screen the film, but the motion was rejected (Singh, 5 June 2008). Khan played in the film a tourist guide in Delhi later revealed as a terrorist, whereas the lead female actress, Kajol, played a Kashmiri blind girl and the story's archetypal Mother. The title of the movie was derived from the Sufi 'fanaa' that in Arabic refers to the dissolution or annihilation of the self to enter Enlightenment. Ironically, the sole screening of the film in Gujarat concluded with a man's self-immolation in protest (*The Hindu*, 21 June 2006). SM's musical palimpsest is therefore the recycled tale of simultaneous 'effacing' of glamour and the religious subject's self-obliteration for virtuous 'Truth's' sake. In this sense, Salim's choice to die in the aftermath of this electronic musical feast foretells the coming of a hallucinogenic post-modernity, in which everything is deconstructed and reconstructed so as to adapt. Likewise, the message Gujarat suicidal subjects articulated is that there has to be a limit to post-modernity's 'clonial' project that happily makes pop heroes out of film utopias (Cronin 2003:131–5; Tzanelli 2010b).

SM's transition to the quiz show's studio at this point rejects this suicidal limit, reiterating instead the power of romantic love and family affection. The contrived coincidence of the final question's content is in itself a demonstration of the power of 'tele-intimacy' in contemporary mediascapes (Sontag 2003). The protagonists' loss of family is alleviated by a global ethnos of sympathetic spectators in the cinematic frame and outside it, in humanity's cinema auditoriums. What family audiences watch from afar reveals itself as the core of the cinematic tale, to endorse a new beginning for Jamal and Latika's love story: the symbolic resonance of collective amnesia. Forgetting the name of Dumas' literary hero obliterates the past social identity of SM's sole heroine, so that she is reborn as a post-modern subject. Mumbai's hypermobile Latika is the new *Homo Faber* – not the passive sex worker but the human who is acting on her destiny. Only then the (Western) name of

India's absent 'Father' ceases to matter, and Mumbai's pseudo-Westernised game makers such as Prem Kumar are rendered obsolete.

What will turn out to be the unsuccessful retrieval of Aramis' name stands for SM's alternative hermeneutics of recovery – of the new symbolic Mother and Latika in the flesh, rather than as an apparition. A demonstration of tele-intimacy grants SM with a moral resolution: Latika reaches Jamal by mobile as his last quiz aid, but they both suffer from an inexplicable amnesia that goes back to their classroom lessons in literature. Just as Jamal and Salim, or Jamal and Latika, the eternal couple of literature and history deconstructs moral fables and however unwillingly assists the scriptwriter, the cinematic auteur and the music composer to graft novel audio-visual journeys. As de Certeau argues, travel itineraries 'create and destroy the paths they take' (1986:37). As much as literature maps particular 'spatial trajectories' (de Certeau, 1988:115), its cinematic equivalents can act as effective urban palimpsests that rearrange old parables and meanings. It is telling that Jamal eventually gets the answer right by 'pure luck' – a joking rendition of what audiences may perceive as an Orientalist attribute – the very moment his brother dies elsewhere in a bath of blood and money whispering 'God is Great'. Salim's implication in a criminal gang ensures his entrapment in Mumbai's affiliative network, reflecting a mafia-like adherence to kinship obligations and responsibilities. The scene in Javed's dark and women-packed hideout that precedes Latika's luminous escape communicates precisely this 'heritage' oxymoron, whereby those networks externally recognised as hyper-mobile preserve normative fixities.

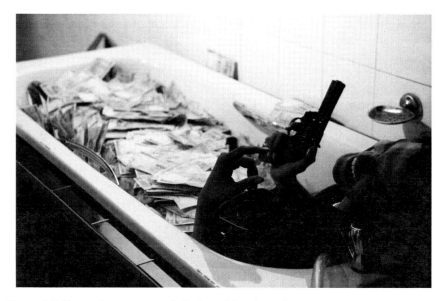

Figure 5.7 Crime does not pay: Salim's anti-heroic ending
Source: Warner Bros/Photofest.

'Aaj Ki Raat' is skilfully succeeded by 'Millionaire's' (A.R. Rahman, featuring Madhumitha) syncopated electronic rhythm to prologue the finale. The trans style blends into the previous tragic scene, recalling once more Deleuze and Guattari's (1980:402–3) note that music and drugs are mostly recognised as elements of the nomadic structures that attempt to restore holistic selfhood through experiments with shattering effects. Salim's aerial ethos proves to be 'out of place' in this concluding techno-trance *motif*, further obscuring the identity of Mumbai's actual post-modern 'architect'. If indeed 'terror's' twin ascription as social movement and affect provides a plausible field for group 'psychological diagnostics', Salim's angry profiling exposes the ways racism naturalises both for political reasons (Spivak 2004:92). Salim's indecorous end signals the death of Manichean conceptualisations of travel that polarise social groups, homogenise individual *ēthe* and ignore syncretic possibilities in favour of antiquated oppositions between 'good' and 'evil' (JanMohammed 1985:19–20).

The reunification of Jamal with Latika overwrites Salim's *hubris* through a series of cinematic flashbacks and through Susanne D'Mello's vocals in the returning 'Latika's Theme'. The irretrievable Face of the 'Mother' – the recognition of ethno-cultural alterity – is replaced with Mumbai's uneven urban transformation that bathes the lovers in street lights outside the studio. In these scenes Mumbai's 'stranger' is accepted in its many forms through the generation of audio-visual bonds with cinematic spectators, who are allowed to figure as actors in a global economy of human suffering through distant, broadcast messages (Kyriakidou 2008; Chouliaraki 2008). The sacralisation of global memory landscapes in digital domains emphasises the diversity of roots and routes in imaginative travel. Personalising this connection through the couple's admission that 'this is our destiny', and reinforcing the message with the selection of the final answer from SM's first scene ('It is written') is how far Boyle is prepared to go. The movie's credits act as a wake-up call for the spectator, shifting through pop rhythms and movement, audio-visual perception and engagement. The spectator is transferred to Mumbai's train station, where Latika and Jamal front a group of dancers; altogether, they perform in the rhythms of the film's final track and global hit, 'Jai Ho!', which forms the theme of the next chapter.

6 The frail dialogics of pop participation

On 'knowing the use of tools'

The concluding song and dance sequence occupies a central place in SM's national and transnational *technopoetics* and deserves in-depth analysis. *Téchne* is the crux of reproductive consumption and communicates with practical knowledge of one's available tools, but their creative use separates the genius from the common human (Merton and Barber 2004:43–6; Morley and de Rond 2010:3–4). In post-modern environments of music production, *technopoetic* innovation is overdetermined by combinations of technological mastery and sagacious inspiration. Lead innovator in 'Jai Ho!' is A.R. Rahman, but the song was a product of dialogues within SM's artistic community.

The song was originally written for the soundtrack of *Yuvvraaj* (dir. Subhash Ghai 2008), a film about the overconfidence of contemporary youth. When Boyle approached Rahman to compose SM's soundtrack, it was decided that 'Jai Ho' would be included in the deal but accompanied with a choreographed dance sequence at the end credits. Rahman composed the song using Logic Pro, a digital audio workstation and MIDI sequencer software application created by Apple Inc. For the bassline and the 'trancey, arpeggiated' musical line Rahman used ES2 pre-sets, whereas for the chorus vocals he created a 'robotic, stair-stepping pitch-bend effect' with Logic's Pitch Correction plugin to achieve the 'exaggerated tuning effect' (Cellini, undated). The lyrics were written by Gulzar in combinations of Hindi, Urdu and Punjabi. The lyrics in Spanish were included in the song 'to go along with Rahman's Latin American touch of music' (ibid.). According to India-EU Film Initiative (undated) this inclusion 'really makes the song quite unique and international'. Despite the Latin American layer, the song was deemed to communicate a version of Sufism or Tasawwuf, as it is known in the Muslim world, with an emphasis on Hindu Bhakti also underlining the novel's and the movie's cosmology. Gulzar's lyrics were thought to 'reflect the quintessential Ghalib thought, named after the giant Urdu poet Mirza Ghalib who talked of insufferable pain but also found it enjoyable if one was in love' (ibid.). As a good-luck-wishing song, for Rahman it communicated a vision of the whole world celebrating Jamal's victory as 'he succeeds in the end' (Associated Press, 17 February 2009).

Talking of India breaking sound barriers, Rahman contended that 'earlier there was a kind of an aversion in the West when you played anything that didn't fit in with their culture. However, now they're open to our music; and the acceptance of the *Slumdog Millionaire* track is evidence of this' (ibid.). The comment reverses the tale of fortuitous Eastern synchronisation with the lands of progress, suggesting instead that the West has to keep apace with Eastern developments in the pop scene. Rahman's revision of formulaic responses to former centres of power could be considered as practical Orientalism, 'the translation of hegemonic ideology into everyday practice so that it infiltrates the habitual spaces of ordinary experience' (Herzfeld 2005:96). Following the song's win at the Oscar ceremony, Rahman reiterated that '[Jai Ho!] was like a prayer…like the film Slumdog suggests everything has its own destiny' (Meena, 24 February 2009). It may be naïve to read this as clandestine fatalism, when Rahman's art-work is defined by techno-hermeneutics. Indeed, just as the polyvocal production and feel of the film, the song contains a mix of 'multiple *motifs* from the traditional pieces on the soundtrack' with 'big drums and blasting horns' (Winistorfer, 13 January 2009). Of the three singers credited, Sukhwinder Singh is the principal vocalist, whereas Vijay Prakash sang the words 'Jai Ho' in a high pitch, Mahalakshmi Iyer sang the Hindi words between the 'Jai Ho' chants and the portions of the verses not sung by Singh, and Tanvi Shah sang and wrote the song's Spanish lyrics (Rediff India Abroad, 5 March 2009).

The music and the lyrics are not merely in agreement with the cinematic performance but an aesthetically integral part of it. Note how the beginning of the credits scene functions as an introduction to the cinematic back stage: actors and dancers rush to line themselves up for the music, assuming the right position and positionality in this post-cinematic narrative. Boyle marked the scene as the most difficult to shoot because 'railways are the lifeblood of India…they won't stop for anyone' (Slumdog Dreams, 2009). Whereas initially the scene's kinaesthetic staging takes precedence over its auditory significance, the song and the music eventually blend into Mumbai's cityscape and dance routine as mediators of new Eastern civilities. Today enmeshed into global leisure systems, such civilities subdued *risqué* physicality and sensuality to professionalised instruction. This educational processing made local genres and cultural idioms more accessible to images of cultural propriety in various societies around the world (Gagné 2013). There is a strong link between such Orientalising processes and the European emergence of tourism (Dann and Parrinello 2009): professionalised instruction in dancing conforms to the principles of *scholé* in tourist development as both study (first meaning of *scholé*, subsequently reserved for middle-class tourists) and free time (second meaning, associated with proletarian 'waste' of paid holiday) (Lanfant 2009:105, 113). The credits' informality places such carefully crafted public images under scrutiny, removing the curtain separating back stages of learning from the front, while simultaneously regionalising (Bollywood dancing) and globalising (through other music and dance styles) the performers' 'schooling'.

The scene's de-mediating allure falls flat intentionally in what Diekmann and Hannam (2012) recognised as the film's mobile platform: squeezed between two trains, the young performers enact a utopian artistic community that revises 'slumdog' cosmologies of old Bollywood film.

This highly contested narrative could in fact be read as another representation of Indian affordances, as its Bollywood routine is not disconnected from the cinematic heroes' journey. Instead, we should view it as yet another aspect of the Everyman's (and woman's) route to India's equivalent of the 'American dream' *dalits* enjoy on the big screen (Liebes 2003). Also, Latika's embodied dexterity in the scene suggests that social mobility is possible even for those designated by birth for 'prostitution'. SM's narrative economy functions as a documentary-like dialogue with the viewer. Contra Vaughan's (1999:80) distinction between documentary and narrative on the basis of meaning, SM's Bollywood scene displays a paralinguistic repertoire characterised by excess of meaning, just like any documentary. One may even argue that Boyle and his associates worked towards bridging the gap between dialogic analyses of social-historical reality and the interpretative possibilities of art-work (Bordwell 1989:64–5; Renov 2004:135). The couple's dislocation from the slum activates a distinctive form of cultural energy associated with the Caribbean 'limbo' dance or 'gateway' as a process of bodily dismantling and rebirth that produces the catalytic cultures of the New World (Harris 1981; Glissant 1989). Though originally recognised as having African roots, today such utopian scenarios symbolise forced or voluntary migrations of global diasporic communities (Walcott 1974) and increasingly also *Unheimlichkeit* as a generative value within artistic neotribes.

The world as home (replay): dance mobilities

Despite the global criticism of 'Jai Ho!' and the film's 'feel good' modality, SM's musical conclusion problematises social conventions, by allowing audiences to speculate on the story's 'thereafter', when family and community loyalties, generational clashes or class structures reinstate real(ist) structures the dance routine suspends (Banerjea 2000 on bhangra). This 'recession' of the cinematic tourist gaze in favour of a shaky diasporic ethics partially guides the debate on SM's purported 'cultural imperialist' agenda: in line with the compassionate political discourse on slum tourism, most of such argumentation was based on interpretations of the post-colonial subject's 'silence' (Spivak 1992, 1999) or the cinematic object's (slum citizens) epistemological absence (Herzfeld 2002). As this is explored in the concluding chapter, here I treat the credits as a cultural product in their own right. For, once we step outside such political argumentation, it is easier to examine how the scene's utopian resolution combines two aspects of Bollywood's global branding: dance and a progressively more hybridised music.

As the lyrics become articulated through embodied posturing and dance styles, we enter a new Babelic plane in which no genre – including Bollywood or kathak – stands alone. The lyrics of the song's generic wish ('Jai Ho' as 'hail' or 'Hallelujah') border on sensual surrealism, as they invite one's 'love' to come 'under the canopy' and the 'blue brocade sky' to taste the honey of the night. The exalted singer proceeds to praise his sweetheart's 'dark black kohl' as 'some black magic', and her 'downcast eyes' as two lit-up diamonds (Inkspill, 1 January 2009). We therefore encounter the emergence of coloured and exoticised references to *la femme universelle* from the Orientalist cabinet of curiosities, ready to be incorporated into global illusion industries (Stavrou Karayanni 2004; Buonaventura 2010; Tzanelli 2013a:ch. 5). Outlining an at once withdrawn and hyper-feminised subject, the song drafts the history and hybrid futures of gendered and racialised poetics. There are other subtle discursive connectivities to tease out from 'Jai Ho's!' aural and embodied creolisation, as all three dance and music styles (bhangra, tango and salsa) of the dance routine are aurally classified under 'World Music'.

Each of these dance styles has its own functionality within global and national lifestyle systems. Nationally, each of them proffers glimpses to specific socio-cultural articulations, as 'every dance exists in a complex network of relationships to other dances and other non-dance ways of using the body...in socially meaningful ways' (Desmond 1994:36). Bhangra remains closer to 'common' Punjabi regional cultures that spilled into everyday social functions, and from there into cinematic or staged tourist representations of 'India'. Bhangra first sprang in the central northern areas of the region to celebrate the harvest – a practice that was ended by the Partition in 1947. The style attained a standardised form by the 1980s, but its folkloric version, which was mainly danced by men (*c.* 1950), was exported to other countries by Punjabi emigrants. By the 1990s a newer style called 'bhangra' was being staged by the Punjabi Diaspora and was often characterised for its Western stylistic importations and impurities and the use of pre-recorded audio mixes. A mobile cultural form, bhangra amasses multiple 'texts' simultaneously enabling a hegemonic 'hermeneutics of recovery' (community-building, reification of Punjabi identity) and an intersection of multiple diasporas 'with the national spaces that they [are] continuously negotiating and challenging' (Gopinath 1995 in Connell and Gibson 2004:355). As the basis of the overall dance routine, bhangra defers to what Giddens (1992) terms 'plastic sexuality', directly expressed sexuality that leaves no space for innuendos. Lined up in front of the camera, the dancers (including Latika and Jamal) mediate collective contentment rather than individual uniqueness or desire, pure club *ecstasis* or extension (Malbon 1999) in old migrant collectivity's stead.

The insertion of tango in the segment is another exercise in contemporary lifestyle mobilities. The intervention develops as a sensual form of answerability involving 'posing' and 'counter-posing' on the screen, rather than a dance routine (Gagné 2013:8). While it visually draws on stylised tourist brochures of tango classes, its sonic dimensions suggest two additional themes: one connects to fast renditions of Argentinian tango known as *milonga* that in contemporary halls preserves old gender orders as an aesthetic additive. Notably, 'Jai Ho's!' fast music specifies *milonga* as stylistic selection, even if the heroes merely

The frail dialogics of pop participation 119

Figure 6.1 Mobility romance: Latika and Jamal's unification in VT (Mumbai's central train station)
Source: Warner Bros/Photofest.

pose for the camera. Contemporary *milonguero* codes support the image of an ideal female partner as the 'light woman' (*mujeres livianas*) – a kinaesthetically imperceptible but predictable Baumanesque pilgrim, who can instantly respond to her male leader's choreographic improvisation. Yet, instead of tying this phenomenon to allegories of colonised feminisation (Carozzi 2012), one might treat SM's concluding polyphonic 'dance event' as an artistic rendition of heterosexual answerability (Wieschiolek 2003:121 on salsa): just like its Bollywood counterpart that places man and woman side-by-side, the *milonguero* shot gestures towards a fortuitous gender agreement in India's mobile spaces (train station). Otherwise put, 'Jai Ho!' hints at a generational divide that in this particular instance connects *milonga* poising to multiple mobilities of airports, motorways, media representations and tourism (Featherstone et al. 2004).

At the same time, the overarching presence of a Eurasian discourse on female beauty supported by the makers of SM remains symmetrical to orthodox *milonga* rules that allow beautiful young women to climb up the dance hierarchy fast. Thus SM's tango (counter-)posing reinforces a European aesthetic hierarchy, as the *milonguita's* 'lightness' claims descent from the 'ethereal quality expected from ballet performers since the 19th century' (Carozzi 2012:24–5). This reinstatement of European hierarchy is nevertheless debated through the position of the scene within the overall cinematic plot. Following gendered representations of *milonguitas* as 'docile women', who eventually abandon oppressive men (Savigliano 1995), Latika as 'Jai Ho's!' hybrid performer chooses the Eurasian Jamal over the 'Oriental' Maman. Arming them with technological extensions, tango custom portrays female dancers 'in love' as 'heavy', just like 'truck drivers' (Carozzi 2012:26).

The salsa musical innuendos of the track are followed by allusions to the relevant dance style. The style – the most popular and hybridised of all three in the scene – conforms to the principles of 'non-representational theory' (Thrift 2007): not only is it not danced in the credits, it is embellished with affective power by a female chorus prompting the imaginary interlocutor in Spanish to dance ('*Baila!*') with them, whatever their problems may be ('*los problemos lo que sean*') (Inkspill, 1 January 2009). As racialised and gendered articulation, this representational gap is harmonised with Latika's absent presence for the greatest part of the film: the scene forecloses choreographic representations of feminised parasexuality, thus also excluding direct individual expression by the heroine on the screen (Gagné 2013). The 'salsa innuendos' of the credits transpose a dance genre and its accompanying music into new liminal zones of pleasure represented in SM by Mumbai's train station. Erasing the memory of Latika's scarring by Javed's gang – perhaps in more direct correspondence to traditional 'neighbourhood' (*el barrio*) norms in Latin American communities of 1950s, 60s and 70s New York (Wieschiolek 2003) – Mumbai's train station becomes integrated into travelling lifestyles that have recently attained global presence in e-tourism and blended tourism initiatives (Tzanelli 2010b:134–40; Tzanelli 2013a). Notably, the actual filmed site, Chhatrapati Shivaji or Victoria Terminus (VT) in Mumbai is a World Heritage site and former terrorist target, blending conceptions of heritage with ideas of tourist legacy.

On the one hand, the credits' aesthetics of sexuality tease the spectator and the listener by amplifying Latika's central role in the consumption spaces of the dance floor while using Jamal to exemplify a new form of romantic masculinity, which challenges domestic hierarchies and the stereotype of the crude man harassing female tourists (Tzanelli 2011:132–3). In this scenario, imagined salsa dance routines generate space for the expression of refined individuality – a fantasy space that evokes popular phantasmagorias rather than colonial phantoms. On the other hand, just as most new dance mobilities, the dance routine's actual participants do not represent marginalised social groups (Pušnik and Sieherl 2002). Just as the salsa chorus' fleeting sonic protest in Spanish, Latika's fading in and out of focus summarises what contemporary lifestyles do to the city's social fabric. We may view SM's choreographic credits as social commentary on Mumbai's social mobility patterns: who could afford to stage such polished performances if not the up-and-coming urban middle classes who can train the body to project cultural capital (Urquìa 2005; Tzanelli 2010b:ch.5)? An artistic parable of DaMatta's (1991) 'safety valve' in Brazilian social movements, SM's combined aural and embodied performance communicates Mumbai's new civilised *dispositif*, in which the resentful migrant *Karna* has no place (Wacquant 2004 on habitus). The overall scene projects Mumbai's cosmetic cosmopolitanism as white feminine desire for inclusion in the highest ranks of a global value hierarchy – but a not-too-white desire, so that it does not lose its exotic flair (Nederveen Pieterse 2006:1250; Archibugi et al. 1998; Gowan 2003). But as a form of social dancing salsa has become part of an entertainment industry 'specifically orientated towards the gaze of others that needs to be policed' (Nagai 1991:37; Tzanelli 2011:145; Gagné 2013:6). We are back to 'O'Saya's' mobile context, in which modern Mumbai's human refuse is swept away by 'aesthetic' *gendarmes* for the benefit of global visitors.

However unsuccessful the credit's de-mediating action (Strain 2003:2), it proved rife with the potential to generate new social stages. The proliferation of DIY videos of its dance routines on You Tube and other social media platforms further ramifies the analysis of 'Jai Ho!'s global consumption. The phenomenon connects to sociological considerations of the effects that Web 2.0 growth has on understandings of consumption as creative act, a form of 'public art' or even a new cultural citizenship statement (Stevenson 2003; Boyd and Ellison 2007; Gauntlett 2011). The online 'prosumerist demand' (Toffler 1980a; Ritzer and Jurgenson 2010) for more video-recorded versions of 'Jai Ho!' dance routines amplified the power of professionalised music networks, tying a rather specific hybrid product to other hybrid forms of world music and dance (Feld 2000). Just as 'Ringa, Ringa's' proliferation of You Tube versions led to connections between SM's Bollywood routines to belly dancing genres, 'Jai Ho!'s prosumer proliferation led to felicitous connections between different music and dance genres. The DIY ethos of this prosumer movement, which matched the rise of network socialities as one of SM's underlining messages, broadened the recognition of A.R. Rahman's art-work and of Rahman as a cosmopolitan artist (Qiongli 2006:386).

The politics of 'Jai Ho!' mobility

But what within the film acts as an open interpretative frame was mobilised by different interest groups for disparate purposes because of its malleability. Such re-contextualisations shaped SM's kinaesthetics, excluding or significantly modifying also the context of aesthetic movement. The song's mobility dissonance, its split routes between the *belle artes*, sports and political negotiation, reminds us that mobility in and of itself exerts power that may dominate, contest, convert or liberate *only in context* (Cresswell 1999; Adey 2010:115–19). In 2009 the music company that holds the song's copyright (Super Cassettes Industries) received approximately $200,000 from the governing Indian Congress for the use of 'Jai Ho!' in the national campaign for the Indian General Elections. Vice-Chairman of the advertising firm Precept Harinda Singh claimed that the tune and the title of the song were used in the campaign because of its projection of a multicultural feel the Congress wished to communicate in the tradition of Bollywood songs (often used in elections). At the forthcoming polls the contest was expected to be between Congress and the main opposition Hindu nationalist BJP. The stakes were high, for, if neither party won a clear majority with its allies, smaller regional parties would play a crucial role in shaping the country's political landscape. On the eve of the elections Senior BJP leader, Prakash Javadekar, told Reuters that the song 'will ensure [Congress] defeat because it will remind every Indian that millions of people still have to stay in slums because of faulty Congress policies' (BBC News, 5 March 2009).

The song connected different material sites, ideological spaces and shadowy political practices to 'retail opportunities' and pleasure zones such as that of the Olympic Games – a tourist-leisure system based on offshoring labour and culture (Urry 2014:94–5). The track also figured as part of a medley with 'Jiyo Utho Badho Jeeto' in the 2010 Delhi Commonwealth Games Opening Ceremony. Rahman had promised to go beyond Shakira's soccer anthem 'Waka Waka' with the composition and 'he delivered a powerful performance, backed by a spectacle of dancers' (*The Times of India*, 3 October 2010). Dedicated to Mahatma Ghandi and with a title based on the motto of the games, 'Come out and play', 'Jiyo Utho Badho Jeeto' sketches the portrait of an audio-visual tourist, who can act as a child-consumer in new cultural industrial environments (Dann 1989). The live performance of 'Jiyo Utho Badho Jeeto' was followed in the Opening Ceremony by fireworks and 'Jai Ho!' as a ceremonial wish. An editor from Sify wrote that during the performance of 'Jai Ho!' 'the chant at Jawaharlal Nehru Stadium, many would swear, was magical' (Sify, 3 October 2010). The performance of the song in this conjunction showcased a Eurasian synergy – not in Nehru's spirit of non-European state alliance, but in Ghandi's vision of cross-cultural connectivity. In reality, both leaders' versions of Indian ethics figured in a Tardean-like display of creative repetition of *dispositif* for the nation and the world alike. The *chronic* and *kairotic* versions of time, the slow and fast mobilities of culture, figured in the aesthetic space of the same mega-event: Guangzhou Asian Games Opening and Closing Ceremonies Operation Centre invited Ravi K. Tripathi, a young singer from Lucknow to sing 'Jai Ho!'. Immediately after the show Ravi received an offer from the Chinese government to perform in 15 shows in major cities across the country. 'We have no major cultural ties with China', he noted, 'but you will be surprised to know that Raj Kapoor is a household name there and his *Awara Hoon* is a popular song' (DNA India, 14 November 2010).

The comment acknowledged the global circulation of cultural flows rooted in rather particular social-national histories with the help of Asia's budding cultural industries. In this instance, regional privilege takes a back seat, and cultural industrial sectors (of Beijing, Hong Kong, Mumbai or Delhi) speak on behalf of a whole nation *and* their transnational artistic communities. Still, 'Jai Ho's!' insertion into Delhi's display of diachronic cultural opulence was based on blends of Indian aesthetic fixities and mobilities: the opening and closing ceremonies of the Asian Games encompassed an amalgamation of Hindustani classical, Carnatic and folk music and performances of various customs ensnared into embodied narratives of the lives of the masses in India as seen through a train window. Art director Omung Kumar's portrayal of a common man's life, routines and materialities such as the bangle shops, politicians campaigning, Bollywood and the cycle shop, spoke a popular language transcending the slow vision of custom (Achal, 3 October 2010). The incorporation of a Ghandi effigy and of spiritual traditions such as yoga that crossed over to the domain of mass consumption and tourism mobilities matched the more traditional performances of Beijing 2008 (Tzanelli 2010c). This performative and artistic correspondence bears witness to transnational borrowings within industrial business networks, supporting the existence of mobile 'Olympic caravans' and 'artistic nomadism' as well as their contingent political mobilisation by political centres (Cashman and Harris 2012; Tzanelli 2013b:ch.1). When political mobilisation happens, such artistic flows become reintegrated into national *technopoetic* structures. Ultimately, a shift towards decentralised modes of commodification and cultural invention in capitalist societies ensures that such artistic professionals generate Olympic art-work on the borders of national and transnational imaginaries (Cunningham 2005; Thrift 2006; Currah 2007).

The political and mega-event spaces through which the song was channelled, and the online participatory media platforms in which its original form was pluralised seem to outline an ever-expanding 'semiotic democracy' (Fiske 1987, 1989). Nevertheless, even at a purely signifying level, such an analysis promotes misunderstandings on the nature of fan reception, because it encourages uncritical conflation of political activism with the 'hermeneutic unpredictability' of television and cinematic fans (Murray 2004:21). It could also be suggested that by placing the product (CD, MP3 and internet versions) and its intangible properties (melody, lyrics) under semiotechnological scrutiny, research effectively decentres human creators (leading or amateur artists) from the production of meaning, replacing them with heterogeneous representational and informational technologies or linguistic values (Langlois 2012). An example of the absolute triumph of capitalism, this decentring of human voices – native and non-native, poor and affluent – highlights that the world of art in the globalised, digital era is organised around three poles: language, technology and the field of power formations. This powerful triangle conditions socio-cultural action through techno-cultural assemblages that constantly broadcast new meanings in line with new regimes of truth (Foucault 1980:131).

Semiotechnological considerations aside, it may still be useful to employ human-centred epistemologies to grasp the expansion of 'Jai Ho!'s popularity in combined media platforms – especially those of mega-event industries and electoral campaigning. Harvey et al. (2009) employed the concept of 'alter-globalization' to explore the possibilities offered by sport to develop an anti-neoliberal, anti-neoconservative, anti-imperial or anti-capitalist alternative to globalisation. Not all these movements are radical or progressive, nor do they always promote the inclusion of individual polities in global communities: alterglobalization can easily lapse into anti-globalisation (see Tzanelli 2011 on *ressentiment* or Kahn and Kellner 2007 on nationalist anti-globalists). One may question the relevance of such movements to the project of commercialised Olympic art, which can be either conservative or radical, depending on the socio-cultural context (Tzanelli 2013b:ch.1). As SM's original context recedes in the background, the biopolitics of 'Empire' are caught in their own self-policing limitations. By this I mean that by regulating the human resources of artistic industrial communities through various political and economic channels, we are only left with the residue of diverse policy-planning(s). Thereafter, art as we know it, unwillingly or contingently feeds into strategies of (re-)articulation in national electoral politics or in transnational sport polities.

From politics to artistic poetics: pop palimpsests

Human agency is located at various stages of the song's creation and recreation, constantly negotiating distinctions between what we classify as spontaneous translation, done on the spot, and specialist translation, done by professionals (Reeves 2002; Cronin 2013:42). The distinction, which is present even in the emotional and stylistic ambience of Hindi tracks such as 'Aaj Ki Raat', corresponds to the twin function of English – as a language of global communication and the basis 'for constructing cultural identities' (Graddol 2001:27 in Cronin 2013:43). The semiotechnological channels through which 'Jai Ho!' was subsequently disseminated in English also suggest an unpredictable globalisation of the concluding scene's sanitised urban sentiment that recreates the film's rhetorical horizon of expectation in a different language (Crystal 2006). The same observation applies to the proliferation of web pages from which one retrieves translations of SM's lyrics in English, and which oscillate from 'homemade' mediations of the song to authoritative 'texts' produced by 'reliable' translators. Dispensing with a priori definitions of intentionality in the electronic release of such scripts – as opposed to the commercial intentionality of cultural industries that co-opted the song – 'Jai Ho!' manages to bring forth (*pro-duce*) potentials both in the producer and the de-territorialised environment in which millions of users act as 'readers' (Ingold 2011). Unlike the principle of single recognised 'authorship' applying to SM's industry of cultural experts (songwriters), such individual interventions usually emerge in multi-user sites rather than sites individually mastered.

The tale of translation and transliteration does not end here. From the moment 'Jai Ho!' was embraced by the digital masses, it was inscribed onto a separate popular palimpsest. This palimpsest is sustained by the principle of creative reproduction, as this is legitimately supported by artistic leadership. These musical remixes are instances of cultural adaptation beyond colonial boundaries: SM's gendered 'clonial' phantom dies a beautiful death in these domains, with eulogies crafted by young pop stars giving new meanings to old cosmetic cosmopolitan agendas. American girl group Pussycat Dolls translated and included the song into their second album, Doll Domination 2.0. The translation, which was in fact transliteration across different cultural planes (for Nicole Scherzinger an interpretation rather than a remix), was written by Evan Bogart, Ester Dean, Ron Fair, Gulzar, E. Nuri, D. Quinones, A.R. Rahman, Nicole Scherzinger and Tanvi Shah. Scherzinger explained that she was reluctant to cover 'Jai Ho'. Despite Jimmy Iovine and Ron Fair's support, and their asking her to see the movie and listen to Rahman, it was not before her tour in London on the eve of the Oscars that the project kicked off (James, 24 March 2009). Although the song was recorded in London, Scherzinger and Rahman corresponded via webcam. Its recording with English lyrics bore a different key signature, with all vocals coming from Scherzinger. Whereas the music and the 'Jai Ho!' phrase remained the same, the lyrics communicated female sexuality more directly ('I got shivers when you touch my face...just keep it burnin', yeah baby, just keep it comin') (MetroLyrics, 'Jai Ho!' (You are my destiny), undated), disconnecting the performance from its original Bakhti spirituality. In this respect, Scherzinger's remix was reminiscent of nominalisation tropes in art: inversing 'proper' interpretation, the remix involved a process of naming that granted the product with a new ontology (Barthes 1979). The *Pussycat Dolls* remix introduces issues of feminine subjectivity in a song that originally emphasised spiritual uplifting and a near Platonic version of affect.

The official video of 'Jai Ho! (You are my destiny)', today circulating on You Tube channels (e.g. xuxuahbeijinhoS, 14 October 2009) develops in the same direction, promoting adaptation as a form of cross-cultural fertilisation. Properly considered as 'structural hybridisation' (Nederveen Pieterse 1997) that conforms to contemporary Western conceptions of sexual liberation, the subtext of its kinaesthetic visuals portrays ideas of a mobile white female human. The video's introduction exemplifies the modern mobile subject of air travel that visits liminal spaces such as that of the train station or the airport (Urry and Larsen 2011:29). It is shot in the shady space of a train platform through which a hyper-feminised Scherzinger, complete with a crop top (akin to Indian *choli*), a *bindi* (a bright dot of red colour or a small ornamental stone applied in the centre of the forehead close to the eyebrows, today used by women of many religious beliefs in India) and Indian-inspired jewellery, runs. In line with the new American poetics of womanhood, the performance draws on Western consumption trends that incorporate yoga sessions, Bollywood-style exercise and fashionable adaptation of *bindi, meh(e)ndi* (henna body art) and colourful Indian-style garments (Maki, 7 November 2011). Such adaptations are assisted by the rejection of tradition by global migrant communities, and an articulation of new – especially, but not exclusively – middle-class professionalism (Nederveen Pieterse 2004:88).

This mobile platform of SM articulates desire and a public feminine presence through half-electronic vocals, which nevertheless populate the sonic background. This is so, because the video switches from Scherzinger's 'soulful R&B voice and hitting all the (incredibly) high notes on this Eastern-themed piece of pop' (BBC Newsround, 4 June 2009) to a group performance inspired by Bollywood choreography, which recalls SM's credits. At the same time, the video incorporates shots of the singer-tourist pursued by a stranger in an undefined 'Oriental bazaar', akin to that which world music enters when famous world musicians are commoditised (Erlmann 1996:475). In line with Mazumdar's (2007:95) 'virtual city' of the neoliberalisation era, the scene generates metonymies to window shop displays, arcades and the 'hyperstimulus' of Mumbai as a global post-colonial city *available to the global flâneuse* (Friedberg 1993, 1995; Patke 2000). The music video was filmed at a railway station in Vienna and was directed by Thomas Kloss (Rap-Up, 13 March 2009). Wien Westbahnhof (Vienna Western Station) is a major Austrian railway station, the starting point of the West railway (Westbahn) for trains to Salzburg, Munich, Frankfurt, Zürich, Budapest, Bucharest, Belgrade and a node of transport in Europe. Wien Westbahnhof was selected as a main *motif* for a collector's commemorative coin, depicting the Empress Elisabeth (Western Railway commemorative). The building's architectural style, which was inspired by Romantic historicism, functions as an ambivalent presence in the song: just as the eponymous Eastern stranger it hosts, it has shed its attachment to nationalist patriotic symbolism in favour of new tourist mobilities (Tzanelli 2013b:ch.3 on France).

In this sense 'Jai Ho!'s' video background provides a revisionist history 'that will attempt the impossible: to look forward to its own death by tracing that which resists and escapes the best human effort at translation across cultural and other semiotic systems, so that world may once again be imagined as radically heterogeneous' (Chakrabarty 2000:45–6). But its audio-visual articulation also adopts a two-dimensional stance, whereby the female band and its lead voice occupy with little clothing the phantasmagoric foreground but the ethnic singer fills the background in a sober black costume. Although, in the original release the phrase 'Jai Ho!' was sang by Vijay Prakash, the new video depicts – against a vague Oriental architectural complex – Rahman, who sings in back-up. As the musical creation's most recognised face, he is contextually represented as a Bollywood celebrity; his star's 'auratic' essence can only be accommodated in an authentic heritage ambiance. The substitution of the original singer communicates an ambivalent message: digital and artistic mobilities acquire 'faces' that can be legitimately synchronised – that is, Westernised – under specific social conditions. Here the video's audio-visual poetics of adaptation align with the politics of assimilation as the only way Eastern fixities can be 'managed' and accepted in Western markets.

This programmatic statement is turned on its head when we consider global perceptions of standard Bollywood practices: back-up singing is commonly accepted and used in films as part of the economy of performance. The industry's art-work is closer to Asian theatre and ancient myths, therefore accepting such conventions as a form of modernisation. But in Eastern cultures aurality commanded respect, as opposed to embodied performance that was denigrated as a form of 'prostitution'. After decades of struggle, Bollywood succeeded in countering such forms of customary prejudice by merging aural and embodied performance, while also retaining in the background the memory of their gendered and racialised difference. Rahman's appearance in the video clip goes against Western conceptions of respectable performance and might easily be recognised by external audiences as 'kitsch'. Ethnicised kitsch and feminised pop come together in the video that, ironically, is shot in those regions from which the term emerged.

Adorno and Horkheimer (1991) criticised kitsch for being a style derivative of high art and imitative to such an extent, that it destroys innovation and uniqueness. As a form of art, kitsch originates in a reaction to revolutionary (artistic) consciousness, in which the nineteenth-century working- (and subsequently middle-)classes saw a prelude to the destruction of tradition and morality. Kitsch principles are organised around sentimental attachment to embeddedness and find expression in reproduction. Walter Benjamin, alone amongst the Frankfurt School theorists, stressed that the modern 'mechanical age' expresses a desire to bring things closer spatially and humanly. '[It overcomes] the uniqueness of every reality by accepting its reproduction' (Benjamin 1992:217). When the 'aura' of art-work is gone, the copy acquires its own value. More recent analyses of the kitsch have endorsed the importance of reproduction, imitation and repetition as attributes of a *sui generis* mode of art (Binkley 2000). Bourdieu called this 'the taste of necessity': a cheap due to lack of resources, yet accurate reproduction of conventional aesthetic forms (Bourdieu 1984:371–2). Rahman's appearance in the video is certainly not kitsch but mobilises a reproductive sonic practice that in the Asian pop context has its own value and history as a piece of resistance, rather than conformity to prejudicial custom.

Ultimately, Rahman's back-up and Scherzinger's hyper-sensualised performance counter heritage fixities, asserting a distant tourist archetype in their stead. Let us not forget that Vienna hosted the first European Centre for Research and Documentation in the Social Sciences: founded and maintained by Polish academics fleeing Nazi persecution, the group bequeathed social sciences the first Simmelian conception of the tourist as a 'collective alien' (Ostrowski 1988:5). This collectivised type was introduced into the structure of the visited society as 'a wanderer who comes today and goes tomorrow' (Simmel 1969 in Przeclawski et al. 2009:179). The definition suggested that we need to move away from a notion of 'authentic place' and 'authentic practice' corrupted by tourism, and towards 'cultural involution', loosely invoked where tourism promotes local and global awareness (Franklin and Crang 2001:8). Vienna is also the renowned cradle of positivism, that as social science did not just exalt methodological precision but promoted a better understanding of the scientific basis of *belle arts* such as music. As the civilisational cradle of Orientalist research, the East held the key to such art's mathematical foundations. The father of modern racism, Gobineau, commented on Eastern dance's mesmerising effect and 'hypnotic intoxication', explaining that 'its repetitive nature and unchanging rhythms exhale a delightful torpor upon the soul' (Buonaventura 2010:192). Like its repetitive music, Bollywood dance is choral as much as it is individualised and subjected to mathematical motifs. In this respect, Rahman the global artistic nomad represents positivism's original mobile ethos or *dispositif* as a form of creative repetition across lifeworlds. Similarly, SM's credits and Scherzinger's 'mesmerising' group performance transliterate an Eastern *dispositif* into a Eurasian mass culture ritual. What certainly begins as 'structural hybridisation' could be read as its cultural equivalent in 'Jai Ho's!' creative synergy.

How can one reconcile the joy of dancing, pop singing and digital recreation with the ugliness of SM's slums? Perhaps here we can detect one of the roots of the general discontent with a film and its overall industry, which both promotes the utopian parables of Bollywood's phantasmagoria and questions Mumbai's social structures. Just as Hutnyk's (1996) dissection of the viral spread of knowledge about Calcutta as 'Indobabble', Mumbai's cinematic and digital depictions control tourist ways of seeing and sensing the world from afar with a specific toolkit 'of technologies, techniques and aesthetic sensibilities and predispositions' (Franklin and Crang 2001:8). Nevertheless, we must bear in mind that films forge their own 'sign industries' in unexpected ways, facilitating new entrepreneurship in liaison with or at the expense of old artisanal networks. More correctly, such emerging sign industries tend to encompass artisanal, filiative networks into what often becomes demarcated as their new rationalised business (Tzanelli 2010a:ch.1). The next chapter illuminates how, within Mumbai's socio-cultural horizons and in India's cluster of state-polities, SM's industry of multi-sensory signs facilitated one such blended form of filiative-and-affiliative networking. Much like Hardt and Negri's (2000) imperial contingent that becomes impregnated with multitudes (Hardt and Negri 2004), SM's industry mutated first into new (slum) tourist business, and then into social activism against poverty-as-passivity. Implicated into cosmetic agendas that were promoted by the city's administration and global capitalist business, these new touring cultures have acquired a very strong digital face. But as much as their websites claim to give a voice to slum citizens, their custom allows the subaltern to deconstruct the *ethological* complex for which SM artists faced such criticism about their own intentions.

Part III
A plural slumdog *kósmos*

7 Tourist modernities
Slumdog Millionaire's multiple sites as fields

Plural temporalities and *tornadóros'* counter-gaze

The previous part's analysis of SM in terms of artistic text and context unveiled its multiple interpretative perspectives, allowing us to glance and listen to Indian modernity's images and echoes and the artistic workings of Mumbai's *pangosmiopoiesis*. Part III unpacks the film's wider societal impact, focusing especially on the unintended consequences of its production and consumption chains. This chapter in particular investigates its implication in the enactment of multiple temporalities in SM's twin screened heritage sites: the Taj Mahal and the Indian slum. From this split temporal frame I proceed to examine the maintenance of different tourism mobilities, heeding that this perspectival dualism corresponds to (a) different consumption trends and (b) different aesthetic(-ised) conceptions of belonging in the nation, the city and the world. Just's (2000) suggestion that *kósmos* as the world can only be understood from a local perspective – as it is always meaningfully enacted within local or regional contexts is pertinent. This connects to Nederveen Pieterse's (2006) thesis that cosmetic cosmopolitanism is based on the production of a gloss (the Urdu courtesan) that overlays local reality (wanted or unwanted mobilities). What happens when such conflicting realities, however grim or dark, are essential ingredients of the gloss?

SM's implication in Mumbai's tourism mobilities has to be placed within a global context of disorganised capitalist structuration and economic neoliberalisation (Lash and Urry 1987; Urry 2014:22–3). This structural embeddedness was communicated through complaints that Boyle's 'romantic poorist' fable damaged the image of an emerging superpower (Kapur, 7 November 2008). In this respect, the SM controversy illuminates challenges faced by most growing world economies that can develop further, not just by blocking effective re-shoring of resources, but also by making nation-states complicit to undemocratic secrecy (contra Urry (2014:178) who suggested that national players matter less these days). The slogan 'India Shining', which was coined for the 2004 general election campaign by the then ruling nationalist Bharatiya Janata Party (BJP) – the very party that used Rahman's 'Jai Ho!' in electoral promotion – was orientated towards the production of a cosmopolitan gloss.

132 A plural slumdog kósmos

The work of presenting 'Shining India' to a global audience 'is performed as much by domestic boosters like Gurcharan Das or Bollywood stars such as Amitabh Bachchan, as by its visiting US commentators like Thomas Friedman' (Corbridge and Shah 2013:335), the father of India's McWorld (Barber 2003, 2010). It is through such performances that India's 'network capital', its tourist 'currency' in Eurasian domains and beyond (what Larsen and Urry (2008:93) would identify with practices of engendering and sustaining global social relations and to generate 'emotional, financial and practical benefit'), is currently managed for the market as much as it aspires to be a 'government of the market' (Foucault 1997, 2007; Bærenholdt 2013:26). According to the Ministry of Tourism, between 2000 and 2008 the country experienced an increase in foreign tourist arrivals from 2.65 to 5.38 million per annum, with accompanied foreign exchange earnings growth placing tourism in third position as a foreign financial inflow generator. India's major marketers attribute this rise to the 'Incredible India' promotion (Geary 2013:37).

The 'Shining India' motto can strategically enclose both the promotion of heritage tourism and the recent digital boom in the country's regional knowledge economies, including e-tourism. This raises questions on the organisational adjustment of Mumbai's plural lifeworlds (slum, tourist, bureaucratic/political) but also the accompanying temporal rifts this might introduce (fast tourism/digital marketing vs slow heritage/lifeworld mobilities). Urry (2014:8–9) includes virtual environments in contemporary offshoring and the de-localising of production, consumption and sociability. We observe unprecedented shifts from localised agency to structured decision-making within mobility systems governed by corporate capital. These virtual(-ised) changes condition tourist economies and host-guest interactions. Even for an examination of Mumbai's SM-related tourism, we must consider what conditions the passage from *kairós* to *chrónos* – or what Kirschenblatt-Gimblett (1997) divides into historic, heritage and visitor times that roughly parallel three types of authenticity.

> Historic time, which can be thought of as real time or 'stopped clock', is the point in which an event being judged in terms of authenticity takes place or occurs. This moment (or period) cannot be repeated…whether the event be an individual touristic experience … or 'historic' in the usual sense …. Heritage time can be thought of as a "rewound the clock" in which those attempting to present an authentic experience from another age constantly move the clock back (or theoretically, forward) to the point at which other factors … can be created to add to the authenticity of the experience. Finally, personal or 'crystal ball' time can almost be thought of as a 'transcendence' of time …. The experiential [tourist] moment can be simultaneously in the past, present and even future.
>
> (Jamal and Hill 2002:83–4)

The model explicates more social occurrences than the tourist experience: the whole 'Shining India' discourse can, for example, pass from *chrónic* to *kairótic* planes or from personal/everyday to heritage time in politics. More importantly, when we examine Mumbai's and India's tourist industries and mobilities, the model seems to suggest that these neat categories are more malleable than at first sight.

This temporal exposition is intended as a link between the projection of *dispositif* and habitus in the film by SM artists and their critics and their emergence and manipulation in tourism markets by different Western and Eastern actors. One might argue that such manipulations assume the mantle of activism with a cautionary note: not all action transforms into agency and not all 'positive' views on activism – philanthropic or otherwise – are progressive or disinterested. We must also consider how interplays of *chrónos* with *kairós* in everyday life – or negotiations of folk custom and official history (Herzfeld 1987; Sutton 2000; Guichard 2013:77) – impinge on Mumbai's and India's SM-related tourist industries. Though ethnic and class habitus and its products (i.e. crafts and indigenous art-work) as tourist commodities inhabit heritage time, they communicate with industrial calibrations of historic memory. At the same time, industrial conditions and the positioning of workers in regional, national and global spheres may provoke reactions (action and activism), leading to the emergence of a *dispositif* we encounter in other spheres of human activity (strike, protest). Coding the slum's terrible 'picturesque' presupposes that the dispossessed native human toils while middle-class visitors watch (Bell and Lyall 2002:33–5).

My move from Bourdieu's tight social ordering and expansive network 'capitalism' to Tarde's diffusionist paradigm of social disposition addresses the changes globalisation introduces to human experience and articulations of the self and collective identity. As I argue later, disparate actors in Mumbai's tourist industry and adjacent activist cultures exemplify a particular version of the *tornadóros,* the tourist industrial crafter or worker, who uses embodied and digital technologies of gazing *and being gazed at*. The primacy of vision, which customarily connects to European colonial imaginaries (Adler 1989:367; Jay 1993; Bauman 1994:151; Edensor 1998:64), is recalibrated by disenfranchised or activist subjects so as to validate – if not institutionalise – a counter-gaze. Thereafter, this counter-gaze might also transform into a marketing technique for the various (privileged) *tornadóroi* who have a say in the city's tourist marketing. The counter-gaze of the slum-dwellers is different in that it can both reciprocate the visitor's gaze (see Maoz's (2006) mutual gaze) and exclude ocular, or at times also other sensory, connectivity with visitors. Because it may be impossible to examine all the virtual and terrestrial sites in which dominant gazes, tourist performances and counter-gazes occur, I use as guide SM's focus on Mumbai's heritage markers: the Taj Mahal, its media industrial architecture and the filmed slums. Within each one of them we observe how social fields operate to consolidate reputable versions of heritage or advance the city's new (digital, tourist) legacies. Due to its heterogeny and disarticulation, tourism may not even comprise a uniform industry (Lew 2011; MacCannell 2012:184). Practical and definitional restrictions make me revert to the concept of 'sign industry' (Tzanelli 2010b) to explore Mumbai's institutional and business convergences between various industries with a special focus on clusters of signs. These signs contextually refer to ideas of human ecosystems, cultural habitats and their inhabitants' corresponding lifestyles.

The connection between habitats, their corresponding habitus and the emergence of *dispositif* should not be passed in silence. As much as it highlights the role of human *éthoi* in the production of urban and rural destinations, it might become implicated in unspoken inclinations of global tourists and tourist industries to primitivism and racism. As Blanton (2011) and Jamal et al. (2003) point out from two different perspectives (urban ecology and environmentally-geared tourism), environmental racism hides in the noblest intentions to conserve and develop. But the suggestion that, especially in slum places, racism single-handedly regulates exclusion from the city or the nation's socio-cultural community may not be correct. MacCannell (2012:190), who highlights that maintaining the 'purity' of the tourist bubble prompts the removal of city residents such as manual labourers, who might produce visually discordant messages, seems to suggest the involvement of other social variables in such cosmetic exclusions – or conditional inclusions or 'museumifications'. We cannot avoid delving into these new sightseeing rituals with an emphasis on second-order simulations and representations of slum life (MacCannell 2011).

Bourdieu (1998) warns that 'habitus' and 'field' are ontologically complicit because different power alliances collude (*collusio*) in *ex post festum* rationalisation of a tacit form of belief – what he terms, in a manner compatible with Merton's sociology (1948:506) *illusio*. He would suggest that 'the competitive game is a polarised "field of force"…consisting of opposed positions determined by reciprocal relations in a network of objective relations…rooted in an unequal distribution of different forms of capital: economic, cultural social and symbolic' (Albertsen and Diken 2003:3). Instead of considering *collusio* in relation to straightforward habitus transfers from plane to plane, I examine it in terms of a more spontaneous distribution of *dispositif* outside the main fields of domination. Habitus transfers from artworlds to lifeworlds might be restricted to monetary imperatives (securing tourism-cash flows), whereas the manifestation of *dispositif* – or its customary immanence in slum lifeworlds – might have historic depth transcending monetary demands. A propensity to collective recognition in terms of lifestyle, habitats and customs clashes with India's turn to *pangosmiopoiesis* as an externally manifested instantiation of inner beauty. In the following parts we will see how essentialisations of disenfranchised habitus activate a *dispositif* in these slum industrial communities, which agrees contingently with the Western European phenomenological heritage of gazing.

Agra: rejecting film-induced tourist development

SM's potential contribution to the country's tourism mobilities is examined through a particular prism: the filmed sites. A small portion of the film, dominated by the scene at the Taj Mahal, was shot in Agra. Former capital of Hindustan, Agra is a city on the banks of the river Yamuna in the northern state of Uttar Pradesh. The city is a major tourist destination because of its many splendid Moghul-era buildings – most notably the Taj Mahal, Agra Fort and Fatehpūr Sikrī, all three of which are today UNESCO World Heritage sites (Edensor 1998). Though most of the slum scenes were shot in the slums of Juhu and Versova in the northern borders of Mumbai, filming some in Maharashtra airport near Dharavi, Mumbai's mega-slum, conflated landscapes and affirmed how cinematic heterotopias can affirm sites as cosmological loci: what mattered most was that this was a slum story (see also Bolan (2010) on cinematic spatial displacement). Some scenes were shot in ND (Nitin Desai) Studios, Karjat, Mumbai, Maharashtra. With over 22 years in the film industry and 85 films under his belt, award-winning production designer Nitin Chandrakant Desai proved essential for the finalisation of the Taj Mahal scenes. His studio advertises on the web its foundation through Desai's collaboration with Oscar winning director Oliver Stone, when he was sourcing locations for his film *Alexander* (2004) (Nitin Desai Studios, undated).

This multi-site complex affirms the coexistence of at least three asynchronous lifeworlds – one of Indian heritage proper (Taj Mahal), a second connected to the county's budding spectacular technological mobilities (Maharashtra, Bollywood) and a third connected to new tourist sites amenable to global conceptions of 'dissonant heritage' (slums) (Dann and Seaton 2001). And whereas these lifeworlds present the project of Indian post-modernity as an unfinished business, pronouncements of transitional development by powerful regional constituencies merely articulate the usual disenchantment with neat progression, while trying to hide that the 'temporary' is in fact integral to, or a permanent feature of modernisation (Faubion 1988; Nederveen Pieterse 1998). Such digitally advertised spaces highlight the uneven speeds of Mumbai's development but also draw special attention to the zones of contemporary urban dynamism in Asia. Again, we deal with intricate Eurasian and Transatlantic-Asian aesthetic blends and cloned (or clonial) styles of consumerism that forge unique versions of post-modern life. As Raymond Lee suggested, 'even in countries that still rely on Western technology for "progress", the ascendancy of local knowledge may create new syncretic levels of discourse and practice' (Lee 1994:41 in Nederveen Pieterse 1998:77–8). While these blends promote optimistic views on local progress, they are always informed by plural, internally contested tropes of memory as well as the adjacent politics of class and consumption.

In tourism markets the collaboration between ND Studios and Boyle bears little capital *per se* but is used in indirect ways to consolidate such capital. Of particular focus in this section is Taj Mahal's role in staging (or not) SM and tourism mobilities. Media sources inform us that the British director managed to film a few shots there, but when he tried to complete the scenes, he found out that the production was no longer welcome. Resorting to improvisation that reflects stereotyping of the 'Oriental other' as a manipulator of impressions, he and his team conjured up a fake documentary crew to get the essential footage. 'I can't remember if they posed as Indian or German or a mixture of both', says Boyle: the trick was to pick production members who did not visit the place before, so that security would not recognise them. 'We had to do a bit of stealth' he concludes (Horn, 9 November 2009). Though the incident prompts us to examine the global emergence of *dispositif* themes in reverse (Westerners as tricksters) outside their Oriental(-ist) archaeologies, its source (*Los Angeles Times*) also incites suspicion of external media (American) staging. All the same, the production's exclusion from the heritage site generated a fruitful collaboration between Boyle and Desai, stage producer for the Indian show *Kaun Banega Crorepati?*. 'Since I've done a lot of reading on the monument, it was easy for me', Desai the serendipist explains. 'We created the interiors and also a *dargah* [Islamic shrine, mausoleum] for a scene' (Joshi, 21 January 2009).

Tourist development of heritage sites is a contentious issue: not only does it necessitate legal negotiations with third, 'alien' parties (holiday companies and multi-national corporations), it calls for the development of a new hospitality ethos, which remains regulated by the site's 'rightful' national custodians (nation-state, localities). Especially in cinematic tourist regimes territorial claims on open land are framed these days in terms of spatial representations that emerge from regimes of simulation (Couldry 2003b; Peaslee 2011; Tzanelli 2013a). Mediated representations of simulations have become in today's global economy a form of cultural capital in the most conventional Bourdieusian fashion (Couldry 2003a). We cannot determine whether the global mediation of a *faux* Taj Mahal angered native crowds – the move's iconographic resonance can be perceived as iconoclastic in a Muslim non-representational context. However, the monument's plural meaning within India's multi-ethnic and multi-religious polity is affected by foreign media symbols and the languages of global mediascapes (Edensor 1998; Clifford 1988:15). Emplotted in nation-building fables, beautiful architectural sites such as the Taj enclose migration narratives, founding myths and cinematic-like stories with 'golden ages of splendour' (the nation's *ánodos* or uplifting in the world (Campbell 2008:27)), inner decay (*káthodos* or fall (ibid.)) and regeneration (Hutchinson 2004; Hutchinson 2005:ch.1; Smith 1999, 2004; Tzanelli 2008b:ch.6). Architectural achievements comprise the spectacular aspects of political archplots, which showcase the nation's macro-cosmic victories after a series of manipulations of reality.

Such manipulations appeal to the utopian dream of *kósmos*, a beautiful pure world that did not survive the advent of modernisation, but was corrupted by the forces of progress (Berman 1981). This 'structural nostalgia' (Herzfeld 2005:109) encloses the seeds of nation-building's communitarian logic, which is essentially restorative and shared both by the state and its subjects in an unspoken complicity. To counter colonial denigrations of Hindu and Muslim cultures, nationalist uses of the Taj present its Muslim origins in a more 'positive' light: the building's Moghul Age is designated as India's 'Second Golden Age' and syncretic cults such as the Bakhti and the Sufi are exalted for their progressive outlook. In this re-writing of history, the Taj becomes a pan-religious

Tourist modernities 137

creation of hybrid nature (Edensor 1998:88). Its transformation into a tourist-cinematic 'node', that incorporates cultures from East and West, is another interesting technique of strategic hybridisation. But claims to this utopian mysticism, though mesmerising to less knowledgeable visitors, are provoking for radicalised nationalists. Extremist narratives ignore present social divides and continue to accuse some ghostly Muslim 'invaders' for destroying Hindu culture and promoting barbarism, thus recycling 'fixed' ancestral identities in terms of civilisational difference (Thapar 1993:6).

In post-colonial Indian fundamentalisms the focus on religion as an othering tool produces a suspicious discursive historicisation, obscuring social inequalities within the 'Hindu group' in favour of a narrative on Hindu-Muslim or Hindu-Christian conflict (Thapar 1999, 2004). By-passing issues of caste discrimination allows nationalists to ignore the mistreatment of the *dalits* by the upper castes or pervasive socio-cultural discourses of 'untouchability'. SM as a film seems to deliberately blend conceptions of physical dirt as matter out of place, religious conflict and class inequality, sieving all these through a covert critique on the neoliberalisation of Mumbai's economy and polity. Many scholars have considered globalisation as a process triggering new racialisations of the world. These racialisations rely on ever-complex classifications of human types and characters through intersectional difference on the basis of geographical rezoning and other socio-spatial divisions (Winant 2004; Ellison and Burrows 2007; Dikötter 2008; Law 2010; Tzanelli 2011). But how much of this detrimental process should be attributed to neoliberalisation, and how much is the product of domestic economic and political greed? Neoliberal machines and machinations are a generic globalisation applique that can be superimposed on national polities or adapted to domestic politics. In Mumbai's social landscape neoliberalisation interacts and intersects with forces that extend beyond those of the old post-colonial excuse, enmeshing transnational and national economic and political enterprise in varied degrees and with varied consequences. We may remember Beck's (2002:21) observation that cosmopolitanisation does not take place only across national boundaries, but activates processes that change national societies from within (Sassen 2000). Not all cosmopolitanisations are progressive and humanising: some are geared towards eradication of difference.

One would expect that, since Uttar Pradesh is the leftist hub of India, a socialist director such as Boyle would be a welcome visitor. The very expectation sounds naïve without considering that extra advertising for a globally admired monument is virtually redundant. Boyle's disarming northern English habitus might have generated the wrong impressions in the press: constantly highlighting the country's charming but disruptive ethos, 'whatever-it-takes spirit', lack of precision and exactness (Horn, 9 November 2009) or performing 'stealth' in the Taj is not good business strategy. A group of post-colonial units entertaining global recognition for their heritage treasures can perceive such enthusiastic comments and performances as slander. Although, as is the case with most nationalist structures, the Indian nation (*rashtra*) is separated from the nation-state as a cultural community residing a piece of land with which it shares an organic and emotional relationship (Basu et al. 1990:78), the separation might be obscured in public articulations of belonging. The self-same need to exclude from intimate understandings of identity occurs both at the level of locality and that of the national centre (Herzfeld 2005:3–7). There is no way one can fix the factors that contribute to sustainable film-induced tourism in today's hyper-neoliberal destinations (Dredge and Jamal 2013), so we need to consider factors that extend beyond the usual economic imperatives. It may be significant that the Taj continued to be advertised as a sort of India's spiritual 'mediated centre' (Couldry 2003b) that attracted visitors as famous as Princess Diana, but no effort was made to enhance the monument's glamour by serious connections to SM (Holden, 25 March 2013). Contravening Boyle's joking reflections on India's social chaos, UNESCO classifies the monument (inscription: 1983) as a world heritage site under criterion i:

> Taj Mahal represents the finest architectural and artistic achievement through perfect harmony and excellent craftsmanship in a whole range of Indo-Islamic sepulchral architecture. It is a masterpiece of architectural style in conception, treatment and execution and has unique aesthetic qualities in balance, symmetry and harmonious blending of various elements.
>
> (UNESCO, undated)

The emphasis on aesthetic harmony and symmetry appeal to European conceptions of landscape prescribed on to a colonial 'dual motion' of de-territorialising and then re-territorialising space as 'world heritage'. Heritage nominations are managed by national centres, so we can safely assume that the Taj Mahal was elevated into a heritage marker thanks to India's urban centre and capital (Harrison 2005:8; Williams 2005:132; Salazar 2013:280). The meaning of 'landscape', 'scenery' and 'nature', interchangeably used to express the pleasure gained from enjoying natural, semi-natural or cultural landscapes, roughly follows Western modern and modernist shifts from 'land' to 'landscape' (Mitchell 1994; Tuan 1996:30; Urry 2004; Korstanje 2013:56). But the alignment of landscape representations with Western European institutionalisations of urban and rural space management also reifies the Taj as 'an object of sensuous and voluptuous pleasure' (Parry 1993:299) in the tourist trade. Edensor's (1998:22–8) ethnographic documentation of global visitors to the site reveals the use of a specific repertoire of terms and phrases for the monument, which blends feminised and sexualised imagery. Sexist discourse turns rape to prostitution – indeed, not only does it promote labelling and social isolation, it may also push victims to this very corner (prostitution). Conforming once more to the Urdu character of a raped woman, the Taj emerges as yet another form of *dispositif*. It is therefore pertinent to highlight the social content of SM's filmed Taj scenes: unprofessional tour guiding, inaccurate information about the monument's history, systematic shoe and car theft and shameless exploitation of Western compassion. After the film's release, such imagery could only be perceived as crude Orientalist discourse that symbolically strips off the beautiful 'whore' to examine her poor black underbelly.

There are nevertheless other reasons for this ubiquitous marketing silence, including widespread fears of travel safety: before the November 2008 terrorist attacks on the Taj Mahal Palace and Tower, as well as several sites in Mumbai, luxury hotels that conformed to India's image as a glamorous tourist destination were operating at near-capacity. But after the November events, most tourist business in the affected areas had to slash prices, including those offering rooms at the Taj Mahal Tower (Sesser, 21 February 2009). The national ignominy of a great *lieux de memoire* turning into a target for nebulous Islamist organisations and a reproduced Bollywood site, while American tourists stood as visitors to benefit from the 25 per cent dip of the rupee against the dollar, was unbearable. For a region of pronounced socialist leaning, the American tourist contingent could also become coterminous with the very mobile threat for which the Taj Mahal became infamous. The scattered riots against the film were probably connected to such post-colonial-capitalist shifts from intimate national heritage to cinematic tourist legacies. The terrorist rupture in Western – and today largely digitised – control of such globally mobile spaces must have been perceived as failure to survey human traffic in tourist enclaves (Edensor 1998: ch.2). Just as SM's story of Salim the mobile vagabond, the Taj would eventually be validated as a symbolically polluted space, if it developed links to clonial cinematic images of 'poorist' crime. Beck's (1992, 1999) realist conception of risk as a para-environmental theme communicates with the anthropological parable of Indian 'dirt' as disorder. Tourism's dirty and risky business should be handled by more suitable labour.

The blindness of memory: Mumbai's new heritage tourisms

To properly explore the expansion of tourism in Mumbai we must place it in the context of a progressive bureaucratisation of Indian tourism. The creation of the Indian Tourism Development Corporation (ITDC) as part of the Ministry of Tourism in 1966 marked a definitive transition in government approaches towards tourism and paved the way for its corporatisation. The process culminated with the launch of neoliberal reforms in 1991 that facilitated the globalisation of the Indian tourism industry. The new Corporation's aims and objectives included the provision of managerial services in India and abroad and tourism development, including consultancy and project implementation (see the Indian Tourism Development Corporation's website). These goals could overlap with the development of slum labour hubs into touristic bubbles for the new tourist gaze, ear and nose. However, this would necessitate a redefinition of old aesthetic norms so as to pronounce that there is beauty in hardship, social deprivation and even physical dirt, in which children like Jamal and Salim have to grow. This is easier said than done: though on the way to becoming a superpower, India still negotiates its position *vis-à-vis*

Western norms of perfection. Civilisational achievement in technology comes easier than the eradication of status insecurity. The promotion of global metropolitan art-work that focuses on the lifeworlds of deprived urban areas might delink such social milieus from the old project of the nation-state that dictated the folklorisation of marginality. Expansive media networking certainly promotes national awareness through the external recognition of local marginalities. But is colonial fear and prejudice exorcised across India's multi-culture, or do they still inform to some extent the country's social services and promote cultural closure in tourist projects?

A slide from context to textual imperatives is necessary. SM's filming locations project a spatial arrangement of audio-visual narratives, which adheres to the principles of cosmopolitanism as a cosmetic and political project. The film's overt (via image, sound and lyrics) and covert (via situating art-work in designated areas such as those of a studio) spatial distribution, challenges perceptions of the living environment. A narrative shift from the slum to India's revered heritage (Taj Mahal), then back to a reconstructed slum, a Bollywood-like studio setting, and finally Mumbai's transport node (VT), promotes mind-walking in which social divisions and fields are bound to be questioned. The ensuing criticism is likely to disincentivise official action and investment in slum tourism development; priorities are given to other social mobility and environmental concerns. As a result, other non-state agents kick in to capitalise on the 'bounty', or sincerely help in local growth.

In the European context Irimiás (2012) expresses similar concerns over the management of connections between international film productions and tourist destination marketing. As urban image-making is dependent upon complex glocal socio-cultural interpretation (Roesch 2009), the motion picture's success can evade consideration, just because the host 'interprets' its potential 'somewhere else'. SM could be classified as a missed ITDC target: in early 2009, press sources record Ashok Amritraj, producer of 100 films in Hollywood and voting member of the Academy of Motion Picture Arts and Sciences (AMPAS) (the body that awards the Oscars), making a faint reference to such possibilities. Dismissing accusations that SM is 'poverty porn', he recalled that the first time he attended the Oscars the winner was *Gandhi* (1982), with SM being the second film shot in India to win the Oscar. 'Isn't it interesting that both films were directed by men from Britain?' he mused, while global media channels pointed out that *Gandhi* was co-produced by director Richard Attenborough with India's National Film Development Corporation (*Rediff News*, 4 March 2009). Intentionally or not, especially Mumbai's slum tourism development presents us here with a missed articulation between corporations. Although SM fell into the category of movies that enhanced awareness of place, the aims of relevant development initiatives were contradictory: on the one hand, the film connected to international initiatives in educational tourist trips to India's slums, but on the other it created destination image cushions that agreed better with Mumbai's illusion mega-industry. Building an urban image in mediascapes can both obscure and reinforce a well-delineated urban identity so as to attract 'the right' investors, tourists and migrants (Macionis 2004; Hudson and Ritchie 2006; Egedy and Kovács 2009; O'Connor et al. 2009; Croy 2010; O'Connor et al. 2010). But also inversely, the displacement of filmed activities in safer areas enables the production of new allegories of time-space dislocation (Tzanelli 2010b; Tzanelli 2013a). Ironically, relocating the slum to the cinematic market enhances the translatability of its cultural formations (local cultures), which otherwise remain inaccessible to, and not invested in by foreign visitors and professionals. The neoliberal triumph was assisted by SM's recognition as an inauthentic extension of the novel, as it transformed it into a more accessible educational vehicle in the wake of global pro-slum activism. This observation, which certainly connects to the ways 'authenticity' is guarded in literary tourist sites (Fawcett and Cormack 2001; Earl 2008) also sheds light on some global critiques of the movie. Although Riley and Van Doren's (1992) argument that media channels act as 'vehicles of recognition' to facilitate destination image development is still valid, battles over the promotion of the 'correct' representations can disrupt the fair development of the cinematic sites (Croy and Heitmann 2011:198).

But does this spatio-temporal distanciation also contribute to the creation of an educational utopia 'elsewhere' – a common theme in the creation of the post-modern or 'nowhere' place in film? (Croy and Heitmann 2011:199; Buchmann 2006; Sydney-Smith 2006). We can excavate more missed articulations if we highlight the uneven development and national regard of Mumbai's spectacular film industry (Bollywood) *vis-à-vis* foreign film and tourist development. The history of the Bollywood industry's growing number of production, human resource needs and transnational audiences was not supported by the central government until 1998, when it received formal industry status with the initiative of Culture Minister Sushama Swaraj, and in 2000, when the bank of India began to provide loans for film production. The Nehruvian heritage ensured for a long time that only realistic films would be endorsed as products that promote socio-political awareness and what was perceived as a sound path to modernisation. The all-too-familiar aesthetic clash between 'high' and artistic on the one hand, and 'low' and popular culture on the other was enacted on Indian ground as a backdrop to home-grown nationalist discourse (Gellner 1983:57, 72; Gellner 1998; Chatterjee 1986). The political search for the alleged 'eternal' Indian culture did not agree with Bollywood's pop cosmologies of love and revenge, which in a post-Partition landscape resonated better with the masses of illiterate working-class migrants and refugees. Bollywood's archplots better enacted what Herzfeld (2005:96) examines as practical Orientalism – the very 'translation of hegemonic ideology into everyday practice' Rahman espoused in his commentary on Easternisations of Western artscenes.

Reworking narratives of modernism (Gellner 1998:25–30; Smith 1971; Hutchinson 2005:60), Bollywood film transformed into a domestic observatory on how hegemonic ideologies of nationhood inhabit the spaces of an everyday sociality that defines meaningful human togetherness throughout

142 *A plural slumdog* kósmos

mankind's history (Tzanelli 2008b:164). Nehru's political-cultural project upset India's economic agenda even more from the 1990s, when mounting import bills led to a bailout deal with the International Monetary Fund that required economic restructuring, including deregulation, privatisation and trade liberalisation. Nehruvian echoes of civility are also traced in new liberal policies that emphasise specialisation in advanced technologies and management, as well as deregulated urban trade to attract foreign capital investment. Mumbai is one of the main urban nodes affected by this change that favours mostly the educated middle classes. Educational attainment and the professionalisation of new knowledge economies, such as those of new technologies (internet, digital cinema) and tourism, has changed both the cosmological and economic structure of cultural industries (Nelson and Deshpande 2013). Having to keep pace with these changes has led to further diversification of Bollywood scenarios and the way the industry communicates with foreign investors and affiliate business (Morcom 2008). Notably, a similar trend is noticed in cultural traffic that ensures the catering of blended forms of tourism, including backpacking, heritage tourism, voluntourism and more recently cinematic tourism.

As is the case with other nation-states, one of the consequences of neoliberal globalisation in urban India has been the rapid retrenchment of the state from social services and the liberalisation of real estate markets that opened up the public arena to the establishment of profitable partnerships with private agents (Glasze 2005). Such public-private partnerships fuel new fears based on perceived dangers of social identities residing at the margins of urban respectability, with slums and their poor populations at the top of such agendas (Bauman 2005b; England and Simon 2010). Reactions to imagined geographies of social refuse-as-terror communicate with space-time geographies of power (Massey 1994; Pain 2009). In India's urban neoliberalisation it is precisely these loose, 'un-gated communities' that have been acting over at least the last decade as mobility hubs, increasingly attracting global tourist clientele – in opposition to privileged gated communities that have been transformed into emotional and material fixities for the mobile professional classes. Mumbai's new urban planning communicates with this mobility paradox, suggesting unexpected and, at times optimistic interchanges between Indian heritage and its legacies.

Serendipity and new anthropophagies

To this background one may add other considerations of urban competition, amply endorsed in neoliberal contexts. Mumbai's new slum tourism follows in the steps of other so-called 'poorism' holidays, such as those offered in New Delhi via the non-profit Salaam Baalak Trust fronted by Mira Nair's *Saalam Bombay*. The Trust specialises in tours concerned with children living at or near the city's train station. Since 1988 the NGO has been 'rehabilitating' children and involving them in 'meaningful ventures', such as conducting walking tours in New Delhi's new built and living heritage for which they are paid tips by tourists. 'It's a unique way of engaging people in the lives of children in distress' according to Mohammed Javed, a former street kid acting today as tour guide (Lal, 13 September 2009). Framed around ideas of a life-changing, life-opening experience, according to Ethical Traveler executive director Jeff Greenwald, these tours need to be interactive. 'If not, this is the modern equivalent of watching people suffer in public coliseums' (Bly, 2 October 2009). So, the question remains: how are such tours legitimated as ethical choices when they are based on a proximate *consumption* of slum communities? The consolidation of 'east-oriented geo-politics' (Italiano 2012:14) in such terrestrial, and progressively also digital enterprises, demotes the subaltern to nothing more than a highly lucrative source of income for those controlling the means of digital production (Ranciére 2004:7–9). In the adjacent field of volunteer tourism, such consumption options are rendered literally untouchable, like Jamal's trip though the public latrine so as to achieve a brief encounter with celebrity (Fassin 2012; Reas 2014). Just as SM's audio-visual touring, any broadcast holiday package to Mumbai's slumscapes includes a fundamental contradiction: to 'know' and 'learn' about them, one has to 'devour' them with all their senses, to engage in a sort of cognitive 'anthropophagy', of which Western modernity is constantly accused (Edwards 1999; Tzanelli 2011:8–9).

That is how we arrive at today's development crossroads that nearly burned SM to the altar of compassion. Virtual communication of the tourist gaze is the pinnacle of post-modern articulation: Lash and Urry (1994) suggest that it sustains economies of sign through which memory becomes commoditised. In fact, even the performance of slumming in Mumbai by international journalists updates the archetypical Benjaminian *flâneur* (Gilloch 2007), better connecting it to Reality Tours persistent invocation of reality online. The website of this company, which still monopolises Mumbai slumming (but see Mumbai Magic 2013 as a new competitor), is a valuable critical spyglass into Indian post-modernity's ethics of tourist gazing, providing no fast-food neo-liberal or Marxist answers. We may in fact begin by asking what reporters – the regular 'junkhunters' – are supposed to report without travelling to such zones of exception. Yet, when Nigel Richardson of *The Telegraph* notes that he found 'touring a place like Dharavi [Reality Tours' business focus] to be an education' (Richardson, 22 January 2009), we cannot but note how his commentary invokes disconcerting linkages between edu-tourist and middle-class philanthropic pursuits from nineteenth-century journeys to London and Paris shantytowns (Holdnak and Holland 1996; Seaton 2012). Stan Sesser of *Asia News* appears persuaded by a certain Mayur Dixit's argument that slums are the symbol of old India of the 2,000 community slums. 'Too much poverty and too few jobs', he says, explaining that he does not need to watch SM to 'get the point'. Interestingly, Sesser remarks that as the image of new India's billionaires and buzzing technology companies has taken a hit because of SM, many educated slum-dwellers such as Dixit plan to benefit 'by leading visitors around [their] neighbourhood and catering for the international appetite for

144 *A plural slumdog* kósmos

slum tourism' (Sesser, 21 February 2009). Later the same day he visited Dharavi with Reality Tours to be updated on the company's progress. Reality Tours have been running since 2006, but their condemnation by a TV programme as 'poverty tourism' and the threats of Minister of Tourism, Kumari Selja, to have them shut down certainly contributed to their media staging as one of Maximum City's controversial tourist businesses (Richardson, 22 Janurary 2009).

In 2009, Selja unveiled plans to extend the 'Incredible India' campaign to the domestic tourism sector with US $12 million out of a total budget of US $200 million allocated to the campaign. The previous year the Ministry of Tourism had already launched a campaign with a purpose of educating local populations into adopting good etiquette when dealing with foreign tourists (ICMR, undated). Indian actor Aamir Khan was recruited to endorse the 'Atithidevo Bhava' campaign, which was supposed to supplement 'Incredible India' as an integrated communication strategy for attracting global tourists with the help of professional actors (HolidayIQ.com 2009). This Sanskrit rendition of 'Guests are like God' supports the secularised conceptions of pilgrimage we encounter in European cosmologies of travel (Coleman and Eade 2004). The campaign attuned to Western civility standards, while selling *chrónic* or native heritage capital such as yoga (also Singh 2012). Although, just as slum histories, such intangible products have been part of slow tourism mobilities, the marketing campaign was not interested in addressing the realist aspects of the relationship between natives and visitors, producers and consumers, which is predicated upon an unwritten social contract that seals the tourist's respect for native creativity. The interaction is entrenched in the structural logic of work, which, in the absence of fair affective and material remuneration, begins to resemble *douleiá* or slavery (Deacon 2007; Gregg 2009). The ethics of work frame industrial humanity's self-image as a community of carers while also defining its relationship with leisure economies. Leisure economies enable cultural mobilities that ought to be beneficial for cultural givers and native workers (Derrida 1994; Derrida and Dufourmantelle 2000). Even in the 2009 campaign's Hindu cosmology, which strangely resembles the European Christological spirituality, we note the presence of a hegemonic script that excludes so as to beautify the country, by individualising and aestheticising spiritual tourist experiences (Ranciére 2004:4). In this programme that now welcomes corporate Bollywood contributions, there is little space for those populations whose culture originally inspired Indian film of the *masala* range.

This is where independent tourist business steps in to close the gap between fierce competition and labour recognition: Krishna Pujari, one of Reality Tours' directors and owners, highlighted that the company was accused initially of selling poverty. But when later he and his partner, Chris Way, started financing Dharavi's educational projects, donating 80 per cent of their profits to the slum, showing sensitivity by limiting tour groups to six people and forbidding photography, local reception improved. Way estimated that in late 2009 Reality Tours sales were up by 25 per cent after SM's release and the gradual rebound of tourism after the terrorist attacks (Bly, 2 October 2009). During Sesser's visit to Dharavi, Pujari was watching SM on his laptop and noting that the movie 'was lighting a fire on his business …. "I'm getting 10 to 15 calls a day from the media all over the world"', he continued, while painting in bright colours Dharavi's 10,000 small-scale industries (with an estimated $665 million in annual revenue) and the presence of less crime in the slum than in the city 'because there is a sense of community' (Sesser, 21 February 2009). In the slum's recycling area 'old ink vats, cooking oil containers and paint tints were being returned to gleaming perfection, while scraps of trashed plastic were converted into pristine pellets and twisted aluminium was returned to ingots' (Richardson, 22 January 2009). It is rather amazing how a community living in soot turns darkness and junk into shining consumption materials. The old BJP 'India Shining' motto seems to communicate with the new 'Incredible India', despite their varied inception by different political affiliations.

The near-Edenic image of a crowded migration node emulates aspects of nationalist communitarianism, minus its exclusive logic, so as to turn the slum's residual Babel into spectacular Mumbai's core ingredient. This is nothing other than the equivalent of an appeal to a pro-filmic reality, a strategy of de-mediating mediation that strips real gazing of its distance (Vaughan 1999:79; Strain 2003:2–3). Persistent admiration of Dharavi's recycling industry in the international press approximates such hermeneutics of recovery, and reminds us how close ethnographies come to the cult of nationalism (Herzfeld 1987, 2005). Mazumdar's (2007) divide between the spectacular cinematic city and the city of ruins also comes to mind, generating essential links between Mumbai's new slum tourist and global media industries. To unpack the rather important statement on 'community' we may draw on the suggestion that industrial modernity's tourist potential is hidden in aestheticisations of its material remains (Edensor 2005a). In opposition to the tightly regulated tourist enclaves of globally sanctioned heritage such as the Taj (Edensor 1998:45–53), slums are living places on the social margins, which can accommodate transgressive and playful activities. But the ways Dharavi operates as a tourist destination does not always conform to Edensor's theory: despite the lack of official surveillance mechanisms, save occasional police visits, slum tourist spaces appear to be regulated by residents. Finally, it is not advisable to conflate tourism policy with art-work as such, as the latter is not created for the improvement of the former.

Of importance is the persistence and cosmological significance of local regulatory mechanisms I explore through conceptions of the 'counter-gaze'. Close, but not identical to Maoz's 'mutual gaze' (2006), slum 'counter-gazing' surveys the cultural ethos and historical depth of Mumbai's slum visitor economy, suggesting that a dip into 'reality' in relevant research should not be limited to the tourist 'questioning gaze' (Bruner 2001) or 'reverse gaze' (Gillespie 2006). It is suggested that slum tourists' questioning gazes are manufactured by multiple local and non-native agents, hence 'reality' (as in Dyson 2012:257, 269) is nothing more than a Eurasian phenomenological mirage. Dharavi's 'counter-gaze' is a sort of camera-like recording and replaying of *what is perceived of* as Western civility though Indian views of cosmological unity. While this camera-like vision resembles Boyle's and his associates' art, it emerges independently from it. The reasons behind depriving visitors of their right to produce their photographic memories of the tour are complex and entwined with the politics of guest performances, as well as the hosts' deferred synaesthetic performativity. Rather than referring to digital technologies – with which Dharavi residents are all too familiar – we may revert to conceptions of *technopoesis* as an assemblage of humans, tools and self-narratives to understand how communal activism grows beyond nationalist pursuits. Depriving visitors of their primary representational tools coerces them to reconstruct their experience of the tour *from memory* – a memory already ridden with profitable misconceptions of dark industrial spaces and practices. Though modifying the colours of the journey (darkness turns into symbolic brightness-optimism), this strategy amplifies the visitors' respect for local *téchne*. As we saw in Part I, even Boyle and his associates adopted this contentious optimistic narrative, possibly knowing less of its political origins.

Since 2008 the Western preference to experience the 'reality' behind the British film has persuaded many to shun Goa's beaches and Rajasthan's palaces for a 'slumdog tour'. Tourists follow Ganesh Tikonkar, a Reality Tours guide, for up to three hours exploration of the life of slum-dwellers. The highlights include a stop at a stall of six toilets serving 16,000 people 'and a stroll inside a river so black that it oozes rather than flows' (The Indian Express, 22 January 2009). Quite often, tourists return convinced that the movie is a fairy tale and reality 'a little darker, a little grittier' (The Indian Express, 22 January 2009). Still, the tour allows visitors to find what Deval Sanghavi of a Mumbai-based NGO describes as 'thriving, diverse communities who live together peacefully' (ibid.). The post-modern shift from gazing landscapes and their peoples to performing tourism and philanthropy (Perkins and Thorns 2001) promises to blur the boundaries between hegemonic consumers and disenfranchised hosts (Blocker 2009). There is always an 'allegorical' (Tzanelli 2010c:221) or 'philological imperative' (Doueihi 2011 in Cronin 2013:131) that not only pins down changing fields of meaning in technological environments, but also effectively transposes (i.e. transliterates) ethnic forms and styles into the global market.

One wonders what it is like to live in Dharavi and what leads interviewees such as Dixit to hail new Mumbai's progress. The notion of the slum is rather hazy in India's urban context, as slum spaces tend to incorporate plural citizenships, lifestyles and mobilities. The definite class divide in Juhu says little about life in its slum: many Bollywood celebrities and famous Indian personalities call its affluent parts 'home' ('The Beverly Hills of Bollywood') as its aesthetic appeal and busy-yet-peaceful surroundings make it a great place to live. But its slum area is also better organised than in previous decades. The Juhu Citizen Welfare Group is the outcome of many years of NGO involvement and activism by Juhu residents. Formed in 2002 as 'The Juhu Seatizen' and formalised in 2003 with its own monthly newspaper (*The Juhu Citizen*), it now attracts voluntary support from the whole of North-west Mumbai – a development also advertised on the community's website (Juhu Citizens Welfare

Group 2013). Notably, the website's photo gallery includes highly ordered, clean and beautiful sites and humans, indicating local image awareness and diverse living experience.

Dharavi is an even more exceptional case, with many commentators regularly describing it as 'a node on the global economy' or 'an amazing mosaic of villages and townships from all over India' (Dyson 2012:258). We must generally account for the fact that real estate in India's financial capital is ranked amongst the world's most prohibitively expensive, pushing various social groups into slums like Dharavi. Snuggled between Mumbai's two main suburban railway lines that connect the ends of the city, Dharavi's little spaces can cost as much as US$40,000 (Lal, 13 September 2013). It is reported that its tiny condominiums host 55 per cent of the city's population (Swanson, 16 May 2011). Still, the tourist boom and its generous digital advertising resurrect some ghosts that modern professionals find difficult to exorcise. On such occasions, conceptions of environmental racism implode into transnational risk politics, as the following chapter suggests.

8 The virtual journeys of *Slumdog Millionaire*

Dharavi's e-magined anamnestic solidarity

This chapter explores the digital dimensions and social consequences of Mumbai's tourist enterprise. E-touring problematises the presence of chrono-diverse lifeworlds, inviting netizens to participate in the protection of different human experiences of time or parallel modernities (Tzanelli 2008b:ch.4; Virilio 2010:28). Commercialisation creates a thin cosmopolitan crust that on-site visitations break, leaving some tourists full of admiration for the locals' 'industriousness', but horrified by their living conditions. The realisation that SM's autographic products are handed over to chains of allographic production – otherwise put, the tribulations of the local workforce can only be communicated by tourist business digitally (Goodman 1976) – reiterates ideas of globalisation as adaptation of surfaces to commercial demands. However, e-tourist initiatives may also sensitise tourist prosumers, who actively produce with no interest in the consequences of their actions (Toffler 1980b). This is achieved through online promotions of new consumption norms that direct internet *flâneurs* towards responsibilisation and beneficial co-production of Dharavi's 'public image'.

Dharavi's new e-mage (electronic image) promotes a felicitous chrono-spatial exchange of different *tornadóroi* (old industrial for new artistic and digital labour) to dignify the site's socio-cultural presence (Dyson 2012:265). Old *tornadóroi* toiled under unsafe conditions to support humanity's industrial progress, whereas the new *tornadóroi* re-imagine these pasts under the safe conditions of post-modernity while giving tours to foreigners or creating relevant websites. Both social types discard versions of utopia as the restoration of a natural condition lost in the past and consider it as intentional product of rational action, 'the outcome of "human contrivance" or social "engineering" through which the good society might be realised in the future' (Yar 2014:8). The contribution of new *tornadóroi* is essential for the maintenance of 'anamnestic solidarity' with Mumbai's industrial pasts and the promotion of a better future for the slums (Lenhardt 1975:136; Pensky 1989:356–58; Tzanelli 2007:254). Setting the tourist guilt for global contractual oblivion against Western modernity's debt to industrial labour consolidates a 'pure' connection with the dead and dying cultures of the slum (Ricoeur 1999). Akin to artificial resuscitations of patriotism in global reconciliation cultures with their own slum problems, this activism is proffered as a sort of 'compensation for damages' (Duvenage 1999:8–9) inflicted upon humans by contemporary governmobility's biopolitical grammar. This articulation of an old civilisational *debt* raises anew powerful 'universalist demands of liberal principles and the need for a robust political identity, including a shared [post-colonial, post-national] history' (Tzanelli 2007:254; Mizstal 2003; Habermas 1996) beyond the nation-state, in mobile sites of tourist solidarity.

To this end, alongside any promotions of anodyne touring, Reality Tours website enacts a labour utopia that reiterates the category of human as a noble creative worker, who can produce from rubble. Nevertheless, Reality Tours utopian topography is not imagined as an 'other-worldly realm', but at least in the first instance as a transformation of the plane of the actual, 'its immanent reconfiguration into new possibilities' (e.g. Yar 2014:4). Real collective biographies of migration play a significant role in this. Industriousness is stressed on the website, corroborating the presence of guild consciousness and 'a sense of camaraderie that permeates this unique settlement everywhere one goes, with Tamils, Muslims, south Indians, Maharashtrians, Konkanis, potters, leather-workers, plastic recyclers, goldsmiths, garment workers, craftsmen working with the common goal to disgorge themselves from this Dickensian wretchedness' (Lal, 13 September 2013). It is true that family businesses in Dharavi pay tax and some are wealthy enough to buy into the slum's few residential uprises. But on-site visitations by tourists cannot always capture such nuances. The proof is in the gazing: 'Most tourists come here expecting to see us begging, but are surprised to see us busy and doing quite well here', says slum resident Brij Rai (Lal, 13 September 2013). It seems that this labour utopia has also been embraced and now performed by Dharavi's gazed upon residents.

But the staging of labour *digitopias* or digital utopias is a different issue (Urry 2011:139–41; Tzanelli 2012a, 2013a, 2013b). Many constituencies stress how marketing and ethical imperatives clash by definition – hence we should dismiss such websites and their on-site options as shameless capitalist exploitation. More favourable commentators, such as Anand Giridharadas, columnist for *International Herald Tribune*, attribute poverty to the 'failure of empathy', as those with means to make a difference 'are far away, geographically and mentally'. Atma Programs executive collaborator with Reality Gives, Bronwyn McBride, states that the company 'does a lot of good here', but Dharavi NGO Director of Community Outreach Programme, Nirmal Chandappa, accuses Reality Tours of masquerading profitmaking as charity. From outside the slum, Jockin Arputham, President of Mumbai-based Shack/Slum Dwellers International (SDI) that represents the urban poor in 20 countries in Asia, Africa and Latin America, describes the tours as 'crime against poverty', an affront 'to the dignity of slum dwellers' (Forster, April 2009). All factions agree on one thing: the company's tours fill a gap left by overstretched NGO activism and poor government support (Swanson, 16 May 2011). Wray's and Pujari's profitable activism counteracts government attempts to close Dharavi's recycling operations 'for health reasons' – a move fiercely opposed by residents as this is their sole source of income (Sesser, 21 February 2009). The community's recycling activities are an essential constituent of most Reality Tour options, constantly reminding Western visitors that regional officialdom seeks to modify labour *digitopias*. In effect, these tours replace one conception of 'risk' (contamination, disease) with another (removal of local income resource, hence eradication of a particular type of labour). As recycling is enmeshed into digital presentations of a wider range of 'old' professions not practiced in 'more developed' Western contexts, the website promotes a hermeneutics of recovery familiar to Western tourist visitors. Dharavi labour tasks are represented as an extension of 'beautiful creativity', not a patchwork of dirty professions.

In Western Enlightenment contexts cosmologically familiar to visitors, teleological narratives of social mobility and hierarchy promoted first the scientific *ergonomy* (*érgon*=work, *nómos*=law) of industrialised modernity. The initial prioritisation of industry's *ergonomic* principles side-lined the *ergopoetic* aspects of 'primitive' cultures and their contribution to civility. *Ergopoesis* refers to the *ergetic* ability humans possess to learn while doing (Funkenstein 1986:290; Trey 1992; Ricoeur 2005:157, 260–2), connecting to a range of Dharavi's know-how labour activities. Arendt's critique of the individualisation of action, which is not grounded in social co-presence and an agreement with others supported by dialogue (Benhabib 1992), could also be read here against a critique of modernity's consumerist logic that leads to reproductive exploitations of work (Bauman 2005a; Davis 2008:56). Reality Tours website turns slum professions into sights worthy of multi-sensory consumption, but moralises the tourist's right to proximity/co-presence through charitable giving to the gazed sites. But before delving into Reality Gives initiatives, let us deconstruct snapshots from Reality Tours proposed journeys.

The slum's digital *tórnos*

The most potent hermeneutic tool e-tourist business possesses is the digital cosmetics of its website. To consider contemporary alterations of *pangosmiopoiesis* we need only take a closer look at the design of such e-business (Jensen 2013, 2014), which includes various combinations of text, video and dialogue. The promise to 'dissect Dharavi' through a signature tour suggests the adoption of a clinical gaze that appeals to Western consumers (Foucault 1976; Urry 2002). Although tourists are not allowed to photograph the slum, a video directed by Andrew Johnson is embedded in the 'See the real India!' page. The video commences with hypermobile images of a moving train, which are succeeded by a moving vision following Pujari (as guide) and one of his customers. 'How big is this?' the traveller asks, and before too long we traverse the narrow streets of the shantytown. The guide explains more about development initiatives in the slum, including teaching computer skills and English to locals. The tour immediately cuts to more streets; a door is opened by Way to a kindergarten full of children casting inquisitive looks at the lens. Way stresses that teaching adopts a child-centred expressive approach and is delivered by locally recruited teachers. Some wide-screen distant shots of children running on piles of garbage that recall SM's airport scenes are backed by Way's statement that the purpose of the tours is to dispel negative images of the slum. Fast-track images of local residents or children, and Dharavi's busy streets are permeated by noise and unidentified chanting, while Way and Pujari continue to advertise the company's contribution to the slum. A succession of other human types are blended into images of tourists and heritage sightseeing ('we are trying to show the reality of Mumbai'). These include tourist *testimonios* that juxtapose local to Western experience, articulating a 'counterpoint' or opposite visions of the social world that match SM's fictional documentary narrative (of tourist gazes vs. slum-dwellers' labour). In this fashion, the video projects multiple autobiographies of travelling the world on the screen (Desforges 2000; Tzanelli 2012a; Germann Molz 2012). Pujari declares his love for this vibrant place, while we watch groups of young hyperactive children running around a room. 'I want to show you this friendly community…the hard-working people, the humble people', he says (and we watch Pujari hugging a rather embarrassed man).

Deconstructing the order of digitised spatial geographies, the camera immediately rewinds in fast-forward style to show Dharavi's spaces and conclude with a shot from above in a busy computer class. The edu-tourist vision is exchanged with an intimate encounter with residents involved in such development initiatives: the suggestion is that the website's digitised voices are local. 'Nowadays, if you want a good job you need English plus computers', explains a local man in fluent English, confirming the presence of a digital/social divide (Warschauer 1999). As Stewart (2000) and Castells (1997) highlight, in our contemporary digital era the concept of social inclusion does not refer merely to adequate share of resources but also to human participation in collective life chances and the maintenance of a healthy civil society. Project Director Jonny Clarke appears, to discuss the enabling programme and the plans concerning expansion of such teaching initiatives beyond Dharavi, to schools across Maharashtra. An aerial shot of the slum's rooftops allows us to assume a God's eye view, transforming the clip's original clinical into a mathematical vision.

Despite its positive take on human socialities, the video refrains from sublimating Dharavi's scapes. It is as if pure human beings inhabit a plane corrupted by indifference, industry and refuse. A Tardean (1903) variable of Mumbai lifeworlds emerges in the cyber-sphere, which conforms to the rules of digital reproduction and creative repetition (a 'rewinding' of sightseeing but remotely, 'from afar' and 'above') (Tzanelli 2013a:172–3; Szerszynski and Urry 2006). This allows for endless replication of difference rather than sameness, and the replacement of identicality with cultural variability that is managed and marketed by global networks in 'responsible ways'. Function might be prioritised over value in such simulations of sociality, but there are also cases of synergy between the two – a choice occasionally depending on the network's

(Reality Tours) regulators. In all cases however, such websites support a sort of 'cultural translation' as an autographic – in reality allographic – practice, an activity that is primarily the work of a maker (rather a guild or network of makers) or artisan – 'an activity [that is] routinely unacknowledged work of others' (Cronin 2013:6): the digital professionals. Notably, the video's *digitopian* parable emulates global care as a matter of family intimacy via technologised visions of social inclusion. As Warschauer (2002) explains, social inclusion is a prominent concept in European discourse, with reference to the extent that families and communities are able to control their own destinies. For once, Reality Tours suggests, the disenfranchised do not take the back seat but proffer a voice, however subjected to market imperatives.

These days, the fortunes of cultural translation have become inseparable from the technologies that make long-distance trade possible (Cronin 2013:17). Consequently, the ethics of technological mobilities are integrated into a touristic *technopoesis*, constantly flagging the potency of the media, as well as what can be perceived of as fair distribution of their control (Couldry 2007). Perhaps the fact that English acts as *lingua franca* in such cyber-spheres can address anxieties regarding the expansion of Eastern cultural systems westwards (see Bernal 1991 on Africanism in Europe and Goody 2006 on Islam). Though, when conceptions of 'the Orient' as Islamic heritage are replaced with the slum's migrant working-class abjection, old racisms may still dominate (in the form of traditional biopolitics) consumer milieus, our technological framework and its context need updating. As much as every intellectual technology reflects an *ethos* (McGrath 2001; Carr 2010), it remains a malleable tool in human hands. The Reality Tours video addresses *technopoesis* as a system of at least three overlapping ecologies: a physical one (of movement), a symbolic ecology marked by competition over definition (who defines the conditions of the slum) and a media ecology overlaying the other two (Carey 1999). These three ecologies are situated within spatio-temporal boundaries, just as Mumbai's slum ecology, which is historically lived, practiced, and produced 'through bodies in motion' (Hay 2006:47). If photography is out of question for tourists, it is not precluded from the website, as the video and its numerous images of children and natives at work betray. Reiterating the presence of a communal 'family' unravelled by modern life in industrialised countries (hence, essentialising *technopoesis* through biological-emotional bonds), photographing is inextricably linked to the modern activity of tourism (Sontag 1971:8–9; Chalfen 1999:216–17; Tzanelli 2011:84–5). As a steady nature-culture bond, it cannot be excluded by business altogether.

The video clip seeks to assert human commonality, while alerting digital visitors to the gaping inequalities of the city. There is a distinction to be made between what is called 'universal', what is 'uniform' and the 'common' (Julien 2008:213) – differentiations that have real life consequences and implications. The universal does not alter its premises wherever it is studied in the universe, whereas the uniform has universal impact, because of skilfully engineered ease of access, as is the case with e-tourism consumption. But the common is *fons* or source – what is potentially shareable because of its global intelligibility – rather than *fundus* – the sediment, once everything else has been removed or diluted in the cup of globalisation. The *fundus* lingers like the viral presence of fundamentalist discourse, which grows on historical resentment and unequal distribution of resources (Nietzsche 1990; Honneth 2007). Hence, the common corresponds not to the 'ready implementation of a blueprint', but to a form of 'weaving' or production through interactivity (Ingold 2000). Cronin follows up this trail of thought:

> As becomes all too apparent when you travel abroad, being similar to someone…does not mean that you necessarily have everything in common with them. This construed nature of the common, which is conflated and processual, must be at the core of any digital humanism, if the latter is not to be indiscriminate, "massive" and manipulatory in its effects.
>
> (2013:138)

Tourist hyper-real spaces such as Reality Tours might initially harbour the suspicion that communal life is trapped into the final act of a Faustian drama, in which human agency succumbs to consumerism's 'kinetic inferno' (Sloterijk 1989 in Cronin 2013:94; Bauman 2010). The Faustian drama warns us that everything – from virtual visits to the slum, to finding appropriate guides and booking holidays in Mumbai's slums – can easily become processed into an accelerated programme that systematises even the localities chrono-diverse narratives (Jensen 2010; Virilio 2010).

This is not so in Reality Tours offerings, which promise a return home after successive visits to recycling facilities, pottery-making, embroidery, poppadom-making and bakery shops, soap factories and leather-tanning sites 'with an enlightened sense of purpose' (Reality Tours 'Slum Tours', undated). It is as if we, the neo-nomad 'tourists', are relocated into a time before the woes of authoritarian oppression and urban division, to a world in which community triumphed over modernity's evils, and guests were free to revert to their carefree childhood (Dann 1989). Dharavi's 'Short' and 'Long Tour' options are prefaced by the presence of Dharavi's ethno-religious mosaic, 'and this diversity is apparent in the temples, mosques and churches that stand side-by-side'. An array of highlights includes visits to recycling plants, factory rooftops (an exercise akin to the video's aerial vision), the craft-spaces of bakery, poppadum and pottery as well as inspecting a resident's house. Though determined to stay away from historical accounts of the community's development, such visits promote meticulous 'seriating' (Bhabha 1994: 22; Bal 2003:21), hence associations between the values of transparent realism and Western individualist elitism. Stressing the presence of old crafts conforms to European discourses of (in-)tangible heritage (Lange 2003:436) with a twist: we are not transposed into the West's or Europe's old time but watch the coexistence of the then with the Indian now, Dharavi's very own fast digital mobilities. The blend of Indian crafts invites mobile anthropophagy, which is not McDonaldised like

Jamal's trip to the restaurant's back stage, but invites consumption of the slum's labour 'aura' (Benjamin 1992).

Thus, *chrónos* comes to the rescue of Mumbai's *digitopia* so as to insert an alternative, heritage time into tourist activities, which agrees with the experiential time of being 'elsewhere' (Kirschenblatt-Gimblett 1997; Jamal and Hill 2002:92). Digital and prospective terrestrial *flâneurs* traverse Mumbai's intimate surface, as this is shaped in biscuits, poppadoms and clothes and marketed to the globe. Slum crafts are often considered products of migrant mobilities that partake in mediated tourist consumptions (Tzanelli 2012b). Polanyi (1966) speaks of an 'art of knowing' we cannot capture without looking back to the milieus of tacit knowledge that produced such crafts, whereas Giddens' (1984) concept of 'knowledgeability' encapsulates the early phases of such artisanship. Incorporated into new knowledge economies (internet and tourism), Dharavi's living crafts become developmental tools in the hands of localities on the one hand, and synaesthetic tools for global tourists on the other. With a steady rise on ecological and cultural tourism, global demand for 'authentic' artefacts extends to the consumption of the locality, as well as its artisanal rituals and microcosms. This prompts a chain effect, whereby local cultures seek to insert their culture and its products into global markets (e.g. Robertson 1992, 1995) – a process inducing multi-directional flows of labour, image, craft and ritual performances for tourists (Little 2000; Moore 2004:81–3).

These flows are better organised in websites advertising relevant tourism. Not only do such sites disseminate representations of locality, they might allow local artisans (if involved) to rework the slum's cosmological representations (Nash 1993; Steiner 1994; Marcus and Myers 1995; Phillips and Steiner 1999; Herzfeld 2001:104–9, 2004). We must assess Reality Tours manipulations in this virtual contingent, which is managed by various international and local agents. Digital and terrestrial offers of a piece of this market paradise extend to spectatorships of Kamathipura, the true equivalent of SM's Pilla Street, apparently talked about only 'in hushed tones' – even though 'it has been the subject of countless films, literary projects and art pieces' (Reality Tours 'Long Tour', undated). The shame of flesh-trading becomes integrated into Mumbai's spectacular Arcades of the cinema and the fast mobilities of the internet (Patke 2000; Benjamin 2002; Gilloch 2007). The strategy consolidates the proverbial Eurasian node of commerce we encountered in Scherzinger/ Rahman's 'Jai Ho!' video clip. As Virilio explained, the 'nodal' has succeeded the 'central' in electronic environments of 'tele-localization', enhancing a 'techno-centric' logic that eradicates secular oppositions of city, country and the state: we are a global village (Virilio 2010).

Unlike Virilio's anti-humanist stance, I recognise the power of human agency in networks that develops over time. Though for example there are offers by the company of 'Sightseeing by Car' that match the internet surfer's distant engagement with other cultures (Page 1991; Turner 1993:154) and reproduce Baudrillard's (1988) driver and Eco's (1987) consumer archetypes, who enjoy landscape through their windscreen, or dispose of certain elements of it such as humans 'in much the same way as any other consumer object' (Bennett 2005:38), some tourists opt for on-foot pilgrimages. And pilgrimages they are – not only because the visitor is positioned as an affective subject communing in Dharavi's humble foodstuff or traversing its markets and temples, but also because (s)he has to confront their plural realities with little mediation. Just like exploring and donating to Dharavi's recycling project, opting for a 'Bicycle Tour' is advertised as an eco-friendly option, allowing pilgrims to enjoy 'the cool weather of the early morning', while watching 'some devotees performing puja…jog or do yoga before the heat of the day arrives' (Reality Tours, Bicycle Tour, undated). Situated between a feminist 'life politics' that shapes Western leisure consumption (Rojek 2010; Fullagar 2012:101) and sympathetic pilgrimage (Singh 2012), the tour promotes well-being as complementary edu-tourist activity. The tour's promise of a multi-sensory experience incorporates VT (CTS) Station both as site of the November 2008 'terrorist attacks' and a filmed SM site. It thus suggests that Mumbai can make allowances for civilised vagabondage – that *flânerie* can demonstrate urban civility in terrorism's stead. The logic of civilised terror permeates most tours, with terrible or demonstrative (as cinematic spectacles) stops and sites, including the *dabbawallah* operation (akin to cinematic Jamal's chai delivery), the *dhobiwallahs* or sheet washer-men in outdoor laundries, or the workers at the Red Lights District. Such stops blend into other spectacles such as the flower markets catering for worship practices. Terror and pilgrimage occupy the same imagined space in the journey – or as Wood (1986) explains, the stranger becomes constitutive of social 'monstering', at once an object of fear, revulsion (as in monsters) and fascination (Latin *monstrare*=to show). Cycling becomes an accessory of the spectacular city even in spaces once ruined by 'strangers', imagined or real ethnic others. The website's spectacular text leaves nothing at the marginalia, but encloses heritage temples and humble residences to produce a node of business, traffic, new pilgrimage, terror, capital and media (Lash and Urry 1994; Castells 1996; Harvey 1999:83–4; Urry 2007:212; Tzanelli 2013a:63).

These multisensory journeys also have their limitations: as already mentioned, to combat accusations of voyeurism, Reality Tours does not allow cameras – a practice vociferously endorsed by residents (Forster, April 2009; Howard, 21 March 2010; Swanson, 16 May 2011). The website also advertises a 'clear tips policy', stating that there is no such obligation, but those who want to tip 'can discreetly put an amount (we suggest that 10% of tour cost is a generous amount) in an envelope at the end of the tour' (Reality Tours, 'Why reality?', undated). The note marks a digital transposition of old civility norms that fed into stereotyping of the 'Orient' and its peoples as treacherous and unreliable in any negotiations (Said 1978). As White (1978) explains, the expansion of knowledge into those parts of the world traditionally regarded as places of savagery for the European imagination, led to a progressive de-spatialisation of the concept of wilderness, with a compensatory process of physical deterioration. Yet, *phýsis* (human nature) and native culture continued to be conflated in the minds of Western travellers, who saw in indigenous haggling or asking for tips a sign of moral degeneracy (Goldberg 1993; Stoler 1995; Stone 2004). The 'no tips' policy ensures Western travellers that business is professionally conducted by native guides ('all from humble backgrounds and...keen and fun to interact with'), while also eliminating any moral discomfort concerning monetary reciprocity.

Honesty and reliability aside, visitors also have to do their part. A pep talk reflecting other e-rules is reportedly given to tourists that 'under no circumstances [should they] show any form of disgust at what [they] might encounter, not to flinch from being touched, and at no time should [they] cover [their] mouths or noses' (Forster, April 2009). Even the Reality Tours website appropriates these dominant discursive forms of propriety (what tourists can or cannot do) that circulate within the community, and turns them into a cinematic-like *testimonio* of the slum, which may involve editing oral accounts and calling into being voices living at the social margins (Beverley and Zimmerman 1990). The website's community *testimonio* beautifies tourist synaesthesia, by filtering all senses through a sanitised tourist gaze that is acceptable to slum-dwellers. Peculiarly then, the disenfranchised appear to dictate Reality Tours policy of sensory policing so as to change harmful images of the slum. Behind such e-*testimonios* hides some compromise, such as that found in the ubiquitous note on all tour's right sidebar on where and when visitors can reach 'clean toilets'. At the same time, touch-friendly policy suggests the community's sensitivity towards a different type of marginalisation within Indian culture: touchability translates into global recognition of slum-dwellers as non-*dalits*, hence whole worthy human beings. Touchability is also promoted through impeccable images of slum kids, whose hair is tied up in ribbons and well combed, and who attend NGO-sponsored or other schools outside the slum (Forster, April 2009). The suggestion that Western tourists should stop feeling 'self-conscious about paying to see poverty' because 'residents are far too busy to notice' (Howard, 21 March 2010) can be as offensive as avoiding contact with them.

Reality Tours charitable involvement shows that any cultural adaptation can be cloned in community enterprise – an observation highlighting how even institutional indifference can generate its own micro-bioethics. Highlighting the status one occupies in the global socio-cultural field has been *sine qua non* in first-line legal defence of indigenous rights and status. As Moreton-Robinson (2006:386) explains, status partook in the development of global variations of inequality through the institutionalisation of 'biopower' Foucault 1997, 2003). If the nation state and its regional authorities calibrate modes of governmentality relying on individual responsibility, communities can also implement it on the tourist gaze. Foucault's governmentality defines the ways humans are turned by state apparatuses into miniatures of economic self-regulation *in toto* (Burchell 1993:275–6; Rose 1989, 1998:135; Lemke 2001:198; Tzanelli 2011:ch.5). But slum performances of this plausible Western *homo economicus* – the 'entrepreneur of himself [*sic*], being for himself [*sic*] his own capital, being for himself his [sic] own producer [...] the source of his [sic] earnings' (Foucault 2007:226) – can also de-individualise this process and transform it into a *collective ethos*. The power of governmobility rests on such interpellating movement (Jensen 2013).

There are other consequences of this marketing of *dispositif* evident in the displacement of sustainable tourist development to global consumers. Strategic marketing suggests to Mumbai's slum tourists that they too have a role to play: to embody what Illouz (2008:95) sees in the *homo communicans*, the subject that 'reflexively monitors his words and emotions, controls his self-image and pays tribute to the other's point of view'. The strategy preys on older debates concerning genre and verisimilitude in Indian cinema, which regarded Western dispositions as 'cold' and disengaged from community values (Thomas 1985:126). As a sort of digital *carnivalesque*, this strategic game makes emotional capitalism work better than any self-betterment incentive in tourist mobilities (Bauman 1992b:167; Elliott 2004:109; Tester 2004:176). Cloning took place in indirect ways from the outset between Reality Tours/Gives donation invitations and slum communities, which prompted business to reciprocate for using their facilities and sites as cultural capital. Reality Tours Paypal donation option seals a happy marriage between 'cold media' (McLuhan 1962), which favour participation to causes from afar, and 'cold intimacy', which favours distant emotional engagement (Illouz 2007; Bauman 2009:17).

Such technologies have a new improved equivalent in Dharavi via its 'hot' media sites. Quinn's (2007) suggestion that localities are always implicated in complex encounters and negotiations with their guests matches concept of the 'mutual gaze'. As Maoz explains, the local gaze 'is based on a more complex, two-sided picture, where both the tourist and local gazes exist, affecting and feeding each other' (Maoz 2006:222). Her ethnographic work in India also revealed that localities perceive tourists as being hedonistic, shallow, rude and 'badly educated and easily deceived' (ibid. 225) – a viewpoint occasionally cropping up in international press commentary by educated slum-dwellers. But the twin response to gazing as submission or internalisation and resistance or rejection might also unveil the workings of 'staged authenticity' online (MacCannell 1973). What is wilfully perceived as reciprocity and hospitality is in fact a form of veiled resistance, a resentful gaze back at the source of tourist gazing, which can only be represented as embodied labour or embodied performativity. As Herzfeld notes, 'the increasing inferiority of the non-reciprocating guest reaches its extreme in the selfish and insensitive tourist, who finds that "the natives are friendly" but fails to understand that this friendliness masks an enduring contempt' (Herzfeld 1992:61; Tzanelli 2010a:116; Urry and Larsen 2011:204–5). Such masterful concealment of what can prove rather damaging for one's self-image and business, shows how online projections of 'cultural intimacy' (Herzfeld 2005) would rather preclude open affective intimations – these are better left to the hosts (Tzanelli 2008a). Spectacularly staged by third parties committed to delivering honest and sustainable services to global visitors, alternative simulacrums of sociality may also be re-appropriated by local interest groups geared towards activism or sustainable development (see Shah 2013 on emulations of upper class habitus by the dispossessed). Though not truly drawing on SM's archplot, this strategy reinstates a disenfranchised *dispositif*, on which SM's cinematic and musical scripts were based.

Junktivism: Looking backwards to a (tourist) future

Reality Gives' website extends a global invitation to tourist visitors and web-surfers to 'help out' with projects including support for disabled children, new mothers and community job seekers. Appealing to the modern ethos of middle-class tourists – aesthetically reflexive agents who 'know' how to consume the right 'signs' (Giddens 1994; Beck 2002a; Lury 2004:38; Howland 2008:84–6) – the website suggests a variety of ways to 'volunteer from home', by making a website for Bombay underground or writing blog posts to outline their tour's experience (Reality Gives undated). Incentivising visitors to join the venture, the organisers ask for a full curriculum vitae and details of the envisaged support. Just as Reality Tours control of any slum-related merchandise (T-shirts, tote bags and even photographs and postcards), Reality Gives' invitation to philanthropy is thoroughly professionalised.

The recycling project, which is repeatedly mentioned on the main website's tour options, is less prominent on its sister charity's website. Generally, the NGO's contribution on recycling is not as strong as that of other initiatives such as *Dharavi Diary*. This project's website is fashioned as an initiative backed by intellectually accomplished individuals and international creative producers. A full presentation of the project's team reveals the participation of an Indian film-maker (Nawneet Ranjan); a San Francisco-educated programme advisor who starred in renowned Western films (Diane Baker); a UNICEF and UNESCO-involved strategist combining activism, technology and culture (Lina Srivastava); a product designer with an MBA (Malavika Tewari); a Boston-based editor known for his award-winning documentaries, including *Dharavi Diary* (Michael G. McCarthy); a Mumbaikar photographer (Vidu Chandan); a Mumbaikar cinematographer (Jai Singh); a San Francisco-educated music composer and editor (Grace Tsai); an interactive app designer and film-maker based in San Francisco (Romy Randev); and two game designers (Purnima Iyer and Deepti Raavi) (Dharavi Diary, undated). *Dharavi Diary* advertises itself online as a platform for a slum innovation project that backs a 'Recycling Design Workshop' in Dharavi 'to empower people to enhance their skills and monetize their creativity'. Connected to Dharavi's recycling project, it stresses the slum-dwellers' innovation as a survival skill, promising to awaken their dormant entrepreneurial vein by interactive means. Just like Reality Tours and SM, its team interpellates two versions of the *tornadóros*: as a more affluent post-modern digital artist and cinematographer and as a primordial working-class scavenger of technological ruins. A serendipitous venture, *Dharavi Diary* started with a short documentary film following the lives of people from Dharavi. Its cinematic style borrows from thanatourist and dark tourist tropes, as the site's discourse reveals:

> Let us set the scene. Dharavi is Asia's largest slum with over one million people packed into a maze of impenetrable dark alleys and corrugated shacks. All along the squalid streets, hundreds of barefoot street children, scurry back and forth, hauling bundles of recycling waste. From every alley comes the sound of hammering, drilling and soldering. In every shack, dark figures sit waist-deep in piles of car batteries, computer parts, fluorescent lights, ballpoint pens, plastic bags, paper and cardboard boxes, wire hangers, and other leftovers from our ever growing consumer culture.... But right now a powerful minority control the entrepreneurial opportunities in the slum and exploit cheap labour. Everyday the workers risk their lives recycling the city's waste, working in the cramped factories sorting through the syringes and smelting the hazardous waste. The short film followed a community of these sorters. It was a huge success, screening to audiences around the world at international film festivals.... We invite you to re-imagine the slum; re-imagine the chaos as dynamism and the disorderly layout as organic; re-imagine the ramshackle construction as innovative design and the lawlessness as cooperativeness without formal policing; and re-imagine the desperation of slum dwellers as drive and enthusiasm to make a better life for themselves.
>
> (Dharavi Diary, undated)

Accompanied by a two-minute video clip observing a volunteer sewing with natives, its visual discourse blends the genres of travel autobiography and urban biography (Desforges 2000; Tzanelli 2012a). Reminding us that the tourist gaze may borrow from older systems of nostalgia, the website's discourse veers between anomic *flânerie's* creative destruction and an ordered, mechanical gaze (Squire 1994:6; Crang 1997:148; Crang 1999:238; Coleman and Crang 2002). Just like Boyle's art-work, the *Dharavi Diary* relocates the spectacle within the city of ruin, prompting us to transcend divisions between craft (the flesh and steel of industrial society) and art (the space of mind and imagination) in a techno-romantic fashion (Coyne 1999; Tzanelli 2011). Devoid of conspicuous music, the visual materials fixate the gaze upon labour tasks performed by women as global mobility goods. From such visual narratives Mumbai emerges as a spectacular node of new heritage hubs, which 'emanate' from industrialisation and the industriousness of the disenfranchised, when in fact such performances are staged cultural capital. There are many ways to stage authenticity as MacCannell (1989) has explained, and quite a few of them might involve simulatory co-production of hosts and guests. This effect can be achieved by mobilising technological tools and their users as both gazed objects and actors-actants. We are back to the twin conceptualisation of *techno-poesis* as filiative (by organic communities) and affiliative (by transnational artists and digital designers) networks. According to Florida (2003), many cities have become 'creative' not only in the sense that they host arts and cultural events, but that they attract high-tech business. But today, though increasingly segregated from Mumbai's privileged spaces, such highly active areas enclose their own idea of 'creative commons' that is progressively digitised and globally disseminated.

Here virtual touring and its constructed global *flânerie* replace the heritage of poverty with new mobile legacies of slum gazing and consuming. The city's privileged 'gated commons' lose over its underprivileged 'open commons', suggesting that spatial subjectivities are not fixed, and that the terror of poverty has very high cultural capital in global markets, including that of tourism (De Kadt 1979; Britton 1989; Britton 1991; Bouhalis 2003; Jeffrey et al. 2012). For these marginalised communities culture has to acquire digitised formats that might initially (before the tourist's visit) or permanently (for non-travelling *flâneurs*) replace traditional patterns of exchange and host-guest interaction (Rantanen 2005:8; Ritzer 2011). Both Juhu's and Dharavi's websites suggest to digital visitors travels in space and time, with detailed excursus on the localities' pasts and activities situated in their turbulent present. Through such complex virtual and terrestrial interactions, initially manufactured and promoted as types of difference or *dispositif* by global capitalist agents (of e-tourism), localities may arrive at new micro-regional cultural assemblages and self-narrations no corporate agent could anticipate (Tomlinson 1999:9; Nederveen Pieterse 2004:65; Wise 2008:19; Castells and Miller 2009:57). Culture does not figure as transformative *praxis* only from the standpoint of artistic leaders, it is also an unending structural activity undertaken by any human being, a globally shared mode of being-in-the-world (Lukács 1968; Beilharz 2002:148; Tzanelli 2008a; Tzanelli 2010b:145–6). Unlike the musings of SM, it is impossible to separate in this context art's contribution to 'identity politics' and the articulation or reframing and challenging unequal regional, class or ethnic relations (Salazar 2007; Vannini et al. 2009:462). Such complex virtual-terrestrial connectivities are practically and normatively established to facilitate the integration of individual and collective actions into the way that 'institutions [should] actually work' (Tomlinson 1999:27).

A detailed analysis of Dharavi's virtual site could be the focus of a different study. Suffice it to conclude with some reflections on the national significance of the slum's recycling project as this appears in the international press. Dharavi's project is illustrative of 'contested urbanism' (Boano et al. 2013), a situation whereby the urban realm turns into a battleground between top-down and bottom-up forces that exercise spatial, political and social resistance. Dharavi's eco-political insertion into such battles is broadcast in so many conflicting ways, that what emerges amounts to Ryan and Kellner's (1990) exposition of the plurality of cinematic plots – if not, more specifically, to SM's take on fragmented nation-building. The fact that India is yet to formalise waste collection in its municipalities certainly adds fuel to the journalists' fire. Akin to America's scroungers (Ferrell 2005), Mumbai's so-called 'ragpickers' fill an essential ecological gap in urban consumerist cultures at grassroots level, setting an example for other cities to follow. For example, similar initiatives emerged in India's eastern city of Chennai (Madras), where Paperman, a non-governmental organisation, looks to 'Mumbai's 13th Compound' (i.e. Dharavi's recycling project) for inspiration (Moore, 23 August 2013). The city's electronic waste (e-waste) is reportedly making its way through a disorganised system of *kabadiwallahs* to piles in Deonar landfill, with serious environmental implications. Toxic lead, cadmium and other retardants slowly release toxins to the groundwater, or, when incinerated, into air.

A great deal of this refuse is generated by the material base of virtual mobilities consumed by more affluent populations. Urry reminds us that a distinct feature of our 'weightless', virtual world is that digital connections are enabled by materialities: 'computer products made of metals, especially aluminium, plastics, rare earth metals, wiring, cables, glass and so on' (Urry 2014:128). But as much as these materialities enable global virtual traffic, they also generate massive amounts of waste necessitating organised policy-making on refuse. In 2011 the Ministry of Environment and Forests introduced a series of E-waste Management and Handling Rules that placed the disposal burden solely on producers and consumers, making the function of *kabadiwallahs* within and without Dharavi a necessity (Lobo, 11 August 2013). Whereas Mumbai in particular has 17 dismantlers/recyclers listed on the Maharashtra Pollution Control Board (MPCB) site, the actual collection and disposal/dismantling is left to scavengers and ecologically aware companies such as the Sony-founded Ecoreco. Lack of national surveys on e-waste and general waste, and no real enforcement of e-rules, explains why the '13th Compound' thrives locally and is dignified in the national and international press. This valorisation, which hides corruption under local solidarity, invites sociologists to question how its strata or temporal, social and spatial layers came together in a single social script or *graftó* (from *grafi*, writing).

A stratigraphy of corruption

The materiality of virtual connectivity encroaches on Mumbai's sustainable futures in indirect ways: on the one hand, it generates jobs for the slum precariat as e-waste pickers; on the other, it enables the expansion of new estate markets that thrive on offshoring professionals, slum eviction, gentrification and social exclusion. The UN estimates suggest that the population of Mumbai will double over the next decade. As Dharavi's land represents approximately $10 billion in dead capital, the state has been coaxing slum-dwellers to bulldoze its tenements and provide flats of 225 sq. ft. to its evicted families in compensation (The Economist, 19 December 2007). After several delays, Maharashtra Chief Minister Prithviraj Chavan gave an in-principle approval to a proposed plan to redevelop the 151-hectare slum colony into a planned modern township. 'We have been directed by the government that the project should be launched before the code of conduct for the next parliamentary elections come into force', reveals a senior government official working on the project (Suryawanshi, 11 August 2013). To tackle the issue of size, the authorities subdivided 4 sectors into 13 sub-zones, and in the spirit of privatisation, handed over the project to successful bidders such as Ernst & Young that act as management consultants in sectors 1 to 4 (Ruparel, 10 August 2013).

Dharavi Redevelopment Authority (DRA) received several objections and applications by local business to 'self-develop' (Ashar, 8 August 2013). The fear of permanent eviction from a site residents have been calling 'home' with relocations into one of the tall buildings in the area but far away from their community, appears to resuscitate customary memory over official development on the one hand, and the pronouncement of individual interests over those of the city's or the community's sustainable futures on the other. Unlike China's economic growth, India's boom did not promote formal sector employment, leaving many in poorly paid contractual wage labour. Whilst public concern over poor people's vulnerability was expressed through nation-wide schemes framed in the language of rights (Right to Food, Information, Work), a parallel discourse concerning 'the threat of dissent from *les classes dangereuses*' was disseminated by the 2005 liberalising National Rural Employment Guarantee Act (NREGA) (Corbridge and Shah 2013:337).

Since Nehru's dams and hydroelectric projects did not deliver formal sector jobs, and neither did land reform sufficiently unlock the productivity of agriculture to stimulate economic development in rural and urban areas, slums turned from a temporary migration stop into a permanent residence for the disenfranchised. The downward spiral produced extremist political formations such as the Maoist-inspired Naxalite movement in Jhakhand, which continues to feed into an underground guerrilla warfare geared towards economic redistribution and a classless India. Despite the party's public denouncement by the government as one of the country's security challenges, the Maoist struggle to create new social relations seems to appeal to the masses that have been uprooted from their former homes and ploughed into a precarious labour landscape. Dharavi seems to have embraced this Maoist project due to its promotion of ideals of kinship and community. As is the case in other regions, the Nehruvian heritage is echoed in divisions between regular salaried (*naukri*) and insecure contractual (*kam*) work, with each corresponding to ideas of honour (*ijjat*) and shame (Parry 2013). Associations of the informal, 'shameful', sector with Maoist principles reinvents caste segregation in terms of danger as pollution, turning slums such as Dharavi into new terror zones. It is as if Nehruvian socialism produced another *tórnos*, originally 'destined' to 'automatically and mechanically eliminate every social ill' (Gouldner 1948:399), but eventually producing its own ideological Nemesis.

The Naxalite promotion of relations of intimacy with the locals recreates an anti-Nehruvian utopian rurality based on pseudo-Ghandian distortions of deep ecology in the form of family bonds and affection and the sense of shared moral worth (see DaMatta 1991 on collective production of the corrupt 'person' and isolated 'individual'; Shah 2013 on the Naxalite spread in rural India; Tzanelli 2011:chs 1 and 5 on comparable historical cases in Europe).

Reproducing the contradictions within the development of the 'Kerala model' of communism, the Naxalite promise to resolve caste and labour inequalities in Mumbai's slums appeals to natural-like kinship bonds but views environmental struggles as bourgeois, brahmanic and patriarchal projects that consolidate social discrimination. At the same time, science and technology, which for mainstream communists are vehicles for self-reliance and popular participation at grassroots level, go against Naxalite collaboration with peasants and indigenous peoples that rely on untainted by industry environments for their livelihood. The genesis of 'ecological Marxism' in the 1970s and 1980s, as well as Prime Minister Indira Ghandi's decision to support Kerala's green movement and struggle to save the evergreen rainforest in the region ('Silent Valley'), further complicated things. The fledging environmental movement associated with it 'was regarded by many as an attempt by the industrialised West to invent new barriers to the development of poor nations' (Madhusoodanan 2003:43–4). Even though environmental politics are not identity politics, indigenous movements around the world might even connect to religious groups, as is the case in Kerala, the Mexican Zapatistas or Brazilians Kayapo (Tzanelli 2013a:172). The Naxalite post-independence manifesto is such an anti-colonial, anti-bourgeois concoction it could only survive by not openly opposing industrial polluting (hence the livelihood of the largely migrant slum-workers). But silent connections between its environmental components and deep ecological visions bring them closer to the rise of Hindu nationalist fundamentalism, whose eco-fascism (of the 'blood' and 'soil' heritage variety) produces 'enemies' out of all sorts of strangers (including Christians, Muslims and Westerners) (Madhusoodanan 2003:52–3).

In today's Dharavi such utopian resurrections have real consequences: customary discourse conforming to local Maoist-based (Communist Party of India) ideas of 'flourishing' before state intervention seems to regard sanitation, scarce water supply and local political corruption as necessary means to an end. As much as such realities are based on utopian rhetoric, they can be tied to dystopian futures, in which resource shortage and climate change support 'an increasing emphasis on local "warlords" and relatively weak national or global forms of governance' (Urry 2011:149). International journalists feel that they have to tip-toe in this minefield of lax morality by pronouncing Dharavi's *dispositif* as 'mostly friendly, almost invariable courteous', even if 'sometimes bitter or suspicious' of strangers (The Economist, 19 December 2007). Local suspicion reveals more strata, if we consider that in the 2012 municipal elections the Congress – in 2013 in power – lost six seats to Shiv Sena in Dharavi. This prompted the ruling party to speed up Dharavi's development into an urban paradise to recapture the lost ground. Sena spokespersons stress that the residents of the slum have not been taken into consideration before the implementation of the redevelopment scheme, adding that the government appropriates their proposals (Suryawanshi, 11 August 2013).

Placed within this war of political attrition and local activism, the e-tourist and e-activist websites of the previous section obtain an extra role as

164 *A plural slumdog* kósmos

international interest mediators. Unlike the case of other global cities such as Bangkok (Herzfeld 2006), Dharavi's anomaly has a beautifying role to play in regional monetary traffic (airport and hotel revenues) and capitalist networks (e-tourism and slum tourism). Its contingent connection to cinematic art (SM) did not, as intended by SM lead artists, configure symbolic resistance to market alienation; on the contrary, its artisan communities appear to be discursively co-opted into 'Shining India's' cosmetic venture to foster ethnic pride, assisting political factions in their populist projects (see for comparison Skoll and Korstanje 2014). Also, unlike other European instances of forced eviction from heritage sites (see Herzfeld 2009 on Coliseum's Monti), Mumbai's global image benefits from the presence of the hazardous '13th Compound' as ecotourist site to be sighted alongside or alternatively to the city's magnificent architecture (temples). Currently, Mumbai's official line adapts to other international imperatives, including sustainability with a sound ecological basis as well as facilitation of hypermodern infrastructures that connect Maharashtra's aeromobilities and Mumbai's twin train lines, without the presence of an outdated historical relic in-between (the slum).

Political ephemeralities aside, Dharavi's redevelopment harmonises with the aims of the Delhi-Mumbai Industrial Corridor (DMIC), a state-sponsored industrial development project coordinated by the government of India, which takes place mainly at the Eastern end of Maharashtra. Conceived of as a global manufacturing and trading node, the Corridor aims to develop an industrial zone spanning across six states in India and including industrial clusters and rail, road, port, air connectivity (see also Wikipedia, 'Delhi Mumbai Industrial Corridor Project', undated). The plan is to develop new industrial cities as 'smart cities' by promoting the convergence of next generation technologies across infrastructure sectors so as to develop DMIC as a 'Global Manufacturing and Trading Hub' (Delhi Mumbai Industrial Corridor, undated). Markedly, e-tourist and artistic activists, such as those of Reality Tours and Dharavi Diary are also facilitators of such blended business traffic: their novel responsible *ethos* highlights a paradigmatic shift towards articulating what local and regional authorities might pass in silence. Against Mumbai's spatial cleansing, their political convictions and professional imperatives ensure commitment to a particular type of conservation as propagated by Carey (1999). However, the gap between virtual privilege and slum poverty is too big to bridge just by well-meaning gestures. Media ecologies struggle to service human ecologies under the demands of cosmetic cosmopolitanisation (Beck 2002b; Nederveen Pieterse 2006), often consigning slum-dwellers to a state of natural exception, where only kinship bonds can help. In this equally suspect ecological network, Dharavi's slumdog *tornadóroi* appear to make *téchne* from the crumbling surface of the city's *pangosmiopoiesis* with the support of the only proximate socialities that they can trust 'at home'.

9 Slumdog economies of modernity

Tourist reality and ghosts of things past

The multiple and convoluted journeys of SM are interpretative ventures: they allow the sociologist to inspect ontological mirages that are digitally wired on big screens and computer monitors, and to produce knowledge based on perceptions of the social world (Dann 2002). One of the basic tenets of the present study concerns the ways individual and collectivised perception allows the observer – a tourist, a noetic traveller, and an experimental *synaesthete* – to produce realities, as well as how these realities affect fellow humans. Tourists are metaphors of society, exploring, understanding and enriching the world with their voracious need to apprehend phenomena.

Knowledge comes in different forms affecting productions of the self and society. SM's parable of modernity allowed whole communities to experience and reinterpret it for themselves and others. But where large communities are involved, serendipitous apprehensions of social reality collide with nationalist *Poltergeists*. Mirages always suggest that the essential components of collective biography or history, our knowledge of what we are, as well as the environment we inhabit, are malleable and exposed to external modification. The rescue mission is bound to have consequences: in liquid tourist environments, the spaces of spectacular modernity such as those of Mumbai tend to project ghosts of past sociality that express unresolved anxieties about potential loss of identity and continuity (Ivy 1995). Representative of India's fast-track modernisation, Mumbai's 'slum problem' also figures today as a neoliberal solution, an open tourist business invitation: preserve, conserve and sell. Perversely, the subjection of Mumbai's slums to spatial cleansing by government programmes has strengthened their global recognition as the core of Indian modernity to such an extent, that they are now 'mourned' and placed under emergency rescue programmes by outsiders, because they face institutional eradication within their national 'hearth' (Barreira 2011:154; de Sousa Santos 1999; Kothari 2002). The paradox of global modernisations is that, while pluralising knowledge, it pluralises the urgency to apprehend, resuscitate and protect the dying specimen of our proximate or distant neighbourhoods.

Although slum populations turn into ghostly apparitions allegedly enclosing pre-modern ideals of community and labour, they are living social formations with the capacity to renovate. As such, they present us with yet another 'crypto-colonial' case (Herzfeld 2002), an undefined cultural space produced through the history of the city's 'global iconicity' as a spectacular utopia (Franklin et al. 2000; Mazumdar 2007; Tzanelli 2010b:135). Herzfeld's 'crypto-colonialism' suggests the invisible colonisation of cultures by more powerful agents though discourses of abnormal or faulty development (Baptista 2012:133–6; Ferguson 2006). Such discourses, which are manifest in anthropology's institutional development in Europe and the West, were internalised by developing countries such as Thailand or Greece that escaped colonisation, but not criticism. Surely, the argument has applicability to regional and local development within other, formerly colonised (or not) nation-states. As local 'buffer zones' (Herzfeld 2002:900) enclosing both rural wilderness and danger, but also as and new techno-romantic hubs, Mumbai's slums are caught in such a developmental trap.

Therefore, the question we must answer is not if historicised Indian 'ghosts' exist – their absence would refute collective memory altogether – but who interpellates and institutes their kindness or malice, and to what ends. The nation-states that Urry (2014) elevates to a solution of offshoring crimes have been the primary ghost merchants of modernity before the neoliberal triumph of post-modern business. This dilemma of truly making democracy work in mobile times rests at the heart of the SM controversy – the film, its plural activist fields and tropes and the raging intellectual debate over the 'charitable' ethos of the film's lead artists. Charity and giving have depth in the SM context, pointing to juxtapositions of a cosmetic type of social amnesia in Indian officialdom vis-à-vis a marketable 'anamnestic solidarity' (Lenhardt 1975:136; Fussell 1975; Misztal 2003:45) with Mumbai's migrant labour forces expressed by contemporary mobile (tourist and media) networks through public engagement and support of the city's slum communities. Though the crux of post-Partition war and death does not describe Dharavi's contemporary labour mobilities accurately, it frames the trauma of multiple modernities in Eastern and Western social spheres (Bauman 1989). Any thanatourist sediment in SM and Mumbai's e-tourist agendas can be attributed to the globally shared cosmological resonance of such *Urtexts*; any reaction by localities and migrant *literati* retains thanatourist traces the very moment such groups seek to obliterate them. In this unfortunate war of conviction and attrition, anti-mobility defenders justify the validity of their discourse in two distinctive ways: either through their filiative connections to the Indian nation and its migrant histories, or through personal commitment to more 'authentic' philanthropic causes. Such political pronouncements are tourist modernity's *alter ego*, a voice steeped in guilt and anger for failing to supress its own desire for pleasure, glamorous authenticity and the right to a better life than that of its glorified ancestry (Marcuse 1955; Taylor 2001). In order to conclude SM's serendipitous journeys, I differentiate between the stance of NRI and national discourses on SM as a piece of utopian art and as activist lightning rod on the one hand,

and the actions of SM artists on the other. Both articulate a hermeneutics that Baumanesque pilgrims (migrants and 'tourists') use to discharge a debt produced by Indian-Western civilisational contacts.

NRI and national spirits/ghosts

There are no winners, losers or fair and unfair militants to highlight in the national terrain, but there are prominent 'discourses of the vanishing' (Ivy 1995) to dissect that point to rationalised state 'violence'. Even SM's plural community was not immune to those, as Amitabh Bachchan's angry blogging reveals. On 13 January 2009, he publicly expressed anger for the ways SM 'projects India as Third World dirty underbelly nation and causes pain and disgust among nationalists and patriots...let it be known that a dirty underbelly exists and thrives even in the most developed nations'. The fact that SM was 'authored by an Indian and conceived and cinematically put together by a Westerner' led to its 'creative Globe recognition', when national disgust goes unreported, he concludes (Bachchan – Day 265, 13 January 2009; BBC News, 16 January 2009). Bachchan later suggested that his wording was misconstrued and proceeded to apologise to Boyle for comments 'created by media' (Hindustan Times, 22 January 2009), but the very outburst interpellated his angry Bollywood persona. The Bahchan-*Karna* blogger of global migration routes came on a par with real slum labour and Dharavi as a site enclosing dangerous emotions such as resentment towards affluent, successful strangers.

Equally indicative have been accusations from the slum that the film peddles 'poverty porn' via images of misery and words such as 'slumdog' (M. Singh, 26 January 2009). Tapeshwar Vikshwakarma, a representative of slum-dwellers' welfare group, filed a defamation lawsuit against Rahman and Anil Kapoor because SM allegedly violated the slum-dwellers' human rights (AFP Google News, 22 January 2009). A separate protest organised by Nicholas Almeida, a social activist working in Mumbai, involved protesting slum-dwellers fronted by children. The widely photographed children held up signs with the phrase 'I am not a dog. I am the future of India' (Kinetz, 22 January 2009). The Hindu organisation Janajagruti Samiti and Shiv Sena also protested against the film's portrayal of the Hindu god Rama, arguing that it hurt the sentiments of Hindus (The Times of India, 22 January 2009) and Kanchan Gupta wrote in the conservative *Daily Pioneer* that SM depicts Hindus as 'rapacious monsters' (25 January 2009). The article, which circulated widely on various online channels, attacked Boyle for making a film 'structured...within the matrix of Western lib-left perceptions of the Indian "reality"' which have little or nothing in common with the real India in which we live' (ibid.).

Hindu protests were obviously geared towards defending the religion's ethno-national purity, thus disregarding the violent basis of national memory-work (Adorno 1986; Huyssen 1995, 2000). Like Europe's Holocaust, religious massacres in Asian nation-states comprise modernity traumas constantly manipulated in different factional scenarios (Bauman 1989; Wolin 1989;

Habermas 1997; Klein 2000:140; Edmunds and Turner 2002). SM's Hindu-Muslim riots refer to a page in twenty-century Indian history that underwent excessive manipulation in official historical accounts, where 'violence in itself is never described' (Guichard 2013:68). The 'selective amnesia' of textbook Indian self-narration and European 'solitary amnesias' in community-building flashpoint events critique the political uses of the past (Tzanelli 2007, 2011; Waddington 2010). An overwhelmingly Marxist reading of Hindu and Muslim groups as heterogeneous but consubstantial of a nation, polarised intellectual and political discourse. This was aggravated by the monomyth of a 'Indian nation' dominated by communal conflict and the end of the Hindu Golden Age by Arab invasions, and Muslim and British domination. Gandhi's message of brotherhood and togetherness replicated nationalist strategies of silencing violence in context, including Muslim ransacking of Hindu temples or forced conversions that mirrored relevant Hindu practices (Bhattacharya 2008).

But the emphasis on a word (slumdog) reveals that Indian memory-work is not solely anchored on religious divides. Middle-class protesters and students from Dharavi were offended by uses of the word 'slum' (Echavone and Srivastava, 21 February 2009), whereas the masses of poor families focused on the suffix 'dog'. Such preferential fixation is more attuned to new divides based on class and status and not religion. Not only does being a dog from the slums designate you as a stranger, it shunts you into a space publicly perceived as 'dirty'. As spaces still evading 'proper' surveillance, Dharavi's neighbourhoods have become unenclosed and 'dangerous' sites evoking and inviting pleasure for tourist visitors (Chakrabarty 1991). Yet, largely unacknowledged in global tourist advertising, Dharavi also functions as the unofficial part of what Johnson (1995:63) debates (in the case of Indian temples) as materialised 'circuits of memory', spaces of national memory-work (Edensor 1998:35–40). In a polyphonic society in which religious etiquette informs custom and everyday practice, to be a 'dog' is to be excluded from the national community. Whereas cows are protected and publicly venerated in a society hegemonised by Hindu tradition, dogs are non-domesticated animals nobody cares to display as human friends or 'brothers' (Lévi-Strauss 1964). Respect for dogs in some Islamic religious sects does little to alleviate the slur: Asia is not dog-friendly, with stray canines seen as potentially dangerous (rabid). The public display of Dharavi children in anti-SM protests in global press photography aimed to dispel such harmful 'accusations' of 'outsidedness'. Well-dressed children in front of the lens juxtaposed Dharavi's grim labour past to its bright futural function. This was achieved by stressing those communities' attachment to institutions entertaining universal recognition: the family and the media.

Anger was turned against Western actants in a loose network of (media in our case) nodes fostering shifting (technological) synergies (Hardt and Negri 2000; Castells 2009) instead of a problematic state bureaucracy. Although artists, including film directors, openly involved in developmental projects, demonstrate an understanding of their self-identity and social positionality in development contexts, there is a significant difference between 'development tourism' and 'developmental tourists' (Salazar 2004). As outsiders in the national territories they enter to do work; such artists conform to multiple definitions of 'anomie' by sociologists of crime (Merton 1938b), creative labour (Hesmondhalgh and Baker 2010) and tourism (Dann 1977). Working from translation studies, Cronin points out that the vocabulary of 'fidelity' and 'infidelity' strongly connects to notions of 'licit fixity and illicit movement', just as cheap consumption replicas (e.g. 'McDonaldization of society' (Ritzer 2010)) project the fear of an uncontrolled dissemination of the 'Double'. Appropriating and broadcasting intimate national stories earns transnational artists the badge of the traitor or intruder. Cinematic artists are socially privileged 'wallahs' in a position to both 'terrorise' and 'civilise' through global disseminations of utopian projects.

The assumption that SM is rejected by Indian artists, because outsiders should never make a film about slum-dwellers, was conditioned by the respondents' socio-cultural profile. Alternatively, positive statements were often mediated by SM artists. Beaufoy claimed that Indian film directors such as Shekhar Kapur and Mira Nair were very warm and generous, because the film 'pushed Indian cinema on a notch' (Rose, 13 February 2009). According to other discussants, positionality was conditioned by class, rather than status. This argument was made by Priya Joshi, a professor at Temple University, who saw in Indian middle and upper classes a tendency to identify with sophisticated, global elites, even when they might have been shocked by SM's depictions of poverty. The reference to class taste should be considered applicable to a broader field of consumer preference, binding the fear of immobility at home (job losses) and abroad (unaffordable tourist trips to exotic slum places). For Joshi, the movie also resonates with American audiences, who feel trapped by the global recession and look to feel-good stories for alleviation of their vulnerability (Kischer, 18 February 2009). Still, the controversy over the uses of the word 'slumdog' and the script's approval by the Indian Film Board (IFB) must be treated as a different question. The Board found unacceptable the presence of a police inspector torturing the hero, but added that 'anyone below the level of inspector is fine'. Beaufoy concludes: 'You simply can't go there with Amnesty International-style preconceptions' (Rose 13 February 2009). Given the IFB's communication with tourism policy, the corrective suggests more than intervention in the production of a movie. Perceived as a potential stigma on the country's policing authorities in the context of an international outcry against high levels of corruption in them, SM's plot had to reproduce the domestic political fable of good Indian synchronisation with Western civility codes.

Equally revealing has been the stance of NRI and Indian scholars and literati. Shyamal Sengupta, professor of film at Whistling Woods International Institute in Mumbai labelled SM 'poverty porn' and a 'white man's imagined India', whereas Vikram Doctor, India's *Economic Times* columnist and Aseem Chhabra, Asia Foundation Fellow, stressed SM's appeal to Western spectators (Magnier, 24 January 2009). Suzanna Arundhati Roy, Indian author and political activist best known for winning the 1998 Man Booker Prize for Fiction and her involvement in environmental and human rights causes, has been pretty vociferous about her objections. Her fear that political factions, including the Congress Party, would attempt to take credit for the Oscar-winning film were followed by the ironic commentary that 'theres [sic] a lot of money in poverty.... Politically, the film de-contextualises [Indian] poverty... making...it a landscape.... Cast[ing] an Indian model and a British boy...was like watching black kids in a Chicago slum speaking in Yale accents' (Roy, 2 March 2009). Amongst Roy's previous political causes has been an attack upon the government for armed actions against the Naxalite-Maoist insurgents in India. Controversially, she called the Naxalites 'Ghandians', who fight for emancipation, and cast the then governmental actions as a 'war on the poorest people in the country' (LBN India, 21 October 2009). Roy's political sympathies were never Naxalite, but just like M.I.A.'s actions, her activism earned her the terrorist label. In line with Eagleton's attack on Spivak's alleged 'US market philosophy' (Eagleton 1999:3–4), Roy exposes SM artists as neo-colonial exploiters. It is not entirely clear from her discourse whether the attack is launched on the basis of the film's verisimilitude, or the selection of actors on commercial or crypto-racist criteria. But her discourse of accountability predicated on a medley of imperialist history and post-modern capitalist imperatives is evident (Landry and MacLean 1996). The discourse differs little from claims by Associate Professor in Politics and Public Administration at Ryerson University, Mitu Sengupta, over SM's 'inauthentic' representation of slum children. His analysis stressed the presence of 'strong collaborative networks' in Dharavi, while also emphasising the slum-dwellers' 'lives of value and dignity', and 'a resourcefulness that stretches far beyond the haphazard, individualist survival-of-the-fittest sort shown in Slumdog' (Sengupta, 20 February 2009). Just like Reality Tours' *digitopia*, his discourse calls for a return to fundamental ideals, such as those of community and labour, even if those currently support the basic strata of Mumbai's slum 'corruption'.

A widely debated NRI critique was delivered as a lecture from Mumbai-born and UK-resident author of *The Satanic Verses*, Salman Rushdie, in his capacity as Distinguished Writer in Residence at Emmory University in 2009 (Winn, 23 February 2009). Though generally exploring the state of cinematic adaptation in the West, the lecture focuses on 'replicative consumption' – a phenomenon, according to Rushdie, defined by 'an insatiable process which can sometimes seem voracious, world-swallowing, as if we now live in a culture that endlessly cannibalises itself, so that, eventually, it will have eaten itself up completely' (Rushdie, undated). The 'clonial' accusation seems to echo Jamal's indecorous introduction to Mumbai's McWorld. Placing himself in a non-Indian ecumene ('we now live...'), Rushdie takes us for a fast-track ride to what he categorises as 'good' and 'bad' adaptations. For him, at the heart of the subject of adaptation is the question of essence, as if the text does not represent but calls things into being. He broadly defines adaptation so as 'to include translation, migration and metamorphosis, all the means by which one thing becomes another' (ibid.). Although he later refutes that he debates the film's verisimilitude with regards to the novel or 'real' slum life, his curious reference to 'western movies about India...about blonde women arriving there to find, almost at once, a maharajah to fall in love with' or 'about European women accusing non-maharajah Indians of rape, perhaps because they were so indignant at having being approached by a non-maharajah' are indicative of his intentionality (ibid.). Rushdie's claim compares with academic research on slum and sex tourism, indicating almost unidirectional flows from poor to affluent countries (Tzanelli 2013b:ch.4). Desire is feminised, racialised and denigrated in his discourse, only in reverse: Westerners are rotten fruit. 'Now that sort of exoticism has lost its appeal; people want, instead, enough grit and violence to convince themselves that what they are seeing is authentic; but it's still tourism. If the earlier films were raj tourism, maharajah-tourism, then we, today, have slum tourism instead' (ibid.). His accusation of 'first world director' Boyle's exoticisation of 'the third world', appeals to a civilisational debt that double post-colonial standards obscure. More correctly, Boyle's appeal to the immanent, original traveller of Indian history – what corresponds to Seaton's model of 'metensomatosis' but with psychic-intellectual extensions – is critiqued as faulty, commercialised version of travel to the 'other's' past – a *vade-mecum* text inventing the external world (Seaton 2002:148).

To consolidate this claim, Rushdie resorts to cinematic *belles-lettres* texts producing worthier mindsets to apprehend the world: the names of Bergman, Fellini and Buñuel are dropped in, alongside those of Peter Jackson as 'a better writer than J.R.R. Tolkien' – all of them are associated with the European artistic traditions of 'dark realism and historically embedded discourse and allegory'. Unable to digest cinematic reproduction, Rushdie eventually confesses a preference for theatre, which is 'so present, the play's being right there in front of you makes it such an insistently declaratory form...and what is true of the theatre in general is doubly true of epic theatre' (ibid.). His Brechtian takes on art appeal to socialist montage, swinging between abstraction and specificity, theory and empiry, but with empirical reality more prominent than its theoretical underpinnings (Brecht 1964 [1936]; Tzanelli 2011:139). For him, adaptation is a metaphor 'as a carrying across, which is the literal meaning of the word...and of the related word "translation", another form of carrying across' (Winn, 23 February 2009). Just like texts, whole communities or nations must find ways to adapt, identifying 'the things we cannot ever give up unless we wish to cease to be ourselves' (ibid.). Rushdie's shift from cinematic technology's epistemic foundations to ontological processes of identity-building replicates a realist fallacy under attack in philosophical circles (Bhaskar 1989). As a Mubaikar migrant, Rushdie seems to interrogate two different things at the same time – cognitive processes in artistic innovation and the essence of transnational self-narration. He evidently feels that SM fails to translate across cultures the problems of the Indian margins. His concluding observations are marked by yet another shift towards the Indian nation that 'has lived through an era of bad social adaptations, of appeasements and surrenders on the one hand, of arrogant excesses and coercions on the other' (Rushdie undated).

And so, we return to the endless search for differentiating *fons* from *fundus*, which can sustain a healthy polity in 'fast', globalising times (Julien 2008:213). Rushdie's support of utopian communitarianism is not 'conservative' in narrow political terms, but is certainly nostalgic. Perhaps critics of his analysis, such as Parthasarathy (2009:1), who sees such literati as 'smallholders of cultural capital' or 'doxosophers', articulate some truths, given Rushdie's alignment with high artistic registers and his consideration of 'bad' tourist film-making along these lines (Urry 1995:134–5). Yet, when Parthasarathy proceeds to outline how Western and Eastern value systems mirror each other, and how Jamal's display of 'knowledgeability', which secures his status and class mobility, reflects real social changes in India, he does not avoid the techno-romantic trap altogether. The desire expressed within the film world 'to move beyond the working class and lower sectors of society' was also propagated by Tejaswini Ganti, an anthropologist and Bollywood expert at New York State University (Magnier, 24 January 2009). By pronouncing their support of such cosmopolitanising processes (Beck 2002b), these analysts try to erase old *tornadóroi's* phantoms, but not without consequences – for, in their place, some new hauntologies emerge to interrogate post-modern 'alienation'.

A hole in our phantasmagoric wall: celebrity giving

The coming of the digital age has not taken away the gleam of nostalgia from new artistic projects. Most of these 'projects' or 'programmes' embed emotional-ideational fixities in new technocratic and *technopoetic* mobilities, producing an amalgam of old and new realities. Despite the good intentions of their makers, some of these projects resuscitate old paradigms and lifeworlds in Frankenstein forms. In 2000 the government of New Delhi invested in a project under the name 'A Hole in the Wall'. An outdoor five-station computer kiosk was fitted in one of the poorest slums; it consisted of computer booths and monitors, which protruded through walls for the benefit of street children with limited educational opportunities. No teachers or instructors were made available – in-line with the idea of unfettered learning development – a Western educational paradigm that had taken strong hold over curricula across the world. No community organisation was involved in running the kiosk, possibly because such involvement was not solicited. The results of the project were mixed: some slum kids did learn to use the computer and even surf the internet, but disrupted internet access and no special educational provision in Hindi meant few could understand the content provided. Families that provided for their kids' education reported that they skipped school to visit the kiosk. All in all, learning to use the facilities did not fulfil any particular purpose, as the kids never used their knowledge for future professional betterment (Warschauer 2002). The project was hailed by both researchers (Mitra 1999) and government as groundbreaking, but only after its transposition into the UK teacher-supervised educational curriculum did it obtain some practical value for schoolchildren (Tobin, 16 March 2010). The change had little to do with the intelligence of users and everything to do with the delivery style; it said less about government intentionality and everything about careful design and consideration of consequences (Jensen 2013, 2014): the experts were still experimenting.

The project's charitable spirit, which reportedly inspired Swarup's novel *Q&A*, haunted SM in other ways: technology aside, its makers' charitable intentions instigated a debate on Western giving and Indian good parenting, with particular reference to the young slum actors. Although the debate appeared in Western and Eastern channels as a 'slum' phenomenon, it mirrored Western psychopathologies of parenting as a gateway to wider debates on cultural reciprocity in mobile settings (tourism). The involvement of slum kids provided the global press with the opportunity to explore progress in family values, but in India's Naxalite framework this produced new colonial phantoms. Deep down, this was a political discourse over cultural value hierarchies with little consideration over the alleged 'crime's circumstantial evidence' or political (right-wing or left-wing) ideology. Herzfeld insists that 'the absence of kinship seems to be one of the defining characteristics of the West's view of itself' (Herzfeld 1992:68). Even the claims of whole political units to operate on strictly rational, bureaucratic principles, sidesteps the dependency of the 'rational upon the symbolic' (ibid.:148; Sutton 2000:175; Schneider 1977). As slum protests over SM's content prove, the symbolic domain of inter-group relations transforms into a theatrical stage upon which such relations are actualised and constantly reproduced through patterns of reciprocity codified in the language of (not) belonging (Ranciére 2004:58). Kinship and family relations become potent metaphors of responsibility or indebtedness, creating a moral grammar for international relations (Herzfeld 2001:231).

Scholarly transitions from film, literary theory and cultural industry to the plane of development can be a problematic exercise in realist discourse. Take for example current discussions of volunteer tourists as contemporary 'Heroes' in Joseph Campbell's (2008) theoretical tradition: if not unpacked methodologically, the metaphor never becomes a rigorous sociological model, leaving readers to consider its validity and applicability as a conceptual framework. Tomazos and Butler's (2010) consideration of analogies between real-time tourists and fictional similes certainly draws attention to the universal power of myth in society. The 'tourist', volunteer or not, is the product of our postmodern global socialities. Eliade's consideration of myth (1989) acknowledges the realist application of heroic metaphors but does less to explain how these connect to artistic creativity and the human capacity to construct utopian imaginaries. We may choose to read SM as pure entertainment or a covert critique of missionary entertainment in development contexts. But the danger that adjacent philanthropic work can transform into what Hutnyk (1996:215) saw in Calcutta's charity tourism as 'an extension of the logistics of the commodity system...that masquerades as a (liberal) project of cultural concern' is imminent. In both cases (entertainment and charity) the movie and its makers took on the mantle of compassionate celebrities, turning, in Sontag's words (2003) 'philanthropy...[into] wholesale rather than a retail enterprise, concentrating not on individuals but on an abstract Mankind and on the all-embracing systems that purportedly misshaped so many lives'. With the restoration of the image of the artist as an investor in cultural translatability with redemptive powers (Latour 1998:434–5; Cronin 2013:65), charity projects have become gigantic in scale and ambition (Magnet 2000:vii-x). The artist's profile as a mobile subject evokes conceptions of pilgrimage to foreign lands and the promise of translatability to global fans. As human components of offshore mechanisms, such artists are conventionally placed into the secret group of 'powerful "virtual citizens", the "rich class" that...straddles the globe' (Urry 2014:179). Yet, one wonders if such generalisations can produce situational understandings of art or artistic giving. Problems arise when disenfranchised populations – the recipients of charity – are fetishised as theological renditions of alterity. Decolonised charitable projects need to be informed by authentic atheism to reject the system that produces victims such as oppressed minorities or slaves and address the charity's recipients as equal humans (Dussel 1985:59).

When Danny Boyle was interviewed in the aftermath of SM's sweeping of awards, he claimed that 'you can't just fill up with pity and horror if you are going to portray that' – otherwise you miss on other aspects of the slum Mumbaikar's lifeworlds: 'their houses are always open and the extended family really important …. Slum is such a pejorative word in our culture but actually [slums] are very safe, family-orientated places' (Pryor undated). Stranded between the tourist visitor's partial perception and the director's marketing awareness, this utopian discourse reveals something about Boyle: reportedly attached to his family, he was thrown into a setting, where the rules of the game were very different indeed. So, when the dispute over the production's hiring of children hit his door in the aftermath of the film's ten Academy Awards nominations, the director and producer Christian Colson had to issue statements disputing various media accusations that SM exploited slum children. The controversy is at the heart of volunteer tourist discourse, allowing us to conclude this book with some reflections on how producers also consume globally circulating tourist ideals.

Articles in the UK's *Daily Telegraph* and in the *Hindustan Times* quoted relatives of actors saying that Rubina Ali (youngest Latika) and Azharuddin Mohamed Ismail (youngest Salim) were poorly compensated for their acting, given that SM made millions. Various numbers for their remuneration circulated in the press (Horn, 30 January 2009a). *The Telegraph* noted that they received considerably less than the poor Afghan kids that starred in *The Kite Runner* (dir. Marc Forster, 2007) (Nelson and Henderson, 26 January 2009). In their statement, Colson and Boyle revealed how the production looked after the children's welfare, paying the expenses for their elementary and secondary schooling, covering all basic living costs and establishing 'a substantial lump sum' for future college tuition to be released upon completion of their studies.

'It was a difficult moral question', Boyle stated with regards to selecting slum-children as actors. 'Do you exclude kids from the slums? If you exclude them then it feels morally wrong. But if you include them, it raises another set of moral questions – how do you care for them after the movie is finished?' (Horn, 30 January 2009a).

The events proved that you cannot. But let us stay on Boyle's comment, to highlight how often political patronage masquerades in the language of family care. Theorists who have worked towards a normative theory of care and non-contractual values such as trust and responsibility (Williams 2004) stress that historically, the language of care was employed to describe unequal political relations (Tzanelli 2008b:151). I am less interested in whether the gesture of SM leaders was honest or not, and more on the circulation of a *fons* in media channels that elevated a series of 'incidents' to fixed 'Truths' about social intimacy standards – just as Rushdie's discourse assumed that we can all agree on community 'essentials'. Unperturbed, Colson and Boyle proceeded to place the $15,000 prize from SM's award at the Toronto International Film Festival into Ali's and Ismail's trust fund (Horn, 30 January 2009), even though both Ismail's and Ali's fathers continued to complain that the money had run out because the families were plagued by illness and accidents. Such statements prompted Fox Searchlight to complete this welfare programme with additional measures to protect Azhar, Rubina and their families due to 'exposure and potential jeopardy created by unwarranted media attention' (Nelson and Henderson, 26 January 2009).

The problems did not go away: fresh reports from Indian gossip columns claimed that Ismail was slapped by his father when he begged fatigue from travelling back from the Academy Awards in Hollywood. Ali was caught in a custody battle between her stepmother, who raised her, and her biological mother, who wanted to control her daughter's earnings. Western media sources even turned the patronising lens on SM donors, pointing that they would benefit from the paradigm of the Salaam Baalak Trust, which was formed to look after the welfare of street kids that starred in *Saalam Bombay*. Author Arundhati Roy was quoted stressing that 'when a slum child becomes famous and comes into money, all sorts of relatives start coming out of the woodwork laying claims on the money' (Bhowmick, 10 March 2009). A series of examples were presented of kids who tried to make it to Hollywood and failed, kids distracted by the glamour of other stars, and kids that developed into damaged adults (ibid.; Horn, 30 January 2009). In early 2009 Ali's family home was destroyed in a big fire in Mumbai, providing more fuel to the tabloids' fire. Tabloids revisited 'Golden SM moments' in photographs figuring the well-dressed child-stars and Boyle in protective postures next to them. The press criticised Boyle when it discovered that a year after SM's success the children were still living in slums, but when Ali's family was offered a flat as compensation for losing their hut, they turned the offer down 'saying it was not big enough to house all of them' (Mail Online, 5 March 2011). Meanwhile, the British tabloid *News of the World* produced a detailed story stating that Ali's father and brother tried to sell her for $400,000 (Fuller, 21 April 2009). Though the father, Rafiq Qureshi, subsequently denied that he tried to sell his daughter to a Middle Eastern sheikh for £200,000 (in one of the gossip's versions, a trio of undercover British reporters), he was arrested by the Mumbai police, and a huge uproar ensued (Brooks, 20 April 2009). Relatives of the father appear to claim to *The Times of India*: 'Why will he sell her? She is going to earn so much more. Does anyone sell a cow that can still be milked?' (Fuller, 21 April 2009).

Thus, SM's charitable actions became implicated in a series of discussions over practices of giving-as-developing. There is significant difference between sociological conceptions of development as 'an immanent and unintentional process, as in, for example, the development of capitalism' and those in which it figures as 'an intentional activity' (Cowen and Shenton 1996). If we consider SM's industrial actors as a transnational phenomenon or ensemble of heterogeneous elements of global forms and worldviews articulated in specific situations (Collier and Ong 2005), then we must move beyond generic assessments of poverty alleviation and examine who wants to develop what and why. Art as an aesthetic, cultural and financial articulation is also geared towards developing sensitivity for local aesthetics by transliterating situational ethics. Any unintentional stimulation of translocal debates triggers new 'ideas and normative arguments' that form 'new orthodoxies about "best practice"' (Bebbington and Kothari 2006:851). The claim that charitable endeavours are *de facto* superficial – what with the film's travel-like spectacle (Urry 1995:161–2; Mowforth and Munt 1998, 2009) or the two slum actors' 'aestheticised' debut in world premieres and glossy magazines – reverses older scripts of decency: where once upon a time radical circles constructed tourism as an activity 'infused with masculine ideas about adventure, pleasure and the exotic [but] deemed those "private" and thus kept off stage in debates about international politics' (Enloe 1990:20), today's philanthropic giving is criticised for its failure to retain respect for the intimate life of the recipients. Rubina Ali's trafficking could be examined by looking at the ways 'offshoring' processes produce 'states of exception' (Agamben 1998), where normal rules governing the mobility of people, capital or information are suspended (along with certain rights, claims, and forms of citizenship) 'to allow for particular kinds of global financial mobility and inter-regional commodity flows' (Sheller 2012:3). The Compassionate parlance employed by SM's lead artists might be understood as an intentional construction of a gap between the post-colonial cultures the film represents and the global visitors' conceptions of these cultures (Ashcroft 1989:61). But the customary shift from colonialism to development does not always explain India's social change (Crush 1995; Giddens 2002). Akin to expressions of authenticity, self-awareness and vulnerability in today's charity cultures, this trope enmeshes artistic *leitmotifs* into those of the 'risk society' (Beck 1992, 1999).

Aficionados of Marxist theory would claim that the commercialisation of dark tourism traumatises or obliterates subjugated voices and reproduces modern anxieties. But to examine the economies of experience and desire guiding the artist's cinematic pilgrimage is only half of the epistemological journey: like conventional tourism analysis, this neglects to consider how 'those in economic need are accurately aware of the desires of others around the world' (Hannam and Knox 2010:12). While the scope and accessibility of such mediations has served in some ways to support the problematic one-world view proposed by many celebrity-inspired campaigns, it has also proven that, 'as human beings, we can imagine a shared bond…that prevents us from exploiting not only other humans, but the environment on which we all rely to live' (Davis 2010:114). Once again, we are faced with any locality's ability to initiate processes of 'profanation' – not by bloody revolution but by streamlined interception of the very systems of governance that insert humans into technological post-modernity (Agamben 2009:22–3, 44–5). The distress Dharavi's audio-visual children might generate for cinematic tourists compares to the distress experienced by real 'compassionate' defenders of slum destitution (on film as 'socially constructed' truth see Beeton 2006,; Tzanelli 2011; Croy and Heitmann 2011). In this contingent, contemporary art-work might be targeted in the place of historic India's 'imperial agents' (Osterhammel 1997:20–1). Though a positive step, the UN's construction of minimum voluntary standards for 'good corporate conduct' lacks enforcement mechanisms (Fritch 2008) making the organisation of charity vulnerable to private business interests and criticism. Boyle and Colson's institution of development funds for SM's young actors raises questions concerning the effectiveness of citizen participation, especially because it provoked those preoccupied with 'public decency' (Couldry 2007:384).

For centuries, conceptions of childhood have served various political agendas. Aries pioneering argument that the construction of the child as separate from adults, grounded in so-called Western contexts in which binarisms such as 'rationality' and 'irrationality', also fed into Cartesian separations of mind from body (Aries 1962). Attributing the abandonment of Ismael's and Ali's welfare to Boyle and Colson's 'rational choices', replicates a deep Western conservatism regarding development-work-as-childcare. Few seemed to consider how this intervention partook in developmental discourses of 'effective practice' (Sen 1999:158) as provision of the right tools to ensure personal freedom, independence and human flourishing. Boyle's facilitation of 'technical access' to global press reporting for the slum-child actors, particularly in the context of film awards , did match 'social access' (Kling 2000:226) and could easily invoke accusations of subaltern silencing (Spivak 1999; Ranciére 2004). 'Trafficking' SM's iconic slum milieus abroad as a tourist object might do no developmental work in the slums if no funds are streamlined to allow community development; and even then, there is no guarantee the local regulators will not abuse their role. SM's criticisms over lack of 'communicative entitlements', the rightful claims of slum groups to 'be listened to and treated seriously' (Scannell 1989:160), can collapse into the discourse of 'recognition' through equitable resource distribution in such resentful environments (Fraser and

Honneth 2003:158). In an adjacent debate on the cosmopolitan ethics of global digitality, both Bauman (2001) and Touraine (2000) asked to what extent online connectedness can affect the social fabric, concluding in different ways that resources and connectedness or solidarities can suffer anyway. Material and ideational resources play different roles in this game, and their mobilisation in different systemic venues (national, regional, global) can (dis-)empower groups in various ways.

The 'digital divide' debate is introduced in SM's controversy as a sore reminder that national/social peripheries might either be excluded altogether or trafficked with the ever-suspect facilitation of foreign industries, such as those of media or tourism. SM's globally televised childhood armed post-colonial critics with the argument that child development is always labelled as a kinder and more humane form of subjecting 'underdeveloped' people, whose symbolic youth or femininity get in the way of progress (Cannella and Viruru 2004:92; Tzanelli 2008b:159). In tandem, the technologisation of tourism via internet sites that package visits to Mumbai's filmed slums could invoke the belief in scientific notions of the child as the product of sexual desire or the model of 'poverty childhood' that is by default product of a bunch of 'evil doers' – and *hence* corrupted (Kessen 1979:28). Such unwarranted metonymies haunt Western public spheres, reproducing those racialised conditions they often set out to contest (Kessen 1993). Even SM's cinematic narrative dances around these problematic debates: its polarisation of good and evil both contest and resurrect categories invented by the British Raj in India, who bequeathed us definitions of Indian caste and African tribalism as early stages in human development (Cohn and Dirks 1988; Cooper and Stoler 1997).

More importantly, however, these accusations sideline the obligatory circulation of discourses of 'trafficking', 'pornification' and 'sexualisation' in Western and Eastern media circuits. They also do not explain how such discourses now seem to enter India via global travel routes, as processes of bourgeoisiefication-as-cosmopolitanisation affect Indian public spheres. In this light, not only does Ali's alleged 'peddling' by her father or by a 'master of impressions' like Boyle suggest a slow domestic shift in family values, they prompt us to consider how it is fine for the sake of neoliberal expansion to invite film-makers and tourists to 'look at' and 'love' slum kids as they see fit. Perhaps more shocking is the realisation that for an artistic enterprise such as SM, the recruitment of child actors from the UK would have been a bureaucratic nightmare. In UK discourses of 'media sexualisation', children transmute into a category with an entitlement to 'innocence' and in need of various disciplinary and institutional interventions. Yet, 'anti-sexualization texts seem to rework the "laments" that have become part of the way public debate is conducted, not only around sex and sexuality, but around the behaviour of young people, the status of women, representation, and technology' (Attwood 2010:743; Smith 2010:176). The debate can incorporate other psychopathologies such as domestic violence or the aura of celebrity cultures, which are pivotal in impositions of Western conduct on the rest of the world.

Few press sources considered context and social conditions in Ali's twin 'domestic violation' (by her mothers and her father). On the one hand, peripheral social groups place great emphasis on relationships, value children and even consult them in decision-making. Hindu beliefs consider producing and raising children as every individual's *dharma* – a sacred duty akin to inter-generational transmissions of heritage. Only a child can relieve an individual from their debt to gods (*dev rin*), ancestors (*pitri rin*) and teachers (*risi rin*) (Mishra et al. 2005:146). At the same time that moral bondages consolidate heritage discourse on bio-cultural properties (Smith 1995:98), family welfare is determined on the basis of status (caste) and economic growth. Although interventions to control birth rates were more 'effective' in recent years, ethnic, demographic and regional divides continue to affect family planning and practices in Indian terrains (Bharat 2001). The omnipresence of extended family networks and kinship status are based on gender selection: women are greatly disadvantaged by this selectivity and treated as second-rate citizens in comparison with their male siblings. Their function in the kinship system is that of mobility enablers, 'things' that change hands through profitable exchange with other powerful kinship managers or 'things' discarded (murdered, ostracised) as useless. Physical beauty might be a bonus in marriage pacts (a custom discarded in some Indian middle-class and urban milieus) but in our case Rumina's beauty is associated with her new celebrity status. Rumina's status finds its perfect equivalent in children rescued by voluntourist initiatives around the world, in individualised acts of giving that make the developed tourist a better human (see Reas 2014).

The transnational context in which this digital mediation of heritage took place is appropriate for a return to the analysis of *hau* (=gift): Mauss (1954) and others (Sahlins 1972; Davis 1992) highlighted that because donors and gifts are bound in a magical way, the recipient of the gift (Boyle and associates) *is obliged* to reciprocate the giver's (Ali family) gesture (to 'lend' their daughter for film-making). Ali's celebrity value was also responsible for the war between her mothers, who wanted to 'milk the cow'. The rationale of 'milking' should be placed in the context of a ubiquitous rivalry between family members over the control of scarce resources (Scheper-Hughes 2013:26–7 on Brazilian slum culture). Such mobility practices lie at the heart of criticism of SM as an effective form of counter-gazing that involves all senses in a synaesthetic performance of sociality. A return to cultural *fons* with the help of the gift's (children) magical properties, bore the potential to relocate marginal voices to media centres within and without the country. Through such ritualistic exchange, marginalised Indian cultures could reclaim a Western 'debt' buried under the rubble of an externally imposed industrial modernity.

10 Conclusion

This book commenced an investigation by pronouncing the validity of film-making as a social metaphor-model – a hypothesis that leads in Chapter 9 to the conclusion that SM's multiple journeys into 'darkness' and 'brightness' reveal less about Indian and more about Western socio-cultural transformations. SM's Mumbai presents us with transitions from multiple modernities to multiple realities in Schutzian terms, while also highlighting that these realities are always communicated by different constituencies (Valera and Harré 1996; Dean 2007). Through the multiple controversies connected to SM, different interest groups sought to negotiate their place on a globalised plateau. At all times we deal with 'negotiation' over the definition of events: cosmologies involve cultural constructs embedded in shared pasts but always in motion and reconstruction through intercultural contacts. Thus, *pangosmiopoiesis* or aesthetic globalisation (Urry 1995:145) acts as a metaphor that models the social world (reality) and generates more metaphors about society (good, bad, fair, unfair) – in other words, it is a phenomenological vehicle prompting understandings of 'Self' and 'Other' in aesthetically reflective ways. SM proffers a textbook case of multiple articulations of cinematic text and context, in which perceptions of 'beauty' as the good life order the social world (*kósmos*) as a whole ('*pan*'). Thus the argument that *pangosmiopoiesis* attends to surfaces should not lead us to confuse surface with superficiality, artistic formation or articulation of political resonance with artistic formalism. Conceptualisations of form-surface often contribute to understandings of alien cosmological registers in post-colonial zones, but they also guide cultural hybridisations. Although this *problématique* is not entirely dependent on Boyle's film, SM as an event instigated mobilities of humans, ideas, travel and art that promoted cultural hybridisations.

But when one considers perceptions of hybridity as 'dirty mixing' (of races-as-cultures), hybridisation is not good in and of itself. Any party can reach such a conclusion, as theories and studies of tourist exchange suggest. In instances of cross-cultural contact such as those of SM's media and tourism mobilities, we have serendipitous interpretations of socio-cultural phenomena, hence agential actions over pre-existing structures – of inequality, corruption or kindness (Archer 2000, 2003). Merton and Barber's exploration of serendipity as happy accidental discovery made them question ideas of ill-fortune and unexpected evil, which have great poignancy for those who place value on a predictable, rational universe (Merton and Barber 2004:150). The very presence of institutional organisation and bureaucracy in communal life aims to eliminate ill-fortune, ensuring that our social world is ordered in plausible, beautiful ways (McCreery 1995:160). In a book flagging serendipity as the basis of any justification of different fortunes and just deserts, SM's virtual and real journeys can only be explored in relation to individual and collective perceptions of good and evil. Collective agency is based on teleological cosmologies resembling SM's emphasis on what 'is written' in the cards – only the end is in fact determined by contingent social action. The *telos* of the events in Mumbai's slumscapes is telling: Indian order is to be restored only when a foreign aesthetic import of *pangosmiopoiesis* (surely a dirty, effeminate version of what an Indian superpower should be), ironically represented by male Westernised artists such as Boyle and Rahman, is no more.

SM's text also communicates with globalisation contexts with a particular orientation towards material and ideational circumstance in other ways (Bhaskar 1989:52). As is the case with most Western and hybrid Bollywood drama, cinematic heroes individualise collective social action and disseminate *dispositif*. In SM the woes of the main characters allow the spectator to view Boyle's critical realist tale of violence as *a domestic, Indian issue* – an unfortunate turn of events, given that Mumbai has reportedly been target for various terrorist organisations, primarily separatist forces from Pakistan. Over the past few years there have been a series of attacks, including explosions in local trains in July 2006, and the unprecedented attacks of 26 November 2008 that coincided with SM's imminent release. Gale (2008:9) observes that with global events such as 9/11 and 7/7 we might have reached the end of tourism as we know it. Additional evidence on environmental pollution across the world seconds his thesis, turning Mumbai's cinematic dystopia of slum abandonment and segregation into an anti-tourist banner. But SM-induced tourism in the heart of Mumbai's 'poverty terrorland' counters this: the film suggests that there is throbbing, mobile life amidst garbage. Exchanging the slow historical spectrum of post-Partition film-making for the new fast mobilities of cinematic celebrity and tourism also ameliorated its critical reception, but only for so long.

SM's lead artists' cultural roots and situational roles in global digital and industrial transformation cast them as accomplices of an 'exploitative capitalist machine' with little qualification over the specific context of 'exploitation'. Travelling to India's slum territories to collect 'signs' for art-work could easily be labelled an edu-tourist activity, a personal development portfolio of activities that allow the tourist to treat foreign cultures as 'objects' (Holdnak and Holland 1996). Beaufoy never figured in media reporting as a 'nomad from affluence' (Cohen 1973) or as an 'alternative' volunteer tourist (Wearing 2001) – an observation that suggests more careful evaluation of his travels to Mumbai as cinematic labour and lifestyle travel (Cohen 1996, 2003; S.A. Cohen 2011). Boyle and Coulson's proactive volunteer activism was nevertheless attacked for its interference with India's 'future': the very children the nation-state excludes from its developmental horizon and, subsequently, as adolescents and adults labels 'terrorists'. In SM's interpretative horizons, young slum actors assumed the ideational role of future social investment in India's global prestige and domestic heritage, despite their actual exclusion from society. To be nourished by a bunch of foreign artists could only be treated with resentment or contempt. This conflation of family reciprocity with exchange is symbolised in Rumina Ali's exchange for fame and money. Debates around the rise of a 'network society' remind us that people are increasingly socially positioned in accordance with their place in media networks (Van Dijk 1999:78) – hence the discussion on cinematic children as property changing hands to accommodate different interests has real implications. Even critical artistic interventions such as those of SM activists reiterate the relocation of intimacy in the marketplace, flooding the public sphere with private concerns and rituals (Bauman 2003b).

The politics of Indian nationalist heritage shed light on the management of collective self-narration in commercial fields such as that of cinematic tourism – a combined field of media representations and global industrial investment in Indian economy and culture. Here the expression of indignation by radical proponents of the 'cultural imperialist' thesis finds surprising replication in defensive official policies of heritage. In a country steeped in rich history but affected by traumatic memories of colonisation, nationalism and forced migrations, yesteryear's Ghandian urge to safeguard the nation's inner spiritual realm against invasions of Western technocratic *civilité* are bound to reassert themselves in periods of tension (Chatterjee 1986, 1993). If one also considers how in media and tourist industries the convergence of economic and socio-cultural interests can be 'crafted' to secure interdependencies (Castells 1996:151–68) that reduce risk of failure and manage to 'silence' critical voices from without (Garnham 1990:160–2; Tzanelli 2010b:ch.1), then the attack upon SM's enterprise necessitates re-evaluation. Technologies of governance connected to Indian officialdom may reinforce digital nationalism as a form of 'soft power' over diverse minorities (Nye 2004). Soft power finds an update in the 'Shining India' campaign, which borrows from post-Nehruvian technologisations of intercultural communication – also one of the aims of SM's overall project. But the idea of 'reaching out' is not specifically Indian, as even the United States recruited Hollywood artists into its 'soft' arsenal as specimen of the 'American way' (Cronin 2013:111, 124). Bollywood or Bollywood-like representations and their unexpected cultural industrial products (internet slum tourism) can be selectively embroiled into a more official program of 'brand nationalism' prioritising Indian spiritual qualities (Volcic and Andrejevic 2011; Irimiás 2012). Here network *technopoesis* can revert to national *technopoesis*, reinventing fictional Jamals as the nation's original *tornadóroi* for the benefit of the nation-state – a phenomenon no less evident in Nehru's modernisation model through strategic and selective alliances with 'the West' (Parekh 1991). The ensuing dialogical conflict of ideas and practices favours a sort of violent creation, as it produces for the subaltern something new (Hitchcock 1993; Tzanelli 2008b:72).

We need to bear in mind that today the management of human and technological resources by national and transnational institutions, or tourist and artistic organisations, takes place under post-imperial conditions. New economic realities are defined mostly by de-territorialised power and judicial regimes that assert new orders, norms and ethical 'truths'. Consequently, the penetration of human psyches ceases to be the job of an identifiable capitalist class or nation-state and becomes attached to bio-political managements of 'fairness' and humanitarian righteousness by corporations and post-industrial mergers (Hardt and Negri 2000). In this arrangement, leading artistic labour may operate under corporate management but still contribute to the 'multitude' (Hardt and Negri 2004) by producing utopian alternatives to a damaging social system, which then feed back into real social action. As Kumar (1991) has repeatedly suggested, the philosophical project of modernism is fundamentally utopian and recuperative of a social ethos that remains a work in progress even in post-industrial contexts. The technological tools such artistic communities mobilise might have played a key role in securing the new capitalist hegemonies but are now turned 'into a weapon of liberation from these oppressive forces' (Miller 2011:156; Yar 2014:34–7). Yet, such *Nebengeschäfte* (ancillary business) is deemed to replicate the (apparently amoral) logic of new knowledge economies (slum tourism) (Calabrese 2005). It is wilfully forgotten that, in the age of 'Empire', any moral reckoning with the subaltern passes through various agendas that cannot be harmonised even within a single nation-state (Lash and Urry 1987).

One might argue that by cancelling charity projects one disrupts the healthy function of public spheres that are based on artistic dialogics (Arendt 1990). It may be wrong to dismiss outright the economic or cultural role of Western celebrity activism or ethical consumerism 'as models of fund and consciousness-raising that provide charities with such immense possibilities to garner support, and donors the opportunity to participate as members of a global community' (Davis 2010:114). Just as common tourists, today charitable celebrities are invited to complement conventional gazing with performing (Perkins and Thorns 2001). Not only does this prompt one to examine art-work as a form of 'moral labour', it also begs a dispassionate investigation of the link between moral and monetary projects. Let us not forget that 'human beings produce facts but they do so through collective labour orientated towards both material and ideational objects, which seeks to intervene in and accumulate knowledge of a natural world irreducible to this labour' (Corrigan, 23 January 2014).

Just like SM's cinematic journeys, its industry's artistic activism reflects the 'generic processes' through which 'public spheres' can emerge in imagining, empathising, vocalising and investing identities through narratives (Plummer 2003:81–3). Ateljevic (2008) proposes a rectification of subaltern silencing through a more careful consideration of 'transmodernity' as 'the emerging socio-cultural, economic, political and philosophic shift' in the cultural and material development of a pluralised human history (Ghisi in Ateljevic 2008:280). Transmodernity recognises hope in human sociality and promises to replace colonialism's antiquated world orders, which constantly masquerade cultures in terms of feminised victimhood or macho militarism. Above all, however, a new transmodern condition discards both the theological basis of the clash of civilisations (Huntington 2002) and the resentment of a world split between Jihad and McWorld (Barber 2003), acknowledging vulnerability as part of our shared humanity (Beck 1999, 2005; Dussel 1985, 1995; Cole 2005). Naturally, the realist conundrums of such global articulations – no less constrained by financial prerogatives and impositions (Sassen 2002a) – might contravene imaginative planning (for a better future for Mumbai's slum-dwellers). Sen's (1992, 1999) 'capabilities model' is put to a test when we are called to consider the 'fundamental diversity of human beings' as a universal value: one may account for several instances in our twentieth and twenty-first century global history in which structures of corporate control were generated as interconnected and multiple with the inscription of normality/abnormality, denying child/family/community knowledge and accepting instead the language and knowledge of experts (Silin 1995) – including those involved in regional administration and activism. But controversially, one may ask if the rights of a disenfranchised socio-cultural group should always override those of another residing more privileged geographical and social domains. Here the conception of 'communicative entitlements' needs broadening so as to include other forms of democratic participation that exceed 'fair treatment' exclusively designed (often by their abusers) for the poor or disadvantaged.

Derrida's phantasmology and Spivak's ethics of subaltern silence merit new consideration in such mobile Indian sites, in which the spiritual slow time of heritage and the fast mobilities of slum tourism collude behind a *Weltanschauung* that transcends divisions of 'high' and 'low' culture (Gellner 1983; Herzfeld 2005). Western takes on the ordinariness of culture as an agential force that activates an interface between the Marxist superstructure and individual or communal action may be a utopian model, but it is a useful model (Williams 1958, 1974, 1983 and 1999). And yet, if too defensive, even 'culture' can kill, humiliate and exclude – not just slum-children, poor families or 'developing ethnicities', but also first-class art. Do we wish to promote a utopian project based on harmful manipulations of 'merit' in the name of 'equal' progress?

Bibliography

Achal, A. (3 October 2010) 'CWG opening ceremony: As it happened', *The Hindu*. Available at: www.thehindu.com/sport/article811224.ece (accessed 13 July 2013).
Adey, P. (2010) *Mobility*. London: Routledge.
Adler, J. (1989) 'Travel as performed art', *American Journal of Sociology*, 94(6): 1366–1391.
Adler, J. (1992) 'Mobility and the creation of the subject', International Tourism: Between Tradition and Modernity Colloquium, Nice: France, 407–415.
Adler, P. A. and Adler, P. (1999) 'Transience and the postmodern self: The geographic mobility of resort workers', *The Sociological Quarterly*, 40(1): 31–58.
Adorno, T.W. (1986) 'What does coming to terms with the past mean?' in T. Bahti and G. Hartman (eds) *Bitburg in Moral and Political Perspective*. Bloomington, IN: Indiana University Press,114–129.
Adorno, T.W. (2001) *The Stars down to Earth and Other Essays on the Irrational Culture*. New York: Routledge.
Adorno, T.W. and Horkheimer, M. (1991) *The Dialectic of Enlightenment*. New York: Continuum.
AFP Google News (22 January 2009) '"Slumdog" stars sued for "defaming" India's slum-dwellers'. Available at:www.google.com/hostednews/afp/article/ALeqM5hK QWmfCUcwj1P5o8cSIxGLwRBwaw (accessed 15 September 2013).
Agamben, G. (1998) *Homo Sacer*. Stanford: Stanford University Press.
Agamben, G. (2009) *"What is an Apparatus" and Other Essays*, translated by D. Kishik and S. Pedatella. Palo Alta, CA: Stanford University Press.
Ahmad, A. (1992) *In Theory*. London: Verso.
Albertsen, N. and Diken, B. (2003) '"Artworks"' networks – Field, system or mediators?', Department of Sociology, Lancaster University On-line Papers. Available at: http://comp.lancs.ac.uk/sociology.soc105bd.html (accessed 30 March 2012).
Alcock, S.E. (2010) 'The stratigraphy of serendipity', in M. de Rond and I. Morley (eds.) *Serendipity*. Cambridge: Cambridge University Press, 11–26.
Alexander, J.C. (2006) 'Cultural pragmatics: Social performance between ritual and strategy' in J.C. Alexander, B. Giesen and J.L. Mast (eds) *Social Performance, Symbolic Action, Cultural Pragmatics and Ritual*. Cambridge: Cambridge University Press, 29–90.
AlexanderJ.C. and Smith, P. (2001) 'The strong program in cultural theory: Elements of structural hermeneutics', in J. Turner (ed.) *Handbook of Social Theory*. New York: Kluwer, 135–150.
Altman, R. (1999) *Film/Genre*. London: British Film Institute.

Bibliography

Anastasiou, D. and Schäler, R. (2010) 'Translating vital information: Localisation, internationalisation and globalisation', *Syn-Théses*, 3:11–25.

Anderson, B. (2006) *Imagined Communities*, London: Verso.

ANI (31 January 2009) '"Slumdog millionaire" seeks inspiration from Bollywood of 70s, says expert', Thaindian News. Available atwww.thaindian.com/newsportal/entertainment/slumdog-millionaire-seeks-inspiration-from-bollywood-of-70s-says-expert_100149354.html (accessed 9 July 2013).

Appadurai, A. (1986) 'Towards an anthropology of things', in A. Appadurai (ed.) *The Social Life of Things*. Cambridge: Cambridge University Press, 3–63.

Appadurai, A. (1990) 'Disjuncture and difference in the global cultural economy', *Public Culture*, 2(2): 1–24.

Appadurai, A. (1996) *Modernity at Large*. Minneapolis, MN: University of Minnesota Press.

Archer, M. (1995) *Realist Social Theory*. Cambridge: Cambridge University Press.

Archer, M. (1996) *Culture and Agency*, 2nd edn. Cambridge: Cambridge University Press.

Archer, M. (2000) *Being Human*. Cambridge: Cambridge University Press.

Archer, M. (2003) *Structure, Agency and the Internal Conversation*. Cambridge: Cambridge University Press.

Archibugi, D.Held, D. and Köhler, M. (eds) (1998) *Re-Imagining Political Community*. Cambridge: Polity.

Arendt, H. (1958) *The Human Condition*. Chicago: University of Chicago Press.

Arendt, H. (1973) *The Origins of Totalitarianism*. New York: Harcourt.

Arendt, H. (1990) *Lectures on Kant's Political Philosophy*. Chicago: University of Chicago Press.

Argyrou, V. (2005) *The Logic of Environmentalism*. Oxford: Berghahn.

Argyrou, V. (2013) *The Gift of European Thought and the Cost of Living*. Oxford: Berghahn.

Aries, P. (1962) *Centuries of Childhood*, translated by R. Baldick. New York: Alfred A. Knopf.

Aristotle (1996) *Poetics*, translated by L. Heath. London: Penguin.

ARRamanMusicVideos (2006) 'AR Rahman's The Banyan theme (2006) | Santosh Sivan'. Available at: www.youtube.com/watch?v=0SROrHIMwT4 (accessed 29 August 2013).

Ashar, S. (8 August 2013) 'A big thumbs down to Dharavi revamp plan', *Mumbai Mirror*. Available at: www.mumbaimirror.com/mumbai/civic/A-big-thumbs-down-to-Dharavi-revamp-plan/articleshow/21690898.cms (accessed 1 September 2013).

Ashcroft, W.D. (1989) 'Is that the Congo? Language as metonymy in the post-colonial text', *World Literature Written in English*, 29(1): 3–10.

Associated Press (17 February 2009) 'Indian composer identifies with "slumdog" hero'. Available at: www.today.com/id/29245892#.Ud7NPPnVCSo (accessed 11 July 2013).

Ateljevic, I. (2008) 'Transmodernity: Remaking our (tourism) world?', in J. Tribe (ed.) *Philosophical Issues in Tourism*. Bristol and Toronto: Channel View Publications, 278–300.

Ateljevic, I. and Doorne, S. (2005) 'Dialectics of authentication: Performing "exotic otherness" in a backpacker enclave of Dali, China', *Journal of Tourism and Cultural Change*, 3(1): 1–17.

Atkinson, R. (2006) 'Padding the bunker: Strategies of middle-class disaffiliation and colonization in the city', *Urban Studies*, 43(4): 819–832.

Atkinson, R. (2007) 'Ecology of sound: The sonic order of urban space', *Urban Studies*, 44(10): 1905–1917.
Atkinson, R. and Blandy, S. (2005) 'International perspectives on the new enclavism and the rise of gated communities', *Housing Studies*, 20(2): 177–186.
Attwood, F. (2010) 'Sexualization, sex and manners', *Sexualities*, 13(6): 742–747.
Averill, G. (1996) 'Global imaginings', in R. Ohmann (eds.) *Making and Selling Culture*. Hannover: Wesleyan University Press, 203–223.
Bachchan, A. (13 January 2009) 'Official blog of Amitabh Bachchan – Day 265'. Available at: http://srbachchan.tumblr.com/ (accessed 15 September 2013).
Bachelard, G. (1994) *The Poetics of Space*. Boston: Beacon Press.
Bachelard, G. (2000) *The Dialectics of Duration*. Manchester: Clinamen Press.
Bærenholdt, J.O. (2013) 'Governmobility: The powers of mobility', *Mobilities*, 8(1): 20–34.
Bærenholdt, O., Haldrup, M., Larsen, J. and Urry, J. (2004) *Performing Tourist Places*. Aldershot: Ashgate.
Bagguley, P. and Hussain, Y. (2008) *Riotous Citizens*. Aldershot: Ashgate.
Baker, R. (1995) 'Combative cultural politics: Film art and political spaces in Egypt', *Alif: Journal of Comparative Poetics*, 15: 6–38.
Bakhtin, M.M. (1968) *Rabelais and His World*. Cambridge: MIT Press.
Bakhtin, M.M. (1981) *The Dialogic Imagination*, edited by M. Holquist. Austin, TX: Texas University Press.
Bakhtin, M.M. (1984) *Problems of Dostoevski's Poetics*. Manchester: Manchester University Press.
Bakhtin, M.M. (1986) *Speech Genres and Other Essays*, edited by C. Emmerson and M. Holquist, translated by V.W. MaGee. Austin: University of Texas Press.
Bakhtin, M.M. (1990) *Art and Answerability*, edited by M. Holquist, translated by V. Liapunov. Austin: University of Texas Press.
Bal, M. (2003) 'Visual essentialism and the object of visual culture', *Journal of Visual Culture*, 2(1): 5–32.
Bal, M. (2010) *Of What One Cannot Speak*. Chicago: University of Chicago Press.
Balaji, M. (2009) 'Owning black masculinity: The intersection of cultural commodification and self-construction in rap music videos', *Communication, Culture and Critique*, 2: 21–38.
Banerjea, K. (2000) 'Sounds of whose underground? The fine tuning of diaspora in an age of mechanical reproduction', *Theory, Culture and Society*, 17: 64–79.
Banerjee, S. (24 September 2009) 'Bollywood? No thanks: Loveen Tandan', *DNA India*. Available at: www.dnaindia.com/entertainment/1292747/report-bollywood-no-thanks-loveleen-tandan (accessed 13 August 2013).
Banks, M. (2001) *Visual Methods in Social Research*. London: Sage.
Baptista, J.A. (2012) 'Tourism of poverty: The value of being poor in the non-governmental order', in F. Frenzel, K. Koens and M. Steinbrink (eds) *Slum Tourism*. London: Routledge, 125–143.
Barber, B. (2003) *Jihad versus McWorld*. London: Corgi Books.
Barber, B. (2010) 'Terrorism and the new democratic realism', in G. Ritzer and Z. Atalay (eds.) *Readings in Globalization*, Oxford: Wiley Blackwell, 305–306.
Barlow, J.P. (1996) 'Declaration of the Independence of Cyberspace'. Available from https://projects.eff.org/~barlow/Declaration-Final.html (accessed 8 April 2015).
Baron, Z. (19 February 2009). 'Sri Lankan government responds to alleged M.I.A. slur: "It's best that she stay with what's she's good at"', *The Village Voice*. Available

188 Bibliography

at: http://blogs.villagevoice.com/music/2009/02/sri_lanka_respo.php#more (accessed 30 June 2013).

Barreira, I.A.F. (2011) 'Social movements, culture and politics in the work of Brazilian sociologists', *Latin American Perspectives*, 38(3): 150–168.

Barth, F. (1981) *Process and Form in Social Life, I*. London: Routledge & Kegan Paul.

Barthes, R. (1979) *The Eiffel Tower and Other Mythologies*. New York: Hill and Wang.

Basic Lexicon of Ancient Greek Online (2013) 'ΛΗΜΜΑ ἦθος'. Available at: www.greek-language.gr/greekLang/ancient_greek/tools/lexicon/lemma.html?id=120 (accessed 12 June 2013).

Basu, K. (2012) 'Slum tourism: For the poor, by the poor', in F. Frenzel, K. Koens and M. Steinbrink (eds) *Slum Tourism*. London: Routledge, 66–82.

Basu, S. (2000) 'The bleeding edge: Resistance as strength and paralysis', *Indian Journal of Gender Studies*, 7(2): 185–202.

Basu, T. (1990) *Khaki Shorts, Saffron Flags*. New Delhi: Orient Longman.

Baudrillard, J. (1988) *America*, translated by C. Turner. London: Verso.

Bauman, R. (2010) 'The remediation of story-telling: Narrative performance on early commercial sound recordings', in A. De Fina, D. Schriffrin (eds) *Telling Stories*. Washington DC: Georgetown University Press, 23–43.

Bauman, Z. (1989) *Modernity and the Holocaust*. Cambridge: Polity.

Bauman, Z. (1991) *Modernity and Ambivalence*. Cambridge: Polity.

Bauman, Z. (1992a) *Intimations of Postmodernity*. London: Routledge.

Bauman, Z. (1992b) *Mortality, Immortality and Other Life Strategies*. Cambridge: Polity.

Bauman, Z. (1994) 'Desert spectacular', in K. Tester (ed.) *The Flaneur*. London: Routledge, 138–157.

Bauman, Z. (1997) *Postmodernity and its Discontents*. Cambridge: Polity.

Bauman, Z. (1998) *Globalization*. New York: Columbia University Press.

Bauman, Z. (2000) *Liquid Modernity*. Cambridge: Polity.

Bauman, Z. (2001) *The Individualised Society*. Cambridge: Polity.

Bauman, Z. (2003a) *City of Fears, City of Hopes*. London: University of London Press.

Bauman, Z. (2003b) *Liquid Love*. Cambridge: Polity.

Bauman, Z. (2005a) *Liquid Life*. Cambridge: Polity.

Bauman, Z. (2005b) 'Seeking shelter in Pandora's box, or fear, security and the city', *City*, 9(2): 161–168.

Bauman, Z. (2008) *Liquid Fear*. Cambridge: Polity.

Bauman, Z. (2009) *Does Ethics have a Chance in a World of Consumers?* Cambridge: Harvard University Press.

Bauman, Z. (2010) *44 Letters from the Liquid Modern World*. Cambridge: Polity.

BBC News (16 January 2009) 'Bachchan denies Slumdog criticism'. Available at: http://news.bbc.co.uk/1/hi/world/south_asia/7832705.stm (accessed 15 September 2013).

BBC News (5 March 2009) 'Jai Ho "cost Congress $200,000"'. Available at: http://news.bbc.co.uk/1/hi/world/south_asia/7926058.stm (accessed 11 July 2013).

BBC Newsround (4 June 2009) 'AR Rahman feat. Pussycat Dolls – Jai Ho'. Available at: http://news.bbc.co.uk/cbbcnews/hi/newsid_7980000/newsid_7989900/7989946.stm (accessed 13 July 2013).

Beaufoy, S. (12 December 2008) 'Life on the hard shoulder', *The Guardian*. Available at: www.theguardian.com/film/2008/dec/12/simon-beaufoy-slumdog-millionaire (accessed 28 August 2013).

Bebbington, A. (2000) 'Re-encountering development: Livelihood transitions and place transformations in the Andes', *Annals of the Association of American Geographers*, 90: 495–520.
Bebbington, A. and U. Kothari (2006) 'Transnational development networks', *Environment and Planning A*, 38: 849–866.
Beck, U. (1992) *Risk Society*. London: Sage.
Beck, U. (1999) *World Risk Society*, Cambridge: Polity.
Beck, U. (2000) 'The Cosmopolitan perspective: Sociology of the second age of modernity', *British Journal of Sociology*, 51: 79–105.
Beck, U. (2002a) *Individualization*. London: Sage.
Beck, U. (2002b) 'The cosmopolitan society and its enemies', *Theory, Culture and Society*, 19: 17–44.
Beck, U. (2005) *Power in the Global Age*. Cambridge: Polity.
Beck, U. and Beck-Gernsheim, E. (1995) *The Normal Chaos of Love*. Cambridge: Polity.
Becker, H.S. (1982) *Art Worlds*. Berkeley and Los Angeles: University of California Press.
Becker, J. (2004) *Deep Listening*. Bloomington, IN: Indiana University Press.
Bederman, G. (1995) *Manliness and Civilization*. Chicago: University of Chicago Press.
Beeton, S. (2005) *Film-Induced Tourism*. Toronto: Channel View.
Beeton, S. (2006) 'Understanding film-induced tourism', *Tourism Analysis*, 11: 181–188.
Beeton, S. (2010) 'The advance of film tourism', *Tourism and Hospitality: Planning and Development*, 7: 1–6.
Beilharz, P. (ed.) (2002) *Zygmunt Bauman – Masters of Social Thought*. London, California, New Delhi: Sage Publications.
Bell, C. and Lyall, J. (2002) *The Accelerated Sublime*. Westport: Praeger.
Benhabib, S. (1992) *Situating the Self*. New York: Routledge.
Benjamin, W. (1968) *Illuminations*. London: Fontana Press.
Benjamin, W. (1992) *Illuminations*. London: Fontana.
Benjamin, W. (2002) *The Arcades Project*. Cambridge: Harvard University Press.
Bennett, A. (1999) 'Subcultures or neotribes? Rethinking the relationship between youth style and musical taste', *Sociology* 33(3): 599–617.
Bennett, A. (2004) 'Consolidating the music scenes perspective', *Poetics*, 32: 223–234.
Bennett, A. (2005) *Culture and Everyday Life*. London: Sage.
Benson, M. and O'Reilly, K. (2009) 'Migration and the search for a better way of life: A critical exploration of lifestyle migration', *The Sociological Review*, 57(4): 608–625.
Ben-Ze'ev, E. and Lomsky-Feder, E. (2009) 'The canonical generation: Trapped between personal and national memories', *Sociology*, 43(6): 1047–1066.
Berman, M. (1981) *All that is Solid Melts into Air*. New York: Simon & Schuster.
Bernal, M. (1991) *Black Athena: The Afroasiatic Roots of Classical Civilisation, I*. London: Vintage.
Bernstein, E. (2001) 'The meaning of the purchase: Desire, demand and the commerce of sex', *Ethnography*, 2(3): 389–420.
Beverley, J. (1989) 'The margin at the center: On testimonio (testimonial narrative)', *Modern Fiction Studies*, 35(1): 11–28.
Beverley, J. and Zimmerman, M. (1990) *Literature and Politics in the Central American Revolutions*. Austin: University of Texas Press.
Bhabha, H.K. (1994) *The Location of Culture*. London and New York: Routledge.
Bharat, S. (2001) 'On the periphery: The psychology of gender', in J. Pandey (ed.) *Psychology of India Revisited, II*. New Delhi: Sage, 300–355.

Bhaskar, R. (1989) *Reclaiming Reality*. London and New York: Verso.
Bhatt, C. (2000) 'Primordial being: Enlightenment, Schopenhauer and the Indian subject of postcolonial theory', *Radical Philosophy*, 100: 28–41.
Bhattacharya, N. (2008) 'Predicaments of secular histories', *Public Culture*, 20(1): 57–73.
Bhattacharya, P. (26 February 2011) 'Madhuri's ardent admiration for Kathak', *The Daily Star*. Available at: http://archive.thedailystar.net/newDesign/news-details.php?nid=175494 (accessed 4 July 2013).
Bhowmick, N. (10 March 2009) 'What will happen to Slumdog's child stars?', *Time*. Available at: http://content.time.com/time/world/article/0,8599,1883809,00.html (accessed 13 September 2009).
Bianchi, R.V. (2000) 'Migrant tourist-workers: Exploring the "contact zones" of post-industrial tourism', *Current Issues in Tourism*, 3(2): 107–137.
Binkley, S. (2000) 'Kitsch as a repetitive system: A problem for the theory of taste hierarchy', *Journal of Material Culture*, 5(2): 131–152.
Binkley, S. (2004) 'Everybody's life is like a spiral: Narrating post-Fordism in the lifestyle movement of the 1970s', *Cultural Studies <- -> Critical Methodologies*, 4(1): 71–96.
Blanton, R. (2011) 'Chronotopic landscapes and environmental racism', *Linguistic Anthropology*, 21(1): 76–93.
Bleicher, J. (1980) *Contemporary Hermeneutics*. London and New York: Routledge.
Bloch, M. and Adler, S.A. (1994) 'African children's play and the emergence of the sexual division of labour', in J.L. Roopnarine, J.E. Jonson and F.H. Hooper (eds) *Children's Play in Diverse Cultures*. Albany: SUNY, 148–178.
Blocker, J. (2009) *Seeing Witness*. Minneapolis: University of Minnesota Press.
Bly, L. (2 October 2009) '"Slumdog Millionaire" boosts Mumbai tourism', *USA Today*. Available at: http://usatoday30.usatoday.com/travel/destinations/2009-02-19-slumdog-millionaire-mumbai_N.htm (accessed 2 September 2013).
Boano, C., Hunter, W. and Newton, C. (2013) *Contested Urbanism in Dharavi*. Berkeley: University of California Press.
Boden, D. and Molotch, H.L. (1994) 'The compulsion of proximity', in R. Friedland and D. Boden (eds) *NowHere*. Berkeley, CA: University of California Press, 257–286.
Bolan, P. (2010) *Film-induced Tourism: Motivation, Authenticity and Displacement*. PhD thesis: Business School: University of Ulster.
Bollywood.com (undated) '"Slumdog Millionaire" in Hindi will be "Crorepati"'. Available at: http://www.bollywood.com/slumdog-millionaire-hindi-will-be-crorepati (accessed 11 August 2013).
Bolton, S. and Houlihan, M. (2005) 'The (mis)representation of customer service', *Work, Employment and Society*, 19(4): 685–703.
Boorstin, D. (1962) *The Image*. Hammondsworth: Penguin.
Bordwell, D. (1989) *Making Meaning*. Cambridge: Harvard University Press.
Born, G. and Hesmondhalgh, D. (2000) *Western Music and its Others*. Berkeley: University of California Press.
Bose, D. (2006) *Brand Bollywood*. Wallingford: CABI.
Bouhalis, D. (2003) *E-tourism*. London: Pearson.
Bourdieu, P. (1977) *Outline of a Theory of Practice*. Cambridge: Polity Press.
Bourdieu, P. (1984) *Distinction*. Cambridge: Harvard University Press.
Bourdieu, P. (1993) *The Field of Cultural Production*. Cambridge: Polity.
Bourdieu, P. (1996a) *Rules of Art*. Stanford: Stanford University Press.
Bourdieu, P. (1996b) *The State Nobility*. Stanford: Stanford University Press.
Bourdieu, P. (1998) *Practical Reason*. Cambridge: Polity.

Bourdieu, P. and Nice, R. (1980) 'The aristocracy of culture', *Media, Culture & Society* 2(3): 225–254.

Bourdieu, P., Accardo, A., Balazs, G. Beaud, S., Bovin, F., Bourdieu, E. and Boujeois, P. (1999) *The Weight of the World*, translated by P.P. Ferguson. New York: New Press.

Box Office India (undated) 'Box Office 1993'. Available at: www.boxofficeindia.com/showProd.php?itemCat=199&catName=MTk5Mw (accessed 4 July 2013).

Boyd, D. and Ellison, N. (2007) 'Social network sites: Definition, history and scholarship', *Journal of Computer-Mediated Communication*, 13(1). Available at: http://jcmc.indiana.edu/vol13/issue1/boyd.ellison.html (accessed 13 May 2012).

Braidotti, R. (1994) *Nomadic Subjects*. New York: Columbia University Press.

Braidotti, R. (2011) *Nomadic Subjects*, 2nd ed. New York: Columbia University Press.

Braudby, L. (1986) *The Frenzy of Renown*. New York: Oxford University Press.

Brecht, B. (1964 [1936]) *Brecht on Theatre*. London: Shevan Press.

Breihan, T. (18 July 2007) 'Status ain't hood interviews M.I.A', *The Village Voice*. Available at: http://blogs.villagevoice.com/statusainthood/2007/07/status_aint_hoo_28.php (accessed 29 June 2013).

Brittain, C. (2010) *Adorno and Theology*. New York: Continuum.

Britton, S.G. (1989) 'Tourism, dependency and development: A model of analysis', in Y. Apostolopoulos, S. Leivadi and A. Yannakis (eds) *The Sociology of Tourism*, London: Routledge, 155–172.

Britton, S.G. (1991) 'Tourism, capital and place: towards a critical geography', *Environment and Planning D*, 9(4): 451–478.

Brooks, D. (2000) *Bobos in Paradise*. New York: Simon & Schuster.

Brooks, X. (20 April 2009) 'Slumdog Millionaire child star's father denies putting her up for sale', *The Guardian*. Available at: www.theguardian.com/film/2009/apr/20/slumdog-millionaire-child-star-sale (accessed 17 September 2013).

Brown, R.S. (1994) *Overtones and Undertones*. Berkeley: University of California Press.

Broxton, J. (14 November 2008) 'Slumdog Millionaire – A.R. Rahman', Movie Music UK. Available at: http://moviemusicuk.us/2008/11/14/slumdog-millionaire-a-r-rahman/ (accessed 21 February 2013).

Bruner, E. (2001) 'The Masai and the Lion King: Authenticity, nationalism and globalization in African tourism', *American Ethnologist*, 28(4): 881–908.

Buchmann, A. (2006) 'From Erewhon to Edoras: Tourism and myths in New Zealand', *Tourism, Culture and Communication*, 6: 181–189.

Buhler, J., Neumayer, D. and Deemer, R. (2009) *Hearing the Movies*. New York: Oxford University Press.

Buonaventura, W. (2010) *Serpent of the Nile*. London: Saqi.

Burchell, G. (1993) 'Liberal government and techniques of the Self', *Economy and Society*, 22(3): 267–282.

Burns, P. and O'Regan, M. (2008) 'Everyday techno-social devices in everyday travel life: Digital audio devices in solo travelling lifestyles', in P. Burns and M. Novelli (eds) *Local-Global Connections*, Wallingford: CABI, 146–186.

Büscher, M. and Urry, J. (2009) 'Mobile methods and the empirical', *European Journal of Social Theory*, 12: 99–116.

Büscher, M., Urry, J. and Witchger, K. (2011) *Mobile Methods*. London: Routledge.

Butler, J. (1993) *Bodies that Matter*. London: Routledge.

Butler, J. (1997) *The Psychic Life of Power*. Stanford: Stanford University Press.

Calabrese, A. (2005) 'Communication, global justice and the moral economy', *Global Media and Communication*, 1(3): 301–315.

Campbell, C. (2005) *The Romantic Ethic and the Spirit Of Modern Consumerism*. Oxford: Blackwell/Alcuin Academics.
Campbell, J. (1964) *Honour, Family and Patronage*. Oxford: Oxford University Press.
Campbell, J. (2008) *The Hero with a Thousand Faces*. California: New World.
Cannella, G. and R. Viruru (2004) *Childhood and Postcolonization*. New York: Routledge.
Canton, N. (13 January 2009) 'Actor gets offers from Hollywood, Bollywood', *Hindustan Times*. Available at: www.hindustantimes.com/News-Feed/Entertainment/Actor-gets-offers-from-Hollywood-Bollywood/Article1-366029.aspx (accessed 29 August 2013).
Carey, J.W. (1999) 'Innis "in" Chicago: Hope as a shire of discovery', in C. Acland and W. Buxton (eds) *Harold Innis in the New Century*, Quebec, Canada: McGill-Queen's University Press.
Carozzi, M.J. (2012) 'Light women dancing tango: Gender images as allegories of heterosexual relationships', *Current Sociology*, 61(1): 22–39.
Carr, N. (2010) *The Shallows*. London: Atlantic.
Carrier, J. (ed.) (1995) *Occidentalism*. Oxford: Clarendon Press.
Carruthers, M. (1990) *The Book of Memory*. Cambridge: Cambridge University Press.
Carruthers, M. (1998) *The Craft of Thought*. Cambridge: Cambridge University Press.
Carter, P. (1987) *The Road to Botany Bay*. London: Faber and Faber.
Cartmell, D., Corrigan, T. and Whelehan, I. (2008) 'Introduction to adaptation', *Adaptation*, 1(1): 1–4.
Cashman, R. and Harris, B. (2012) *The Australian Olympic Caravan from 2000 to 2012*. Petersham: Walla Walla Press.
Castells, M. (1996) *The Rise of the Network Society*. Oxford: Blackwell.
Castells, M. (1997) *The Power of Identity*. Oxford: Blackwell.
Castells, M. (2004) 'Informationalism, networks and the network society: A theoretical blueprint', in M. Castells (ed.) *The Network Society*, Cheltenham: Edward Elgar, 3–43.
Castells, M. (2009) *Communication Power*. Oxford: Oxford University Press.
Castells, S. and Miller, M.J. (2009) *The Age of Migration*. Basingstoke: Palgrave Macmillan.
Cavarero, A. (2005) *More than One Voice*. Stanford: Stanford University Press.
Cellini, J. (undated) 'Scoring "Slumdog Millionaire" with Logic: An interview with A.R. Rahman', Logic Pro. Available at: htwww.apple.com/logicpro/in-action/arrahman/ (accessed 11 July 2013).
Chakrabarty, D. (1991) 'Open space/public space: Garbage, modernity and India', *South Asia*, 16: 15–31.
Chakrabarty, D. (2000) *Provincializing Europe*. Princeton: Princeton University Press.
Chakravorty, V. (13 April 2013) 'Actor Pran, famous for playing Bollywood villains, is to be recognised with India's prestigious Dadasaheb Phalke award', Mail Online India. Available at: www.dailymail.co.uk/indiahome/indianews/article-2308383/Finally-Ninety-year-old-actor-Pran-famous-playing-Bollywood-villains-recognised-Indias-prestigous-Dadasaheb-Phalke-award.html (accessed 7 July 2013).
Chalfen, R. (1999) 'Interpreting family photography as pictorial communication', in J. Prosser (ed.) *Image-Based Research*. London: Falmer, 214–234.
Chambers, I. (1990) *Border Dialogues*. New York: Routledge.
Chambliss, W. (1978) *On the Take*. Indiana: Indiana University Press.
Chambliss, W. (1989) 'State-Organised Crime', *Criminology*, 27(2): 183–208.
Chatterjee, P. (1986) *Nationalist Thought and the Colonial World*. Minneapolis, MN: University of Minnesota Press.

Chatterjee, P. (1993) *The Nation and its Fragments*. Princeton, NJ: Princeton University Press.
Chion, M. (1994) *Audio-Vision* (New York: Columbia University Press).
Chouliaraki, L. (2008) 'The Media as Moral Education: Mediation as Action', *Media, Culture & Society*, 30(6): 831–852.
Chowdry, G. (2007) 'Edward Said and contrapuntal reading: Implications for critical interventions in international relations', *Millennium*, 36(1): 101–116.
ClarkK. and M. Holquist (1984) *Mikhail Bakhtin*. Cambridge, MA: Harvard University Press.
Clifford, J. (1983) 'On ethnographic authority', *Representations*, 1(2): 118–146.
Clifford, J. (1986) 'Partial truths' in J. Clifford and G.E. Marcus (eds) *Writing Culture: The Poetics and Politics of Ethnography* (Berkeley, CA: University of California Press), 1–26.
Clifford, J. (1988) *The Predicament of Culture*. Cambridge, MA: Harvard University Press
Clifford, J. (1992) '"Travelling cultures"' in L. Grossberg, C. Nelson and P. Treichler (eds) *Cultural Studies*, New York: Routledge, 96–116.
Clifford, J. (1997). *Routes: Travel and translation in the late twentieth century*. Cambridge, MA: Harvard University Press.
CNN Entertainment (12 January 2009) '"Slumdog" defied the odds'. Retrieved from http://edition.cnn.com/2009/SHOWBIZ/Movies/01/12/slumdog.millionaire/ (accessed 12 August 2013).
Cohen, E. (1972) 'Toward a sociology of international tourism', *Social Research*, 39(1): 164–189.
Cohen, E. (1973) 'Nomads from affluence: Notes on the phenomenon of drifter tourism', *International Journal of Comparative Sociology*, 14(1–2):89–103.
Cohen, E. (1996) 'A phenomenology of tourist experiences', in Y. Apostolopoulos, S. Leivadi and A. Yannakis (eds) *The Sociology of Tourism*. London: Routledge, 90–114.
Cohen, E. (2003) 'Backpacking: Diversity and Change', *Tourism and Cultural* Change, 1(2): 95–111.
Cohen, S. (1997) 'More than the Beatles: popular music, tourism and regeneration', in S. Abram, J. Waldren and D.V.L. Macleod (eds) *Tourists and Tourism*. Oxford: Berg, 71–90.
Cohen, S.A. (2010). 'Personal identity (de)formation among lifestyle travellers: A double-edged sword?' *Leisure Studies*, 29(3): 289–301.
Cohen, S.A. (2011) 'Lifestyle travellers: Backpacking as a way of life', *Annals of Tourism Research*, 38(4): 117–133.
Cohen, S.A., Duncan, T. and Thulemark, M. (2013) 'Lifestyle mobilities: The crossroads of travel, leisure and migration' *Mobilities*. Available at: www.academia.edu/2058825/Lifestyle_mobilities_The_crossroads_of_travel_leisure_and_migration (accessed 11 August 2013).
Cohn, B. (1987) 'Social structure and objectification in South East Asia', in B. Cohn, *An Anthropologist Among the Historians and Other Essays*. Delhi: Oxford University Press, 224–254.
Cohn, B. and Dirks, N. (1988) 'Beyond the fringe: The nation-state, colonialism and the technologies of power', *Journal of Historical Sociology*, 1: 224–229.
Cole, M. (2005) 'Transmodernism, Marxism and social change: Some implications for teacher education', *Policy Futures in Education*, 3(1): 90–105.
Coleman, J. (1988) 'Social capital in the creation of human capital', *American Journal of Sociology*, 94: 95–120.
Coleman, J. and Crang, M. (2002) *Tourism*, New York: Berghahn.

Bibliography

Coleman, S. and Eade, J. (2004) 'Reframing pilgrimage' in S. Coleman and J. Eade (eds) *Reframing Pilgrimage*. London: Routledge, 1–26.

Coles, T. (2008) 'Telling tales of tourism: Mobility, media and citizenship in the 2004 EU enlargement', in P. Burns and M. Novelli (eds) *Tourism and Mobilities*. Wallingford, Oxfordshire: CABI, 65–80.

Collier, J.F., Rosaldo, M.Z. and Yanagisako, S. (1982) '"Is there a family?" New anthropological views', in B. Thorne and M. Yalom (eds) *Rethinking the Family*. New York: Longman, 25–39.

Collier, S. and Ong, A. (2005) 'Global assemblages, anthropological problems', in A. Ong and S. Collier, *Global Assemblages*. Oxford: Blackwell, 3–21.

Connell, J. and Gibson, C. (2004) 'World music: deterritorialising place and identity', *Progress in Human Geography*, 28(3): 342–361.

Connell, R.W. (1987) *Gender and Power*. Stanford: Stanford University Press.

Connell, R.W. (1995) *Masculinities*. Berkeley: University of California Press.

Cooper, F. and Stoler, A. (1997) *Tensions of Empire*. Berkeley, CA: University of California Press.

Cooper, G. (2001) 'The mutable mobile: Social theory in the wireless world', in B. Brown, N. Green and R. Harper (eds) *Wireless World*. London: Springer, 19–32

Corbridge, S. and Shah, A. (2013) 'Introduction: The underbelly of the Indian boom', *Economy and Society*, 42(3): 335–347.

Corliss, R. (22 February 2011) 'The 2011 Oscar Race: TIME Picks the Winners', *Time*. Available at: www.time.com/time/specials/packages/article/0,28804,2044968_2052929_2053238,00.html (accessed 15 August 2013).

Corrigan, M. (23 January 2014) 'Roy Bhaskar on the fetishisation of facts', *The Sociological Imagination*. Available at: http://sociologicalimagination.org/archives/14809 (accessed 24 January 2014).

Couldry, N. (2003a) 'Media meta-capital: Extending the range of Bourdieu's field theory', *Theory and Society*, 32(5/6): 653–677.

Couldry, N. (2003b) *Media Rituals*. New York: Routledge.

Couldry, N. (2006) 'In place of a common culture, what?', in N. Couldry (ed.) *Listening Beyond the Echoes*. Boulder: Paradigm, 63–82.

Couldry, N. (2007) 'Communicative entitlements and democracy: The future of the digital divide', in R. Mansell, C. Avergou, D. Quah and R. Silverstone (eds) *The Oxford Handbook on Information and Communication Technologies*. Oxford: Oxford University Press, 383–403.

Cowen, M. and Shenton, R. (1996) *Doctrines of Development*. London: Routledge.

Coyne, R. (1999) *Technoromanticism*. Boston: MIT.

Crang, M. (1999) 'Knowing, tourism and practices of vision', in D. Crouch (ed.) *Leisure/Tourism Geographies*. Oxford: Blackwell, 238–256.

Crang, P. (1997) 'Performing the tourist product', in C. Rojek and J. Urry (eds) *Touring Cultures*. London and New York: Routledge, 137–154.

Cresswell, T. (1999) 'Falling down: Resistance as diagnostic', in J. Sharp (ed.) *Geographies of Domination/Resistance*. London: Routledge, 256–268.

Cresswell, T. (2001) 'The production of mobilities'. *New Formations*, 43(2): 3–25.

Cresswell, T. (2009) *On the Move*. London: Routledge.

Cresswell, T. (2010) 'Towards a politics of mobility', *Environment and Planning D*, 28(1):17–31.

Cronin, M. (2000) *Across the Lines*. Cork: University of Cork Press.

Cronin, M. (2003) *Translation and Globalisation*. London: Routledge.

Cronin, M. (2013) *Translation in the Digital Age*. London: Routledge.
Crossley, N. (2002) *Making Sense of Social Movements*. Buckingham: Open University Press.
Crossley, N. (2003) 'From reproduction to transformation: social movement fields and the radical habitus', *Theory, Culture & Society*, 20(6): 43–68.
Crouch, D. (2006) 'Tourism, consumption and rurality', in P. Cloke, T. Marsden and P. Mooney (eds) *The Handbook of Rural Studies*. London: Sage, 355–364.
Crouch, D. (2009) 'The diverse dynamics of cultural studies and tourism', in T. Jamal and M. Robinson (eds) *The SAGE Handbook of Tourism Studies*. London: Sage, 82–98.
Croy, G.W. (2010) 'Planning for film tourism: Active destination image management', *Tourism and Hospitality Planning & Development*, 7(1): 21–23.
Croy, G.W. and Heitmann, S. (2011) 'Tourism and film' in P. Robinson and P.U.C. Dieke (eds) *Research Themes for Tourism*, Wallingford: CABI, 188–204.
Crush, J. ed. (1995) *The Power of Development*. London: Routledge.
Crystal, D. (2006) *Language and the Internet*. Cambridge: Cambridge University Press.
Cunningham, S. (2005) 'Creative enterprises', in J. Hartley (ed.) *Creative Industries*. Oxford: Blackwell, 282–298.
Currah, A. (2007) 'Managing creativity: the tensions between commodities and gifts in a digital networked environment', *Economy and Society*, 36(3): 467–494.
D'Andrea, A. (2004) 'Global nomads: Techno and New Age as transnational countercultures in Ibiza and Goa', in G. Saint-John (ed.) *Rave Culture and Religion*. New York: Routledge, 256–272.
D'Andrea, A. (2006) 'Neo-nomadism: a theory of post-identarian mobility in the global age', *Mobilities*, 1(1): 95–119.
DaMatta, R. (1991) *Carnivals, Rogues and Heroes*. Notre Dame: University of Notre Dame Press.
Dann, G.M.S. (1977) 'Anomie, ego-enhancement and tourism', *Annals of Tourism Research*, 4: 184–194.
Dann, G.M.S. (1989) 'The tourist as child: Some reflections', *Cahiers du Tourisme*, Serie C, No. 135. Aix-en-Provence: CHET.
Dann, G.M.S. (1996) *The Language of Tourism*. Wallingford: CABI.
Dann, G.M.S. (2001) 'Slavery, contested heritage and thanatotourism', *International Journal of Tourism Hospitality and Administration*, 2(3/4):1–29.
Dann, G.M.S. (2002) 'The tourist as a metaphor of the social world', in G.M.S. Dann (ed.) *The Tourist as a Metaphor of the Social World*, Wallingford: CABI, 1–18.
Dann, G.M.S. and Cohen, E. (1996) 'Sociology and tourism', in Y. Apostolopoulos, S. Leivadi and A. Yannakis (eds) *The Sociology of Tourism*. London: Routledge, 301–314.
Dann, G.M.S. and Seaton, A.V. (2001) 'Slavery, contested heritage and thanatourism', in G.M.S. Dann and A.V. Seaton (eds) *Slavery, Contested Heritage and Thanatourism*. New York: Haworth Hospitality Press, 1–29.
Dann, G.M.S. and Liebman Parrinello, G. (2009) 'Setting the scene', in G.M.S. Dann and G. Parrinello (eds) *The Sociology of Tourism*, UK: Emerald, 1–64.
Danto, A. (1964) 'The artworld', *Journal of Philosophy*, 61: 571–584.
Danto, A. (1999) 'Bourdieu on art: Field and individual', in R. Shusterman (ed.) *Bourdieu: A critical reader*, Oxford: Blackwell, 214–219.
Davis, H.L. (2010) 'Feeding the world a line? Celebrity activism and ethical consumer practices from Live Aid to Product Red', *Journal for Nordic Studies*, 9(3): 67–87.
Davis, J. (1992) *Exchange*. Buckingham: Open University Press.

Bibliography

Davis, M. (2008) *Freedom and Consumerism*. Aldershot: Ashgate.
Dawtrey, A. (30 August 2007) 'Danny Boyle to direct "Slumdog"', *Variety*. Available at: http://variety.com/2007/film/news/danny-boyle-to-direct-slumdog-2-1117971102/ (accessed 11 August 2013).
de Botton, A. (2002) *The Art of Travel*. New York: Pantheon.
de Certeau, M. (1984) *The Practice of Everyday Life*. Berkeley: University of California Press.
de Certeau, M. (1985) 'What we do when we believe', in M. Blonsky (ed.) *On Signs*, Baltimore: John Hopkins University Press.
de Certeau, M. (1986) *Heterologies*, translated by B. Massumi. Manchester: Manchester University Press.
de Certeau, M. (1988) *The Writing of History*, translated by T. Conley. New York: Columbia University Press.
De Kadt, E. (1979) 'Social planning of tourism in the developing countries', *Annals of Tourism Research*, 6(1): 36–48.
de Lauretis, T. (1987) *Technologies of Gender*. London: Macmillan.
de Sousa Santos, B. (1999) 'Towards a multicultural conception of human rights', in M. Featherstone and S. Lash (eds) *Spaces of Culture*, London: Sage, 214–229.
Deacon, A. (2007) 'Civic labour or doulia? Care, reciprocity and welfare', *Social Policy and Society*, 6(4): 481–490.
Deagon, A. (undated) 'Feminism and belly dance'. Available at: www.tribalbellydance.org/articles/feminism.html (accessed 12 February 2011).
Dean, J. (2007) 'The net and multiple realities', in S. During, *The Cultural Studies Reader*, 3rd edn., London: Routledge, 520–534.
Debord, G. (1995) *Society and the Spectacle*. New York: Zone.
Deleuze, G. and Guattari, F. (1988) *A Thousand Plateaus*. London: Athlone.
Delhi-Mumbai Industrial Corridor (DMIC) (undated) 'Welcome to DMICDC'. Available at: www.dmicdc.com/Default.aspx (accessed 11 September 2013).
Demiray, B. (2011) 'Cinema on cinema: The kinship between Cinema Paradiso and Zikkimin Kökü, Karpuz Kabuğundan Gemiler Yapmak, Sinema Bir Mucezedir', *Cinej Cinema Journal* 1(1). Available at: http://cinej.pitt.edu/ojs/index.php/cinej/article/view/10 (accessed 15 March 2013).
DeNora, T. (2000) *Music and Everyday Life*, Cambridge: Cambridge University Press.
DeNora, T. (2003) *After Adorno*. Cambridge: Cambridge University Press.
Denzin, N. (1989) *Interpretive Biography*. Newbury Park: Sage.
Denzin, N. (2002) *Reading Race*. London: Sage.
Derrida, J. (1994) *Spectres of Marx*. New York: Routledge.
Derrida, J. (2001) *Acts of Religion*, trans G. Anidjar. New York: Routledge.
Derrida, J. and Dufourmantelle, A. (2000) *Of Hospitality*. Stanford: Stanford University Press.
Desforges, L. (2000) 'Traveling the world: Identity and travel biography', *Annals of Tourism Research*, 27(4): 926–945.
Desmond, J. (1994) 'Embodying differences: Issues in dance and cultural studies', *Cultural Critique*, 26: 33–64.
Dharavi Diary (undated) Available at: www.dharavidiary.com (accessed 3 September 2013).
Diawara, M. (1992) *African Cinema*. Bloomington: Indiana University Press.
Diekmann, A. and Hannam, K. (2012) 'Touristic mobilities in India's slum places', *Annals of Tourism Research*, 39(3): 1315–1336.
Diken, B. and Laustsen, C.B. (2005) *The Culture of Exception*. London: Routledge.

Diken, B. and Laustsen, C.B. (2007) *Sociology through the Projector*. London: Routledge.

Dikötter, F. (2008) 'The racialization of the globe: An interactive interpretation', *Ethnic and Racial Studies*, 31(8): 1478–1496.

DNA India (15 December 2008) 'Rahman advocates free hugs for peace'. Available at: www.dnaindia.com/entertainment/1214284/report-rahman-advocates-free-hugs-for-peace (accessed 15 August 2013).

DNA India (13 January 2009) 'Salaam slum children of Mumbai: Loveleen'. Available at: www.dnaindia.com/entertainment/1221102/report-salaam-slum-children-of-mumbai-loveleen (accessed 12 August 2013).

DNA India (14 November 2010) 'Jai Ho to enthral at Asian Games closing ceremony'. Available at: www.dnaindia.com/sport/1466464/report-jai-ho-to-enthrall-at-asian-games-closing-ceremony (accessed 13 July 2013).

Doezema, J. (2001) 'Ouch! Western feminists' "wounded attachment" to the "Third World prostitute"', *Feminist Review*, 67(1): 16–38.

Donald, S.H. and Gammack, J.G. (2007) *Tourism and the Branded City*. Farnham: Ashgate.

Douglas, M. (1992) *Risk and Blame*. New York: Routledge.

Douglas, M. (1993) *Purity and Danger*. London: Routledge.

Douglas, M. and Wildavsky, A. (1982) *Risk and Culture*. Berkeley: University of California Press.

Dredge, D. and Jamal, T. (2013) 'Mobilities on the Gold Coast, Austalia: Implications for destination governance and sustainable tourism', *Journal of Sustainable Tourism* 21(4): 557–579.

du Rand, G.E., and Heath, E. (2006) 'Towards a framework for food tourism as an element of destination marketing', *Current Issues in Tourism*, 9(3): 206–234.

Duffy, M. (2000) 'Lines of drift: festival participation and performing a sense of place', *Popular Music*, 19(1): 51–64.

Durham, M.G. (2009) 'M.I.A.: A production analysis of musical subversion', paper presented at the annual meeting of the International Communication Association, Chicago, IL, 20 May 2009.

Dürr, E. (2012) 'Encounters over garbage: Tourists and lifestyle migrants at a Mexican dump', *Tourism Geographies*, 14(2): 339–355.

Duruz, J. (2004) 'Adventure and belonging: An appetite for markets', *Space and Culture*, 7: 427–445.

Dussel, E. (1985) *Philosophy of Liberation*. New York: Orbis.

Dussel, E. (1995) *The Invention of the Americas*. New York: Continuum.

Duval, D.T. (2008) '"Claim you are from Canada eh?" Travelling citizenship within global space', in Burns, P. and Novelli, M. (eds) *Local-Global Connections*. Wallingford: CABI, 81–91.

Duvenage, P. (1999) 'The politics of memory and forgetting after Auschwitz and Apartheid', *Philosophy and Social Criticism*, 25(3): 1–28.

Dwyer, C. and Crang, P. (2002) 'Fashioning ethnicities: the commercial spaces of multiculture', *Ethnicities*, 2(3): 410–430.

Dyer, R. (1982) *Stars*. London: British Film Institute.

Dyer, R. (1993) 'The role of stereotypes', in *The Matter of Images: Essays on Representations*, London: Routledge, 11–18.

Dyer, R. (1997) *White*. London: Routledge.

Dyson, P. (2012) 'Slum tourism: Representing and interpreting "reality" in Dharavi, Mumbai', *Tourism Geographies*, 14(2): 254–274.

Bibliography

Eade, J. and Sallnow, M.J. (eds) (1991) *Contesting the Sacred*. London: Routledge.
Eagleton, T. (13 May 1999) 'In the gaudy supermarket', *London Review of Books*, 21(10). Available at: www.lrb.co.uk/v21/n10/terry-eagleton/in-the-gaudy-supermarket (accessed 6 May 2013).
Earl, B. (2008) 'Literary tourism: Constructions of value, celebrity and distinction', *International Journal of Cultural Studies*, 11(4): 401–417.
Echavone, M. and Srivastava, R. (21 February 2009) 'Taking the slum out of "slumdog"', *The New York Times*. Available at: www.nytimes.com/2009/02/21/opinion/21shrivastava.html?_r=0 (accessed 28 January 2013).
Eco, U. (1987) *Travels in Hyperreality*. London: Picador.
Edensor, T. (1998) *Tourists at the Taj*. London: Routledge.
Edensor, T. (2002) *National identity, Popular Culture and Everyday Life*. London: Berg.
Edensor, T. (2005a) *Industrial Ruins*. London: Berg.
Edensor, T. (2005b) 'Mediating William Wallace: Audio-visual technologies in tourism', in D. Crouch, R. Jackson and F. Thompson (eds) *The Media and the Tourist Imagination*. New York: Routledge, 105–118.
Edensor, T. (2011) 'Commuter: Mobility, rhythm, commuting', in T. Cresswell and P. Merriman (eds) *Geographies of Mobilities*. Farnham: Ashgate, 189–204.
Edensor, T. (2014) 'Rhythm and arrhythmia', in P. Adey (ed.) *The Routledge Handbook of Mobilities*. London and New York: Routledge, 163–171.
Edmunds, J. and Turner, B. (2002) *Generations, Culture and Society*. Buckingham: Open University Press.
Edwards, T. (1999) *Contradictions of Consumption*. Buckingham: Open University Press.
Egedy, T. and Kovács, Z. (2009) *The Potential of Budapest to Attract Creativity*. Amsterdam: University of Amsterdam Press.
Eleftheriotis, D. (2001) *Popular Cinemas in Europe*. New York: Continuum.
Eliade, M. (1989) *The Myth of the Eternal Return, or Cosmos and History*. London: Arkana.
Elias, N. (1982) *The Civilising Process: State Formation and Civilisation, II*. Oxford: Blackwell.
Elliott, A. (2002) 'The Reinvention of citizenship', in N. Stevenson (ed.) *Culture and Citizenship*. London: Sage, 47–61.
Elliott, A. (2004) *Social Theory since Freud*. London: Routledge.
Ellison, N. and Burrows, R. (2007) 'New Spaces of (dis)engagement? Social politics, urban technologies and the rezoning of the city', *Housing Studies*, 22(3): 295–312.
Ellul, J. (1964) *The Technological Society*. Toronto: Random House.
England, M.R. and Simon, S. (2010) 'Scary cities: Urban geographies of fear, difference and belonging', *Social & Cultural Geography*, 11(3): 201–207.
Enloe, C. (1990) *Bananas, Beaches and Bases*. Berkeley: University of California Press.
Erlmann, V. (1996) 'The aesthetics of the global imagination: reflections on world music in the 1990s', *Public Culture*, 8: 467–487.
Erlmann, V. (1999) *Music, Modernity and the Global Imagination*. Oxford: Oxford University Press.
Erlmann, V. (2004) 'But what of the ethnographic ear? Anthropology, sound and the senses', in V. Erlmann (ed.) *Hearing Cultures*. Oxford: Berg, 1–20.
Escavone, M. and Srivastava, R. (21 February 2009) 'Taking the slum out of "slumdog"', *New York Times*. Available from www.nytimes.com/2009/02/21/opinion/21srivastava.html?_r=0 (accessed 8 April 2015).
Etzioni, A. (1995) *New Communitarian Thinking*. Virginia: University Press.

Everett, W. (1996) 'The autobiographical eye in European film', *Europa*, 2(1): 3–10.
Fabian, J. (1983) *Time and the Other*. New York: Columbia University Press.
Fabian, J. (1999) 'Theatre and anthropology, theatricality and culture', *Research in African Literatures*, 30(4): 24–31.
Fassin, D. (2012) *Humanitarian Reason*. Berkeley: University of California Press.
Faubion, J. (1988) 'Possible modernities', *Cultural Anthropology*, 3(4): 365–378.
Faulkner, R.R. and Anderson, A.B. (1987) 'Short-term projects and emergent careers: Evidence from Hollywood', *American Journal of Sociology*, 92(4): 879–909.
Fawcett, C. and Cormack, P. (2001) 'Guarding authenticity at literary tourism sites', *Annals of Tourism Research*, 28(3): 686–704.
Featherstone, M. (1990) *Global Culture*. London: Sage.
Featherstone, M. (1991) 'The body in consumer culture', in M. Featherstone, M. Hepworth and B.S. Turner (eds) *The Body*. London: Sage, 170–196.
Featherstone, M., Thrift, N. and Urry, J. (2004) 'Cultures of automobility', *Theory, Culture & Society*, 21: 1–284.
Feifer, M. (1985) *Going Places*. London: Macmillan.
Feld, S. (2000) 'Sweet lullaby for world music', *Public Culture*, 12(1): 145–171.
Ferguson, J. (2006) *Global Shadows*. Durham: Duke University Press.
FergusonK. (1984) *The Feminist Case Against Bureaucracy*. Philadelphia: Temple Press.
FergusonK. (1993) *The Man Question*. California: University of California Press.
Ferrell, J. (2005) *Empire of Scrounge*. New York: University of New York Press.
Fischer, M. (2004) 'Integrating anthropological approaches to the study of culture: The "hard" and the "soft"', *Cybernetics and Systems*, 35(2/3): 147–162.
Fischer, M., Lyon, D. and Zeitlyn, D. (2008) 'The Internet and the future of social science research', in N. Fielding, R.M. Lee and G. Blank (eds) *The Sage Handbook of Online Research Methods*, London: Sage, 519–536.
Fiske, J. (1987) *Television Culture*. London: Taylor & Francis.
Fiske, J. (1989) *Understanding Popular Culture*. London: Routledge.
Florida, R. (2003) *The Rise of the Creative Class*. Melbourne: Pluto.
Forster, J. (April 2009) 'Slumdog Millionaire puts slum tourism in the spotlight', *Development Asia*, 3. Available at: http://development.asia/issue03/feature-01.asp (accessed 1 September 2013).
Fortes, M. (1969) *Kinship and the Social Order*. Chicago: Aldine de Guyter.
Foucault, M. (1976) *The History of Sexuality, vol. I: Introduction*. London: Allen Lane.
Foucault, M. (1979) *Discipline and Punish*. New York: Vintage.
Foucault, M. (1980) *Power/Knowledge*, G. Colin (ed). New York: Harvester Press.
Foucault, M. (1986) 'Of other spaces', *Diacritics*, 16(1): 22–27.
Foucault, M. (1989) *The Order of Things*. London: Routledge.
Foucault, M. (1997) 'The birth of biopolitics', in P. Rabinow (ed.) *Michel Foucault: Ethics*. New York: New Press, 73–79.
Foucault, M. (2003) *Society Must be Defended*. London: Penguin.
Foucault, M. (2007) *Security, Territory and Population*, translated by G. Burchell. Basingstoke: Palgrave Macmillan.
Fox, A. (2004) *Real Country*. Durham: Duke University Press.
Franklin, A. and Crang, M. (2001) 'The trouble with tourism and travel theory', *Tourist Studies*, 1(1): 5–22.
Franklin, S., Lury, C. and Stacey, J. (eds) (2000) *Global Nature, Global Culture*. London: Sage.

Fraser N. and Honneth, A. (2003) *Redistribution or Recognition?* London: Verso.
Freire-Madeiros, B. (2009) 'The favela and its touristic transits', *Geoforum*, 40(4): 280–288.
Frenzel, F. (2012) 'Beyond "Othering": The political roots of slum tourism' in F. Frenzel, K. Koens and M. Steinbrink, *Slum Tourism*. London: Routledge, 49–65.
Freud, S. (1965) *The Psychopathology of Everyday Life*. New York: Norton.
Freud, S. (1991) *The Interpretation of Dreams*. Harmondsworth: Penguin.
Friedberg, A. (1993) *Window Shopping*. Berkeley: University of California Press.
Friedberg, A. (1995) 'Cinema and the postmodern condition', in L. Williams (ed.) *Viewing Positions*. Brunswick: Rutgers University Press, 59–86.
Friedman, J. (1994) *Cultural Identity and Global Process*. London: Sage.
Friedman, T. (2005) *The World is Flat*. New York: Farrar, Straus and Giroux.
Fritch, S. (2008) 'The UN global compact and global governance of corporate social responsibility: complex multilateralism for more human globalisation?', *Global Society*, 22: 1–26.
Frith, S. (1996) *Performing Rites*. Oxford: Oxford University Press.
Frith, S. (2000) 'The discourse of world music', in G. Born and D. Hesmondhalgh (eds) *Western Music and its Others*. Berkeley: University of California Press, 305–322.
Frow, J. (1995) *Cultural Studies and Cultural Values*. Oxford: Clarendon.
Frow, J. (1998) 'Is Elvis a God? Cult, culture, questions of method', *International Journal of Cultural Studies*, 1(2): 197–210.
Fullagar, S. (2012) 'Gendered Cultures of slow travel', in S. Fullagar, K. Markwell and E. Wilson (eds), *Slow Tourism*, Bristol: Channel View, 99–112.
Fuller, B. (21 April 2009) 'Why Danny Boyle had to save his "Slumdog Millionaire" star from being "sold"', *Huffington Post*. Available at: www.huffingtonpost.com/bonnie-fuller/can-326-million-save-slum_b_189406.html (accessed 13 September 2013).
Funkenstein, A. (1986) *Theology and the Scientific Imagination*. Princeton: Princeton University Press.
Fuss, D. (1994) 'Interior Colonies: Frantz Fanon and the Politics of Identification', *Diacritics*, 24(2–3): 19–42.
Fussell, P. (1975) *The Great War and Modern Memory*. New York: Oxford University Press.
Gagné, N.O. (2013) 'Romance and sexuality in Japanese Latin dance clubs', *Ethnography*, Sage Online First (4 July 2013). Available at: http://eth.sagepub.com/content/early/2013/07/03/1466138113490605.abstract (accessed 18 August 2013).
Gale, T. (2008) 'The end of tourism or endings of tourism?', in Burns, P. and Novelli, M. (eds) *Local-Global Connections*. Wallingford: CABI, 1–14.
Gallant, T.W. (1999) 'Brigandage, piracy, capitalism, and state-formation: Transnational crime from a historical world-systems perspective', in J.McC. Heyman (ed.) *States and Illegal Practices*. Oxford and New York: Oxford Berg, 25–61.
Gallant, T.W. (2000) 'Honor, masculinity, and ritual knife fighting in nineteenth-century Greece', *American Historical Review*, 105(2): 359–382.
Game, A. (1991) *Undoing the Social*. Buckingham: Open University Press.
Gammack, J.G. (1999) *Synaesthesia and Knowing*, Perth: Division of Business, Information Technology and Law, Murdoch University.
Gardiner, M. (1992) *The Dialogics of Critique*. London: Routledge.
Garnham, N. (1990) *Capitalism and Communication*. London: Sage.
Garnham, N. (1999) 'Amartya Sen's "capabilities" approach to the evaluation of welfare and its applications to communications', in A. Calabrese and J. Burgelman (eds)

Communication, Citizenship and Social Policy. Lanham: Rowman and Littlefield, 113–124.
Garnham, N. (2000) *Emancipation, Media and Modernity*. Oxford: Oxford University Press.
Gassner, J. (2002) *The Reader's Encyclopedia of World Drama*. New York: Courier Dover Publications.
Gauntlett, D. (2011) *Making is Connecting*. Cambridge: Polity.
Geary, D. (2013) 'Incredible India in a global age: The cultural politics of image branding in tourism', *Tourist Studies*, 13(1): 36–61.
Geertz, C. (1973) *The Interpretation of Cultures*. New York: Basic Books.
Gellner, E. (1983) *Nations and Nationalism*. Oxford: Blackwell.
Gellner, E. (1998) *Nationalism*. London: Phoenix.
Genosko, G. (2008) 'A signifying semiotics', *Public Journal of Semiotics*, 2(1): 11–21.
Germann Molz, J. (2004) 'Playing online and between the lines: Round-the-world websites as virtual places to play', in M. Sheller and J. Urry (eds) *Tourism Mobilities*, London: Routledge, 167–180.
Germann Molz, J. (2008) 'Global abode: Home and mobility in narratives of round-the-world travel', *Space and Culture*, 11(4): 325–342.
Germann Molz, J. (2009) 'Representing pace in tourism mobilities: Staycations, slow travel and The Amazing Race', *Journal of Tourism and Cultural Change*, 7(4): 270–286.
Germann Molz, J. (2012) *Travel Connections*. London: Routledge.
Gibbons, J. (2007) *Contemporary Art and Memory*. London: I.B. Tauris.
Gibson, S. (2006) 'A seat with a view: Tourism, immobility and the cinematic travel guide', *Tourist Studies*, 6(1): 157–178.
Giddens, A. (1984) *The Constitution of Society*. Cambridge: Polity.
Giddens, A. (1987) *Social Theory and Modern Sociology*. Cambridge: Polity.
Giddens, A. (1990) *The Consequences of Modernity*. Cambridge: Polity.
Giddens, A. (1991) *Modernity and Self-Identity*. Cambridge: Polity.
Giddens, A. (1992) *The Transformation of Intimacy*. Cambridge: Polity.
Giddens, A. (1994) 'Living in a post-traditional society', in U. Beck, A. Giddens and S. Lash (eds) *Reflexive Modernization*, Cambridge: Polity, 56–109.
Giddens, A. (2002) *Runaway World*. London: Profile Books.
Giddens, A. and Pierson, C. (1998) *Conversations with Anthony Giddens*. Cambridge: Polity.
Gillespie, A. (2006) 'Tourist photography and the reverse gaze', *Ethos*, 34(3): 343–366.
Gilloch, G. (2007) 'Urban optics: Film, phantasmagoria and the city in Benjamin and Kracauer', *New Formations*, 61(2): 115–131.
Glasze, G. (2005) 'Some reflections on the economic and political organization of private neighborhoods', *Housing Studies*, 20(2): 221–233.
Glissant, E. (1989) *Caribbean Discourse*. Charlottesville: Virginia University Press.
Goffman, E. (1987) *The Presentation of Self in Everyday Life*. Harmondsworth: Penguin.
Goldberg, D.T. (1993) *Racist Culture*. Oxford: Blackwell.
Goldmann, L. (1964) *The Hidden God*. London: Routledge.
Goldmann, L. (1980) *Method in the Sociology of Literature*. Oxford: Basil Blackwell.
Goodman, L. (1976) *The Languages of Art*. Indianapolis, IN: Bobbs-Merill.Goodwin, A. and Gore, J. (1990) 'World beat and the cultural imperialism debate', *Socialist Review*, 3: 63–80.
Goody, J. (2006) *The Theft of History*. Cambridge: Cambridge University Press.

Gorbman, C. (1987) *Unheard Melodies*. Bloomington: Indiana University Press.
Gosh, A. (27 February 2006) 'Mumbai's slums are India's most literate', *DNA India*. Available at: www.dnaindia.com/mumbai/report_mumbai-s-slums-are-india-s-most-literate_1015111 (accessed 1 September 2013).
Gosh, S. and Wang, L. (2003) 'Transnationalism and identity: A tale of two faces and multiple lives', *Canadian Geographer*, 47(3): 269–282.
Gottlieb, A. (1982) 'Americans' vacations', *Annals of Tourism Research*, 9:165–187.
Gouldner, A. (1948) 'Industrial sociology: Status and prospects (Discussion)', *American Sociological Review*, 13(4): 396–400.
Gourgouris, S. (1996) *Dream Nation*. Stanford: Stanford University Press.
Govil, N. (2007) 'Bollywood and the frictions of global mobility', in T.K. Daya (ed.) *Media on the Move*. London: Routledge, 76–88.
Gowan, P. (2003) 'The new liberal cosmopolitanism', in D. Archibugi (ed.) *Debating Cosmopolitics*. London: Verso, 51–66.
Graburn, N.H.H. (1977) 'Tourism: The sacred journey', in V. Smith (ed.) *Hosts and Guests*. Philadelphia: University of Pennsylvania Press, 21–36.
Graburn, N.N.H. (1983a) 'The anthropology of tourism', *Annals of Tourism Research*, 10(1): 9–33.
Graburn, N.N.H. (1983b) *To Pray, Pay and Play*. Aix en-Provence: Centre des Hautes Etudes Touristiques.
Graburn, N.H.H. (2004) 'The Kyoto tax strike: Buddhism, shinto and tourism in Japan', in E. Badone and S.R. Roseman (eds) *Intersecting Journeys*, Chicago: University of Illinois, 125–139.
Graff, H.J. (2001) 'Literacy's myths and legacies: From lessons to the history of literacy to the question of critical literacy', in P. Freebody, S. Muspratt and B. Dwyer (eds) *Difference, Silence and Textual Practice*. Creskill, NJ: Hampton Press, 1–30.
Graham, S. and Marvin, S. (2001) *Splintering Urbanism*. London: Routledge.
Gray, L.E. (2007) 'Memories of the empire, mythologies of the soul: Fado performance and the shaping of saudade', *Ethnomusicology*, 53(1): 106–130.
Gregg, M. (2009) 'Learning to (love) labour: Production cultures and the affective turn', *Communication and Critical/Cultural Studies*, 6(2): 209–214.
Grosz, E. (1999) *Becomings: Explorations in Time, Memory and Futures*. Ithaca, NY: Cornell University Press.
Grosz, E. (2001) *Architecture from the Outside*. Cambridge: MIT.
Grugulis, I. and Stoyanova, D. (2011) 'The missing middle: Communities of practice in a freelance labour market', *Work, Employment & Society*, 25(2): 342–351.
Guattari, F. (1995) *Chaosmosis*. Sydney: Power.
Guichard, S. (2013) 'The Indian nation and selective amnesia: Representing conflicts and violence in Indian history textbooks', *Nations and Nationalism*, 19(1): 68–86.
Gupta, D. (2005) *Learning to Forget*. Oxford: Oxford University Press.
Gupta, K. (25 January 2009) 'Slumdog is about defaming Hindus', *Hindu Nation*. Available at: http://voiceofhindus.blogspot.co.uk/2009/01/slumdog-is-about-defaming-hindus.html (accessed 15 September 2013).
Gupta, R. (2003) *From Homebreakers to Jailbreakers*. London: Zed.
Haas, P. (1992) 'Knowledge, power and international policy coordination', *International Organization*, 46(1): 1–35.
Habermas, J. (1983) 'Hannah Arendt: On the concept of power', in *Philosophical-Political Profiles*. London: Heinemann.

Habermas, J. (1989) *The Structural Transformation of the Public Sphere*. Oxford: Polity.
Habermas, J. (1996) *Between Facts and Norms*. Cambridge: Polity.
Habermas, J. (1997) *A Berlin Republic*. Lincoln: University of Nebraska Press.
Haldrup, M. (2009) 'Banal Tourism? Between cosmopolitanism and orientalism', in P.O. Pons, M. Crang and P. Travlou (eds) *Cultures of Mass Tourism*. Aldershot: Ashgate, 53–74.
Haldrup, M. and Larsen, J. (2003) 'The family gaze', *Tourist Studies* 3(1): 23–46.
Haldrup, M. and Larsen, J. (2006) 'Material cultures of tourism', *Leisure Studies*, 25 (3): 275–289.
Haldrup, M., Koefoed, L. and Simonsen, K. (2006) 'Practical orientalism – Bodies, everyday life and the construction of otherness', *Geografiska Annaler B*, 88(2): 173–184.
Hall, M.C. (2008) 'Of time and space and other things: Laws of tourism and the geographies of contemporary mobilities', in P. Burns and M. Novelli (eds) *Local-Global Connections*. Wallingford: CABI, 15–32.
Hall, S. (1992) 'The question of cultural identity', in S. Hall, D. Held and A. MacGrew (eds) *Modernity and its Futures*. Cambridge and Milton Keynes: Polity and Open University Press, 274–325.
Hall, S. (1996) 'Cultural studies and its theoretical legacies', in S. Hall, D. Morley and K-H. Chen (eds) *Stuart Hall*. London: Routledge, 262–275.
Hand, M. (2012) *Ubiquitous Photography*. Cambridge: Polity.
Hand, M. and Sandywell, B. (2002) 'E-topia as cosmopolis or citadel', *Theory, Culture & Society*, 19(1–2): 197–225.
Hannam, K. (2008) 'The end of tourism? Nomadology and the mobilities paradigm', in J. Tribe (ed.) *Philosophical Issues in Tourism*. Clevedon: Channel View, 101–116.
Hannam, K. and Knox, D. (2010) *Understanding Tourism*. London: Sage.
Hannam, K., Sheller, M. and Urry, J. (2006) 'Editorial: Mobilities, immobilites and moorings', *Mobilities*, 1(1): 1–22.
Hannerz, U. (1990) 'Cosmopolitans and locals in world culture', *Theory, Culture & Society*, 7(2): 237–251.
Hannerz, U. (1996) *Transnational Connections*. London: Routledge.
Hannerz, U. (2002) 'We are who we are and who we want to be', in U. Hedetoft and M. Hjort (eds) *The Postnational Self*. Minneapolis: University of Minnesota Press, 217–232.
Hannerz, U. and Löfgren, O. (1994) 'The nation in the global village,' *Cultural Studies*, 8: 198–207.
Haraway, D. (1988) 'Situated knowledges: The science question in feminism and the privilege of partial perspective', *Feminist Studies*, 14: 575–599.
Hardt, M. and Negri, A. (2000) *Empire*. Cambridge: Harvard University Press.
Hardt, M. and Negri, A. (2004) *Multitude*. New York: Penguin.
Harré, R. (1986) *Varieties of Realism*. Oxford: Blackwell.
Harré, R. (1993) *The Discursive Mind*. Cambridge: Polity Press.
Harrington, A. (2004) *Art and Social Theory*. Basingstoke: Palgrave.
Harris, W. (1981) *Explorations*. Aarhus, Denmark: Dangaroo.
Harrison, D. (2005) 'Contested narratives in the domain of world heritage', in D. Harrison and M. Hitchcock (eds) *The Politics of World Heritage*. Clevedon: Channel View, 1–12.
Harvey, D. (1999) *The Limits to Capital*. London: Verso.
Harvey, D. (2006) *Spaces of Global Capitalism*. London: Verso.

Bibliography

Harvey, J., Horne, J. and Safai, P. (2009) 'Alterglobalization, global social movements and the possibility of political transformation through sport', *Sociology of Sport Journal*, 26: 383–403.

Hay, J. (2006) 'Between cultural materialism and spatial materialism: James Carey's writing about communication', in J. Paker and C. Robertson (eds) *Thinking with James Carey*. New York: Peter Lang, 29–56.

Haythornthwaite, C. and Wellman, B. (2002) 'The Internet in everyday life: An introduction', in B. Wellman and C. Haythornthwaite (eds) *The Internet and Everyday Life*. Oxford: Blackwell, 3–41.

Hebdige, D. (1979) *Subculture*. London: Routledge.

Heidegger, M. (1967) *Being and Time*. Oxford: Blackwell.

Heidegger, M. (1975) 'The origin of the work of art', in *Poetry, Language, Thought*, translated by A. Hofstadter. New York: Harper Colophon.

Held, D. and McGrew, A. (2007) *Globalization Theories*. Cambridge: Polity.

Henning, C. (2002), 'Tourism: Enacting modern myths', in G.M.S. Dann (ed.) *The Tourist as a Metaphor of the Social World*, Wallingford: CABI, 169–188.

Hennion, A. and Latour, B. (1993) *La Passion Musicale*. Paris: Editions Métalié.

Herzfeld, M. (1982) *Ours Once More*. Austin: University of Texas Press.

Herzfeld, M. (1985) *The Poetics of Manhood*. Princeton, NJ: Princeton University Press.

Herzfeld, M. (1987) *Anthropology through the Looking-Glass*. Cambridge: Cambridge University Press.

Herzfeld, M. (1992) *The Social Production of Indifference*. Oxford: Berg.

Herzfeld, M. (2001) *Anthropology*. Oxford: Blackwell.

Herzfeld, M. (2002) 'The absent presence: Discourses of crypto-colonialism', *South Atlantic Quarterly*, 101(4): 899–926.

Herzfeld, M. (2004) *The Body Impolitic*. Chicago: University of Chicago Press.

Herzfeld, M. (2005) *Cultural Intimacy*, 2nd edn. New York: Routledge.

Herzfeld, M. (2006) 'Spatial cleansing: Monumental vacuity and the idea of the West', *Journal of Material Culture*, 1(1/2): 127–114.

Herzfeld, M. (2007) 'Global kinship: Anthropology and the politics of knowing', *Anthropological Quarterly*, 80(2): 313–323.

Herzfeld, M. (2008) 'The Ethnographer as Theorist', in M. Mazower (ed.) *Networks of Power in Modern Greece*. London: Hurst, 147–168.

Herzfeld, M. (2009) *Evicted from Eternity*. Chicago: University of Chicago Press.

Hesmondhalgh, D. (1996) 'Popular music after rock and soul', in J. Curran, D. Morley and V. Walkerdine (eds) *Cultural Studies and Communications*. London: Arnold, 195–212.

Hesmondhalgh, D. (2007) 'Aesthetics and everyday aesthetics: talking about good and bad music', *European Journal of Cultural Studies*, 10(4): 507–527.

Hesmondhalgh, D. and Baker, S. (2010) *Creative Labour*. London: Routledge.

Hindi Lyrics (undated) 'A.R. Rahman: Indian musician, record producer, singer'. Available awww.hindilyrics.net/profiles/a-r-rahman.html (accessed 15 August 2013).

Hindi Lyrics (undated) 'Aaj Ki Raat (1006) song lyrics translation'. Available at: www.hindilyrics.net/translation-Don%20-%202006/Aaj-Ki-Raat.html (accessed 12 July 2013).

Hindustan Times (1 January 2009) 'I sometimes feel like I'm the off-screen "millionaire"': Loveleen', Sawf News Agencies. Available at: www.hindustantimes.com/News-Feed/Archived-Stories/I-sometimes-feel-like-I-m-the-off-screen-millionaire-Loveleen/Article1-362373.aspx (accessed 12 August 2013).

Hindustan Times (22 January 2009) 'Bachchan clears air over Slumdog with Danny Boyle'. Available at: www.hindustantimes.com/News-Feed/Bollywood/Bachchan-clears-air-over-Slumdog-with-Danny-Boyle/Article1-369782.aspx (accessed 15 September 2013).
Hitchcock, P. (1993) *Dialogics of the Oppressed*. Minneapolis: University of Minnesota Press.
Hochschild, A. (1983) *The Managed Heart*. Berkeley: University of California Press.
Hoesterey, I. (2001) *Pastiche*. Bloomington: Indiana University Press.
Hogan, P.C. (2008) *Understanding Indian Movies*. Austin: University of Texas Press.
Holden, E. (25 March 2013) 'Six reasons to visit the Taj Mahal', *Suite 101*. Available at: www.google.co.uk/#q=SIX+REASONS+TO+VIST+THE+TAJ+MAHAL (accessed 4 September 2013).
Holdnak, A. and Holland, S.M. (1996) 'Edu-tourism: Vacationing to learn', *Parks and Recreation*, 31: 72.
HolidayIQ.com (2009) 'Aamir Khan – The New Brand Ambassador of Incredible India Campaign'. Available at: www.holidayiq.com/aamir-khan-for-incredible-india.php (accessed 6 September 2013).
Hollingshead, K. (1992) '"White" gaze, "red" people, shadow visions: The "disidentification" of "Indians" in cultural tourism', *Leisure Studies*, 11(1): 43–64.
Hollingshead, K. (1999) 'Surveillance of the worlds of tourism: Foucault and the eye-of-power', *Tourism Management*, 20: 7–23.
Honneth, A. (2007) *Disrespect*. Cambridge: Polity.
Hooks, B. (1992) 'Eating the Other: desire and resistance', in B. Hooks (ed.) *Black Looks*. Boston: South End Press, 21–40.
Hopkins, A.G. (2011) *Globalisation in World History*. London: Random House.
Horn, J. (30 January 2009) '"Slumdog Millionaire" makers respond to criticism over pay to two young actors', *Los Angeles Times*. Available at: http://articles.latimes.com/2009/jan/30/entertainment/et-slumdog30 (accessed 13 September 2009).
Horn, J. (9 November 2009) 'The answer man', *Los Angeles Times*. Available at: http://articles.latimes.com/2008/nov/09/entertainment/ca-boyle9 (accessed 1 September 2013).
Howard, C. (2012) 'Speeding up and slowing down: Pilgrimage and slow travel through time', in S. Fullagar, K. Markwell and E. Wilson (eds) *Slow Tourism*. Bristol: Channel View, 11–24.
Howard, T. (21 March 2010) 'Slumdog Millionaire tours: Tourists now visit Mumbai slums during India vacations', *Christian Science Monitor*. Available at: www.csmonitoes.com/World/Global-News/2010/0321/Slumdog-Millionaire-tours-Tourists-now-visit-Mumbai-slums-during-India-vacations (accessed 1 September 2013).
Howland, P. (2008) 'Martinborough's wine tourists and the metro-rural idyll', *Journal of New Zealand Studies*, 6–7: 77–100.
Hudson, S., and Ritchie, J.R.B. (2006). 'Promoting destinations via film tourism: An empirical identification of initiatives', *Journal of Travel Research*, 44(3): 387–396.
Humaa.com (undated) 'A.R. Rahman: Short biography'. Available at: www.hummaa.com/music/artist/A+R+Rahman/24 (accessed 15 August 2013).
Humbert, M. (1993) *The Impact of Globalisation on Europe's Firms and Industries*. London: St Martin's Press.
Hunt, P. and Frankenberg, R. (1990) 'It's a small world: Disneyland, the family and the multiple re-presentations of the American child', in A. James, and A. Pout (eds) *Constructing and Reconstructing Childhood*. Sussex: Falmer Press, 107–125.
Hunter, W. (1932) 'The art-form of democracy?', *Scrutiny*, 1(1): 61–65.

Huntington, S.P. (1993) 'The clash of civilizations', *Foreign Affairs*, 72(3): 22–49.
Huntington, S.P. (2002) *The Clash of Civilizations*. New York: Simon & Schuster.
Hurricane (26 April 2009) 'Ringa Ringa lyrics in English', *All Voices*. Available at: www.allvoices.com/contributed-news/3073109-ringa-ringa-lyrics-ringa-ringa-translation-ringa-ringa-in-english-ringa-ringa-song (accessed 4 July 2013).
Huss, H. (2000) 'The "zinc-fence thing": When will reggae album covers be allowed out of the ghetto?', *Black Music Research Journal*, 20: 181–194.
Hutcheon, L. (1988) *A Poetics of Postmodernism*. New York: Routledge.
Hutcheon, L. (1989) *The Politics of Postmodernism*. New York: Routledge.
Hutcheon, L. (2006) *A Theory of Adaptation*. London: Routledge.
Hutchinson, J. (2004) 'Myth against myth: The nation as ethnic overlay', in M. Guibernaeu and J. Hutchinson (eds) *History and National Destiny*. Oxford: Blackwell, 109–124.
Hutchinson, J. (2005) *Nations as Zones of Conflict*. London: Sage.
Hutnyk, J. (1996) *The Rumour of Calcutta*. London and New Jersey: Zed.
Huyssen, A. (1995) *Twilight Memories*. London: Routledge.
Huyssen, A. (2000) 'Present Pasts: Media, politics, amnesia', *Public Culture*, 12(1): 21–38.
Huyssen, A. (2003) *Present Pasts*. Stanford: Stanford University Press.
ICMR (undated) 'The "Incredible India" campaign: Marketing India to the world'. Available at: www.icmrindia.org/casestudies/catalogue/Marketing/The%20'Incredible%20India'%20Campaign.htm#Introduction (accessed 6 September 2013).
Illouz, E. (2007) *Cold Intimacies*. Oxford: Polity.
Illouz, E. (2008) *Saving the Modern Soul*. Berkeley: University of California Press.
Imam, Z. (30 June 2013) 'Shahrukh Khan controversy: Hype and hypocrisy', *The Express Tribune*. Available at: http://blogs.tribune.com.pk/story/15859/shahrukh-khan-controversy-hype-and-hypocrisy/ (accessed 12 July 2013).
IMDB (undated) 'Dev Patel Biography'. Available at: www.imdb.com/name/nm2353862/bio (accessed 11 August 2013).
IMDB (undated) 'Freida Pinto Biography'. Available at: www.imdb.com/name/nm2951768/bio (accessed 11 August 2013).
IMDB (undated) 'Slumdog Millionaire'. Available at: www.imdb.co.uk/title/tt1010048/ (accessed 18 March 2013).
India EU Film Initiative (undated) 'Oscar winning song "Jai Ho!" and its lyrics'. Available at: http://web.archive.org/web/20090414060457/http://www.iefilmi.com/content/oscar-winning-song-jai-ho-and-its-lyrics (accessed 11 July 2013).
India Forums (10 January 2009) '"Slumdog Millionaire" in Hindi will be "Crorepati"'. Available at: www.india-forums.com/bollywood/reviews-reel/7689-lumdog-millionaire-in-hindi-will-be-crorepati.htm (accessed 11 August 2013).
Indian Tourism Development Corporation– 'ITDC' (undated) Available at: http://tourism.gov.in/aboutus/ITDC.aspx (accessed 6 September 2013).
Inglis, D. and Robertson, R. (2005) 'The Ecumenical Analytic: "Globalization", Reflexivity and the Revolution in Greek Historiography', *European Journal of Social Theory*, 8(2): 99–122.
Ingold, T. (2000) *The Perception of the Environment*. London: Routledge.
Ingold, T. (2010) 'Ways of mind-walking: Reading, writing, painting', *Visual Studies*, 25(1):15–23.
Ingold, T. (2011) *Being Alive*. London: Routledge.
Inkspill (1 January 2009) 'Slumdog Millionaire Jai Ho lyrics and English translation'. Available at: www.inskspillz.blogspot.co.uk/2009/01/slumdog-millionaire-jai-ho-lyrics.html (accessed 23 January 2013).

Inoue, M. (2006) *Vicarious Language*. Berkeley: University of California Press.
Irigaray, L. (1974) *Speculum of the Other Woman*. Ithaca: Cornell University Press.
Irimiás, A. (2012) 'Missing identity: Relocation of Budapest in film-induced tourism', *Tourism Review International*, 16(2): 125–138.
Italiano, F. (2012) 'Translating geographies: the Navigatio Sancti Bendani and its Venetian translation', *Translation Studies*, 5(1): 1–16.
Ivy, M. (1995) *Discourses of the Vanishing*. Chicago: University of Chicago Press.
Iwashita, C. (2006) 'Media representation of the UK as a destination for Japanese tourists: popular culture and tourism', *Tourist Studies*, 6(1): 59–77.
Jafari, J. (1987) 'Tourism models: The sociocultural aspects', *Tourism Management*, 8(2): 151–159.
Jamal, T. and Hill, S. (2002) 'The home and the world: (Post)touristic spaces of (in) authenticity?', in G.M.S. Dann (ed.) *The Tourist as a Metaphor of the Social World*, Wallingford: CABI, 77–108.
Jamal, T., Everett, J. and Dann, G.M.S. (2003) 'Ecological rationalization and performance resistances in natural area destinations', *Tourist Studies*, 3(2): 143–169.
James, M. (24 March 2009) 'Nicole Scherzinger says she originally didn't want to cover "Jai Ho"' MTV. Available at: www.mtv.com/news/articles/1607620/nicole-scherzinger-didnt-want-cover-jai-ho.jhtml (accessed 13 July 2013).
James, P. (2006) 'Theorizing nation formation in the context of imperialism and globalism', in G. Delanty and K. Kumar (ed.) *The Sage Handbook of Nations and Nationalism*. London: Sage, 369–381.
Jameson, F. (1986) 'Third-world literature in the era of multinational capitalism', *Social Text*, 15: 65–88.
JanMohammed, A.R. (1985) 'The economy of Manichean allegory: The function of racial difference in colonialist literature', *Critical Inquiry*, 12(1): 59–87.
Jay, M. (1993) *Downcast Eyes*. Berkeley: University of California Press.
Jay, M. (1988) 'The rise of hermeneutics and the crisis of occulocentrism', *Poetics Today*, 9(2): 312–324.
Jeffrey, A., McFarlane, C. and Vasudevan, A. (2012) 'Rethinking enclosure: Space, subjectivity and the commons', *Antipode*, 44(4): 1247–1267.
Jenks, C. (1993) *Culture*. London and New York: Routledge.
Jennings, M., Elland, H. and Smith, G. (eds) (2005) *Walter Benjamin, II: 1931–1934*. Cambridge, MA: Belknap Press.
Jensen, O.B. (2010) 'Negotiation in motion: Unpacking a geography of mobility', *Space and Culture*, 13(4): 389–402.
Jensen, O.B. (2013) *Staging Mobilities*. London: Routledge.
Jensen, O.B. (2014) *Designing Mobilities*. London: Routledge.
Johnson, D.T. (2008) 'Playgrounds of unlimited potential: Adaptation, documentary, and Dogtown and Z-Boys', *Adaptation*, 2(1): 1–16.
Johnson, M. (1997) *Beauty and Power*. Oxford: Berg.
Johnson, M. (1998) 'Global desirings and translocal loves: Transgendering and same-sex sexualities in the Southern Philippines', *American Ethnologist*, 25(4): 695–711.
Johnson, N. (1995) 'Cast in stone: Monuments, geography and nationalism', *Environment and Planning D*, 13: 51–65.
Johnston, B. (2007) 'Merton, Robert K. (1910–2003)', in G. Ritzer and M.J. Ryan (eds), *Encyclopedia of Sociology*. Oxford: John Wiley and Sons, 2958–2961.
Joshi, T. (21 January 2009) 'Slumdog shoot not allowed in Agra, Taj recreated them on set', *MidDay*. Available at: www.mid-day.com/entertainment/2009/jan/210109-Taj-

Mahal-Slumdog-Millionaire-Danny-Boyle-heritage-site-Nitin-Desai-Kaun-Banega-Crorepati.htm (accessed 4 September 2013).
Juhu Citizens Welfare Group (2013) 'About us'. Available at: www.juhucitizen.org/aboutus.htm (accessed 6 September 2013).
Julien, F. (2008) *De l'Universel, de l'Uniforme, du Commun et du Dialogue entre les Cultures*. Paris: Fayard.
Just, R. (2000) *A Greek Island Cosmos*. Oxford: James Currey.
Kahn, R. (2008) *Sacred Violence*. Ann Arbor: University of Michigan Press.
Kahn, R. and Kellner, D. (2007) 'Resisting globalization', in G. Ritzer (ed.) *The Blackwell Companion to Globalization*. Oxford: Blackwell.
Kamath, S. (31 January 2006) 'Netru, Indru, Nalai is back with a bang', *The Hindu*. Available at: www.hindu.com/2006/01/31/stories/2006013102720200.htm (accessed 15 August 2013).
Kandinsky, W. (1977) *Concerning the Spiritual in Art*, translated by M.T.H. Sadler. New York: Dover Publications.
Kapadia-Bodi, M. (2008) 'Rereading in the subaltern: Language, politics, power', Graduate School of Education, University of Pennsylvania. Available at: www.melissakapadiabodi.com/MKBRereadingintheSubaltern.pdf (accessed 30 June 2013).
Kaplan, E.A. (1980) *Women in Film Noir*. London: British Film Institute.
Kaplan, E.A. (1983) *Women and Film*. New York: Methuen.
Kaplan, M. (1995) 'Panopticon in Poona: An Essay on Foucault and colonialism', *Cultural Anthropology*, 10(1): 85–98.
Kapur, A. (7 November 2008) 'The secret of his success', *New York Times*. Available at: www.nytimes.com/2008/11/09/books/review/Kapur-t.html?_r=1 (accessed 3 September 2013).
Karin, A. and Beck, J. (2010) 'Suffering forces us to think beyond the right-left barrier', translated by J. Beck. *Mechademia 5: Fanthropologies*: 251–265.
Kassabian, A. (2000) *Hearing Film*. London: Routledge.
Kaufmann, V. and Mantulet, B. (2008) 'Between social and spatial mobilities', in W. Ganzler, V. Kaufmann and S. Kesserling (eds) *Tracing Mobilities*, Aldershot: Ashgate.
Kaur, R. (2005) 'Cruising on the Vilayeti Bandwagon: Diasporic representations and reception of popular Indian movies', in R. Kaur and A. Sinha (eds) *Bollyworld*. New Delhi, Thousand Oaks, London: Sage, 309–329.
Kearney, M. (1995) 'The local and the global: the anthropology of globalisation and transnationalism', *Annual Review of Anthropology*, 24: 547–565.
Keft-Kennedy, V. (2005) "How does she do that?" Belly dancing and the horror of a flexible woman', *Women's Studies*, 34(3): 279–300.
Kessen, W. (1979) 'The American child and other cultural inventions', *American Psychologist*, 34: 815–820.
Kessen, W. (1993) 'A developmentalist reflections', in G.H. Elder, J. Model and R.D. Parke (eds) *Children in Time and Place*. New York: Cambridge University Press, 226–229.
Kesserling, S. (2008) 'The mobile risk society', in W. Canzler, V. Kaufmann and S. Kesserling (eds) *Tracing Mobilities*. Aldershot: Ashgate, 77–102.
Kinetz, E. (22 January 2009) 'Mumbai residents object to "Slumdog" title', *USA Today/Associated Press*. Available at: http://usatoday30.usatoday.com/life/movies/news/2009-01-22-slugdog-mumbai-protest_N.htm (accessed 15 September 2013).

King, N. (2007) 'Hollywood', in: P. Cook, *The Cinema Book*. London: British Film Institute.
Kippen, J. and Bel, A. (1996) 'Lucknow kathak dance', *Bansuri*, 13. Available at: http://pages.pathcom.com/~ericp/kathak.html (accessed 4 July 2013).
Kirschenblatt-Gimblett, B. (1997) *Destination Cultures*. Berkley: University of California Press.
Kischer, K. (18 February 2009) 'The money and the girl: Temple's Priya Joshi explains why', Temple University Communications. Available at: http://news.temple.edu/news/money-and-girl (accessed 28 January 2013).
Kittler, F. (1997) *Literature, Media Information Systems*. Amsterdam: OPA.
Klein, K. (2000) 'On the emergence of memory in historical discourse', *Representations*, 69(1): 127–150.
Kling, R. (2000) 'Learning about information technologies and social change: The contribution of social informatics', *The Information Society*, 16(3): 217–232.
Kong, L. (1995) 'Popular music in geographical analyses', *Progress in Human Geography*, 19: 183–198.
Korstanje, M. (2008) 'Liquid fears: Contemporary society and its liquid fears', *Antrocom*, 4(2): 169–170.
Korstanje, M. (2011) 'Detaching elementary forms of dark-tourism', *Anatolia*, 22(3): 424–427.
Korstanje, M. (2013) 'The sense, landscape and image. How the tourist destination is replicated in modernist times', *Pasos*, 11(3): 55–65.
Kothari, U. (2002) 'Landless labour and agrarian change in South Gujarat', in G. Shah, H. Streefkirk and M. Rutten (eds) *Labour Relations and Agrarian Change in Gujurat*, Delhi: Sage, 133–149.
Kothari, U. (2005) 'Authority and expertise: The professionalization of international development and the ordering of dissent', *Antipode*, 37: 425–446.
Kothari, U. (2006) 'From colonialism to development: Continuities and divergences', *Journal of Commonwealth and Comparative Politics*, 44(1): 118–136.
Koven, S. (2004) *Slumming*. Princeton: Princeton University Press.
Kracauer, S. (1997) *Theory of Film*. New York: Oxford University Press.
Kracauer, S. (2004) *From Caligari to Hitler*. Princeton, NJ: Princeton University Press.
Krippendorf, J. (1987) *The Holiday Makers*. Oxford: Heinemann.
Kristeva, J. (1991) *Strangers to Ourselves*. New York: Columbia University Press.
Krutnik, F. (1992) *In a Lonely Street*. London: Routledge.
Kuhn, T. (1970) *The Structure of Scientific Revolutions*, 2nd ed. Chicago: University of Chicago Press.
Kumar, A. (23 December 2008) 'Slumdog Millionaire's Bollywood ancestors', *Vanity Fair*. Available at: www.vanityfair.com/online/oscars/2008/12/slumdog-millionaires-bollywood-ancestors (accessed 16 August 2013).
Kumar, A. (2011) 'Changing landscape of moral registers and urban pathology in "Bombay" cinema: Decline of biological family and birth of the individual through *Awara* (1951), *Deewar* (1975) and *Satya* (1998)', *Cinej Cinema Journal*, 1(1). Available at: http://cinej.pitt.edu/ojs/index.php/cinej/article/view/20 (accessed 18 March 2013).
Kumar, K. (1991) *Utopianism*. Buckingham: Open University Press.
Kyriakidou, M. (2008) 'Rethinking media events in the context of a global public sphere: Exploring the audience of global disasters in Greece', *Communications*, 33(3): 273–291.

Lacan, J. (1994) *Four Fundamental Concepts of Psychoanalysis*. London: Vintage.
Lakshmi, P. (30 April 2009) 'The 2009 Time 100 – A.R. Rahman', *Time*. Available at: www.time.com/time/specials/packages/article/0,28804,1894410_1893836_1894435,00.html (accessed 15 August 2013).
Lal, N. (13 September 2009) 'India's new attraction: Slumdog tourism', *Brunel Times*. Available at: www.bt.com.bn/travel/2009/09/13/indias-new-attraction-slumdog-tourism (accessed 6 September 2013).
Landry, D. and MacLean, G. (1996) 'Introduction', in D. Landry and G. MacLean (eds) *The Spivak Reader*. London: Routledge.
Lanfant, F.M. (2009) 'Roots of the sociology of tourism in France', in G.M.S. Dann and G. Liebmann Parinello (eds) *The Sociology of Tourism*. UK: Emerald, 95–130.
Lange, M.E. (2003) 'In search of methodology: From one Other to an-Other', *Cultural Studies/Critical Methodologies*, 3(4): 429–447.
Langlois, G. (2012) 'Meaning, semiotechnologies and participatory media', *Culture Machine*, 12. Available at: www.culturemachine.net/index.php/cm/article/viewDownloadInterstitial/437/467 (accessed 10 February 2013).
Larsen, J. (2005) 'Families seen photographing: The performativity of tourist photography', *Space and Culture*, 8: 416–434.
Larsen, J. and Urry, J. (2008) 'Networking in mobile societies', in J.O. Bærenholdt, B. Granãs and S. Kesserling (eds) *Mobility and Place*, Aldershot: Ashgate, 89–101.
Larsen, J., Urry, J. and Axhausen, K.W. (2006) 'Networks and tourism: Mobile social life', *Annals of Tourism Research*, 34(1): 244–262.
Lash, S. and Urry, J. (1987) *The End of Organized Capitalism*. Madison: University of Wisconsin Press.
Lash, S. and Urry, J. (1994) *Economies of Signs and Space*, London: Sage.
Latour, B. (1993) *We Have Never been Modern*. London and New York: Harvester Wheatsheaf.
Latour, B. (1998) 'How to be iconophilic in art, science and religion', in C.A. Jones and P. Gallison (eds) *Picturing Science, Producing Art*. London: Routledge, 418–440.
Latour, B. (2005) *Reassembling the Social*. Oxford: Oxford University Press.
Law, I. (2010) *Racism and Ethnicity*. London: Pearson Education.
Law, S. (2003) 'Film, memory and nostalgia in Cinema Paradiso (Nuovo Cinema Paradiso)', *Australian Screen Education Online*, 33: 111–116.
LBN India (21 October 2009) 'Govt at war with Naxals to aid MNCs: Arundhati'. Available at: http://ibnlive.in.com/news/govt-at-war-with-naxals-to-aid-mncs-arundhati/103627-3-single.html (accessed 16 September 2013).
Leach, B. (14 January 2009) 'Slumdog Millionaire director Danny Boyle almost became a priest', *The Telegraph*. Available at: www.telegraph.co.uk/culture/film/4238043/Slumdog-Millionaire-director-Danny-Boyle-almost-became-a-priest.html (accessed 19 August 2012).
Lee, M. (2007) 'Understanding human trafficking', in M. Lee (ed.), *Human Trafficking*. Devon: Willan, 1–25.
Lefebvre, H. (1991) *The Production of Space*. Oxford: Blackwell.
Lefebvre, H. (1996) *Writings on Cities*. Oxford: Blackwell.
Leitch, T. (2008) 'Adaptation, the genre', *Adaptation*, 1(1): 106–120.
Lemke, T. (2001) 'The birth of bio-politics': Michel Foucault's lecture at the Collège de France on neo-liberal governmentality', *Economy and Society*, 30(2): 190–207.
Lenhardt, C. (1975) 'Anamnestic solidarity: The proletariat and its manes', *Telos*, 25: 133–154.

Leoussi, A. (2004) 'The ethno-cultural roots of national art', in M. Guibernaeu and J. Hutchinson (eds) *History and National Destiny*. Oxford: Blackwell, 143–159.
Levi, R. (2009) 'Gated communities in Law's gaze: Material forms and the production of a social body in legal adjudication', *Law & Social Inquiry*, 34(3): 635–669.
Levin, T. (2006) *Where Rivers and Mountains Sing*. Bloomington, IN: Indiana University Press.
Lévi-Strauss, C. (1964) *Totemism*, London: Merlin Press.
Lévi-Strauss, C. (1971) 'Race and History' [in Greek], translated by M. Voutiras, in D. Maronitis (ed.) *The Fear of Freedom*. Athens: Papazisis, 171–213.
Lévi-Strauss, C. (1972[1962]) *The Savage Mind*. London: Weidenfeld and Nicolson.
Lew, A. (2011) 'Tourism's role in the global economy', *Tourism Geographies*, 9(3): 148–151.
Lewis, B. (1993) *The Arabs in History*. Oxford: Oxford University Press.
Liebes, T. (2003) *American Dreams, Hebrew Subtitles*. Cresskill, NJ: Hampton Press.
Ling, R. (1997) 'One can talk about common manners' in L. Haddon (ed.) *Themes in Mobile Telephony*. Available at: www.cost269.org (accessed 12 September 2013).
Linke, U. (2012) 'Mobile imaginaries, portable signs: The global consumption of iconic representation of slum life', *Tourism Geographies*, 14(2): 294–319.
Linklater, A. (4 January 2009) 'A film director in a class of his own', *The Guardian*. Available at: www.guardian.co.uk/film/2009/jan/04/danny-boyle-interview-slumdog-millionaire (accessed 24 June 2013).
Little, W. (2000) 'Home as a place of exhibition and performance: Mayan household transformations in Guatemala', *Ethnology*, 39(2): 163–181.
Lobo, J. (11 August 2013) 'The ticking e-bomb', *DNA India*. Available at: www.dnaindia.com/mumbai/1872813/report-the-ticking-e-bomb (accessed 1 September 2013).
Löfgren, O. (1999) *On Holiday*. Berkeley: University of California Press.
Loomba, A. (2005) *Colonialism/Postcolonialism*. London: Routledge.
Low, D.A. (1999) *The Regency Underworld*. Stroud: Sutton.
Löwy, M. and Sayre, R. (2001) *Romanticism against the Tide of Modernity*. Durham: Duke University Press.
Lukács, G. (1968) *History and Class Consciousness*, translated by R. Livingstone. London: Merlin Press.
LukeA. and Freebody, P. (1997) 'The social practices of reading', in C. Luke (ed.) *Feminisms and Pedagogies in Everyday Life*. Albany: SUNY, 185–227.
Lury, C. (2004) *Brands*. London: Routledge.
McCabe, S. (2005) '"Who is a tourist?" A critical overview', *Tourist Studies*, 5(1): 85–106.
MacCannell, D. (1973) 'Staged authenticity: Arrangements of social space in tourist settings', *American Journal of Sociology*, 79(3): 589–603.
MacCannell, D. (1989) *The Tourist*. London: Macmillan.
MacCannell, D. (2001) 'Tourist agency', *Tourist Studies*, 1(1): 23–37.
MacCannell, D. (2011) *The Ethics of Sightseeing*. Berkeley: University of California Press.
MacCannell, D. (2012) 'On the ethical stake in tourism research', *Tourism Geographies*, 14(1): 183–194.
McCreery, J. (1995) 'Negotiating with demons: The uses of magic language', *American Ethnologist*, 22(1): 144–164.
McGrath, A. (2001) *In the Beginning*. London: Hodder and Stoughton.
McIntyre, N. (2009) 'Re-thinking amenity migration: Integrating mobility, lifestyle and social-ecological systems', *Die Erde*, 140(3): 229–250.

212 Bibliography

Macionis, J. (2004) 'Understanding the film-induced tourist', in F. Warwick, G. Croy and S. Beeton (eds) *International Tourism and Media Conference Proceedings*. Melbourne: Monash University, 86–97.

Macionis, N. and Sparks, B. (2009) 'Film tourism: An incidental experience', *Tourism Review International*, 13(2): 93–102.

Macmaster, N. and Lewis, T. (1998) 'Orientalism: From unveiling to hyperveiling', *Journal of European Studies*, 28: 121–135.

Madhusoodanan, G. (2003) 'Greening the Red silently: A case study from India', *Capitalism Nature Socialism*, 14(1): 37–54

Maffesoli, M. (1996) *The Time of the Tribes*. London: Sage.

Magnet, M.2000. *What Makes Charity Work?* Chicago: Ivan R. Dee Publishers.

Magnier, M. (24 January 2009) 'Indians don't feel good about "Slumdog Millionaire"', *Los Angeles Times*. Available at: http://articles.latimes.com/2009/jan/24/world/fg-india-slumdog24 (accessed 28 January 2013).

Mail Online (5 March 2011) 'Slumdog Millionaire child star loses all her Oscar memorabilia as fire rips through slum she still calls home'. Available at: www.dailymail.co.uk/news/article-1363195/Child-star-Slumdog-Millionaire-loses-owns-huge-hut-fire.html (accessed 13 September 2013).

Maki, A. (7 November 2011) 'Cultural Connection: Indians find community, commercial success in Memphis', *The Mephis Daily News*, 126(217). Available at: www.memphisdailynews.com/news/2011/nov/7/cultural-connection/ (accessed 13 July 2013).

Malbon, B. (1999) *Clubbing*. London: Routledge.

Mannheim, K. (1968) *Ideology and Utopia*. New York: Harcourt, Brace & World.

Mannheim, K. (2003) 'The dynamics of spiritual realities', in J. Tanner (ed.) *The Sociology of Art*, London: Routledge.

Manning, S. and Sydow, J. (2011) 'Projects, paths, and practices: Sustaining and leveraging project-based relationships', *Industrial and Corporate Change*, 20(5): 1369–1402

Maoz, D. (2006) 'The mutual gaze', *Annals of Tourism Research*, 33(1): 221–239.

Maoz, D. and Bekerman, Z. (2010) 'Searching for Jewish answers in Indian resorts', *Annals of Tourism Research*, 37(2): 423–439.

Marcus, G. (1998) *Ethnography through Thick and Thin*. Princeton: Princeton University Press.

Marcus, G. and Myers, F. (eds) (1995) *Traffic in Culture*. Berkeley: University of California Press.

Marcuse, H. (1955) *Eros and Civilization*. New York: Beacon Press.

Marcuse, P. (1996) 'Space and race in the post-Fordist city', in E. Mingione (ed.) *Urban Poverty and the Underclass*. Oxford: Blackwell, 176–216.

Massey, D. (1993) 'Power-geometry and a progressive sense of place', in B. Curties, G. Robertson and L. Tickner (eds) *Mapping the Futures*. New York: Routledge, 59–69.

Massey, D. (1994) *Space, Place and Gender*. Cambridge: Polity.

Massey, D. (2005) *For Space*. London: Sage.

MasurkarA. and Bhosale, P. (11 August 2008) 'Why are Juhu slums back? Residents claim AAI "allowing" slums to flourish even after they were demolished by BMC', *Mumbai Mirror*. Available at:www.mumbaimirror.com/article/2/2008081120080811032338439b05f492e/Why-are-Juhu-slums-back-.html (accessed 18 March 2013).

Mauss, M. (1954) *The Gift*. London: Free Press.

Mazumdar, R. (2007) *Bombay Cinema*. Minneapolis, MN: University of Minnesota Press.

Bibliography 213

Mbembe, A. (2001) *On the Postcolony*. Berkeley: University of California Press.
Mbembe, A. (2003) 'Necropolitics', translated by L. Meintjes. *Public Culture*, 15(1): 11–40.
McKee, R. (1999) *Story*. London: Methuen.
McKenzie, E. (2005) 'Constructing the Pomerium in Las Vegas: A case study of emerging trends in American gated communities', *Housing Studies*, 20(2): 187–203.
McLuhan, M. (1962) *The Guttenberg Galaxy*. London: Routledge & Kegan Paul.
McLuhan, M. (1964) *Understanding the Media*, New York: McGraw.
Meena, I. (24 February 2009) 'First reaction from LA: "Please don't go overboard"', *The Times of India*. Available at: http://articles.timesofindia.indiatimes.com/2009-02-24/india/28019066_1_movie-album-rahman-sound-barrier (accessed 11 July 2013).
Meethan, K. (2001) *Tourism in Global Society*. New York: Palgrave.
Meethan, K. (2003) 'Mobile cultures? Hybridity, tourism and cultural change', *Journal of Tourism and Cultural Change*, 1(1): 11–28.
Melucci, A. (1989) *Nomads of the Present*. London: Hutchinson Radius.
Melucci, A. (1995) 'The process of collective identity', in H. Johnston and B. Klandermas (eds) *Social Movements and Culture*. Minneapolis: University of Minnesota Press, 41–63.
Merton, R.K. (1938a) 'Science, technology and society in 17th century England', in G. Sarton (ed.) *Osiris*. Belgium: St. Catherine Press, 363–632.
Merton, R.K. (1938b) 'Social structure and anomie', *American Sociological Review*, 3: 672–682.
Merton, R.K. (1948) 'The bearing of empirical research on the development of sociological theory', *American Sociological Review*, 13(5): 505–515.
Merton, R.K. (1994) 'A life of learning', *American Council of Learned Societies*, Charles Homer Haskins Lecture. Paper 25.
Merton, R.K. and Sorokin, P.A. (1937) 'Social time: A methodological and functional analysis', *American Journal of Sociology*, 42: 615–629.
Merton, R.K. and Barber, E. (2004) *The Travels and Adventures of Serendipity*. Princeton, NJ: Princeton University Press.
Meschkank, J. (2011) 'Investigations into slum tourism in Mumbai: Poverty tourism and the tensions between different constructions of reality', *Geographical Journal*, 76(1): 47–62.
Meschkank, J. (2012) 'Negotiating poverty: The interplay between Dharavi's production and consumption as a tourist destination', in F. Frenzel, K. Koens and M. Steinbrink (eds), *Slum Tourism*. London: Routledge, 144–148.
Metro Lyrics (undated) 'Jai Ho (You Are My Destiny)'. Available at: www.metrolyrics.com/jai-ho-you-are-my-destiny-lyrics-pussycat-dolls.html (accessed 13 July 2013).
Metro Lyrics (undated) 'Paper Planes Lyrics M.I.A'. Available at: www.metrolyrics.com/paper-planes-lyrics-mia.html (accessed 28 June 2013).
Metro Lyrics (undated) 'AR RAHMAN – O… SAYA LYRICS'. Available at: www.metrolyrics.com/o-saya-lyrics-ar-rahman.html (accessed 31 January 2013).
Metz, W. (2007) 'Documentary as adaptation: An intertextual analysis of the Injury to One', *Literature/Film Quarterly*, 35: 307–312.
Meyer, B. and Geschiere, P. (eds) (1999) *Globalization and Identity*. Oxford: Blackwell.
Meyer, J., Boli, J. and Thomas, G. (1997) 'World society and the nation-state', *American Journal of Sociology*, 103(1): 144–181.
Michael, M. (1996) *Constructing Identities*. London: Sage.

Bibliography

Miller, A.H. (1980) *Terrorism and Hostage Negotiations*. Boulder, Colorado: Westview Press.
Miller, V. (2011) *Understanding Digital Culture*. London: Sage.
Minca, C. and Oakes, T. (2006) 'Travelling Paradoxes', in T. Oakes and C. Minca (eds) *Travels in Paradox*. Lanham: Rowman and Littlefield, 1–21.
Mishra, R.C., Mayer, B., Trommsdorff, G., Albert, I. and Schwarz, B. (2005) 'The value of children in urban and rural India: Cultural background and empirical results', in G. Trommsdorff and B. Nauck (eds) *The Value of Children in Cross-Cultural Perspective*. Lengerich: Pabst Science, 143–170.
Misztal, B. (2003) *Social Theories of Remembering*. Maidenhead, Philadelphia: Open University Press.
Mitchell, T. (1996) *Popular Music and Local Identity*. London: Leicester University Press.
Mitchell, W.J.T. (1994) *Landscape and Power*. Chicago: University of Chicago Press.
Mitchell, W.J.T. (1995) *The City of Bits*. Cambridge: MIT.
Mitchell, W.J.T. (2003) *ME++ The Cyborg Self and the Networked City*. Cambridge: MIT.
Mitra, S. (1999) 'Minimally invasive education for mass computer literacy', *CSI Communications*, June: 12–16.
Mitrović, D., Hartlieb, S., Zeppelzauer, M. and Zaharieva, M. (undated) 'Scene segmentation in artistic archive documentaries', Interactive Media Systems Group, Vienna University of Technology. Available at: http://dl.acm.org/citation.cfm?id=1947824 (accessed 22 June 2013).
Mohanty, C.T. (1991) 'Under western eyes: Feminist scholarship and colonial discourses', in C.T. Mohanty, A. Russo and L. Torres (eds) *Third World Women and the Politics of Feminism*. Bloomington, IN: India University Press, 255–277.
Molotch, H. (2004) 'How art works: form and function in the stuff of life', in R. Friedland and J. Mohr (eds) *Matters of Culture*. Cambridge: Cambridge University Press, 341–377.
Moore, H. (1997) 'Interior landscapes and external worlds: The return of grand theory in anthropology', *Australian Journal of Anthropology*, 8(2): 125–144.
Moore, H. (2004) 'Global anxieties: Concept-metaphors and pre-theoretical commitments in anthropology', *Anthropological Theory*, 4(1): 71–88.
Moore, V. (23 August 2013) 'India's Dharavi recycling Slumdog entrepreneurs', Keepinitreal. Available at: http://keepinitrealevanston.wordpress.com/2013/08/23/indias-dharavi-recycling-slumdog-entrepreneurs/ (accessed 1 September 2013).
Morcom, A. (2008) 'Tapping the mass market: The commercial life of Hindi film songs', in S. Gopal and S. Moorti (eds) *Global Bollywood*. Minneapolis: University of Minnesota Press, 63–84.
Moreton-Robinson, A. (2006) 'Towards a new research agenda? Foucault, whiteness and indigenous sovereignty', *Journal of Sociology*, 42(4): 383–395.
Morgan, N. and Pritchard, A. (2005) 'Security and social "sorting": Traversing the surveillance-tourism', *Tourist Studies*, 5: 115–132.
Morley, D. (2000) *Home Territories*. London: Routledge.
Morley, I. and de Rond, M. (2010) 'Introduction: Fortune and the prepared mind', in M. de Rond and I. Morley (eds) *Serendipity*. Cambridge: Cambridge University Press.
Mowforth, M. and Munt, I. (1998) *Tourism and Sustainability*, 1st ed. London: Routledge.
Mowforth, M. and Munt, I. (2009) *Tourism and Sustainability*, 3rd ed. London: Routledge.

MP3 Lyrics (undated) 'Liquid Dance'. Available at: www.mp3lyrics.org/a/ar-rahman/liquid-dance/ (accessed 7 July 2013).
Mulvey, L. (2006) 'Visual pleasure and narrative cinema', in M.G. Durham and D.M. Kellner (eds) *Media and Cultural Studies*. Oxford: Blackwell, 342–352.
Mumbai Magic (2013) 'A-la carte tours'. Available at: www.mumbaimagic.com (accessed 1 September 2013).
Munby, J. (1999) *Public Enemies, Public Heroes*. Chicago: University of Chicago Press.
Murray, C. (1990) *The Emerging British Underclass*. London: Institute of Economic Affairs.
Murray, S. (2004) '"Celebrating the story the way it is": Cultural studies, corporate media and the contested utility of fandom', *Continuum*, 18(1): 7–25.
Murray, S. (2008) 'Phantom adaptations: Eucalyptus, the adaptation industry and the film that never was' *Adaptation*, 1(1): 5–23.
Nagai, Y. (1991) *Ballroom Dance and the Japanese*. Tokyo: Shōbunsha.
Nandy, A. (2001) *The Ambiguous Journey of the City*. New Delhi: Oxford University Press.
Nash, J. (1993) *Crafts in the World Market*. Albany: SUNY.
Nederveen Pieterse, J. (1997) 'Globalization as hybridization', in M. Featherstone, S. Lash, and R. Robertson (eds) *Global Modernities*. London: Sage, 45–68.
Nederveen Pieterse, J. (1998) 'Hybrid modernities: Mélange modernities in Asia', *Sociological Analysis*, 1(3): 75–86.
Nederveen Pieterse, J. (2004) *Globalization and Culture*. Lanham: Rowman & Littlefield.
Nederveen Pieterse, J. (2006) 'Emancipatory cosmopolitanism: Towards an agenda', *Development and Change*, 37(6): 1247–1257.
Nederveen Pieterse, J. (2009) 'Multipolarity means thinking plural: Modernities', *Protosociology*, 26(1): 19–35.
Negus, K. (1999) *Music Genres and Corporate Cultures*. London: Routledge.
Nelson, D. and Henderson, B. (26 January 2009) 'Slumdog child stars miss out on the movie millions', *The Telegraph*. Available at: www.telegraph.co.uk/news/world news/asia/4347472/Poor-parents-of-Slumdog-Millionaire-stars-say-children-were-exp loited.html (accessed 13 September 2009).
Nelson, M.R. and Deshpande, S. (2013) 'The prevalence of and consumer response to foreign and domestic brand placement in Bollywood movies', *Journal of Advertising*, 42(1): 1–15.
Nichols, L.T. (2010) 'Merton as Harvard sociologist: Engagement, thematic continuities and institutional linkages', *Journal of the History of the Behavioral Sciences*, 46(1): 72–95.
Niebuhr, R. (1960) *The Children of Light and the Children of Darkness*. New York: Charles Scribner's Sons.
Nietzsche, F. (1990) *Beyond Good and Evil*, translated by A.J. Hollingdale. London: Penguin Books.
Nitin Desai Studios (undated) 'Origin'. Available at: www.ndstudioindia.com/origin/index.htm (accessed 18 March 2013).
Nora, P. (1989) 'Between memory and history: Les lieux de mémoire', *Representations*, 26(2): 7–25.
Novak, M. (2010) 'The meaning of transarchitecture', *Fen-Om Network*. Available at: issuu.com/salberti/docs/meaning-of-transarchitecture (accessed 5 June 2013).
Nye, J. (2004) *Soft Power*. New York: Public Affairs.

Bibliography

O'Brien, M. (2008) *A Crisis of Waste?* New York: Routledge.

O'Brien, M., Tzanelli, R., Yar, M., and Penna, S. (2005) 'The spectacle of fearsome Acts: Crime in the melting p(l)ot in Gangs of New York', *Theoretical Criminology*, 13: 17–35.

O'Connor, N., Flanagan, S. and Gilbert, D. (2009) '"Stakeholders'" perspectives of the impact of film and television tourism in Yorkshire', *Tourism Review International*, 13: 121–127.

O'Connor, N., Flanagan, S. and Gilbert, D. (2010) 'The use of film in re-imaging a tourist destination: A case study of Yorkshire', *Journal of Vacation Marketing*, 16(1): 61–74.

O'Reilly, K. (2003) 'When is a Tourist? The Articulation of Tourism and Migration in Spain's Costa del Sol', *Tourist Studies*, 3(3): 301–317.

Oakley, A. (1998) 'Gender, methodology and people's way of knowing: Some problems with feminism and the paradigm debate in social research', *Sociology*, 32(4): 707–731.

Obeyesekere, G. (1992) '"British cannibals": contemplation of an event in the death and resurrection of the James Cook, explorer' *Critical Enquiry*, 18: 630–654.

Oliveros, P. (2005) *Deep Listening*. Kingston: iUniverse/Deep Listening.

Ong, W. (1982) *Orality and Literacy*. London: Routledge.

Orr, E.R. (2005) 'The ethics of paganism: The value and power of the sacred relationship', in L.D. Angeles, E.R. Orr and T.V. Dooren (eds) *Pagan Visions for a Sustainable Future*. Woodbury: Llewellyn Publications, 1–38.

Osterhammel, J. (1997) *Colonialism*. Princeton: Markus Wiener.

Ostrowski, P. (1988) 'Understanding Tourism', *Problems of Tourism*, 11(3): 3–20.

Oxy (20 January 2009) 'Review of Slumdog Millionaire', *Zimbio*. Available at: www.zimbio.com/Slumdog+Millionaire/articles/138/Review+of+Slumdog+Millionaire (12 July 2013).

Paechter, C. (2006) 'Masculine femininities/feminine masculinities: Power, identities and gender', *Gender and Education*, 18(3): 253–263.

Page, S. (1991) 'Transport for recreation and tourism'. In B. Hoyle and R. Knowles (eds) *Modern Transport Geography*, London: Belhaven Press, 374.

Page, S. (2009) *Transport and Tourism*. London: Belhaven Press.

Pain, R. (2009) 'Globalised fear? Towards an emotional geo-politics', *Progress in Human Geography*, 33(4): 466–486.

Panofsky, E. (1955) *Meaning in the Visual Arts*. Chicago: University of Chicago Press.

Papastergiadis, N. (2000) *The Turbulence of Migration*. Cambridge: Polity.

Parekh, B. (1991) 'Nehru and the national philosophy of India', *Economic & Political Weekly*, 26(1): 35–48.

Parkhurst Ferguson, P. (1994) 'The flâneur on and off the streets of Paris', in K. Tester (ed.) *The Flâneur*. London: Routledge, 22–42.

Parrinello, G. (2001) 'The technological body in tourism: Research and praxis', *International Sociology*, 16(2): 205–219.

Parry, B. (1993) 'The contents and discontents of Kipling's imperialism', in J. Donald and J. Squires (eds) *Space and Place*. London: Lawrence & Wishart, 221–240.

Parry, J. (2013) 'Company and contract labour in a central Indian steel plant', *Economy & Society*, 42(3): 348–374.

Parthasarathy, D. (2009) 'Of slumdogs, doxosophers and the (in)dignity of labour(ers)', South Asian Studies Programme, University of Singapore (Social Science Research Network). Available at: http://papers.ssrn.com/sol3/papers.cfm?abstract_id=2096954 (accessed 18 June 2013).

Patke, R.S. (2000) 'Benjamin's arcades project and the postcolonial city', *Diacritics*, 30(4): 2–14.
Peaslee, R.M. (2011) 'One ring, many circles: The Hobbiton tour experience and a spatial approach to media power', *Tourist Studies*, 11(1): 37–53.
Peirce, C.M. (1998) 'Harvard lectures on pragmaticism', in N. Houser and C. Kloesel (eds) *The Essential Peirce, vol. I: 1867–1893*. Bloomington: Indiana University Press, 1–106.
Pensky, M. (1989) 'On the use and abuse of memory: Habermas, anamnestic solidarity and the Historikerstreit', *Philosophy and Social Criticism*, 15: 351–380.
Perkins, H.C. and Thorns, D.C. (2001) 'Gazing or performing? Reflections on Urry's tourist gaze in the context of contemporary experience in the Antipodes', *International Sociology*, 16(2): 185–204.
Pers, P. and Salemink, O. (1999) *Colonial Subjects*. Ann Arbour: University of Michigan Press.
Peterson, R.A. and Bennett, A. (2004) 'Introducing the scenes perspective' in A. Bennett and R.A. Peterson (eds) *Music Scenes*. Nashville: University of Vanderbilt Press, 1–15.
Phillips, R. and Steiner, C. (eds) (1999) *Unpacking Culture*. Berkeley: University of California Press.
Picard, M. (2007) 'From Turkey to Bali', in D. Nash (ed.) *The Study of Tourism*. Amsterdam: Elsevier, 167–183.
Pippin, R. (1999) *Modernism as a Philosophical Problem*. Oxford: Blackwell.
Pippin, R. (2005) *The Persistence of Subjectivity*. Cambridge: Cambridge University Press.
Plummer, K. (1995) *Telling Sexual Stories*. London: Routledge.
Plummer, K. (2003) *Intimate Citizenship*. Seattle: University of Washington Press.
Polanyi, M. (1963) 'The function of dogma in scientific research – Response to Kuhn', in A.C. Crombie (ed.) *Scientific Change*. New York: Basic Books, 367–369.
Polanyi, M. (1966). *The Tacit Dimension*. New York: Doubleday.
Prasad, M. (1998) *The Ideology of the Hindi Film*. New Delhi: Oxford University Press.
Prasad, M. (2001) 'Realism and fantasy in representations of metropolitan life in Indian cinema', *Journal of the Moving Image*, 2. Available at: www.jmionline.org/film_journal/jmi_02/article_09.php# (accessed 15 March 2013).
Prasad, M. (2003) 'This thing called Bollywood', *Seminar 525*. Available at: www.india-seminar.com/2003/525/525%20madhava%20prasad.htm (accessed 20 August 2013).
Prasad, M. (2004) 'Realism and fantasy in representations of metropolitan life in Indian cinema' in P. Kaarholm (ed.) *City Flicks*. New Delhi and Calcutta: Seagull, 83–99.
Prashad, V. (2002) *War against the Planet*. New Delhi: LeftWord.
Pratt, M. L. (1992) *Imperial Eyes*. London and New York: Routledge.
Prideaux, B. (2002) 'The cybertourist', in G.M.S. Dann (ed.) *The Tourist as a Metaphor of the Social World*. Wallingford: CABI, 317–339.
Proust, M. (2002) *In Search of Lost Time, vol. I*. London: Vintage.
Pryor, J-P. (undated) 'Danny Boyle talks Slumdog Millionaire', *Dazed Digital*. Available at: http://old.dazeddigital.com/mobile/artsandculture/article/1775/danny-boyle-talks-slumdog-millionaire (accessed 13 September 2013).
Przeclawski, K., Bystrzanowski, J. and Ujma, D. (2009) 'The sociology of tourism in Poland', in G.M.S. Dann and G. Parrinello (eds) *The Sociology of Tourism*. UK: Emerald, 169–194.

Purkayastha, B. and Majumdar, S. (2009) 'Globalization and the sexual commodification of women', in L. Lindio-McGovern and I. Walliman, *Globalisation and Third World Women*. Aldershot: Ashgate, 185–204.

Pušnik, M. and Sieherl, K. (2002) 'Relocating and personalising salsa in Slovenia: To dance is to communicate', *Anthropological Notebooks*, 16(3): 107–123.

Putnam, R. (1993) *Making Democracy Work*. Princeton: Princeton University Press.

Qiongli, W. (2006) 'Commercialization of digital storytelling: An integrated approach for cultural tourism, the Beijing Olympics and wireless VAS', *International Journal of Cultural Studies*, 9(3): 383–394.

Quinn, B. (2007) 'Performing tourism: Venetian residents in focus', *Annals of Tourism Research*, 34: 458–476.

Race, R. (2008) 'Introduction', in J. Eade, M. Barrett, C. Flood and R. Race, *Advancing Multiculturalism Post-7/7*. Newcastle: Cambridge Academic Scholars, 1–6.

Radin, M.J. (1996) *Contested Commodities*. Cambridge: Harvard University Press.

Raghuram, P. (2000) 'Gendering skilled migratory streams: Implications for conceptualizations of migration', *Asian and Pacific Migration Journal*, 9(4): 429–457.

Rajadhyaksha, A. (1998) 'Indian Cinema', in J. Hill and P.C. Gibson (eds) *The Oxford Guide to Film Studies*. Oxford: Oxford University Press

Rajadhyaksha, A. (2003) 'The "Bollywoodization" of the Indian cinema: Cultural nationalism in a global arena', *Inter-Asia Cultural Studies*, 4(1): 25–39.

Rajan, A. (4 March 2010) 'Dance me no nonsense', *The Hindu*. Available at: www.thehindu.com/arts/article145715.ece (accessed 4 July 2013).

Rajan, G. and Mohanram, R. (1995) *Postcolonial Discourse and Changing Cultural Contexts*. Westpost: Greenwood Press.

Ralph, D. and Staeheli, L. (2011) 'Home and migration: Mobilities, belongings and identities', *Geography Compass*, 5(7): 517–530.

Ranciére, J. (2004) *The Politics of Aesthetics*. London: Bloomsbury.

Ranciére, J. (2011) *The Emancipated Spectator*. London: Verso.

Rantanen, T. (2005) *The Media and Globalization*. London: Sage.

Rap-Up, (13 March 2009) 'Video: Pussycat Dolls – "Jai Ho! (You Are My Destiny)"'. Available at: www.rap-up.com/2009/03/13/video-pussycat-dolls-jai-ho-you-are-my-destiny/ (accessed 13 July 2013).

Rathore, T. (25 February 2009) 'A.R. Rahman Slumdog Millionaire review', BBC Review. Available at: www.bbc.co.uk/music/reviews/89jw (accessed 9 July 2013).

Ray, R. (2012) 'Wither Slumdog Millionaire: India's liberalization and development themes in Bollywood films'. www.wbiconpro.com/228-Rita.pdf (accessed 24 May 2013).

Reality Gives–(undated). Available at: www.realitygives.com (accessed 2 September 2013).

Reality Tours – (undated). Available at: http://realitytoursandtravel.com (accessed 1 September 2013).

Reas, P.J. (2014) 'The "must have" tourist experience: An exploration of the motivations, expectations, experiences and outcomes of volunteer tourists in Siem Reap, Cambodia'. PhD thesis: University of Leeds, UK.

Rediff India Abroad (5 March 2009) 'Meet the singers of Jai Ho'. Available at: www.rediff.com/movies/2009/feb/26singers-of-jai-ho.html (accessed 11 July 2013).

Rediff News (2009) 'Playing slumdog Salim'. Available at: http://specials.rediff.com/movies/2009/jan/20video4-slumdogs-salim-speaks-up.htm (accessed 29 August 2013).

Rediff News (4 March 2009) 'The number one film in the entire world'. Available at: www.rediff.com/movies/report/slumdog-is-number-one-film-worldwide/20090304.htm (accessed 6 September 2013).

ReetzChannel (2008) 'Interview with Slumdog Millionaire writer Simon Beaufoy'. Available at: www.reelz.com/article/757/interview-with-slumdog-millionaire-writer-simon-beaufoy/ (accessed 19 January 2013).
Reeves, C. (12 April 2012) 'Screenwriter interview – Simon Beaufoy', ScriptShadow. Available at: http://scriptshadow.blogspot.co.uk/2012/04/screenwriter-interview-simon-beaufoy.html (accessed 19 January 2013).
Reeves, N. (2002) 'Translation, international English and the planet of Babel', *English Today*, 18(4): 21–28.
Rege, S. (2011) 'Exorcising the fear of identity: Interrogating the "Language Question" in sociology and sociological language', in S. Patel (ed.) *Doing Sociology in India*. New Delhi: Oxford University Press, 213–240.
Reid-Brinkley, S.R. (2008) 'The essence of (ex)pectability: Black women's negotiation of black femininity in rap music and music videos', *Meridians*, 8(1): 236–260.
Reijnders, S. (2010) 'Places of the imagination: An ethnography of the TV detective tour', *Cultural Geographies*, 17(1): 37–52.
Relph, E. (1976) *Place and Placeness*. London: Pion.
Renov, M. (2004) *The Subject of Documentary*. Minneapolis: University of Minnesota Press.
Rettie, R. (2009) 'Mobile phone communication: Extending Goffman to mediated interaction', *Sociology*, 43(3): 421–438.
Richards, G. and Wilson, J. (2004) *The Global Nomad*. Clevedon: Channel View.
Richardson, N. (22 January 2009) 'Slumdog Millionaire: On the trail of Mumbai's slumdogs', *The Telegraph*. Available at: www.telegraph.co.uk/travel/destinations/asia/india/4306996/Slumdog-Millionaire-on-the-trail-of-Mumbais-slumdogs.html (accessed 1 September 2013).
Ricoeur, P. (1970) *Freud and Philosophy*. New Haven: Yale University Press.
Ricoeur, P. (1974) *The Conflict of Interpretations*. Evanston: Northwestern University Press.
Ricoeur, P. (1993) *Oneself as Another*. Chicago: University of Chicago Press.
Ricoeur, P. (1999) 'Memory and forgetting', in R. Kearney and M. Dooley (eds) *Questioning Ethics*. London: Routledge.
Ricoeur, P. (2005) *The Course of Recognition*. Cambridge: Harvard University Press.
Riley, R.W. and Van Doren, C.S. (1992) 'Movies as tourism promotion. A "pull" factor in a "push" location', *Tourism Management*, 13(3): 267–274.
Ritzer, G. (2010) *Globalization*. Oxford: Wiley-Blackwell.
Ritzer, G. (2011) *Globalization-The Essentials*. Oxford: Wiley-Blackwell.
Ritzer, G. and Liska, A. (1997) '"McDisneyization" and "post-tourism": Contemporary perspectives on contemporary tourism', in C. Rojek and J. Urry (eds) *Touring Cultures*. London and New York: Routledge, 96–112.
Ritzer, G. and Atalay, Z. (2010) *Readings in Globalization*. Oxford: Wiley-Blackwell.
Ritzer, G. and Jurgenson, N. (2010) 'Production, consumption, prosumption: The nature of capitalism in the age of the digital "prosumer"', *Journal of Consumer Culture*, 10: 13–36.
Robertson, R. (1992) *Globalization*. London: Sage.
Robertson, R. (1995) 'Glocalization: time-space and homogeneity-heterogeneity', in M. Featherstone, S. Lash and R. Robertson (eds) *Global Modernities*. London: Sage, 25–44.
Roesch, S. (2009) *The Experiences of Film Location Tourists*. Clevedon: Channel View Publications.

220 Bibliography

Rojek, C. (1993) *Ways of Escape*. Basingstoke: Macmillan.
Rojek, C. (2001) *Celebrity*. London: Reaktion.
Rojek, C. (2010) *The Labour of Leisure*. London: Sage.
Rolfes, M., Steinbrink, M. and Uhl, C. (2009) *Townships as Attraction*. Potsdam: Universitätsverlag.
Rollins, J. (1996) 'Invisibility, consciousness of the Other and *ressentiment* among black domestic workers', in C. McDonald and C. Sirianni (eds) *Working in the Service Society*. Philadelphia: Temple University Press, 223–243.
Rose, N. (1989) *Governing the Soul*. London: Free Association.
Rose, N. (1998) *Inventing Ourselves*. Cambridge: Cambridge University Press.
Rose, S. (13 February 2009) 'Saturday interview: Simon Beaufoy', *The Telegraph*. Available at: www.telegraph.co.uk/news/celebritynews/4612235/Saturday-interview-Simon-Beaufoy.html/ (accessed 19 January 2013).
Roston, T. (4 November 2008) '"Slumdog Millionaire" shoot was rags to riches', *The Hollywood Reporter*. Available at: www.hollywoodreporter.com/news/slumdog-m illionaire-shoot-was-rags-122290 (accessed 11 August 2011).
Rowe, W. and Schelling, V. (1991) *Memory and Modernity*. London, Verso.
Roy, A. (2 March 2009) 'Caught on film: India "not shining"', *Dawn.com*. Available at: http://archives.dawn.com/archives/108135 (accessed 13 September 2013).
Ruparl, A. (10 August 2013) 'Dharavi development project inches ahead', *The Indian Express*. Available at: www.indianexpress.com/news/dharavi-development-project-inches-ahead/1153592/ (accessed 2 September 2013).
Rushdie, S. (undated) 'A fine pickle: Slumdog Millionaire and film adaptation', Red Room. Available at: http://redroom.com/member/salman-rushdie/writing/a-fine-pick le-slumdog-millionaire-and-film-adaptation (accessed 28 September 2013).
Ryan, M. and Kellner, D. (1990) *Camera Politica*. Bloomington: Indiana University Press.
Sacks, O. (2013) *Musicophilia*. London: Picador.
Sahlins, M. (1972) *Stone Age Economics*, Chicago: Aldine.
Said, E. (1978) *Orientalism*. London: Penguin.
Said, E. (1983) *The World, the Text and the Critic*. Cambridge, MA: Harvard University Press.
Said, E. (1994) *Culture and Imperialism*. London: Vintage.
Said, E. (2000) 'Secular criticism', in M. Rayoumi and A. Rubin (eds) *The Edward Said Reader*. New York: Vintage, 218–242.
Sakakeeny, M. (2010) '"Under the bridge": An orientation of soundscapes to New Orleans', *Ethnomusicology*, 54(1): 1–27.
Salazar, N. (2004) 'Developmental tourists vs. development tourists: a case study', in A. Raj (ed.) *Tourist Behaviour*. New Delhi: Kanishka, 85–107.
Salazar, N. (2007) 'Art as politics: Re-crafting identities, tourism, and power in Tana Toraja, Indonesia by K. Adams (2006)'. www.h-net.org/~travel/ (accessed 26 August 2013).
Salazar, N. (2013) 'The double bind of world heritage tourism', in B. Jansson (ed.) *The Significance of World Heritage*. Dalarna: Dalarna University, 274–291.
Samuels, D.W., Maintjes, L., Ochoa, A.M. and Porcello, T. (2010) 'Soundscapes: Toward a sounded anthropology', *Annual Review of Anthropology*, 39: 329–345.
Sánchez Taylor, J. (2000) 'Tourism and "embodied" commodities: Sex tourism in the Caribbean', in Clift, S. and Carter, S. (eds.) *Tourism and Sex*. London and New York: Pinter, 41–53.
Sandywell, B. (2011) *Dictionary of Visual Discourse*. Surrey: Ashgate.

Sassen, S. (2000) 'New frontiers facing urban sociology at the Millennium', *British Journal of Sociology*, 51: 143–160.
Sassen, S. (2001) *The Global City*. Princeton: Princeton University Press.
Sassen, S. (ed.) (2002a) *Global Networks, Linked Cities*. London: Routledge.
Sassen, S. (2002b) 'The repositioning of citizenship: Emergent subjects and spaces for politics', *Berkeley Journal of Sociology*, 46: 4–25.
Sassen, S. (2003) 'Globalization or denationalization?', *Review of International Political Economy*, 10(1): 1–22.
Savigliano, M. (1995) *Tango and the Political Economy of Passion*. Boulder: Westview Press.
Sawyer, M. (13 June 2010) 'MIA: "I'm here for the people"', *The Observer*, Available at: www.guardian.co.uk/music/2010/jun/13/mia-feature-miranda-sawyer/print (accessed 29 June 2013).
Sayer, A. (1999) 'Valuing culture and economy', in L. Ray and A. Sayer (eds) *Culture and Economy after the Cultural Turn*. London: Sage, 53–75.
Sayyid, S. (2003) *A Fundamental Fear*. London: Zed Books.
Scannell, P. (1989) 'Public service broadcasting and modern public life', *Media, Culture & Society*, 11(1): 135–166.
Schafer, R.M. (1994) *The Soundscape*. Rochester: Destiny.
Scheper-Hughes, N. (2013) 'No more angel-babies on the Alto', Center for Latin American Studies (CLAS). Berkeley: University of California.
Schickel, R. (1985) *Intimate Strangers*. Chicago: Ivan R. Dee.
Schneider, D.M. (1977) 'Kinship, nationality and religion: Toward a definition of kinship', in J. Dolgin, D. Kemnitzer and D.M. Schneider (eds) *Symbolic Anthropology*. New York: Columbia University Press, 63–71.
Schneider, S.M. and Foot, K.A. (2004) 'The Web as an object of study', *New Media & Society*, 6(1): 114–122.
Schneider, S.M. and Foot, K.A. (2005) 'Web sphere analysis: An approach to studying online action' in C. Hine (ed.) *Virtual Methods*, Oxford: Berg, 157–170.
Schulman, J.L. (2004) 'Introduction', in R.K. Merton and E. Barber, *The Travels and Adventures of Serendipity*, Princeton, NJ: Princeton University Press.
Scott, J.C. (1998) *Seeing like a State*. New Haven: Yale University Press.
Seaton, A.V. (2002) 'Tourism as metempsychosis and metensomatosis: The personae of eternal recurrence', in G.M.S. Dann (ed.) *The Tourist as a Metaphor of the Social World*. Wallingford: CABI, 135–168.
Seaton, T. (2012) 'The literary evolution of slumming', in F. Frenzel, K. Koens and M. Steinbrink, *Slum Tourism*. London: Routledge, 21–48.
Sen, A. (1992) *Inequality Reexamined*. Oxford: Oxford University Press.
Sen, A. (1999) *Development as Freedom*. Oxford: Oxford University Press.
Sengupta, M. (20 February 2009) 'Slumdog Millionaire's dehumanizing view of India's poor', *Counterpunch*. Available at: www.counterpunch.org/2009/02/20/slumdog-millionaire-s-dehumanizing-view-of-india-s-poor (accessed 28 January 2013).
Serres, G. (1995) *Genesis*. Ann Harbour: University of Michigan Press.
Serres, M. and Latour, B. (1995) *Conversations on Science, Culture and Time*. Ann Arbor: University of Michigan Press.
Sesser, S. (21 February 2009) '"Slumdog" tour guide', *Asia News*. Available at: http://online.wsj.com/article/SB123517711344337609.html (accessed 5 September 2013).
Shah, A. (2013) 'The intimacy of insurgency: Beyond coercion, greed or grievance in Maoist India', *Economy & Society*, 42(3): 480–506.

Bibliography

Sharpley-Whiting, T. (2007) *Pimps Up, Ho's Down: Hip Hop's hold on young black women*. New York: University of New York Press.
Sheller, M. (2003) *Consuming the Caribbean*. New York: Routledge.
Sheller, M. (2004) 'Demobilising and remobilising the Caribbean paradise', in M. Sheller and J. Urry (eds) *Tourism Mobilities*, London: Routledge, 13–21.
Sheller, M. (2012) 'Mobilities', in G. Ritzer (ed.) *Encyclopaedia of Globalization*. New York: Wiley-Blackwell.
Sheller, M. (2014a) 'Sociology after the mobilities turn', in P. Adey, D. Bissell, K. Hannam, P. Merriman and M. Sheller (eds) *The Routledge Handbook of Mobilities*. London and New York: Routledge, 45–54.
Sheller, M. (2014) 'The new mobilities paradigm for a live sociology', *Current Sociology*, 1–23 (Online First: 23 May 2014). Available at: http://csi.sagepub.com/content/early/2014/05/23/0011392114533211.abstract (accessed 25 September 2014).
Sheller, M. and Urry, J. (2004) 'Places to play, places in play', in M. Sheller and J. Urry (eds) *Tourism Mobilities*. London: Routledge, 1–10.
Sheller, M. and Urry, J. (2006) 'The new mobilities paradigm', *Environment and Planning A*, 38: 207–226.
Shields, R. (1992) 'Spaces for the subject of consumption', in R. Shields (ed.) *Lifestyle Shopping*. London: Routledge, 1–20.
Shilling, C. (1999) 'Towards an embodied understanding of the structure/agency relationship', *British Journal of Sociology*, 50(4): 543–562.
Shohat, E. (1992) 'Notes on the "post-colonial"', *Social Text*, 31/32: 99–113.
Shohat, E. and Stam, R. (2003) *Multiculturalism, Postcoloniality and Transnational Media*. New Brunswick: Rutgers University Press.
Sider, L. (ed.) (2003) *Soundscape*. London: Wallflower Press.
Sify.com, 3 October 2010, http://www.sify.com/sports/commonwealth-games/
Silin, G. (1995) *Sex, Death and the Education of Children*. New York: Teacher's College Press.
Silver, I. (1993) 'Marketing authenticity in Third World Countries', *Annals of Tourism Research*, 20(2): 302–318.
Simmel, G. (2004) *The Philosophy of Money*, edited by D. Frisby. London: Routledge.
Singh, M. (26 January 2009) 'Slumdog Millionaire, an Oscar favorite, is no hit in India', *Time*. Available at: http://content.time.com/time/arts/article/0,8599,1873926,00.html (accessed 15 September 2013).
Singh, O. (25 May 2013) 'Aamir on Narmada: I won't apologise', *Rediff India*. Available at: www.rediff.com/movies/2006/may/25aamir1.htm (accessed 12 July 2013).
Singh, O. (5 June 2008) 'SC rejects Fanaa petition', *Rediff India*. Available at: www.rediff.com/movies/2006/jun/05fanaa.htm (accessed 12 July 2013).
Singh, S. (2009) 'Spirituality and tourism: An anthropologist's view', *Tourism Recreation Research*, 34(2): 143–155.
Singh, S. (2012) 'Slow travel and Indian culture: Philosophical and practical aspects', in S. Fullagar, K. Markwell and E. Wilson (eds) *Slow Tourism*. Bristol: Channel View, 214–226.
Skoll, G.R. and Korstanje, M. (2014) 'Urban heritage, gentrification and tourism in Riverwest and Albasto', *Journal of Heritage Tourism*. Available at: http://dx.doi.org/10.1080/1743873X.2014.890624 (Online first 15 April 2014).
Slemon, S. (1987) 'Monuments of the Empire: Allegory/counter-discourse/post-colonial writing', *Kunapipi*, 9(3): 1–16.

Slemon, S. (1988) 'Magical realism as post-colonial discourse', *Journal of Commonwealth Literature*, 23(1): 157–168.
Slumdog Dreams: Danny Boyle and the Making of Slumdog Millionaire (2009) Blue Ray Extras in *Slumdog Millionaire*. Celador Films and Channel 4, Pathé.
Slumdog Millionaire (2009), dir. Danny Boyle, Blue Ray. Celador Films and Channel 4, Pathé.
Smith, A.D. (1971) *Theories of Nationalism*. London: Duckworth.
Smith, A.D. (1995) *Nations and Nationalism in a Global Era*. Cambridge: Polity.
Smith, A.D. (1999) *Myths and Memories of the Nation*. Oxford and New York: Oxford University Press.
Smith, A.D. (2004) 'History and National Destiny: Responses and Clarifications', in M. Guibernaeu and J. Hutchinson (eds) *History and National Destiny*. Oxford: Blackwell, 195–209.
Smith, C. (2010) 'Review: Papadopoulos, Linda: Sexualisation of young people review', London: Home Office Publication, February 2010, pp. 100', *Participations: Journal of Audience and Reception Studies*, 7(1): 175–179.
Smith, E. (2013) 'Slumdog Millionaire', in *The Danny Boyle Handbook – Everything you need to know about Danny Boyle*. United Kingdom: Emereo Pty Limited, 516–529.
Smith, P. (2008) 'The Balinese Cockfight decoded: Reflections on Geertz, the strong programme and structuralism', *Cultural Sociology*, 2(2): 169–186.
Smith, R. (2007) *Being Human*. New York: Columbia University Press.
Smith, S. and Watson, J. (2001) 'The rumbled bed of autobiography: Extravagant lives, extravagant questions', *Biography*, 24(1): 10–14.
Soja, E.W. (2000) *Post Metropolis*. Oxford: Blackwell.
Solomon, T. (2009) 'Berlin-Frankfurt-Istanbul: Turkish hip-hop in motion', *European Journal of Cultural Studies*, 12(3): 305–327.
SongLyrics (undated) 'A.R. Rahman – Gangsta Blues Lyrics'. Available at: www.songlyrics.com/a-r-rahman/gangsta-blues-lyrics/ (accessed 7 July 2013).
Sontag, S. (1971) *On Photography*. London: Penguin.
Sontag, S. (1991) *AIDS and its Metaphors*. Harmondsworth: Penguin.
Sontag, S. (2003) *Regarding the Pain of Others*. New York: Picador.
Spivak, G. (1985) 'The Rani of Sirmur: An essay in reading the archives', *History and Theory*, 24(3): 247–272
Spivak, G. (1988) 'Can the subaltern speak?', in C. Nelson and L. Grossberg (eds) *Marxism and the Interpretation of Culture*. Urbana: University of Illinois Press, 271–313.
Spivak, G. (1992) *Thinking Academic Freedom in Gendered Post-Coloniality*. Cape Town: University of Cape Town Publishing.
Spivak, G. (1999) *A Critique of Postcolonial Reason*. Cambridge, MA: Harvard University Press.
Spivak, G. (2000) 'The politics of translation', in L. Venuti (ed.) *The Translation Studies Reader*. London: Routledge, 397–416.
Spivak, G. (2003) *Death of a Discipline*. New York: Columbia University Press.
Spivak, G. (2004) 'Terror: A speech after 9/11', *Boundary 2*, 31(2): 81–111.
Spivak, G. (2005) *Other Asias*. Oxford and New York: Wiley-Blackwell.
Spivak, G. (2009) *Outside the Teaching Machine*. New York: Routledge.
Spivak, G. (2012) *An Aesthetic Education in the Era of Globalization*. Cambridge: Harvard University Press.
Spode, H. (2009) 'Tourism research and theory in German-speaking countries', in G.M.S. Dann and G. Parrinello (eds) *The Sociology of Tourism*. UK: Emerald, 65–94.

Squire, S. (1994) 'Accounting for cultural meanings: the interface between geography and tourism studies re-examined', *Progress in Human Geography*, 18(1): 1–16.
Stallybrass, P. and White, A. (1986) *The Politics and Poetics of Transgression*. Ithaca: Cornell University Press.
Stam, R. (2005) *Literature through Film*. Malden: Blackwell.
Standing, G. (2011) *The Precariat*. London: Bloomsbury.
Standing, G. (24 May 2011) 'The Precariat – The new dangerous class', *Policy Network*. Available at: www.policy-network.net/pno_detail.aspx?ID=4004&title=+The+Precariat+%E2%80%93+The+new+dangerous+class (accessed 12 June 2011).
Starpulse.com (undated) 'M.I.A. biography'. Available at: www.starpulse.com/Music/M.I.A./Biography/ (accessed 29 June 2013).
Stavrou Karayanni, S. (2004) *Dancing Fear and Desire*. Canada: Wilfrid Laurier University Press.
Stedman Jones, G. (1971) *Outcast London*. Oxford: Oxford University Press.
Steinbrink, M. (2012) 'We did the slum! Urban poverty tourism in historical perspective', *Tourism Geographies*, 14(2): 213–234.
Steiner, C. (1994) *African Art in Transit*. Cambridge: Cambridge University Press.
Stevenson, N. (1997) 'Globalisation, national cultures and cultural citizenship', *Sociological Quarterly*, 38(1): 41–66.
Stevenson, N. (2003) *Cultural Citizenship*. Maidenhead: Open University Press.
Stewart, A. (2000) 'Social inclusion: An introduction', in P. Askonas and A. Stewart (eds) *Social Inclusion*. London: Macmillan, 1–16.
Stoler, A.L. (1995) *Race and the Education of Desire*. Durham, NC: Duke University Press.
Stoler, A.L. (1996) *Race and the Education of Desire*. Durham: Duke University Press.
Stoler, A.L. (1997) 'Making Empire respectable: The politics of race and sexual morality in twentieth century colonial cultures', in A. McClintock, A. Mufti and E. Shohat (eds) *Dangerous Liaisons*. Minneapolis: University of Minnesota Press, 344–373.
Stoler, A.L. (2006) *Haunted by Empire*. Durham: Duke University Press.
Stone, B.E. (2004) 'Defending society from the abnormal: the archaeology of biopower', *Foucault Studies*, 1: 77–91.
Strain, E. (2003) *Public Places, Private Journeys*. New Jersey: Rutgers University Press.
Strathern, M. (1983) 'The kula in comparative perspective', in J.W. Leach and E. Leach (eds) *The Kula*. Cambridge: Cambridge University Press, 73–88.
Strathern, M. (1988) *The Gender of the Gift*. Berkeley: University of California Press.
Strathern, M. (1991) *Partial Connections*. Madison: Rowman and Littlefield.
Straw, W. (1991) 'Systems of articulation, logics of change: communities and scenes in popular music', *Cultural Studies*, 5(3): 368–388.
Suryawanshi, S. (11 August 2013) 'Dharavi development turns into political battle', *DNA India*. Available at: www.dnaindia.com/mumbai/1872815/report-dharavi-development-turns-into-political-battle (accessed 1 September 2013).
Sutton, D. (2000) *Memories Cast in Stone*. New York: Berg.
Swanson, J. (16 May 2011) 'The pros and cons of slum tourism', CNN Travel. Available at: http://travel.cnn.com/mumbai/play/pros-and-cons-slum-tourism-723332 (accessed 6 September 2013).
Swarup, V. (2006) *Q&A*. Reading: Black Swan.
Sydney-Smith, S. (2006) 'Changing places: Touring the British crime film', *Tourist Studies*, 6: 79–95.
Syfy (3 October 2010) 'Rahman brings CWG ceremony to electrifying climax'. Available at: http://web.archive.org/web/20101006052925/http://sify.com/news/rahman-brings-

cwg-ceremony-to-electrifying-climax-news-national-kkdx4ccdbib.html (accessed 12 July 2013).
Szerszynski, B. and Urry, J. (2006) 'Visuality, mobility and the cosmopolitan: Inhabiting the world from afar', *British Journal of Sociology*, 57(1): 113–131.
Tarde, G. (1903) *The Laws of Imitation*. New York: Henry Holt & Co.
Tate, S. (2011) 'Heading South: Love/sex, necropolitics and decolonial romance', *Small Axe*, 35: 43–58.
Taylor, J.P. (2001) 'Authenticity and sincerity in tourism', *Annals of Tourism Research*, 28(1): 7–26.
Taylor, T.D. (1997) *Global Pop*. New York: Routledge.
Tester, K. (1994) *Media, Culture and Morality*. London: Routledge.
Tester, K. (2004) *The Social Thought of Zygmunt Bauman*. Basingstoke: Palgrave Macmillan.
Thapar, R. (1993) *Communalism and the Writing of Indian History*. Delhi: People's Publishing House.
Thapar, R. (1999) 'Communalism and the writing of ancient Indian history', in R. Thapar (ed.) *Communalism and the Writing of Indian History*. Delhi: PPH, 1–21.
Thapar, R. (2004) 'The future of the Indian past', 7th Lakdawala Memorial Lecture. Available at: www.sacw.net/India_History/r_thaparLecture21022004.html (16 February 2013).
The Banyan (undated) 'Project description: Chennai district (Tamil Nadu)'. Available at: www.ashanet.org/projects/project-view.php?p=604 (accessed 29 August 2013).
The Economist (19 December 2007) 'A flourishing slum'. Available at: www.economist.com/node/10311293 (accessed 4 September 2013).
The Fader (7 August 2007) 'Video+Interview: MIA, "Jimmy"'. Available at: www.thefader.com/2007/08/07/video-interview-mia-jimmy/ (accessed 29 June 2013).
The Hindu (21 June 2006) 'Fanaa: Man who immolated dies'. Available at: www.hindu.com/2006/06/21/stories/2006062107441500.htm (accessed 12 July 2013).
The Indian Express (22 January 2009) ' "Slumdog Millionaire" boosts Mumbai's "slum tourism" industry'. Available at: www.indianexpress.com/news/-slumdog-millionaire–boosts-mumbai-s-slum-tourism–industry/413939/ (accessed 1 September 2009).
The Times of India (30 September 2002) 'A R Rahman: In tune with life'. Available at: http://timesofindia.indiatimes.com/city/A-R-Rahman-In-tune-with-life/articleshow/23791015.cms (accessed 15 August 2013).
The Times of India (27 May 2006) 'Gujarat left out as world sees Fanaa'. Available at: http://articles.timesofindia.indiatimes.com/2006-05-27/ahmedabad/27807929_1_youth-wing-bharatiya-janata-yuva-morcha-amit-thaker (accessed 12 July 2013).
The Times of India (22 January 2009) 'Hindu group demands ban on "Slumdog Millionaire"'. Available at: http://articles.timesofindia.indiatimes.com/2009-01-22/goa/28046633_1_hjs-slumdog-millionaire-hindu-janjagruti-samiti (accessed 15 September 2013).
The Times of India (3 October 2010) 'A R Rahman's grand finale with "Jeeyo, Utho"'. Available at: http://articles.timesofindia.indiatimes.com/2010-10-03/india/28245061_1_theme-song-peppy-sports-anthem-commonwealth-games (accessed 12 July 2013).
Theobald, W.F. (1998) 'The meaning, scope and measurement of travel and tourism', in W.F. Theobald (ed.) *Global Tourism*, 2nd edn. Oxford: Butterworth Heinemann, 3–21.
Therborn, G. (1995) 'Routes to/through modernity', in M. Featherstone, S. Lash and R. Robertson (Eds.) *Global Modernities*. London: Sage, 124–139.
Thomas, R. (1985) 'Indian cinema: Pleasures and popularity', *Screen*, 26(3–4): 116–131.

Thompson, J. (1995) *The Media and Modernity*. Cambridge: Polity.

Thompson, P. (13 February 2008) 'DFA, Adrock Remix M.I.A.'s "Paper Planes" on new EP', *Pitchfork*. Available at: http://web.archive.org/web/20080227234701/http://www.pitchforkmedia.com/article/news/48681-dfa-adrock-remix-mias-paper-planes-on-new-ep (accessed 30 June 2013).

Thompson, P. (2012) 'What is concrete about Ernst Bloch's "concrete utopia"?' in M. Hviid Jacobsen and K. Tester (eds) *Utopia*. Farnham: Ashgate, 33–46.

Thrift, N. (2006) 'Re-inventing invention: new tendencies in capitalist commodification', *Economy & Society*, 36(2): 279–306.

Thrift, N. (2007) *Non-Representational Theory*. London: Routledge.

Tiruchi (20 July 2012) 'Where has all the magic gone?', *The Hindu*. Available at: www.thehindu.com/features/metroplus/article3661883.ece?css=printwww.thehindu.com/life-and-style/metroplus/article3661883.ece%3fcss=print (accessed 9 July 2013).

Tobin, L. (16 March 2010) 'Slumdog reveals learning treasures', *The Guardian*. Available at: www.theguardian.com/education/2010/mar/16/slumdog-millionaire-education-online-independent (accessed 13 September).

Todd, B. (22 September 2008) 'MIA: Interview', *Time Out*. Available at: www.timeout.com/london/things-to-do/mia-interview (accessed 29 June 2013).

Todorov, T. (1990) *Genres in Discourse*. Cambridge: Cambridge University Press.

Toffler, A. (1980a) *Future Shock*. New York: William Morrow and Co.

Toffler, A. (1980b) *The Third Wave*. London: Pan Books.

Tomaselli, K. (2007) '"Op die grond": Writing in the san/d, surviving crime', in K.G. Tomaselli (ed.) *Writing in the San/d*, New York: Altamira Press, 39–58.

Tomazos, K. and Butler, R. (2010) 'The volunteer tourist as "hero"', *Current Issues in Tourism*, 13(4): 363–380.

Tomlinson, J. (1999) *Globalization and Culture*. Cambridge: Polity.

Tonkin, E. (1992) *Narrating Our Pasts*. Cambridge: Cambridge University Press.

Tonkonoff, S. (2013) 'A new social physic: The sociology of Gabriel Tarde and its legacy', *Current Sociology*, 61(3), 267–282.

Touraine, A. (2000) *Can We Live Together?* Cambridge: Polity.

Trey, G. (1992) 'Communicative ethics in the face of alterity: Habermas, Levinas and the problem of post-conventional universalism', *Praxis International*, 11(4): 412–427.

Tribe, J. (2008) 'Philosophical issues in tourism', in J. Tribe (ed.) *Philosophical Issues in Tourism*. Clevedon: Channel View, 3–35.

Truax, B. (2008) 'Soundscape composition as global music: Electroacoustic music as soundscape', *Organising Sound*, 13(2): 103–109.

Tuan, Yi-Fu, (1996) 'Man and Nature', *Landscape* 15(3): 30–36.

Turim, M. (1989) *Flashbacks in Film: Memory and History*. New York: Routledge.

Turkle, S. (2010) *Alone Together*. London: Basic Books.

Turner, B.S. (1993) 'Cruising America', in C. Rojek and B.S. Turner (eds), *Forget Baudrillard?* London: Routledge, 146–161.

Turner, B.S. (1994) *Orientalism, Postmodernism and Globalism*. London and New York: Routledge.

Turner, B.S. (2001) 'The erosion of citizenship', *British Journal of Sociology*, 52(2): 189–209.

Turner, G. (1999) *Film as a Social Practice*. London: Routledge.

Tzanelli, R. (2002) 'Haunted by the "enemy" Within: Brigandage, Vlachian/Albanian Greekness, Turkish "contamination" and narratives of Greek nationhood in the Dilessi/Marathon Affair (1870)', *Journal of Modern Greek Studies*, 20(1): 47–74.

Tzanelli, R. (2004) '"Europe" within and without: Narratives of American cultural belonging in and through My Big Fat Greek Wedding (2002)', *Comparative American Studies*, 2(1): 35–59.
Tzanelli, R. (2006) 'Capitalising on value: Towards a sociological understanding of kidnapping', *Sociology*, 40(5): 929–947.
Tzanelli, R. (2007) 'Solitary amnesia as national memory: From Habermas to Luhmann', *The International Journal of Humanities*, 5(4): 253–260.
Tzanelli, R. (2008a) 'Cultural intimations and the commodification of culture: Sign industries as makers of the "public sphere"' *The Global Studies Journal*, 1(3): 1–10.
Tzanelli, R. (2008b) *Nation-Building and Identity in Europe*. Basingstoke: Palgrave-Macmillan.
Tzanelli, R. (2010a) 'Islamophobia and Hellenophilia: Greek myths of post-colonial Europe', in S. Sayyid and A.K. Vakil, *Thinking Through Islamophobia*, New York: Columbia University Press, 213–230.
Tzanelli, R. (2010b) *The Cinematic Tourist*. London: Routledge.
Tzanelli, R. (2010c) 'Mediating cosmopolitanism: Crafting an allegorical imperative through Beijing 2008', *International Review of Sociology*, 20(2): 215–241.
Tzanelli, R. (2011) *Cosmopolitan Memory in Europe's 'Backwaters'*. London: Routledge.
Tzanelli, R. (2012a) 'Domesticating sweet sadness: Thessaloniki's glyká as a travel narrative', *Cultural Studies – Critical Methodologies*, 12(2): 159–172.
Tzanelli, R. (2012b) 'Domesticating the tourist gaze in Thessaloniki's Prigipos', *Ethnography*, 13(3): 278–305.
Tzanelli, R. (2013a) *Heritage in the Digital Era*. London: Routledge.
Tzanelli, R. (2013b) *Olympic Ceremonialism and the Performance of National Character*. Basingstoke: Palgrave Pivot.
UNESCO (undated) 'Taj Mahal'. Available at: http://whc.unesco.org/en/list/252 (accessed 4 September 2013).
Urquia, N. (2005) 'The rebranding of salsa in London's dance clubs: How an ethnicised form of cultural capital was institutionalised', *Leisure Studies*, 24(4): 385–397.
Urry, J. (1995) *Consuming Places*. London: Routledge.
Urry, J. (2000) *Sociology Beyond Societies*. London: Routledge.
Urry, J. (2002) *The Tourist Gaze*, 2nd edn. London: Sage.
Urry, J. (2003) *Global Complexity*. Cambridge: Polity.
Urry, J. (2004) 'Death in Venice', in M. Sheller and J. Urry (eds) *Tourist Mobilities*. London: Routledge, 205–215.
Urry, J. (2007) *Mobilities*. Cambridge: Polity.
Urry, J. (2011) *Climate Change and Society*. Cambridge: Polity.
Urry, J. (2014) *Offshoring*. Cambridge: Polity.
Urry, J. and Larsen, J. (2011) *The Tourist Gaze 3.0*, 3rd edn. London: Sage.
Uteng, T.P. and Cresswell, T. (2008) *Gendered Mobilities*. Aldershot: Ashgate.
Valera, C. and Harré, R. (1996) 'Conflicting varieties of realism: Causal powers and the problems of social structure', *Journal for the Theory of Social Behaviour*, 26(3): 313–325.
Van Dijk, J. (1999) *The Network Society*. London: Sage.
Van Dyck, K. (2000) 'Greek poetry elsewhere', *Gramma*, (Special Issue on Contemporary Greek Poetry), 8: 81–98.
Van Schendel, W. (2005) *The Bengal Borderland*. London: Anthem Press.
Vannini, P., Hodson, J. and A. Vannini (2009) 'Toward a technography of everyday life', *Cultural Studies – Critical Methodologies*, 9(3): 462–476.
Vardiabasis, N. (2002) *Story of a Word* [in Greek]. Athens: Livani.

228 Bibliography

Vattimo, C. (1988) *The End of Modernity*. Cambridge: Polity.
Vaughan, D. (1999) *For Documentary*. Berkeley: University of California Press.
Veijola, S. (2009) 'Tourism as work', *Tourist Studies*, 9(2): 83–87.
Veijola, S. and E. Jokinen (1994) 'The body in tourism', *Theory and Society*, 11: 125–151.
Veijola, S. and A. Valtonen (2007) 'The body in tourism industry', in A. Pritchard, N. Morgan, I. Ateljevic and C. Harris (eds) *Tourism and Gender*. Wallingford: CABI, 13–31.
Venuti, L. (2000) 'Translation, community, utopia', in L. Venuti (ed.) *The Translation Studies Reader*. London: Routledge, 468–488.
Vertovec, S. (2010) *Transnationalism*. London and New York: Routledge.
Vertovec, S. and Cohen, R. (2002) *Conceiving Cosmopolitanism*. Oxford: Oxford University Press.
Vesselinov, E., Cazessus, M. and Falk, W. (2007) 'Gated communities and spatial inequality', *Journal of Urban Affairs*, 29(2): 109–127.
Vidal, H. and Jara, R. (eds) (1986) *Testimonio y Literatura*. Minneapolis: Institute for the Study of Ideologies/Literature.
Virilio, P. (2010) *L'Administration de la Peur*. Paris: Textuel.
Vogt, J.W. (1976) 'Wandering: Youth and travel behavior', *Annals of Tourism Research*, 4(1): 25–41.
Vogt-William, C. (2009) 'British-Asian music between resistance and commercialization', in M. Meyer (ed.) *Word and Image in Colonial and Postcolonial Literatures and Cultures*. London: Rodopi, 237–260.
Volcic, Z. and Andrejevic, M. (2011) 'Nation branding in the era of commercial nationalism', *International Journal of Communications*, 5: 598–618.
Wacquant, L. (2004) *Body and Soul*. New York: Oxford University Press.
Waddington, D. (1992) *Contemporary Issues in Public Disorder*. London: Routledge.
Waddington, D.P. (2010) 'Applying the Flashpoints Model of Public Disorder to the 2001 Bradford Riot', *British Journal of Criminology*, 50(2): 342–359.
Wager, J.B. (1999) *Dangerous Dames*. Athens: Ohio University Press.
Walcott, D. (1974) 'The muse of history' in O. Coombes (ed.) *Is Massa Day Dead?* New York: Doubleday, 1–27.
WallersteinI. (1974, 1980) *The Modern World System, vols. I-II*. New York: Academic Press.
Warschauer, M. (1999) *Electronic Literacies*. London: Longman.
Warschauer, M. (2002) 'Reconceptualizing the Digital Divide', *First Monday*, 7(7). Available at: http://firstmonday.org/ojs/index.php/fm/article/view/967/888 (accessed 9 September 2013).
Wearing, S. (2001) *Volunteer Tourism*. Oxford: CABI.
Weber, M. (1985) *The Protestant Ethic and the Spirit of Capitalism*, translated by T. Parsons. London: Unwin Hyman.
Weber, M. (2002) 'Basic sociological terms', in C. Calhoun, J. Gerteis, J. Moody, S. Pfaff and I. Virk (eds) *Classical Sociological Theory*. Oxford: Blackwell, 280–290.
Webopedia (2013) 'Segment'. Available at: www.webopedia.com/TERM/S/segment.html (accessed 22 June 2013).
Weidman, A. (2006) *Singing the Classical, Voicing the Modern*. Durham: Duke University Press.
Welk, P. (2004) 'The beaten track: Anti-tourism as an element of backpacker identity construction', in G. Richards and J. Wilson (eds), *The Global Nomad*. Clevedon: Channel View, 77–91.

Wellman, B., Quan-Hasse, A. and Boase, J. (2003) 'The social affordances of the Internet for networked individualism', *Journal of Computer-mediated Communication*, 8(3). Available at: http://jcmc.indiana.edu/vol8/issue3/wellman.html (accessed 15 May 2012).
Wenning, M. (2009) 'The return of rage', *Parrhesia*, 8: 89–99.
Westerhausen, K. (2002) *Beyond the Beach*. Bangkok: Thai Lotus Press.
White, H. (1978) *Tropics of Discourse*. Baltimore: John Hopkins University Press.
Wieschiolek, K. (2003) 'Ladies, just follow his lead! Salsa, gender and identity', in N. Dyck and E. Archetti (eds) *Sport, Dance and Embodied Identities*. New York: Berg, 115–138.
Wikipedia (undated) 'Agra'. Available at: http://en.wikipedia.org/wiki/Agra#cite_note-2 (accessed 18 March 2013).
Wikipedia (undated) 'Delhi Mumbai Industrial Corridor Project'. Available at: http://en.wikipedia.org/wiki/Delhi_Mumbai_Industrial_Corridor_Project#cite_note-1 (accessed 11 September 2013).
Wikipedia (undated) 'Dharavi'. Available at: http://en.wikipedia.org/wiki/Dharavi (accessed 18 March 2013).
Williams, C. (2008) 'Ghetto-tourism and voyeurism: Forays into literary and non-literary slumming', *Favela Bulletin of Latin American Research*, 27(4): 400–440.
Williams, F. (2004) *Rethinking Families*. London: Calouste Gulbenkian Foundation.
Williams, K. (2005) 'The meanings and effectiveness of world heritage designation in the USA', in D. Harrison and M. Hitchcock (eds) *The Politics of World Heritage*. New York: Channel View, 132–137.
Williams, L. (1984) 'When the woman looks', in M.A. Doanne and L. Williams (eds) *Re-vision*. Maryland: American Film Institute, 83–99.
Williams, R. (1958) *Culture and Society*. London: Chatto and Windus.
Williams, R. (1961) *The Long Revolution*. Harmondsworth: Penguin.
Williams, R. (1974) *The Country and the City*. New York: Oxford University Press.
Williams, R. (1983) *Culture*. London: Fontana Press.
Williams, R. (1999) *The Country and the City Revisited*. Cambridge: Cambridge University Press.
Winant, H. (2004) *The New Politics of Race*. Mineapolis: University of Minnesota Press.
Winistorfer, A. (13 January 2009) 'Album Review: A.R. Rahman – Slumdog Millionaire', *Prefix*. Available at: www.prefixmag.com/reviews/ar-rahman/slumdog-millionaire-music-from-the-motion-picture/24412/ (accessed 11 July 2013).
Winn, J. (23 February 2009) 'Salman Rushdie: Scenes in Slumdog Millionaire "Impossible"', The CelebrityCafe.com. Available at: http://thecelebritycafe.com/features/25008.html (accessed 1 September 2013).
Wise, J. (2008) *Cultural Globalisation*. Oxford: Blackwell.
Witmore, C. (2006) 'Vision, media, noise and the percolation of time: Symmetrical approaches to the mediation of the material world', *Journal of Material Culture*, 11(3): 267–292.
Wolff, J. (1983) *Aesthetics and the Sociology of Art*. Basingstoke: Macmillan.
Wolff, K.H. (ed.)/Simmel, G. (1959) *Georg Simmel, 1858–1918*. Columbus: Ohio State University Press.
Wolin, S.S. (1989) *The Presence of the Past*. Baltimore: John Hopkins University Press.
Wood, R. (1986) *Hollywood – From Vietnam to Reagan*. New York: Columbia University Press.

Woodiwiss, M. (1988) *Crime, Crusades and Corruption*. London: Pinter.
Wright, N.S. (2010) 'Bollywood eclipsed: The postmodern aesthetics, scholarly appeal, and remaking of contemporary popular Indian cinema'. PhD thesis: University of Sussex, UK. Available at: http://sro.sussex.ac.uk/2360/ (accessed 24 May 2013).
xuxuahbeijinhoS (14 October 2009) 'The Pussycat Dolls – Jai Ho (Official Music Video HD)', You Tube. Available at: www.youtube.com/watch?v=imWEDyUXAzM (accessed 13 July 2013).
Yar, M. (2000) 'From actor to spectator: Hannah Arendt's "two theories" of political action', *Philosophy and Social Criticism*, 26(2): 1–27.
Yar, M. (2014) *The Cultural Imaginary of the Internet*. Basingstoke: Palgrave Macmillan.
Young, R.C. (1995) *Colonial Desire*. London: Routledge.
Yuval-Davis, N. (1997) *Gender and Nation*. London: Sage.
Zeitlyn, D. (2001) *Reading in the Modern World, Writing and the Virtual World*. Canterbury: CASC Monographs. Available at: http://casc.anthropology.ac.uk/CASCMONOG/RRRweb/ (accessed 8 February 2011).
Zeitlyn, D. (2003) 'Gift economies in the development of open source software: Anthropological reflections', *Research Policy* (special issue: Open Source Software Development), University of Kent at Canterbury. Available at: http://lucy.ukc.ac.uk/dz/ (accessed 29 March 2012).
Žižek, S. (2002) *Welcome to the Desert of the Real!* New York: Verso.
Zumkawala-Cook, R. (2008) 'Bollywood gets funky: American hip-hop, basement bhangra and the racial politics of music', in S. Gopal and S. Moorti (eds) *Global Bollywood*. Minneapolis: University of Minnesota Press, 308–330.

Index

13th Compound 161, 164
26 November 2008 terrorist attacks 139, 144, 155, 181
7/7 (London bombing) 108, 181, 218 (bibl.)

A Hole in the Wall 172–173
A.R. Rahman Foundation 50
Aaj Ki Raat (music track) 65, 110–111
absence: epistemological 117; Latika's 101; of Beaufoy's dialogue artistry 65; of dialogue 108; of Indian 'ghosts' 166; of kinship 173; of remuneration 144; of resentment, 103
Academy of Motion Picture Arts and Sciences (AMPAS) 140
acceptance: modes of 29; of Slumdog Millionaire 116; official 91
actants: actors 159; Western, 168
activism 7, 37, 72, 80, 133, 149, 184, 195 (bibl.): academic 58; artistic 30, 37, 183; as 'cultural imperialist' propaganda 13; Boyle's 58, 181; celebrity 183; Dharavi's 22, 146; M.I.A.'s 89, 170; NGO 146, 149–150; of local interest groups 158, 163; political (mega-events) 123; privileged 57; pro-slum 141, 149; Reality Tours xxi, 149; social (SM) 128, 133; volunteer 181
activist(-s) xxii, 30, 35: *artist–* 12, 30, 33; *artistic–* 164; *Arundhati Roy* 169–170; *M.I.A.* 51, 88–89; *SM*, 182
adaptation 7, 21, 192 (bibl.), 206 (bibl.), 207 (bibl.), 210 (bibl.), 231 (bibl.), 215 (bibl.), 220 (bibl.); and Bollywood aesthetics 14–16, 61, 73, 102, 111, 125; and Boyle 45–46; and colonialism 17, 67, 106; community 156, 170; and genre 27–29, 56–57, 59, 67–68, 170–171; and globalisation 7, 13, 87, 92, 97, 148; and tourism 16, 18, 28–29, 41–42, 91–92, 156, 171; as impure art 19, 21, 34, 42, 62, 97; as metaphor 10–11, 94, 171–172; as trafficking 8, 97–98; as translation 9
aeromobilities 164
aesthetics 120, 158 (bibl.), 204 (bibl.), 218 (bibl.), 229 (bibl.), 230 (bibl.): SM 15; Aristotelian 28; necropolitical 58–60; local 176; and communities 7, 14; music, 14, 25
affiliation 51, 102; blood 55; genre 59; kinship 33; political 145; relations of 8
affordances 38–39, 101, 229 (bibl.): educational 104; Indian 117; linguistic 102; socio-cultural 61
agency (-ies) 17–18, 133, 186 (bibl.), 211 (bibl.), 222 (bibl.): pedagogical 30; human 34, 124, 153–154; structure and– 43; Jamal's 60; localised 132; collective 181
Agra Fort 135
alamgiriat xxii, 9
Alexander (dir. Oliver Stone, 2004) 135
Ali, Rubina (actress, b. Mumbai, 1999) 174–176
alienation: market 164; of global social movements 84; post-industrial 44; post-modern 172
Allah 69, 84, 108
allegory (-ies) 12, 14, 16, 44
alterglobalization 123, 204 (bibl.) *see* globalisation, movement (-s)
ambiguity 14, 84, 88, 91, 103, 104: diasporic 84; politicised 59; visual 99
ambivalence 10, 19, 74, 79, 80, 188 (bibl.) *see* ambiguity: psycholographic 63; cosmological 67; stereotypical 111

Index

amity, axiom of 39
amnesia: collective 112; selective 109, 168, 202 (bibl.), 206 (bibl.), 227 (bibl.); social 166; solitary 105
Amnesty International 169
Amritraj, Ashok (producer. b. Chennai, Tamil Nadu, 1956) 140
Angelus Novus 44
ánodos 136
nomaly: Dharavi's 164; social 67
answerability 99, 118, 119, 187 (bibl.)
anthropophagy 95, 142–143: mobile 153
Anwar (*Skins* character) 47
apparition (-s) 113: ghostly 166; nostalgic 65; visual 65
apprehension (-s), 6: nuanced 26; serendipitous 165
Aramis (*Three Musketeers* hero) 86, 113
arc 144: ethological 21; narrative 25, 74; Racist-Christological 9
archaeology: of domestications 10; trans-disciplinary, of contemporary urbanity 108; of bio–power 224 (bibl.)
archetype (-s) see arc, character, habitus: cinematic, 16
archplot 17, 62, 91, 93, 158 see arc, cosmology: Bollywood's 141; film 18, 62, 87; political 136; SM 49, 67
Aristotle (ancient Greek philosopher, 384BC, Stagira 322, Euboea) 59, 186 (bibl.)
art (-s), xxii, 6, 7, 12, 21, 29, 30, 38, 40, 43, 51, 62, 68, 80, 83, 100, 104, 146, 159, 174, 176, 180, 184, 185 (bibl.), 187 (bibl.), 189 (bibl.), 190 (bibl.), 195 (bibl.), 201 (bibl.), 203 (bibl.), 204 (bibl.), 205 (bibl.), 208 (bibl.), 210 (bibl.), 211 (bibl.), 212 (bibl.), 214 (bibl.), 216 (bibl.), 220 (bibl.), 224 (bibl.), 229 (bibl.): activist 89; Bollywood 14; Brechtian takes in 171; cinematic 79, 164; embodied 96, 125; –form of democracy 19; global 11; high 57, 127; institutional theory of 41; marketable 92; mode of 127; nominalisation tropes in 125; of government 32; of knowing 154; of tornadóroi 16; of trading 99; of travel 32, 196 (bibl.); Olympic 123; post-colonial, 45; utopian, 11, 166; world of, 123. See also articulatio, articulation, art-world, art-work, lifeworld, multitude, téchne, tornadóros, tourism
articulation (-s) xxii, 12, 21, 30, 33, 86, 100, 108, 125, 133, 140, 141, 149, 160, 180, 216 (bibl.), 224 (bibl.): audio-visual 25, 126; cinematic 72; conservative 32; expressive 40; financial 78, 106, 176; global cultural 4, 78, 176; global financial 32; global 184; Jamal's, 84; linguistic 75; migration 31; of modernity/post-modernity 16; post-modern 143; public 138; racialized and gendered 120; SM 104; social 110; socio-cultural 118; tourism, 31. See also affiliation, art, assemblage(-s), city, cityscape, community, filiation, mobility, pilgrim, pilgrimage, semiotechnologies, technology, tourism
artscapes 24: *soundscapes-as-* 98; Western 107
Artwork (also as art-work) 7, 9, 11, 13, 14, 24, 30, 31, 37, 41, 42, 44, 49, 51, 70, 90, 99, 117, 126, 127, 145, 177, 181, 183, 185 (bibl.): A.R. Rahman's, 34, 50, 116, 121; Beaufoy's 78; Bollywood 27; Boyle's 45, 58, 66, 80, 159; cinematic 16, 27, 108; impure 19; indigenous 133; M.I.A.'s 89; metropolitan 140; Olympic 123; post-modern 61; professional 8; SM 37, 39, 57, 106; Swarup's 78. *See also* art, articulation, pangosmiopoièsis
Asian Games 122, 197 (bibl.)
Assemblage (-s) 31, 36, 99, 109, 146, 194 (bibl.): audio-visual 108; micro-regional 160; musical 90, 98; open-ended 31; semiotechnological 34; techno–cultural 123; techno-cultural 26. See also affiliation, articulation, mobility, music, semiotechnologies, technology
athinganos 81
audio-vision 24, 193 (bibl.). *See also* synaesthesia
authenticity 16, 18, 21, 44, 47, 73, 88, 98, 176, 190 (bibl.), 191 (bibl.), 199 (bibl.), 207 (bibl.), 211 (bibl.), 221 (bibl.). 225 (bibl.): and tourism 132, 141; cultural 14; glamorous 166; local 79; staged 94, 157, 159; strategic 28; stylistic 28. *See also* adaptation, heritage, phenomenology, reality, tourism
awalim 97

Bachchan, Amitabh Harivansh (actor, b. Allahabad United Provinces, 1942) 62–63, 73, 77, 81, 82, 100, 104, 111, 132, 167, 187 (bibl.), 188 (bibl.), 205 (bibl.). *See also:* Bollywood, Karna, ressentiment
Bakhti 125, 131. *See also:* Sufi, Sufism
band (-s): American music 28; female 126; musical 89
Bangalore 9, 47
bāṇīs 69
barbarism 108, 137
Beaufoy, Simon (screenwriter, b. Keighley, 1967) xxii, 6, 19, 20, 26, 28, 41, 42, 43–45, 51, 57, 58, 60, 64, 65, 67, 68, 70, 78, 83, 85, 105, 169, 181, 188 (bibl.), 219 (bibl.), 220 (bibl.)
beauty 8, 139, 207 (bibl.): as the good life 180; colonised 49; female 119; inner 134; physical 179; Rumina's 179; startling 65. *See also* kósmos, pangosmiopoìeisis
beggars 44, 58
behaviour (-s) 10, 16, 178, 220 (bibl.), 227 (bibl.): anti-social 109; organised 110; typical set of 16; worthy 78. *See also* character, dispositif, habitus
Beijing 122, 123, 218 (bibl.)
being-in-the-world 41: *mode of* 160
Belgrade 126
Bengal 103, 227 (bibl.)
Bergman, Ingmar (director, b. Uppsala, 1918 – d.2007, Fårö) 171
bhangra 117–118, 230 (bibl.)
Bharatiya Janata Party (BJP) 112, 121, 131, 145
biography 196 (bibl.), 205 (bibl.), 206 (bibl.), 223 (bibl.), 224 (bibl.): cinematic 103; collective 165; disreputable 62; Jamal's, 60, 103; nation–state 106; personal 16; social 69; urban 62, 159
biopower 156, 224 (bibl.)
Black Friday (dir. Anurag Kashyap, 2004) 58
bloodline 33. *See also* heritage, legacy
blueprint, 12, 153, 192 (bibl.)
Bollywood 12, 14–15, 17, 19, 20, 27–28, 29, 32, 44, 55, 56, 58, 63, 71, 74, 87, 139, 186 (bibl.), 187 (bibl.), 190 (bibl.), 192 (bibl.), 202 (bibl.), 209 (bibl.), 214 (bibl.), 215 (bibl.), 217 (bibl.), 218 (bibl.), 230 (bibl.): action thriller 96; adaptation 111; archplots 141; artist 96; celebrity fandom 82, 146; choreography 62, 127; corporate contributions 144; dancing 117; drama 181; expert 172; fame 77; film (-s) 97, 117; global brand 100; global branding 117; melodrama 76, 86; norm 64; persona 167; phantasmagoria 128; productions 68; scenarios 142; sign universe 73; stars 61, 66, 74, 132; tracks 97, 121; villain 100. *See also* (cultural) industry (-ies)
Boogie Woogie (Indian TV show, 1996–2014) 49
Boyle, Danny (director, b. Radcliffe, 1956) xxii, 6, 11, 19, 27, 28, 38, 40, 41, 42, 43, 44, 45–46, 47, 51, 57, 58, 60, 61, 63, 64, 65, 67, 68, 69, 73, 74, 75, 77, 78, 80, 82, 83, 85, 86, 87, 93, 96, 97, 105, 109, 110, 115, 116, 117, 131, 135, 136, 138, 146, 159, 167, 171, 174, 175–77, 178, 179, 180, 181, 191 (bibl.), 200 (bibl.), 205 (bibl.), 208 (bibl.), 210 (bibl.), 211 (bibl.), 217 (bibl.), 223 (bibl.)
Bradford 43, 83, 228 (bibl.)
brand (-s) 70, 190 (bibl.), 197 (bibl.), 205 (bibl.), 211 (bibl.), 215 (bibl.), 227 (bibl.): Bollywood's global 100; India's 79; nationalism 182; of environmental discourse 19; personality 62; urban 45
branding 201 (bibl.), 228 (bibl.): *global* 117
Brick Lane (dir. Sarah Gavron, 2007) 46
bricollages 100
brightness 146, 180
brothel 23, 55, 62
Bucharest 126
Budapest, 126
Buñuel, Luis Portolés (film–maker, b. Calanda, 1900 – d. Mexico City, 1983) 171
Burma 103

Calcutta 15, 29, 47, 173, 206 (bibl.): as 'Indobubble' 128' as elusive representation 40
camera (-s) 16, 26, 43, 71, 77, 94, 95, 102, 106, 109, 110, 118, 119, 151, 155, 220 (bibl.): digital 40; static 78; techniques 69; Western 68; work 16, 26, 40, 42, 45, 56, 63, 74, 91. *See also* assemblage, technopoesis, tornadóros
capabilities 184, 200 (bibl.)
capacities 34, 39

capital 134, 135, 142, 155, 191 (bibl.), 193 (bibl.), 194 (bibl.), 203 (bibl.), 227 (bibl.): corporate 132; cultural 38, 81, 91, 120, 136, 157, 159–160, 172; dead 161; heritage native 144; monetary 27; network 62, 132; social 104; symbolic 95. *See also* capitalism, character, dispositif, habitus, homo communicans, homo economicus
capitalism 123, 176, 200 (bibl.), 203 (bibl.), 207 (bibl.), 210 (bibl.), 212 (bibl.), 219 (bibl.), 228 (bibl.); disorganised 56; emotional 157; global 106; network 133; tourism 18. *See also* articulation, assemblage, city, network
carnivalesque 79, 93, 94: digital, 157
celebrity 62, 66, 76, 82, 143, 172, 177–178, 179, 181, 183, 195 (bibl.), 198 (bibl.), 220 (bibl.)
centre (-s), 19, 24, 106, 111, 116: administrative 6; colonial 67; cosmological 5; media 179; mediated 138; national 22, 33, 138; political 31, 123; urban 46, 79, 101
character (-s) 12–13, 17, 19, 27, 43, 47, 60, 61, 65, 73, 104, 106, 181, 227 (bibl.): active 43, 72; angry 95; group's 5, 61; human 57, 59, 81, 137; Indian 33, 64; industrial 63; Latika's 98; Salim's 107; SM 61, 67; socio-cultural 59, 61; Urdu 138; vanishing 80; violent 75. *See also* arc, archetype (-s), archplot (-s), Aristotle, dispositif, habitus, junktivism, junctivists (-s), Karna, nostalgia, stereotype (-s), type (-s)
charity (-ies) 49, 50, 80, 159, 158, 166–167, 173–174, 176, 177, 183–184, 21 (bibl.)
Chavan, Prithviraj (National Congress politician, b. Indore, Madhya Pradesh, 1946) 161
Chembur Pradeep Motwani 47
Chhatrapati Shivaji or Victoria Terminus (VT) 119, 120, 140, 155
child 59, 84, 85, 179, 184, 190 (bibl.), 191 (bibl.), 196 (bibl.), 205 (bibl.), 208 (bibl.), 215 (bibl.): actors 46, 47, 49, 76; -consumer 132; good-mannered 106
childhood 20, 45, 60, 67, 89, 104, 110, 177, 186 (bibl.), 192 (bibl.), 205 (bibl.): collective, 78; English 82; India's slum 105; Jamal's 63, 84, 86, 94; Mittal's 49; Salim's 86; utopia 104

children 18, 32, 49, 79, 80, 81, 92, 142–143, 151, 152, 167, 182, 190 (bibl.), 197 (bibl.), 214 (bibl.), 215 (bibl.), 222 (bibl.): as objects of consumption 80, 90; carefree 153; Dharavi 168, 177; disabled 158; gypsy 81; homeless 87; middle-class 47; of darkness 6; photographed 167; slum 47, 80, 88, 170, 174–175, 184; stars 175; street 87, 97, 159, 172; well-dressed 168; young 43
Choli Ke Peeche (music track) 96–97
Chopra, Aditya (director, screenwriter and producer, b. Maharastra, Mumbai, 1971) 112
Chopra, Priyanka (actress, b. Jamshedpur, Bihar, 1982), **111**
choreography 96, 100: Bollywood 61, 96–97, 125
Christian (-s), 163, 205 (bibl.)
chrónos 21, 77, 132, 133, 154. *See also*: kairos
chronotope 30, 44, 94, 107
citizens 85, 187 (bibl.): slum 117, 128, 146; second–rate 179; virtual 174
citizenship (-s) 4, 29, 33, 46, 61, 110, 178, 194 (bibl.), 197 (bibl.), 198 (bibl.), 201 (bibl.), 208 (bibl.), 217 (bibl.), 221 (bibl.), 224 (bibl.), 226 (bibl.): cultural 121
city 4, 6, 26, 32, 40, 44, 45, 68, 71, 77, 80, 83, 87, 95, 101, 104, 105, 106, 108, 111, 120, 128, 131, 133, 134, 135, 143, 145, 147, 152, 154, 159, 161, 162, 164, 166, 186 (bibl.), 187 (bibl.), 197 (bibl.),198 (bibl.), 201 (bibl.), 21 (bibl.), 214 (bibl.), 215 (bibl.), 217 (bibl.), 221 (bibl.), 229 (bibl.): absent presence 86; cinematic 62, 109, 145; cultural intimacy 86; global xxiii, 77; Maximum 144; mega- 21; north Indian 49; of ruins 71, 145; post-colonial 126; residual 79; spectacular 155; virtual 71, 126; zones, 85. *See also* capitalism, cityscape (-s), intimacy, phantasmagoria, presence, tourism
City of Joy (dir. Roland Joffé, 1992) 68
cityscape 40, 78, 94,: global 91; polyphonic 41; Mumbai's 64, 67, 95, 116; ever-expanding 110
civilisation (-s) 19, 64, 66, 189 (bibl.), 198 (bibl.): ancient 70; clash of 10, 184; human 93; manliness and 16; race and 81; science and 106; Western European 7; Western 19; world 80;

see also civility, mobility, modernity, technology, terrorism

civility 80, 86, 92, 102, 142, 150: codes of 49, 169; European 99; global 110; India's late-modern 104; industrial 85; self-fashioned 58; urban 155; Western 144, 145, 169

class 62, 96, 143, 186 (bibl.), 199 (bibl.), 211 (bibl.), 224 (bibl.): and gender 106; capitalist 183; middle- 64, 68, 71, 116, 121, 125, 127, 133, 158, 168, 179; politics of 135; professional 142; rich 174; service 106; social 57; upper 169; working- 64, 87, 95, 142, 152, 172

cleansing 106: spatial 164–165, 204 (bibl.)

climax 224 (bibl.): audio-visual 110; technological 111

collusio 134. *See also* dispositif, habitus

colonialism 33, 42, 55, 80, 176, 184, 193 (bibl.), 208 (bibl.), 209 (bibl.), 212 (bibl.), 216 (bibl.): European 17. *See also* capitalism, colonisation, crypto-colonialism, post-colonialism, presence (absent)

colonisation (-s) 4: of India 48; invisible 166; memories of 182

colour (-s) 5, 44, 66, 104, 146: antithetical 60; bright 145; ethereal 109; red 125; sepia 59; sublime 65. See also phenomenology, race, racism, (dark/slum) tourism

Colson, Christian (producer, b. Buenos Aires, 1968) xxiii, 43, 174

comedy 27, 45, 73, 92: carnivalesque 79

commons 109, 207 (bibl.): creative 160; gated 160; open 160

communication (-s) 9, 25, 45, 62, 82, 96, 104, 144, 187 (bibl.), 191 (bibl.), 192 (bibl.), 197 (bibl.), 200 (bibl.), 201 (bibl.), 202 (bibl.), 204 (bibl.), 209 (bibl.), 214 (bibl.), 219 (bibl.), 228 (bibl.), 229 (bibl.): global 124; intercultural 31, 33, 182; proximate/distant 35, 39; theorists 68; virtual 143

communitarianism: nationalist 115; utopian 172; village 108

community 4, 5, 21: artistic xxii, 36–51, 51, 57, 115, 117; cultural industrial xxii; imagined 13, 16. See also: articulation, assemblage, neotribe, semiotechnology (ies)

compassion 79, 92, 99: altar of 143; global politics of 62; televised 28; Western 139

complexity (-ies) 22, 36, 84, 227: ethno-cultural 67; interpretative 60; post-modernity's 4

conduct: code of 161; good corporate 177; Western 178

connectivities: discursive 118; layered 33; virtual-terrestrial 160; world 19

Constable Srinivas (SM hero) 58

consumer (-s) 9, 24, 45, 62, 144, 162, 188 (bibl.), 195 (bibl.), 199 (bibl.), 216 (bibl.): global 88, 100, 157; hegemonic 146; privileged 16; Western 150.

consumerism 27, 71, 135, 153, 192 (bibl.), 196 (bibl.): ethical 183

consumption 9, 14, 17, 28, 30, 33, 46, 56, 58, 70, 95, 131, 195 (bibl.), 198 (bibl.), 211 (bibl.), 231 (bibl.), 219 (bibl.), 222 (bibl.): aestheticised 72; audio-visual 17; class 135; cultural 11; e–tourism 152; global 121; language of 16; lifestyle 87; mass 123; multi-sensory 150; of slum communities 143–145; reproductive 115, 170; tourist 21, 22, 27, 99, 154; Western 125. See also capitalism, mobility (-ies), neoliberalism, netizens, synaesthesia, technology, tourism

contrapuntalism 30

convergence (-s) 90, 182: business 134; institutional 9; of téchne/érgon 5

corporation (-s) 75, 140, 183, 206 (bibl.): cultural 12; ITDC 139–140; multi-national 136; telecommunication, 62

corruption 3–5, 18, 58, 62, 77, 89, 161, 169, 180, 230 (bibl.): administrative 56; bureaucratic 6; developmental 85; Orientalist 3; political 26; slum 170; social 87; stratigraphy of 161–164.

cosmology (-ies) 17, 61, 73, 180: European 144; Hindu 144; movie's 115; pop 141; slumdog 117. *See also* archplot, phenomenology

cosmopolitanism 37, 140, 202 (bibl.), 203 (bibl.), 215 (bibl.), 227 (bibl.), 228 (bibl.): aesthetic 26; cosmetic 120, 131. *See also* activism, pangosmiopoièisis, synaesthesia

creativity 32, 195 (bibl.), 198 (bibl.): artistic 33, 38, 77, 173; beautiful 150; cinematic 42; collaborative 7; native 144; popular 25; symbolic 16, 34; technological 3

crime 29, 47, 58, 71, 105, 109, 110, 145, 149, 173, 192 (bibl.), 200 (bibl.), 216

236 *Index*

(bibl.), 224 (bibl.), 226 (bibl.), 230 (bibl.):'poorist' 139; and kitsch 96; border, 103; offshoring, 166; Salim's character 63, 100–101; sociologists of 169
cciminality 74, 96, 104
crypto-colonialism 166, 204 (bibl.)
Curtis, Cliff (actor, b. Rotorua, Bay of Plenty, 1968) **65**
custom 122, 123, 128, 134, 168, 179: family 64; folk 133; prejudicial 127; scopophilic 27; tango 120; *see also* character, conduct, ethological, habitus
cyber-sphere 15, 151, 152

D'Mello, Susanne (singer, song writer, vocal arranger, lyricist) 114
dabbawallah 155
dakaitee 104
dalit (-s), 18, 117, 137, 156
dance, 45, 61, 65, 196 (bibl.), 200 (bibl.), 209 (bibl.), 215 (bibl.), 218 (bibl.), 227 (bibl.), 229 (bibl.): eastern 127; hybridised 27; Indian classical 48; Latika's 96–97; limbo 117; liquid 109; mobilities, 117–121; river 86
darkness, 62, 65, 71, 141, 145, 146, 180, 215 (bibl.): children of 4; terrorist 58
death 30, 60, 67, 77, 114, 126, 166, 216 (bibl.), 222 (bibl.), 223 (bibl.), 227 (bibl.): beautiful 124; violent 78
debt (-s) 40: post-colonial 19; trope of 33; civilizational 38. See also economy (-ies), exchange, gift, reciprocity (-ies)
decency 176–177
Delhi Commonwealth Games 2010, 122
Delhi, New 142, 143, 172
Delhi–Mumbai Industrial Corridor (DMIC) 164
Democracy (-ies), 56, 67,166, 194 (bibl.), 206 (bibl.), 218 (bibl.): global 10; semiotic 123; third-world 90
depth 14, 56, 104, 166: chronological 93; emotional 74, 85; historical 62, 101, 134, 145; post-colonial 63
Desai, Nitin Chandrakant (production designer, b. Mulund, Mumbai) 135–136, 215 (bibl.)
destiny, 11, 27, 47, 74, 79, 114, 116, 206 (bibl.), 211 (bibl.), 223 (bibl.): Jamal's 110; Latika's 112 *See also* determinism, éthos (-e), karma, phenomenology, serendipity, teleology

determinism: biological 19; techno– 38
Devdas (dir. Sanjay Leela Bhansali, 2002) 97
development, 55, 136, 173, 176, 189 (bibl.), 191 (bibl.), 194 (bibl.), 195 (bibl.), 209 (bibl.), 213 (bibl.), 215 (bibl.), 218 (bibl.), 220 (bibl.), 221 (bibl.). 224 (bibl.), 230 (bibl.): child 178; city's 77; communal-technological 108 ; community's 153, 178 ; destination image 141; Dharavi's 164; diachronic (of slum tourism); 57–58; economic 162; ethographic 59; fair 62, 141; faulty 166; language of 42; linear narrative 29; material 184; of Indian tourism 4; of poor nations 164; sustainable 158; tourism 18, 139; tourist 116, 134, 157; urban 105; Western European discourses of 21; work 13
Dharavi (Mumbai slum) 22, 36, 58, 80, 105, 135, 143, 144, 145, 146, 147, 148, 149, 150, 151, 153, 154, 155, 157, 158, 159, 161, 162, 163, 164, 166, 168, 170, 177, 186 (bibl.), 190 (bibl.), 196 (bibl.), 197 (bibl.), 213 (bibl.), 220 (bibl.), 224 (bibl.), 229 (bibl.): recycling project 160–161; virtual site 160; website 160
Dharavi Diary, 158–159
Dharavi Redevelopment Authority (DRA) 162
dharma 179
dhobiwallahs 155
dialogics 115, 200 (bibl.), 205 (bibl.): artistic 183
diaspora (-s), 33, 36, 48, 187 (bibl.): multiple 118; Punjabi 118; South Asian 20
Dickens, Charles (novelist, b. Landport, 1812 – d. Higham, 1870) **58**
difference (-s) 13, 20, 27, 41, 64, 72, 137, 160, 168, 176, 186 (bibl.), 196 (bibl.), 197 (bibl.), 202 (bibl.), 204 (bibl.), 207 (bibl.): civilisational, 137; cultural 17, 21, 108; discourses of 28; ethnic 106; generational 78; internal 77, 91; intersectional 137; professional 102; racialised 126; replication of 151; social, 106, 110. *See also* hybridity, hybridisation
digitopia (-s) 149, 150, 154, 170
discourse (-s) 3, 16, 20, 28, 30, 33, 47, 55, 80, 82, 96, 97, 100, 108, 132, 135, 159,

162, 163, 166, 170, 171, 200 (bibl.), 201 (bibl.), 204 (bibl.), 209 (bibl.), 226 (bibl.), 229 (bibl.): allegorical 81; Beaufoy's 45, 51; biological 33; Boyle's 51; citizenship 61; colonial 92, 214 (bibl.); comparative 84; confrontational 13; conservative 85; developmental 177; environmental 19; ethological 5; Eurasian 119; European 152, 153; fatalist 74; fundamentalist 21, 153; heritage 179; metaphorical 100; mobility 30; moral 81, 102; nationalist 141; normative 21; of recognition 177; of the vanishing 167, 207 (bibl.); of trafficking 178; Orientalist 81, 139; peripheral 51; political 12, 57, 117, 168, 173; positivist 26; post-colonial 99, 218 (bibl.), 222 (bibl.) post-feminist 68; realist 173; religious 84; Rushdie's 175; sensitive 44; serendipitous 6; sexist 138; socio-cultural 137; stereotypical 71; utopian 7, 32, 174; visual 159, 220 (bibl.); volunteer tourist, 174; Western European 21, 49
dispositif 17, 122, 127, 133, 134, 136, 138, 157, 163: Bollywood 181; civilised 120; Dharavi's 163; disenfranchised 158; good 69, 86; human 100; Indian 17; individualised 58; micro–sociology of 13; Tardean 57. *See also* articulation, character, habitus
divide (-s), 103, 104: class 146; digital 101, 151, 178, 194 (bibl.), 228 (bibl.); ethno-religious 83; generational 119; racialised 28; regional and demographic 179; religious 68, 168; social 137, 151; theological 56
Dixit, Madhuri (actress, b. Maharastra, Mumbai, 1967), 96–97
documentary (-ies), 44, 66, 71, 83, 117, 151, 159, 207 (bibl.), 213 (bibl.), 219 (bibl.), 228 (bibl.): Boyle's 60; realist 68; techniques 59, 71, 75
domestication 10, 13, 80
Don (dir. Chandra Barot, 1978) 111
Don: The Chase Begins Again (dir. Farhan Akhtar, 2006) 111
doxosophers 172, 216 (bibl.)
drama 47, 48, 92, 201 (bibl.): Bollywood 181; Faustian 153; melo- 45; Sanskrit, 97. *See also* comedy, genre, melodrama

drugs 46, 47, 114
Dumas, Alexander (playwright and novelist, b. Villers-Cotterêts, Aisne, 1802 – d. Puys, Seine-Maritime, 1870) 67–68, 113

Eccleston, Christopher (actor, b. Pendleton, 1964) 63
ecology (-ies) 152: deep 162; human 164; media 152, 164; symbolic 152; urban 134
economy (-ies) 191 (bibl.), 207 (bibl.), 221 (bibl.): global 114, 136, 147, 186 (bibl.), 211 (bibl.); Indian 182; Mumbai's 137; narrative 117; of performance 126; political 98; service 109; visitor 145. *See also* capitalism, exchange, gift, reciprocity
ecosystem (-s): balanced 81; human 134; industrialised 25
edu–tourism 20, 57, 205 (bibl.). *See also* tourism
Elizabeth (dir. Shekhar Kapur, 1998) 50
embeddedness 127: institutional 42; structural 131
emotion (-s) 89, 157: dangerous 167; destructive 84; familial 95; intense, 42
empathy 50, 108 : failure of 149; tourist 92
Enlightenment 18–19, 30, 112, 185 (bibl.), 190 (bibl.): dialectic of 34; Western 150
environment (-s), 63, 165, 177, 195 (bibl.), 206 (bibl.): cultural industrial 122; de-mediated 31; de-territorialised 124; digital 39, 72; disorderly and threatening 74; epistemic 42; hybrid production 12; industry 163; liquid tourist 177; living 140; media 43; mediated 32; new social media 35, 107; physical 104; post-Fordist 102; post-modern 115; realist 57; resentful 177; social 38, 103; socio-cultural 61; sonic 100; technological 39, 70, 146, 154; virtual 132
ethics xxii, 55, 57, 59: de-territorialised 29; developmental 21; diasporic 117; global 56; Indian, 122; of global digitality 178; of technological mobilities 152; of tourist gazing 143; of work 144; situational 176; Spivak's 184. *See also* aesthetics. dispositif, habitus
ethnicity (-ies) 35, 96, 104, 210 (bibl.)

ethnography (-ies) 145, 193 (bibl.), 212 (bibl.), 219 (bibl.): music 25; post-colonial 19
ethnoscapes, 51, 69, 98
ethos (-e) 21, 37, 47, 48, 57, 63, 103, 114, 152: aerial 12; charitable 166–167; collective 157; cultural 145; disruptive 137; DIY 114; hospitality 136; mobile 127; modern 158; responsible 164; social 183; Sufi 50. *See also*: aesthetics. character, *dispositif*, ethics, habitus
Europe 10, 19, 58, 79, 81, 84, 97, 103, 126, 152, 153, 162, 166, 167, 192 (bibl.), 198 (bibl.), 205 (bibl.), 227 (bibl.)
evil 5–6, 21, 62, 64, 67, 77, 102, 104, 114, 153, 178, 215 (bibl.): unexpected 181
exchange (-s) 5, 80, 182, 195 (bibl.): cross-cultural 7; organised 94; Rumina Ali's 182; foreign 132; chrono-spatial, 148; patterns of 160; profitable 179; ritualistic 179; industrial 12; pure 33, 88; cultural 37, 88; host-guest, 92; human 39
exclusion (-s) 3, 32, 62, 79, 80, 134, 182: cosmetic 134; everyday 61; social, 81, 161
excrement 62, 81: human 82; slum 82
experience (-s), 10, 16, 17, 21, 40, 41, 47, 48, 60, 70, 71, 77, 80, 83, 90, 106, 107, 108, 144, 146, 158, 177, 212 (bibl.), 217 (bibl.), 218 (bibl.), 219 (bibl.): abnormal 89; aesthetic 24; anti-tourist 88; contemporary 34, 217 (bibl.); harrowing 6; human 78, 133, 148; individualised 21; intimate 43; life 3; life-opening 143; living 147; multi-sensory 155; ordinary 116; past 42, 77; personal 41, 51, 66; sensory 26; situated 8; subjective 38, 61; tourist 21, 143, 193 (bibl.); traumatic 77–78; travel 41; Western 151

fable (-s): *domestic political* **169**; *moral* **113**; *nation–building* **136**; *romantic poorist* **131**
family (-ies), 15, 49, 51, 65, 80, 85, 86, 112, 152, 172, 175, 179, 192 (bibl.), 194 (bibl.), 203 (bibl.), 205 (bibl.), 210 (bibl.), 229 (bibl.): biological 95, 209 (bibl.); communal 152; Dumas 67; evicted 161; extended 174; heterosexual 100; Irish Catholic 45; M.I.A.'s 88; middle-class 48; Muslim 106; nation- 84, poor 168, 184; real 84
Fanaa (dir. Kunal Kohli, 2006) 111–112
fans 50, 89: Bollywood 27; cinematic 123; global 174
fatalism, 74, 116
Father Thomas (Q&A hero) 68
Fellini, Federico (director and scriptwriter, b. Rimini, 1920 – d. Rome, 1993) 171
femme attrapée 64, 109
femme fatale 64
femme universelle 118
fetishisation (-s) 28, 194 (bibl.): musical 98; historical 60
field 6, 39, 83, 114, 131, 134, 140, 143, 169, 185 (bibl.), 190 (bibl.), 194 (bibl.), 195 (bibl.): activist 38, 166; commercial 182; communicative 67; digital 40; semantic 20; social 34, 38, 133; socio-cultural 123, 156
figure (-s): borderline 103; dark 159; fictional 66; literary-cinematic 106; mother 85; nomad 107; star 79
filiation 51: relations of 8; bonds of 102; hegemonic 8; kinship 33. *See also* affiliation, assemblage, kinship, network, technopoesis
Film (-s) 7, 8, 11, 17, 18, 19, 20, 22, 23, 24, 25, 26, 32, 38, 40, 44, 45, 46, 47, 49, 50, 51, 55, 56, 57, 60, 64, 66, 67, 68, 70, 115, 116, 117, 120, 121, 124, 126, 128, 131, 133, 134, 135, 137, 139, 166, 167, 169, 171, 173, 174, 176, 177, 181, 185 (bibl.), 187 (bibl.), 195 (bibl.), 199 (bibl.), 201 (bibl.), 208 (bibl.), 209 (bibl.), 215 (bibl.), 216 (bibl.), 220 (bibl.), 224 (bibl.), 226 (bibl.): acclaimed 6; Bollywood 29, 58, 71, 117, 141, 218 (bibl.); Bombay 71; Boyle's 180; documentary 59, 158; Hindi 49, 2014 (bibl.), 217 (bibl.); Indian 144; Oscar-winning 170; prestige 62; realistic 141; sociology of film 29; Western 71, 158
flânerie 155: anomic 159; global 160; horizontal 106; types of 71; urban 96
flâneur (-s) 188 (bibl.), 216 (bibl.): Benjaminian 143; cinematic 97; internet 148; middle-class 71; non-travelling 160; terrestrial 154
flashbacks 77, 226 (bibl.): cinematic, 114; Jamal's 59; memory 58. *See also*

experience, flashpoint, memory, mind-walking
flashpoint (-s) (also as 'flashpoint events' or 'flashpoint model') 83, 168, 228 (bibl.)
flavours 28: *travelling* **27**
flows 12, 31: aesthetic 7; artistic 123; commodity 176; cosmological 13, 57; cultural 15, 25, 111, 122; global 7; media 25; multi–directional 154; political 4; tourism-cash 134; tourist 21; unidirectional 171
fons 152–153, 172, 175: cultural 179
formations 5: cultural 141; fluid 80; political 162; power 34, 123; social 16, 166; tourist 22
fortune (-s) 152, 214 (bibl.): ill 181; quiz 101
Fox Searchlight Pictures 3, 175
Frankfurt 126, 127, 223 (bibl.)
Free Hugs 50, 197 (bibl.)
freedom 56, 196 (bibl.), 211 (bibl.), 221 (bibl.), 223 (bibl.): holistic 108; personal 177; precarious 87
fremdenverkern 7–8
Full Circle (travel show, 2006–2008) 48
fundus 153, 172

Gandhi (dir. Richard Attenborough, 1982) 140
gangs, 96, 216 (bibl.): brotherhood 71; criminal 86; irregular 103; local 3
Gangsta Blues (music track) 101, 223 (bibl.)
gaze 17, 21, 79, 121, 201 (bibl.), 203 (bibl.), 205 (bibl.), 211 (bibl.), 212 (bibl.), 217 (bibl.): analytical 100; carefree 94; cinematic tourist 24, 71; cinematic 29; clinical 150; controlling and organising 106; counter- 129, 133, 145–146; feminine 71; horizontal and vertical (tourist) 106; inward-looking 63; local 157; mechanical 159; mutual 157–158; resentful 157; slum tourist 59; spectator's 26; tourist 9, 80, 89, 101, 117, 139, 143, 151, 156, 169, 227 (bibl.); visitor's 22; Western tourist 78
gazing 26, 27, 30, 149, 157, 183, 217 (bibl.): counter- 145, 179; digital technologies of 133; environmental tourist 58; phenomenological heritage of 134; real 145; slum 160; tourist 143
gender, 35, 42, 56, 62, 101, 106, 189 (bibl.), 192 (bibl.), 194 (bibl.), 196 (bibl.), 212 (bibl.), 216 (bibl.), 224 (bibl.), 228 (bibl.), 229 (bibl.), 230 (bibl.): agreement 119; complementarity 64; inequalities 99; order 64, 118; roles 71; selection 179; stereotypes 92
genealogy (-ies) 34: Bollywood 15; Eastern 97
genre (-s) 27, 28, 56, 87, 97, 157, 158, 185 (bibl.), 187 (bibl.), 210 (bibl.), 226 (bibl.): belly dancing 121; comical 73; dance 120; film's 14; gangster 102; heritage 68; local 116; music 24, 29, 50, 101, 215 (bibl.), of adaptation 67; SM's 59–60
geography 191 (bibl.), 207 (bibl.), 216 (bibl.), 223 (bibl.)
geo–politics 143, 216 (bibl.)
Ghalib, Mirza (Urdu poet, b. Agra, 1797 – d. Delhi, 1869) 115
Ghandi, Mahatma (Mohandas Karamchand) (politician, b. 2 October 1869, Porbandar, Kathiawar Agency, British India – d. 30 January 1948, New Delhi) 31, 122, 123
Ghandi, Indira Priyadarshini Nehru (politician, b. 19 November 1917, Allahabad, United Provinces, British India (today Uttar Pradesh) – d. 31 October, New Delhi) 163
ghetto, 206 (bibl.), 229 (bibl.)
ghettoization 105, 109
gift 33, 56, 179, 186 (bibl.), 195 (bibl.), 213 (bibl.), 224 (bibl.), 230 (bibl.): of European/Eurasian thought 38–39; *See also* economy (-ies), exchange (-s), giving, heritage, reciprocity (-ies), technopoesis
giving 166, 179: artistic 174; as-developing 176; celebrity 172; charitable 51, 150; philanthropic 49, 16; Western 173
globalisation (also as globalization): 9, 10, 12, 42, 72, 101, 123, 124, 133, 137, 139, 153, 187 (bibl.), 188 (bibl.), 186 (bibl.), 191 (bibl.), 194 (bibl.), 200 (bibl.), 204 (bibl.), 205 (bibl.), 206 (bibl.) 208 (bibl.), 213 (bibl.), 215 (bibl.), 218 (bibl.), 219 (bibl.), 221 (bibl.), 222 (bibl.), 223 (bibl.), 224 (bibl.), 226 (bibl.), 229 (bibl.): aesthetic 180; as adaptation 7, 13, 92, 93, 148; consumer 95; cultural 19; economic 19; metaphors of 20; neoliberal 142; political 19;

post-colonial 67; Western cosmologies of 73. *See also* alterglobalization, beauty, glocalisation, mobility, pangosmiopoieisis
glocalisation (also glocalization) 23, 72, 219 (bibl.)
Goa, 146, 195 (bibl.)
good 5, 11, 20, 62, 77114, 178, 180, 181, 215 (bibl.). *See also* cosmology, evil
guest (-s) 93, 144, 153, 157, 159, 202 (bibl.): gullible tourist 91
guilt 44, 166: compassionate 28; tourist 148
Gujarat 112, 209 (bibl.), 225 (bibl.)
Gulzar (poet, lyricist and director, b. Sampooran Singh Kalra Dina, Jhelum District (Pakistan), 1936) 115, 124
Gunga Din (dir. George Stevens, 1939) 68

habit (-s) 21, 41, 57, 88. *See also* character, custom, habitus
habituation 29, 120, 133
habitus 12–13, 59, 73, 75, 134, 195 (bibl.): black masculine 101; class 133, 158; disenfranchised 134; embodied 38; ethnic 61; ethno-racial 63; Eurasian 64; improvised 76; macro-social cultural 48; melodramatic 20; northern English 137; psychosocial 56; radical 30. *See also* character, custom, dispositif, habit
hauntology (-ies) 172: ethno-national 4; Indian 4
heritage, 7, 33, 55, 68, 72, 80, 113, 120, 132, 133, 179, 184, 195 (bibl.), 204 (bibl.), 220 (bibl.), 222 (bibl.), 227 (bibl.), 229 (bibl.): dark tourist 82; dissonant 57, 58, 135; domestic 182; European cultural 61; globally sanctioned 146; India's architectural 65; India's, 149, 142; intangible 33, 153; Islamic 152; living 143; national 17; nationalist 182; Nehruvian 141, 162; phenomenological 134; post-colonial 32, 85; tangible 33; world 139; World 92. *See also* kinship, legacy, network, time
hermeneutics 70, 89, 150, 167, 185 (bibl.), 190 (bibl.), 207 (bibl.): double 23, 89; human 34; M.I.A.'s 89; of recovery/suspicion 46, 82, 113, 118, 145; religious 96; social 60; techno- 116

hero (-es), 13, 49, 58, 60, 69, 70, 71, 74, 75, 77, 78, 84, 86, 87, 95, 110, 117, 169, 192 (bibl.), 195 (bibl.), 215 (bibl.): anti- 38, 46, 63; cinematic 4, 117, 181; disenfranchised 49; female 64, 67–68; fictional 38; lonely 79; main 6, 50, 61, 62 ; masculine 68 ; mobile 38 ; movie 82; pop 112; romantic 104; slumdog 111, 186 (bibl.); SM 47, 73; travelling 38; volunteer tourists as 173–174, 226 (bibl.)
heroine 118: main 6
heterotopia (-s) 70–71: cinematic 135
Hindi 75, 97, 115, 172, 190 (bibl.), 206 (bibl.), 214 (bibl.), 217 (bibl.)
hip hop 51, 222 (bibl.), 223 (bibl.), 230 (bibl.)
history 21, 42, 72, 73, 82, 83, 102, 110, 113, 118, 127, 136, 138, 141, 165, 166, 182, 191 (bibl.), 196 (bibl.), 198 (bibl.), 199 (bibl.), 201 (bibl.), 202 (bibl.), 204 (bibl.), 206 (bibl.), 211 (bibl.), 215 (bibl.), 223 (bibl.), 225 (bibl.), 226 (bibl.), 228 (bibl.): city's 44; Edenic futural 32; global 184; imperialist 170; Indian 168, 171; official 133; post-colonial 149; post-national 149; revisionist 126
Holocaust 188 (bibl.): Europe's 167
Holy Mother 66
home 14, 29, 36, 40–42, 44, 51, 66, 96, 108, 109, 111, 117, 146, 153, 158, 162, 164, 169, 201 (bibl.), 207 (bibl.), 211 (bibl.), 212 (bibl.), 218 (bibl.): Ali's family 175
homo communicans 157
homo economicus 156
homo faber 112
hospitality 45, 136, 157, 196 (bibl.)
host (-s) 91, 93, 126, 140, 157, 159, 202 (bibl.): disenfranchised 146; -guest 5, 92, 132, 160; slum tourist industry 13; W3B 73; Who Wants to be a Millionaire? 75
hustler (-s) 88
hybridisation 48, 64: aesthetic 56; cultural 61, 77, 180; strategic 137; structural, 61, 125, 126. *See also* glocalisation, globalisation, pangosmiopoiesis
hybridity 64, 180, 231 (bibl.): Bollywood 14, 27; ontological 64; artistic 77
hypermobility, 9, 65

Index 241

icon (-s) 84: female 77; global 91, 103; romanticised 108
iconography 68: SM's, 23
ideal (-s) 30, 31: community 29; fundamental 170; muscular-masculine 53; of kinship and community 163; of nature 15; pre-modern 166; tourist 174
identification (-s) 10, 39, 84, 98, 200 (bibl.), 205 (bibl.): anthropomorphic 45; self– 13; total 26
identity (-ies) 14, 22, 23, 27, 65, 75, 83, 91, 94, 110, 114, 138, 165, 192 (bibl.), 193 (bibl.), 194 (bibl.), 196 (bibl.), 198 (bibl.), 202 (bibl.), 207 (bibl.), 213 (bibl.), 219 (bibl.), 227 (bibl.), 228 (bibl.), 229 (bibl.): artistic 38; Beaufoy's 44; Boyle's British 85; collective 133, 213 (bibl.); cosmopolitan 48; cultural 78, 200 (bibl.), 203 (bibl.); Muslim 111; of Third World women 99–100; political 149; Punjabi 118; Roma 81; Salim's 'professional' 107; Salim's wallah 104; self– 37, 168, 201 (bibl.); social 9, 62, 90, 112; socio-cultural 36; urban 141
ideology 7, 57, 212 (bibl.), 217 (bibl.): hegemonic 116, 141; neoliberal 34; political 173
ideoscapes 13, 51: Mumbai's 107
idiom (-s): local 12; ethnic 30; artistic 30; cultural 116. *See also* articulation
imagery 71, 139: childhood 84; sexualised 138
imaginary (-ies) 22, 41, 211 (bibl.), 230 (bibl.): artistic 61; art-work 61; colonial 133; homeland 36, 51; NRI 14; transnational 123; utopian 173
immigrant (-s) 90: first–generation 103
immigration 91
immobility (-ies) 41, 169, 201 (bibl.), 203 (bibl.)
imperative (-s) 62: allegorical 108, 227 (bibl.); business 47; capitalist 97, 170; consumerist 16; doxic 30; economic 138; ethical 149; industrial 80; international 164; kairotic 21; market 12, 29, 152; media 20; monetary 134; philological 146; professional 164; representational 46; textual 140; Western 14
imperialism 201 (bibl.), 207 (bibl.), 2016 (bibl.), 220 (bibl.)
Incredible India 132, 144–145, 205 (bibl.), 206 (bibl.)
India 3, 4, 5, 6, 9, 14, 15, 18, 20, 28, 31, 33, 36, 40, 41, 43, 44, 46, 48, 50, 55, 64, 67, 72, 73, 74, 799, 80, 85, 88, 89, 90, 91, 96, 97, 100, 102, 104, 105, 106, 108, 111, 113, 116, 117, 119, 122, 125, 128, 132, 138, 139, 140, 141, 143, 146, 147, 153, 157, 160, 161, 162, 165, 167, 169, 170, 171, 172, 175, 176, 177, 178, 181, 182, 185 (bibl.), 189 (bibl.), 196 (bibl.), 196 (bibl.), 202 (bibl.), 205 (bibl.), 206 (bibl.), 210 (bibl.), 212 (bibl.), 214 (bibl.), 216 (bibl.), 218 (bibl.), 219 (bibl.), 220 (bibl.), 221 (bibl.), 222 (bibl.): classless 162; government of 164; la longue durée of 61; northeast 103; northern 9; prestige of 62; real 57, 150; refractions of 68; urban 56, 65, 142
Indian National Congress 112
Indian Tourism Development Corporation (ITDC) 139, 206 (bibl.)
Indians 205 (bibl.), 212 (bibl.): south, 149; non-maharajah, 171
individualism 42, 82, 229 (bibl.)
Indonesia 48, 220 (bibl.)
industriousness 148, 149, 159
innovation (-s) 127: aesthetic 8; artistic 16, 171; Bollywood structural 74; ideational 39; individualised 7; slum 158; synaesthetic 28; technological 4; technopoetic 115
interdependency (-ies) 182: global 34; of cinematic archplots with cosmology 17; socio-economic, 93
interface 26, 184, 223 (bibl.): representational 55
internet 7, 23, 89, 98, 101, 123, 142, 154, 172, 195 (bibl.), 199 (bibl.), 204 (bibl.), 229 (bibl.), 230 (bibl.)
Internet Movie Database (IMDB) 3, 23, 48, 206 (bibl.)
interrogation (-s) 19, 21, 41, 59, 73, 74, 75, 101,
intersections 8, 15, 18, 22, 36, 41, 118, 187 (bibl.)
intimacy 40, 162, 182, 201 (bibl.), 204 (bibl.), 221 (bibl.): cold 157; cultural 86, 157; ethno-cultural 78; family 152; illusion of 66; Mumbai's 109; national 15; of Western encounters 11; sexual 98; social 175; tele– 112
Islam 49, 84, 152
Ismail, Azharuddin Mohamed (actor, b. Mumbai, 1998) 174, 175
Iyer, Mahalaxmi (Mahalakshmi) (backup singer) 110, 116

242 *Index*

Jackson, Michael Joseph (pop singer, b. Gary, Indiana, 1958 – d. Los Angeles, 2009) 49
Jackson, Peter (director, producer and scriptwriter, b. Wellington, 1961) 171
Jai Ho! (music track) 61, 110, 114, 115–128, 131, 154, 188 (bibl.), 197 (bibl.), 206 (bibl.), 207 (bibl.), 213 (bibl.), 218 (bibl.), 230 (bibl.)
Jaipur 47
Janajagruti Samiti 167
Javadekar, Prakash (BJP politician, b. Pune, 1951) 122
Javed (SM anti-hero) 47, 100, 106, 107, 108, 109, 110, 111, 113, 120
Jiya Se Jiya (music track) 50
Jiyo Utho Badho Jeeto (music track and anthem) 122
journalist (-s) 12, 15, 22, 25, 60, 160: –artist 44; hack 88; international 143, 163
journey (-s) 4, 6, 41, 57, 81, 146, 150, 155, 202 (bibl.), 215 (bibl.), 224 (bibl.): (auto)biographical 61; audio-visual 113; bus 107; cinematic heroes' 117; cinematic 183; cognitive 46; cosmological 21; emotional and social 58; epistemological 177; experiential 37, 63; expressive 16; imaginative 14; individual 79; inner 38, 48, 72; multiple 165, 180; nineteenth-century 143; real 181; reflexive 44; serendipitous 167; SM's 5; tourist 91; train 106; virtual 148; Wilford E. Deming's 15; writer's 45
Juhu (Mumbai slum) 22, 32, 40, 44, 47, 78, 79, 80, 84, 110, 135, 146–147, 160, 208 (bibl.), 212 (bibl.)
junktivism 158

kabadiwallahs 161
Kabir (poet, b. Varanasi, 1440 – d. Maghar, 1518) 69, 86
kairós 21, 77, 132–133. *See also* time (-s), chrónos
Kajol (Mukherjee) (actress, Maharashtra, 1974) 112
kam 163
Kapoor, Anil (actor and producer, b. Chembur, 1956) 59, 75–76, 167
Kapoor, Raj (actor, producer and director, b. Peshawar, 1924 – d. Mumbai, 1988) 62–63, 122

Kapoor, Shekhar (director, b. Lahore, 1945) 50
karma 27
karna 63: Bachchan- 167; resentful migrant 120
kathak 97, 117, 190 (bibl.), 209 (bibl.)
káthodos 136
Kaun Banega Crorepati? (Indian quiz show) 3, 136
Khal Nayak (dir. Subhash Ghai, 1993) 96–97
Khan, (Mohammed Hussain) Aamir (actor, producer, director, scriptwriter and television presenter, b. Maharashtra, 1965) 112, 144, 205 (bibl.)
Khan, Irfan (Sahabzade Ali) (actor, b. Jaipur, 1962) 3, 59
Khan, Shah Rukh (actor, producer, television presenter, b. New Delhi, 1965) 111
kinaesthetics 121
kinship 33, 34, 39, 162, 173, 199 (bibl.), 204 (bibl.), 221 (bibl.):
kitsch 11, 96, 126–127, 190 (bibl.): quasi-colonial 96
Kloss, Thomas (director, b. Vienna, 1956) 126
knowledge 3, 17, 21, 31, 34, 45, 51, 71, 74, 77, 91, 99, 101, 128, 155, 165, 183, 199 (bibl.), 202 (bibl.), 203 (bibl.): child/family/community 184; embodied-acting 56; iconological 101; intercultural 25; intimate Indian 76; local 45, 135; methodology of 30–31; native 8; ontological 100; personal 59; practical 115; professional 61; regional 132; tacit 154; technological 102
knowledgeability 154, 172
Koppikar, Isha (actress, b. Maharasthra, 1976) 111
kósmos 8, 12, 131, 136, 180: Greek 31. *See also* beauty, pangosmiopoieisis, lifeworld
Kudalkar Laxmikant Shantaram (composer, b. Bombay Presidency (Maharashtra), 1937 – d. 1998) 96
Kumar, Omung (producer, designer and art director) 122
Kumar, Prem (*Q&A* character) 59, 73, 110, 113
Kumari, Selja (National Congress politician, b. Chandigarh, 1962) 144

labour 5, 37, 59, 92, 103, 122, 150, 154, 166, 170, 183, 190 (bibl.), 196 (bibl.), 202 (bibl.), 209 (bibl.), 216 (bibl.), 220 (bibl.): aesthetic 11; artistic 183; cheap 159; child 89; cinematic 181; contractual wage 162; creative 43, 169, 204 (bibl.); digital 148; embodied 88, 157; industrial 148; manual 106; migrant 16, 166; moral 183; peripheral 89; physical 5; slum 139, 167; slum-dwellers' 151; technological 58, 89; traditional 16; women's 99; workers' 90; working-class 87

land (-s) 20, 30, 31, 116: Dharavi's 161; foreign 11, 174; open 136; real 41

andscape (-s) 24, 30, 81, 85, 91, 135, 138, 146, 154, 170, 190 (bibl.), 209 (bibl.), 214 (bibl.), 226 (bibl.): auditory 25; British 44; cinematic 46; film's 85; Indian 6, 33; memory 114; natural 26; political 106, 122; post-Partition 141; precarious labour 162; social 137

language 9, 16, 34, 84, 184, 186 (bibl.), 195 (bibl.), 201 (bibl.), 204 (bibl.), 207 (bibl.), 208 (bibl.), 211 (bibl.), 219 (bibl.): cyber-stratification of 15; English 15; global, of translation 99; Indian 17, 22; local 102; of bureaucratic rationalisation 92; of criminal resentment 96; of cultural hybridisation 61; of development 42; of family care 175; of global communication 124; of global mediascapes 136; of not belonging 173; of rights 162; popular 123

Latika (SM heroine) 3, 47, 48, 58, 59, 60, 62, 64–66, 67, 71, 77–78, 85, 86, 94, 95, 96, 98–100, 102, 104, 109, 110, 111, 112, 114, 117, 118, 119, 120: rape of 101; youngest 174

'Latika's Theme' (music soundtrack) 65, 106, 109, 114

law (-s) 95, 103, 150, 200 (bibl.), 203 (bibl.), 211 (bibl.), 225 (bibl.): domain of 21; state 104; practical 42; Sufism's outer 50; abstract 85; Indian 92

leadership: artistic 124; forms of 39; social production of 39

legacy (-ies) 33, 142, 202 (bibl.), 203 (bibl.), 226 (bibl.): audio-visual 94; colonial 10, 18; tourist 120, 133, 139. *See also* community, heritage, kinship, nationalism

leitmotifs 176

lens 151, 168: patronising 175; SM's allegorical 102; theoretical 36; Western 68

lieux de mémoire 37, 139, 215 (bibl.)

lifestyle (-s) 91, 134, 146, 211 (bibl.): consumption 16; contemporary 8, 120; travelling 120, 191 (bibl.)

lifeworld (-s) 41, 42, 77, 91, 127, 134, 140, 172: asynchronous 135; chrono–diverse 148; India's 94; Mumbai 151; plural 132; rural 38; slum Mumbaikar's 174; stratifications of 32; urban 38, 105

light 58, 67, 101, 141, 215 (bibl.): fluorescent 159; morning 82; positive 136; street 114

liminality 45

Liquid Dance (music track) 65, 107–108

listening 55, 58, 101, 189 (bibl.), 196 (bibl.): deep 25, 189 (bibl.), 216 (bibl.). *See also* soundscape (-s)

locality (-ies) 15, 22–23, 26, 27, 61, 77, 79, 136, 138, 153, 157, 160, 166, 177: subaltern 13; consumption of 154

London 46, 47, 88, 125, 143 : East 87

longue durée, la 61

Lucknow 122, 209 (bibl.)

Luhrmann, Baz (Mark Anthony) (director, Sydney, 1962) 50

lyrics 13, 24, 29, 61, 65, 80, 88, 90, 96, 97, 98, 99, 101, 107, 111, 115, 117, 123, 140, 204 (bibl.), 206 (bibl.), 213 (bibl.), 215 (bibl.), 223 (bibl.): English 125; SM's 124; Spanish 116; techno- 110. *See also*: articulation, music, synaesthesia

M.I.A. (Mathangi (Maya) Arulpragasam), songwriter, record producer, singer, rapper, fashion designer, visual artist, and political activist, b. Sri Lanka, 1975) 40, 41, 51, 87–89, 90, 91, 170, 187 (bibl.), 197 (bibl.), 224 (bibl.), 226 (bibl.)

machismo 101, 103, 106, 109

Madhumitha (Swapna Madhuri) (singer, b. Hyderabad, 1984) 107, 114

mafia: Mumbai's 6; underworld 56

Mahabharata 61, 63

Maharashtra 36, 48, 79, 135, 151, 164

Maharashtra Pollution Control Board (MPCB) 163

Maharashtrians 149

244 *Index*

Malaysia 48
Malik, Jamal (SM hero) 3, 6, 20, 43, 47, 57, 58, 59, 62, 63, 64, 65, 67, 68, 69, 70, 72, 73, 75, 77, 78, 82, 83, 84, 85, 86, 91, 92, 93, 94, 95, 96, 98, 101, 102, 103, 104, 105, 106, 107, 106, 109, 110, 111, 112, 113, 114, 115, 118, 120, 139, 170, 172: cinematic 155; Eurasian 119; fictional 182
Malik, Salim (SM anti-hero) 3, 43, 47, 49, 58, 59, 60, 62, 63, 67, 74, 78, 82, 83, 84, 85, 86, 87, 91, 93, 95, 96, 100, 102, 103, 104, 106, 107, 108, 110, 112, 113, 114, 179, 184, 218 (bibl.): repentant 111
Maman (SM anti-hero) 96, 100, 104, 106: Oriental 119
marginality 37: ethnic 28; fetishized 95; folklorisation of 140; Jamal's 60
market (-s) 8, 42, 155, 197 (bibl.), 202 (bibl.), 214 (bibl.), 215 (bibl.): aesthetic 12; cinematic 141; cultural 12; emerging 48; flower 155; gambling 74; global 61, 108, 146, 154, 160; government of the 132; movie 32; music 28, 98; new estate 161; real estate 142; street 94; tourism 133, 135; Western 126
masala 27, 144
materiality (-ies) 56–57, 80, 122, 161: urban 63
matrix 167: lyrical 28; mobility 41
Mausam & Escape (music track) 86, 107
McGregor, Ewan Gordon (actor, b. Perth, 1971) 63, 82
media 22, 23, 108, 145, 152, 155, 167, 168, 178, 183, 193 (bibl.), 194 (bibl.), 196 (bibl.), 198 (bibl.), 201 (bibl.), 202 (bibl.), 206 (bibl.), 209 (bibl.), 210 (bibl.), 212 (bibl.), 214 (bibl.), 215 (bibl.), 217 (bibl.), 218 (bibl.), 222 (bibl.), 225 (bibl.), 226 (bibl.), 229 (bibl.): American 89; Asian (Bollywood) 7, 49; fair 56; global 156; SM 6; Western 7
mediascapes 73, 98, 140: contemporary 112; global 136
mélange 215 (bibl.): compositional 50; dialogical 48; global 61
memory (-ies) 17, 33, 40, 51, 73, 89, 120, 126, 143, 189 (bibl.), 192 (bibl.), 197 (bibl.), 200 (bibl.), 201 (bibl.), 202 (bibl.), 206 (bibl.), 209 (bibl.), 210 (bibl.), 215 (bibl.), 217 (bibl.), 219 (bibl.), 220 (bibl.), 223 (bibl.), 224 (bibl.), 226 (bibl.), 227 (bibl.): audio-visual 78; blindness of 139; childhood 86; circuits of 168; collective 166; coloured 67; creative role of 77; customary 162; elicitations of 38; ethno-nationalist 5; historic 133; main 71; official national 23; old 37; painful 84; personal 79; photographic 146; screen 78; transpersonal 72; traumatic 182; tropes of 137. *See also* amnesia, articulation, history
merchants: dream 93; primary ghost 166
merit 4, 101, 184
metaphor (-s) 9, 10–11, 12, 14, 33, 46, 62, 65, 106, 165, 171, 195 (bibl.), 204 (bibl.), 207 (bibl.), 214 (bibl.), 217 (bibl.), 221 (bibl.), 223 (bibl.): Benjaminian 44; book's 20; global 95; Heideggerian 84; methodological 6; -model 180; potent 173; word and sound 99
metempsychosis 38, 221 (bibl.)
metensomatosis 38, 171, 221 (bibl.)
methodology 22, 210 (bibl.), 216 (bibl.): of knowledge 30
migrant (-s) 9, 16, 63, 103, 141, 167, 197 (bibl.): adolescent 95; destitute 38; first-generation 103; labour 4; Mumbaikar 171; second-generation 47; vagabond 11; working-class 141
migration(-s) 8, 31, 33, 36, 41, 66, 170, 189 (bibl.), 192 (bibl.), 194 (bibl.), 211 (bibl.0, 216 (bibl.), 218 (bibl.): coerced 19; collective biographies of 167; forced 182; global 51; post-colonial 47; professional 18, 24; tourism-related 16; voluntary 91, 117. *See also* migrant (-s), immigration, mobility, tourist (-s), vagabond (-s)
mimicry 94: colonial 92
mind–walking 46, 60, 72, 77, 104, 206 (bibl.)
mission 20, 32, 37, 60: alternative 104; rescue 165
Mittal, Madhur (actor, b. Agra, 1987) 3, 49
mobilisation 100, 178: political 24, 31, 123; professional 38
mobility (-ies) 7, 24, 30, 35, 36, 80, 185 (bibl.), 187 (bibl.), 196 (bibl.), 197 (bibl.), 1098 (bibl.), 202 (bibl.), 203 (bibl.), 207 (bibl.), 208 (bibl.), 210 (bibl.), 211 (bibl.), 218 (bibl.),

222 (bibl.), 225 (bibl.): artistic 11, 126; audio-visual reproduction of 55; blended forms of 15; cinematic tourist 29; civilised 82; class 172; contemporary professional 39; corporeal 41, 60; cosmological 17; criminal 88; dance 117, 120; Eurasian professional 15; Eurasian tale of 46; fast 16, 122, 154, 181, 184; global financial 176; global 9, 99; heritage 132; human 19, 51, 103; inner 38, 70; intellectual 103; intersecting 61; labour 59, 105, 166; lifestyle 71, 118, 194 (bibl.); media, 180; migrant 5, 154; pilgrimage 77; popular 21; post-industrial 8; sedentary 107; slow 21, 41, 110, 122; SM's staging of 49; social 64, 102, 117, 150; spatial 87; status 172; synaesthetic 38; technological 135, 152; terrorist 108; theories of 6; tourism 5, 131, 134, 144, 180, 201 (bibl.), 222 (bibl.); tourist 16, 59, 123, 126, 157, 227 (bibl.); virtual 161; work-related 48
mocking 78, 80, 92
modernisation (-s) 77, 126, 136, 141: global 165; India's fast-track 165; national industrial 31; permanent feature of 135
modernity (-ies) 70, 71, 79, 111, 150, 151, 185 (bibl.), 186 (bibl.), 188 (bibl.), 189 (bibl.), 192 (bibl.), 198 (bibl.), 199 (bibl.), 201 (bibl.), 203 (bibl.), 211 (bibl.), 215 (bibl.), 219 (bibl.), 220 (bibl.), 226 (bibl.), 228 (bibl.): (post-) industrial 7; articulations of 16; artistic 97; Asian 31; Bollywood–induced 17; city's passage to 26; competing 26; early 7; India's 91; Indian 15, 32; industrial 10, 62, 145, 179; late 94; liquid 31, 72, 102, 108; local 4; multiple 166, 180; parallel 148; post-colonial 48, 72; romantic critique of, 57; sexist traditions of, 64; slumdog economies of 165; tourist 131; Western 143. *See also* globalisation, mobilities, modernisation
Modi, Narendra (BJP politician, b. Vadnagar, Mehsana District, 1950) 112
Monsoon Wedding (dir. Mira Nair, 2001) 46
montage 95, 100: socialist 171

monument (-s) 91, 92, 93, 136, 137, 138, 207 (bibl.), 222 (bibl.)
moods 28
morality 67, 95, 127, 224 (bibl.), 225 (bibl.): lax 163
Mother (SM heroine) 78, 83, 84, 85–86
motif (-s) 69, 108: choral 107; electronic 88; hip–hop 101; main 126; mathematical 127; multiple 116; techno–trance 114
motion (-s) 9, 89, 112, 152, 180, 207 (bibl.), 223 (bibl.): dual 138; linear 72; of travel 18, 72; organic 67
movement (-s) 5, 7, 15, 16, 27, 30, 40, 41, 45, 46: activist 35; artistic 30; corporeal 26; emotional 30; inner 11; Naxalite 162; pilgrim's 20; political 29, 39; social 83, 84, 114, 121, 188 (bibl.), 195 (bibl.), 204 (bibl.)213 (bibl.); technological 18
Mozart of Madras 50
multiculturalism 56, 85, 218 (bibl.), 222 (bibl.)
multi–site 41: as methodology 22–23; Mumbai's 43
multitude 128, 183, 203 (bibl.): mobile 19
Mumbai 3, 4, 5, 6, 9, 12, 13, 14, 16, 17, 19, 20, 21, 23, 24, 25, 26, 27, 29, 30, 31, 32, 36, 37, 41, 43, 44, 47, 48, 49, 55, 57, 58, 60, 61, 62, 63, 64, 67, 70, 72, 75, 76, 77, 78, 79, 80, 81, 82, 83, 84, 94, 95, 96, 97, 100, 101, 102, 103, 104, 105, 106, 107, 108, 109, 110, 112, 113, 114, 116, 119, 120, 121, 122, 126, 128, 131, 132, 133, 134, 135, 137, 139, 140141, 142, 143, 145, 146, 147, 148, 2152, 153, 154, 155, 157, 159, 160, 161, 163, 164, 165, 166, 167, 169, 170, 174, 175, 176, 178, 180, 181, 184, 190 (bibl.), 196 (bibl.), 197 (bibl.), 202 (bibl.), 205 (bibl.), 208 (bibl.), 213 (bibl.), 215 (bibl.), 219 (bibl.), 225 (bibl.), 229 (bibl.): as city of 'bits' 40; as city of ruin and as virtual city 71–72; the reality of 151
Munich 126
music 13, 18, 29–31, 35, 40, 51, 61, 65, 87, 89, 91, 96, 97, 100, 107, 108, 110, 114, 115, 116, 117, 127, 159, 187 (bibl.), 189 (bibl.), 190 (bibl.), 191 (bibl.), 193 (bibl.), 194 (bibl.), 196 (bibl.), 198 (bibl.), 199 (bibl.), 200 (bibl.), 202 (bibl.), 204 (bibl.), 209 (bibl.), 214 (bibl.), 215 (bibl.),

217 (bibl.), 219 (bibl.), 220 (bibl.), 224 (bibl.), 226 (bibl.), 228 (bibl.), 230 (bibl.): electronic 79: film 25, 28; folk 122; hybridised 27; Indian 50; scores 25; Tamil 49; violin 86; –work 26 *see* work; world, 24, 28, 50, 95, 118, 121, 125. *See also* articulation, synaesthesia

Muslims 149, 163

Muslim–Hindu massacres 6, 78, 82

mysticism: imagined 45; Sufi 50; utopian 137

myth (-s) 21, 77, 198 (bibl.), 202 (bibl.), 204 (bibl.), 206 (bibl.), 223 (bibl.), 227 (bibl.): ancient 126; founding 136; Indian 27; tourist 88, 191 (bibl.); universal power of 173

Nair, Mira (director, b .Rourkela, 1957) 46, 47, 142, 169

National Rural Employment Guarantee Act (NREGA) 162

Nationalism, 72, 182, 191 (bibl.), 201 (bibl.), 202 (bibl.), 207 (bibl.), 218 (bibl.), 223 (bibl.), 228 (bibl.): cult of 145

nature 5, 9, 19, 40, 68, 153, 199 (bibl.), 212 (bibl.), 219 (bibl.), 226 (bibl.): human 43, 155; hybrid 137; ideals of 15; Islam's non-representational 84; liquid modernity's dis-embedded 108; of community 94; of creativity 32; of criminal networks 109; of culture 33; of fan reception 123; of human interaction 39; of Indian modernity 31; of the common 153; power of 31; repetitive 127; sounds of 24

naukri 162

Naxalite (-s) 162–164, 170

Nehru, Jawaharlal (First Prime Minister, b. Allahabad, 1889 – d. New Delhi, 1964) 31–32, 62, 63, 85, 102, 122, 142, 162, 182, 216 (bibl.)

neighbourhood (-s) 109, 143, 165: Dharavi's 168; traditional 120

neoliberalisation 131, 137, 143

neotribe (-s) 117, 189 (bibl.)

network (-s) 29, 30, 32, 39, 42, 71, 72, 93, 104, 105, 118, 134, 168, 179, 185 (bibl.), 189 (bibl.), 191 (bibl.), 192 (bibl.), 204 (bibl.), 210 (bibl.), 215 9bibl.), 221 (bibl.), 227 (bibl.), 229 (bibl.): activist 7, 45; affiliative 33, 100, 113, 159; artisanal 128; artistic 8;

business 123; capitalist 164; creative 41; criminal 9, 46, 101, 109; cultural industrial 111; digital 12–13, 91; ecological 164; family 96, 179; gang 103, 110; global 151; human 37; India's global 62; kinship 16, 94; mafia 102; media 182; mobile social 85, 166; music 121; sex-work 6; tourist 21, 27, 77; urban 17; world music 24. *See also* articulation, assemblage, technopoesis

nexus 22: practical-poetic 99; SM's text-context 62

NGO (-s) (Non-Governmental Organisation (-s)) 87, 142, 146, 159, 158,

Nita (*Q&A* heroine) 65, 95

node(-s) 126, 147, 168: activist 30; aesthetic 29; artistic 80; audio-visual 25; Eurasian narrative 50; Eurasian 154; global manufacturing and trading 164; memory 71; migration 145; Mumbai's transport 140; spectacular 159; tourist-cinematic 137; urban 142

nomad 94, 103, 193 (bibl.), 213 (bibl.), 219 (bibl.), 228 (bibl.): artistic 8, 41, 97, 127; dangerous 7; from affluence 181; travelling 72

nomadology 40, 203 (bibl.)

Non-Resident Indians (NRI) 14, 166, 167, 169

Noorani, Tabrez (producer, b. 1969) 46

norm (-s) 93, 102, 183, 203 (bibl.): aesthetic 139; consumption 149; ethographic 107; neighbourhood 120; old civility 155; Western 140

nostalgia 66, 172, 210 (bibl.): articulations of 25; structural 94, 97, 104, 136; systems of 159

O'Saya (music track) 80–81, 87, 121

offshoring 5–6, 8–9, 10, 28, 122, 132, 161, 176, 227 (bibl.)

Olympic Games 87, 122

ontology 125

orality, 40, 99, 216 (bibl.)

Orient 45, 152, 155

Orientalism 116, 203 (bibl.), 212 (bibl.), 220 (bibl.), 226 (bibl.): practical 141

orphan (-s) 3, 50: maimed 86; mobile 88; working 92

orphanage 86, 87

Oscars 125, 140

otherness 13, 186 (bibl.), 203 (bibl.): colonised 92; cultural 80; ethnic 58

Pakistan 91, 81, 103, 181
Palakkad, Sriram (playback singer, b. 1972) 107
palimpsest 93: archaeological 93; musical 112; pop 124; terrorist 112; urban 75, 113
pangosmiopoiesis 8–9, 10, 11, 48, 59, 66, 131, 134, 150, 164, 180, 181: artistic 51
Paper Planes (music track) 87–91, 213 (bibl.), 226 (bibl.)
paradigm (-s) 32, 172, 175, 203 (bibl.), 222 (bibl.): Indian socio-cultural 57; leadership 40; neo-colonial 40; new mobilities 8, 36; representational 100; social 29, 57; Tarde's diffusionist 133
parenting 85, 173
Partition, Indian-Pakistan (1947) 101, 118
past 4, 30, 31, 34, 51, 59, 72, 77, 83, 90, 97, 108, 132, 148, 171, 180, 185 (bibl.), 206 (bibl.), 225 (bibl.), 226 (bibl.), 229 (bibl.): collective 17; Dharavi's grim labour 168; localities' 160; political uses of the 165; proximate 60
pastiche 14, 1205 (bibl.): audio-visual 24; Boyle's 61; hybrid 73; textual 27
Patel, Dev (actor, b. Harrow, 1990) 3, 47–48, 49, 59, 75, 84, 206 (bibl.)
peproméno 4, 6, 10–11
performance (-s) 11, 21, 100, 107, 108, 122, 123, 125, 132, 137, 143, 154, 159, 185 (bibl.), 188 (bibl.), 202 (bibl.), 207 (bibl.), 211 (bibl.), 227 (bibl.): cinematic 116; economy of 126; embodied 27, 70; guest 146; hyper-sensualised 127; kathak 98; Kumar's stylised 75; material spaces of 24; on-stage 87; oral 17; slum 156; social 25; subaltern group 22; synaesthetic 45, 179; tourist 133. *See also* habitus
performativity 45, 72, 93, 210 (bibl.): embodied 157; mind-body complex of 26; synaesthetic 146; tourist 27
periphery (-ies) 43, 189: internal 18; social 56, 178; implosion of 24; national 23, 44, 46, 64, 178
phaneroscopy 40
phantasmagoria 42, 201 (bibl.): Bollywood's 128; India's 73; Indian 106; Mumbai's 101
phantom (-s): colonial 120, 173; gendered 'clonial' 124; Indian 42; of adaptation 42; old tornadóroi's 172

phenomenology 193 (bibl.): filmic 67
philanthropy 20, 146, 158, 174
photography 32, 40, 84, 144152, 168, 192 (bibl.), 201 (bibl.), 203 (bibl.), 210 (bibl.), 223 (bibl.)
phronesis 57
physicalisation 11, 31
phýsis 155
picture (-s) 15: high-resolution 40; memory 65; motion 140; two-sided 157; world 84; worldview 65
picturesque: Scotland's 64; slum's 'terrible' 133
pilgrim (-s) 20, 155: artistic 11; Baumanesque 119, 167; foreign 33; post-modern 37
pilgrimage 16, 20, 27, 37, 48, 50, 91, 144, 155, 174, 194 (bibl.), 205 (bibl.): cinematic 17, 177; existentialist 77; sympathetic 155; synaesthetic 41. *See also* mobility, travel, tourism
Pilla (Street) 95, 96, 97, 99, 154
Pinto, Freida Selena (actress, b. Maharashtra, 1984) 3, 48, 49, 59, 65, 206 (bibl.)
plot (-s) 3, 43, 47, 61, 68, 86, 104, 106, 169: 'un-realistic' 20; Bollywood 27; cinematic 17, 55, 56, 119, 160; film's 7; Indian 28; musical 88; mythical 107; novel's core 73; Swarup's 41
polity (-ies) 61, 172: foreign 38; colonised 56; individual 123; multi-religious 136; Mumbai's 137; national 55, 103, 137; post-colonial 60, 73; sport 124; state– 128
pollution 162: environmental 182; sound 26; urban 26
poor 184, 187 (bibl.), 188 (bibl.): deserving 57; Indian 45, 221 (bibl.); urban 149
positivism 10, 68, 127
post-modernisation: translocal 31; transnational 31
post-modernity 108, 110, 148: hallucinogenic 112; Indian 32, 135, 143; technological 177; tourist 94. *See also* modernity
poverty 50, 56, 58, 60, 95, 143, 144, 149, 156, 160, 169, 170, 187 (bibl.), 212 (bibl.), 213 (bibl.), 224 (bibl.): -as-passivity 128; representations of 45; slum 85, 164
precariat 224 (bibl.): slum 57, 161

Prakash, Vijay (playback singer, b. Mysore, 1976) 110, 116, 126
Pran (actor, b. New Delhi, 1920) 100–101, 192 (bibl.)
presence 89, 110, 111, 153, 229 (bibl.): absent 80, 86, 120, 204 (bibl.); embodied 67; of digital/social divide 151; of Eurasian discourse 119; of hegemonic script 144; of chrono-diverse lifeworlds 148; of corruption 5; of fundamentalist discourse 153; of guild consciousness 149; of less crime 145; of police 80; of collaborative networks 170; of audience 82; of '13th Compound' 164; phantasmic 42; public feminine 125; static 76
prestige 37: of India's 'network capital' 62; India's global 182
progress 31, 57, 67, 116, 135, 173, 178, 184: company's 144; Enlightenment 57; forces of 136; human 18; industrial 63, 148; meritocratic 3; Mumbai's 146; serendipitous 5; socio-cultural 6; technological 19; Western discourses of 15
proletariat 17, 210 (bibl.): lumpen 79
property (-ies) 80, 88, 182: bio–cultural 179; intangible 123; intellectual 33; Javed's 111; magical 179
prostitute (-s) 9, 65, 95, 96, 97, 98, 197 (bibl.)
prostitution 65, 96, 117, 126, 198
prosumers 148, 219 (bibl.)
protest (-s) 112, 133, 167: angry 63; anti-SM 168 ; non-violent 56 ; slum 173; sonic 120; violent 112
proximity: compulsion of, 107, 190 (bibl.); tourist's right to 150
psychopathology (-ies) 178, 200 (bibl.): Western 173
Pujari, Krishna (Reality Tours co-founder) 144, 145, 149, 150, 151
purity 51, 134, 197 (bibl.): ethno-national 167
Pussycat Dolls (band) 124–125, 188 (bibl.) 218 (bibl.), 230 (bibl.)

Q&A (novel, 2005) 13, 20, 43, 64, 65, 67, 68, 73, 74, 87, 92, 95, 105, 106, 173, 224 (bibl.)
Quantum of Solace (dir. Marc Forster, 2008) 48

racism 34, 42, 50, 114, 127, 134, 152, 210 (bibl.): ecosystemic 81–82; environmental 107, 134, 147, 190 (bibl.)
Rahman, A.R. (A.S. Dileep Kumar) (composer, lyricist, b. Chennai (Madras), 1966) 6, 26, 27, 29, 34, 40, 49–51, 65, 70, 79, 80, 85, 96, 97, 99, 101, 107, 110, 114, 115–116, 121, 122, 124, 125, 126, 127, 131, 141, 154, 167, 181186 (bibl.), 187 (bibl.), 191 (bibl.), 192 (bibl.), 197 (bibl.), 204 (bibl.), 205 (bibl.), 210 (bibl.), 213 (bibl.), 218 (bibl.), 223 (bibl.), 224 (bibl.), 225 (bibl.), 229 (bibl.)
Ram Mohammed (*Q&A* hero) 65, 68, 69, 74, 92, 93, 95, 105, 106
rasas 45. *See also* synaesthesia
rashtra 137
realism 11, 44, 45, 106, 110, 187 (bibl.), 203 (bibl.), 217 (bibl.), 222 (bibl.), 227 (bibl.): Bollywood magical 29; dark 171; SM's 27; social 43, 66; transparent 153
reality (-ies) 10, 11, 13, 39, 59, 60, 67, 71, 80, 81, 92, 99, 127, 136, 143, 146, 151, 163, 165, 172, 190 (bibl.), 197 (bibl.), 212 (bibl.), 213 (bibl.): alternate 73; cinematic 58; economic 183; empirical 171; filmic 58; Indian 167; local 46, 131; multiple 32, 180, 196 (bibl.); plural 155; pro-filmic 145; social 4, 16, 31, 68, 83; socio-historical 117
Reality Gives 149, 150, 158, 218 (bibl.)
Reality Tours 149, 150, 152–155, 158, 164, 170, 218 (bibl.)
reciprocity (-ies) 49, 157, 196 (bibl.): intergenerational 33; monetary 156; cultural 173; family 182; cross-cultural 33; purified 40
recycling 137, 145, 150, 153, 155, 158, 159, 161, 214 (bibl.)
redemption 109: bloody 9; male 64; technological 64
refraction (-s) 6, 68
refuse 18, 151, 161: human 24, 121; social 55, 79, 142
regime (-s): judicial 183; leisure 60; of simulation 136; of truth 123; tourist 136; visual 5
region (-s) 23, 112, 118, 126, 139, 162, 163: back 25; Mediterranean 103; Sind 81
religion 27, 45, 47, 66, 137, 167, 168, 195 (bibl.), 196 (bibl.), 210 (bibl.), 221 (bibl.)

Index 249

repetition 13, 107: blended human and electronic 88; creative 72, 122, 127, 151; ritual 69; stylistic 27
reproduction 25, 100, 127, 187 (bibl.), 195 (bibl.): artistic 73; audio-visual 55; authentic 39; cheap 19; cinematic 171; creative 124; digital 151; global digital 33; habitual 12; impure 62; mocking 21; predatory 34; social 109; working-class stylistic 96
respectability 14, 57, 06: middle-class 68; urban 142
responsibility 37, 99, 113, 175, 200 (bibl.): individual 156; metaphors of 174
ressentiment 123, 220 (bibl.)
rights 176, 184: human 170, 196 (bibl.); indigenous 156; language of 162; slum-dwellers' human 167; Tamil minority 89
rin (dev, pitri, risi) 179
Ringa Ringa (music track) 96–99, 121, 206 (bibl.)
risk (-s) 6, 10, 68, 83, 150, 189 (bibl.), 197 (bibl.), 208 (bibl.): global 108; realist conception of 139; social 82
ritual (-s) 182, 185 (bibl.), 194 (bibl.): adult 90; artisanal 154; bonding 109; Eurasian mass culture 127; everyday 58; innocent consumption 107; lifestyle 57; public 71; romantic gazing 17; sightseeing 134; social 79
roots 24, 42, 47, 48, 51, 106, 114, 128, 189 (bibl.), 200 (bibl.), 210 (bibl.), 211 (bibl.): African 117; ancestral 14; artistic 43; childhood 45; cultural 181; documentary 44; Indo-European 31; national 61
routes 42, 47, 106, 114, 121, 193 (bibl.), 225 (bibl.): artistic community's 51; artistic 43; cinematic 100; global migration 167; global travel 178; market 28; mobility 7, 11; new media 33; trading 24
Roy, Suzanna Arundhati (author and political activist, b. Shillong, Assam (present-day Meghalaya), 1961) 169, 175, 210 (bibl.)
rumour 40, 56, 206 (bibl.)
Rushdie, Salman (author, b. Bombay, 1947) 170–172, 175, 220 (bibl.), 229 (bibl.)

sacrifice: collective 5; self 67, 102
sagacity 45, 101
Salaam Baalak Trust 175
Salzburg 126
Sanskrit 9, 144
Satya (dir. Ram Gopal Varma, 1998) 58, 209 (bibl.)
Say Salaam India (dir. Subhash Kapoor, 2007) 49
scene (-s) 25–26, 59, 70, 71, 73, 74, 85, 86, 90, 91, 92, 101, 102, 105, 106, 107, 108, 109, 110, 111, 113, 114, 119, 120, 124, 125, 134, 159, 95 (bibl.), 217 (bibl.), 224 (bibl.), 229 (bibl.): Agra, 87, 94; airport 150; Bollywood 13, 44; Boyle's favourite 78; cinematic 80; closing 62; concluding 64, 66; dance 27; ending 79; iconic 44, 82; intimate 76, 95; introductory 75, 94, 95; music 27, 189 (bibl.), 217 (bibl.); national 32; opening 58, 79; pop 116; slum 135; SM's Bollywood 117; SM's Pilla 97, 99; SM's social 43; SM's train 88–89; SM's violent 83–84; sub–, 22, Taj Mahal 36, 135, 137; transitional riot 83
Scherzinger, Nicole (Prescovia Elikolani Valiente) (song writer and singer, b. Honolulu, 1978) 124, 125, 127, 154, 207 (bibl.)
scholé 91, 116
scopophilia 27
Searle (Sunshine hero) 65
secrecy: elaborate forms of 5; undemocratic 131
segment (-s) 70–72, 75, 76, 77, 85, 95, 101, 104, 107, 110, 111, 118, 228 (bibl.): Agra 94; cinematic 15, 72, 106; musical 26
segmentation 71, 214 (bibl.)
semiotechnology (-ies) 26, 34, 123–124, 210 (bibl.)
semiotics 100, 201
sentiment 8, 96, 167: aesthetic 56; cosmetic 9; embedded 30; intermediary 56; techno-fetishistic 108; urban 124
Serendip 3
Serendipist: Walpole's 93; Desai 136
serendipity 3, 56, 67, 142, 181, 186 (bibl.), 213 (bibl.), 214 (bibl.), 221 (bibl.): film's 27; Merton and Barber's exploration of 180; Mertonian 73; role of 70

sexuality 35, 42, 178, 199 (bibl.), 200 (bibl.): aesthetics of 120; consumption of 55; female 125; plastic 118
Shack/Slum Dwellers International (SDI) 149
Shah, Tanvi (songwriter and singer) 101, 116, 124
Shakira (Isabel Mebarak Ripoll) (singer, b. Barranquilla, 1977) 122
Shallow Grave (dir. Danny Boyle, 1995) 45, 46, 63, 67, 79, 109
shantytown (-s): Indian 84; London and Paris 143
Sharma, Pyarelal Ramprasad (composer, orchestrator, music director and conductor, b. Gorakh Pur, 1940) 96
Shining India 4, 131–132, 145, 164, 182
shit 8, 64, 82, 90
Shiv Sena 163, 167
Shukla, Saurabh (actor, director and scriptwriter, b. Gorakhpur, 1963) 58
silence 24, 44, 134, 164, 202 (bibl.): post-colonial subject's 117; selective 80; strategic 99; subaltern 184; ubiquitous marketing 139. *See also* performance, synaesthesia
simulacra of sociality 39, 42, 88, 157
Singapore 48
Singh, Manmohan (thirteenth Prime Minister of India, b. Gah, 1932) 112
Singh, Sakhuvinder (singer, b. Sharika Pind, 1971) 116
site (-s) 22, 25, 29, 3, 49, 138, 139, 147, 148, 157, 159, 162, 167, 168, 191 (bibl.): alien 41; Bollywood 139; cinematic 141; dangerous tourist 84; Dharavi's virtual 160; digital 24; disreputable tourist 96; Eastern and Western virtual 23; filmed 18, 120, 134, 155; gazed 150; heritage 91, 136, 138, 164; India's tourist 85; Indian 36; industrial-slum 72; internet 6, 178; landmark 100; leather–tanning 153; material 122; media 157; memory 73; mobile 149, 184; moribund 11; multiple 131; multi-user 124; Mumbai's 24; national 33; of myth 21, 77; terrestrial 133; tourist 135, 141, 199 (bibl.); touristified 27; UNESCO World Heritage 135; Western 28, 14. *See also* internet, multi-site, web
skill (-s) 48, 56, 80, 92, 158: acting 49; computer 150; cricket 49; embodied 110; feminine 92; social 92; technical 101; technological, 67
Skins (UK TV series, 2007–2013) 47
slumming 7, 68, 209 (bibl.), 221 (bibl.), 229 (bibl.): performance of 143; tourist 71; Western 14
slumscapes (Mumbai's), 57, 143, 181
socialism 82, 162, 212 (bibl.)
socio-cultures 48: Mumbai's slum 12
solidarity 84, 108: anamnestic 148, 166, 210 (bibl.), 217 (bibl.); childhood 67; destruction of 95; local 161; social 94, 102; tourist 149
soundscapes 24–25, 26, 95, 220 (bibl.), 221 (bibl.), 222 (bibl.), 226 (bibl.): as-artscapes 24, electronic 81; mesmerising 87; urban 25
soundtrack (-s) 15, 25–26, 29, 115, 116: film 90, 111; music 24; SM's 115
spectacle (-s) 80, 101, 122, 159, 196 (bibl.), 216 (bibl.): 'runaway' 79; beautiful 14; cinematic 155; multi-sensory 99; of slum tourism 59; televised 74; touristified 45; travel-like 176
sphere (-s) 222 (bibl.): global 133; Indian public 178; of cultural consumption 55; public 182, 183, 203 (bibl.), 209 (bibl.), 227 (bibl.); public 64; Western public 178; Western social 166
spirituality 222 (bibl.): Bakhti 125; European Christological 144
Sri Lanka (Ceylon) 3, 88, 89, 90
stage (-s) 50, 97, 124, 176: archetypical social 60; back 95, 154; cinematic back 116; dissonant touring 72; front 93, 101, 107; global 4, 94; new social 121; post-modern 72; televised 65; theatrical 174
stereotype (-s) 63, 93, 120, 197 (bibl.): gender 92; industrial man 63; Orientalist 74; sexist and racist 111
stranger (-s) 4, 7, 15, 16, 91, 125, 155, 163, 168, 209 (bibl.), 221 (bibl.): affluent 167; –enemy 80; eponymous Eastern 126; image of 57; mobile 63; Mumbai's 114; Simmelian peripatetic 38; SM 4
stratigraphy 161, 185 (bibl.)
subaltern (-s) 22, 23, 43, 110, 128, 143, 183, 208 (bibl.), 223 (bibl.)
subjectivity 207 (bibl.), 208 (bibl.), 217 (bibl.): female 97; feminine 125; feminised 97; human 31; spatial 160; traditional 102

sublimation 24, 44, 56
sublime 189 (bibl.): inverted 55; romantic 79
Sucker Punch (dir. Zack Snyder, 2011) 48
suffering 65, 208 (bibl.): European conceptions of 13; human 114
Sufi 136
Sufism 49, 50, 115
Sunshine (dir. Danny Boyle, 2007) 60, 65
surveillance 205 (bibl.), 214 (bibl.): 'proper' 168; media 76; official 145; photographic cultures of 90; state 89, 109; urban 80
Swaraj, Sushama (BJP politician, b. New Delhi, 1952) 141
Swarup, Vikas (diplomat and novelist, b. Allahabad, 1963) 13, 19, 41, 78, 83, 87, 106, 173, 224 (bibl.)
synaesthesia 24, 26–28, 200 (bibl.): tourist 156
synaesthete: real-life 66; experimental 165
synaesthetics 27
synergy (-ies) 151: activist-artistic 33; artistic 28; creative 127; deep 101; Eurasian 123; shifting 168; vocal 26
syngyria 4: globalised 21; post-colonial 73

Taj Mahal, 24, 33, 36, 49, 62, 65, 87, 91, 92, 93, 102, 131, 133, 134, 135–139, 140, 205 (bibl.), 227 (bibl.)
Tandan, Loveen (director, b. New Delhi) 46–47, 187 (bibl.)
tango 118, 119, 120, 192 (bibl.), 221 (bibl.)
Tasawwuf 115
taste (-s) 27, 42, 189 (bibl.), 190 (bibl.): class 169; emergent 19; good 27; of necessity 127
téchne 5, 115, 164: marketable 74; local 146
technique (-s) 17, 25, 34, 46, 59, 60, 66–67, 69, 70, 71, 74, 75, 76, 77, 82, 90, 101, 128, 133, 137, 191 (bibl.)
technology (-ies) 3, 8, 19, 24, 34, 35, 38, 39, 40, 41, 63, 128, 140, 142, 152, 157, 158, 163, 164, 173, 178, 193 (bibl.), 194 (bibl.), 196 (bibl.), 198 (bibl.), 209 (bibl.), 213 (bibl.): (hum)man–made 5; audio-visual 4, 29, 198 (bibl.); cinematic 32, 85, 171; digital 26, 32, 70, 133, 146; hermeneutics as 89; informational and representational 123; mechanical 75; new/old media 18, 22, of action 35; of governance *see* governance; of the eye 30; of vision and control 75; telecommunication 88; theatre 25; Western 15, 111, 135
technopoesis 34–35, 42, 146: artistic 56; as filiative/affiliative 159; digital 40; network 182; post-modern 39; touristic 152. *See also* articulation (-s), assemblage (-s), community (-ies), network (-s)
telos 6, 45, 181
temple (-s) 33, 153, 155, 164: Hindu 168; Indian 168
temporalities: plural 131; slow 37
terror 79, 99, 103, 108, 114, 223 (bibl.): and pilgrimage 155; civilised 155; of poverty 160; refuse-as- 142
terrorism 103, 187 (bibl.), 214 (bibl.)
terrorist (-s) 9, 49, 91, 103, 109, 112, 182
testimonio (-s) 60–61, 189 (bibl.), 228 (bibl.): cinematic-like 156; community 156; tourist 151
Thailand 45, 48, 166
The Banyan (music track, 2006) 50, 186 (bibl.), 225 (bibl.)
The Beach (dir. Danny Boyle, 2000) 45–46, 82, 229 (bibl.)
The Kite Runner (dir. Marc Forster, 2007) 174
The Namesake (dir. Mira Nair, 2007) 47
The Satanic Verses (novel, 1988) 170
The Three Musketeers (novel, 1844) 67–68
theatre 48, 92, 97, 126, 171, 191 (bibl.), 199 (bibl.)
theft 87, 88, 138: petty 77, 87; fear of 7; of history 42, 201 (bibl.)
time (-s) 30, 39, 41, 72, 160, 229 (bibl.): chronic and kairotic versions 122; fast globalising 172; free 118; heritage 132, 133, 154; historic 132; Indian 6; linear conceptions, 76; politics 97; profane 77; quiz's 78; real life 65; rural 86; sacred 21; screen 47; televised show's 74; two separate 4; unities of 28; visitor 132; West's or Europe's old 154
Tollygung/Tollywood 15
tools 34, 38–39, 93, 115, 173: capitalist 29; developmental 154; interpretative 7; representational 146; synaesthetic 154; technological 159, 183. *See also* téchne, technopoesis

252 Index

topos (-oi): childhood 94; diachronic 70. See also heterotopia (-s)
tornadóros (-oi) 16, 131, 133, 158: privileged 15
tórnos 16, 162: digital 150
tour (-s) 16, 142, 125, 146, 148, 149, 150–153, 155, 158, 205 (bibl.), 215 (bibl.): Agra cinematic 94; locally managed 55; mind-walking 104; reality 29; signature 150; slumdog 146; walking 142. See also pilgrimage (-s)
tourism 6, 7, 8, 9, 10, 12, 21, 22, 27, 80, 88, 91, 119, 132, 133, 142, 160, 176, 178, 186 (bibl.), 187 (bibl.), 190 (bibl.), 191 (bibl.), 193 (bibl.), 194 (bibl.), 195 (bibl.), 196 (bibl.), 197 (bibl.), 198 (bibl.), 201 (bibl.), 202 (bibl.), 203 (bibl.), 204 (bibl.), 211 (bibl.), 213 (bibl.), 214 (bibl.), 216 (bibl.), 219 (bibl.), 221 (bibl.), 222 (bibl.), 225 (bibl.), 228 (bibl.), 229 (bibl.): activist music 28; blended 120, 142; cinematic 18, 70, 72, 142; cultural 154, 205 (bibl.), 218 (bibl.); dark 57, 58, 59, 176, 209 (bibl.); e– 120, 132, 160, 164, 190 (bibl.); eco- 24; edu- 20, 57, 205 (bibl.); end of 181, 200 (bibl.), 203 (bibl.); European emergence 116; film-induced 18, 46, 138, 189 (bibl.), 190 (bibl.), 207 (bibl.); heritage 21, 33, 70, 132, 139, 142; Indian 4, 139; internet slum 182; mass 37; philanthropic 58; poverty see also poorism, 144, 224 (bibl.); slum 14, 56–57, 58, 94, 117, 144–145, 164, 171, 183, 184, 188 (bibl.), 199 (bibl.), 200 (bibl.), 210 (bibl.), 213 (bibl.), 224 (bibl.); slum-as-dark 50; terrestrial 18; thana- 59, 82; urban 23; volunteer 28, 142, 228 (bibl.). See also mind-walking, mobility (-ies), pilgrimage (-s), travel (-s)
tourist (-s) 3, 16, 17, 49, 51, 62, 78, 81, 89, 92, 96, 107, 141, 149, 155, 165, 167, 178, 205 (bibl.), 207 (bibl.), 211 (bibl.), 216 (bibl.), 217 (bibl.): adventure 84; American 139; anti- 37; as 'collective alien' 127; audio-visual 72, 122; Baumanesque media 40; cinematic 38, 43, 46, 67, 72, 79, 83, 177, 182, 227 (bibl.); dark 71; development 168–169, 220 (bibl.); developmental 168–169, 220 (bibl.); disreputable 110; diversionary 39; drifter 87; edu- 143;

film 5, 212 (bibl.); global 134, 144, 154; Grand 44; hack 91; insensitive 157; middle-class 116, 158; modern 44; neo–nomad 153; Northern 38; post- 37; post-colonial 18, 43; singer 125; slum 24, 71, 157; vagabond 92; volunteer 173, 218 (bibl.), 226 (bibl.); Western cinematic 97; Western, 156. See also migrant (-s), traveller (-s), vagabond (-s)
tradition (-s) 7, 11, 70, 125, 127: artistic 171; documentary 66; Enlightenment 18; Euro–American cinematic 64; European philosophical 15; Hindu ethno-linguistic 32; Hindu 168; kathak 97; linguistic 81; non-European oral 76; sexist 64; spiritual 123; Western racist 42
trafficking 177–178, 210 (bibl.): cultural 8; drug 88, 103; human 42; Rubina Ali's 176; sex 46, 99, 103
Trainspotting (dir. Danny Boyle, 1996) 45, 46, 63, 64, 74, 82, 109
translation (-s) 4, 7, 41, 124, 126, 169, 170, 171, 193 (bibl.), 194 (bibl.), 195 (bibl.), 204 (bibl.), 207 (bibl.), 219 (bibl.), 223 (bibl.), 228 (bibl.): chains of 13; cultural 152; fixed 10; Hindi 47; of hegemonic ideology, 116, 141
transliteration (-s) 8, 13, 41, 124: global language of 99; plot's 47
travel (-s) 5, 6, 8, 10, 17, 20, 34, 35, 36, 37, 38, 39, 41, 45, 48, 50, 60, 72, 108, 114, 160, 171, 180, 181, 185 (bibl.), 191 (bibl.), 193 (bibl.), 196 (bibl.), 198 (bibl.), 199 (bibl.), 200 (bibl.), 201 (bibl.), 205 (bibl.), 213 (bibl.), 214 (bibl.), 221 (bibl.), 222 (bibl.), 224 (bibl.), 225 (bibl.), 227 (bibl.), 228 (bibl.): art of 32; cinematic heroes' 4; colonial 58; cosmologies of 144; deep 25; experiential 11, 15; genres of 159; imaginative 16, 37, 71, 114; kinship 84; lifestyle 181; non-European traditions of 77; slum 7; virtual 18. See also mind-walking, mobility, tourism
traveller (-s) 8, 16, 35, 40, 72, 150, 171, 193 (bibl.): artistic 42, 80; backpack 45; budget 41; business 24; -come-tourists 17; New Age 107; noetic 165; post-industrial 7; techno 108; Western 156; world 47. See also mobility, tourism, tourist

Tripathi, Ravi K. (Ravikant SriKrishna) (playback singer, b. Lalganj, Pratapgarh, Uttar Pradesh, 1978) 122

trope (-s) 108, 166, 176: colonial 80; dark tourist 60, 78, 159; of debt 33; of labour 58; of memory 135; mobility and nomadism 36

truth (-s) 34, 67, 69, 172, 193 (bibl.): fragile 5; fixed 175; socially constructed 177; ethical 183; emotional 74; personal 77; disciplinary 80; global developmental 88; virtuous 112; regimes of 123; ultimate 38. *See also* experience (-s), phaneroscopy, phenomenology

Turner Prize, 51, 90

underclass 85, 212 (bibl.), 215 (bibl.)
underworld 56, 211 (bibl.): Mumbai 58, 79; criminal 96
UNESCO (United Nations Scientific Committee, est. 1945) 20, 55, 138, 227 (bibl.)
United States 19, 36, 88, 89, 182
universal 152–153
untouchable (-s) 81, 143
Upanishads 61
urbanity 58, 86, 108: India's 63; multicultural 85; Mumbai's 13; segmented 109; tourist 79
Urdu 9, 115
utopia (-s) 148, 212 (bibl.), 226 (bibl.), 228 (bibl.): Platonic 62; labour 149; digital 149; spectacular 166; film's 62, 112; educational 141; family 71; filiative 80; childhood 104; travel 106
Uttar Pradesh, 135, 137

vagabond (-s) 11, 37–38, 49, 51, 89, 92, 101, 107: archetypical 78; disenfranchised 3; mobile 139; puerile 81. *See also* globalisation, migrant (-s), mobility, tourism
vagabondage 51: civilised, 155
value (-s) 6, 12, 24, 26, 68, 73, 78, 91, 102, 127, 152, 152, 170, 179, 187 (bibl.), 198 (bibl.), 200 (bibl.), 214 (bibl.), 216 (bibl.), 227 (bibl.): aesthetic 8, 11, 87; celebrity 179; community 157; cultural 30, 173; Eastern 172; family 47, 173, 178; generative 117; linguistic 123; material 81; non-contractual 175; pedagogical 73; place 181; practical 173; primary 40; slow 77; SM's 8; social 30; traditional 27; Western 172

vanishing 167, 207 (bibl.)
variables 22, 106: human 35; social 134
verisimilitude 47, 77: acting 100; film's 170, 171; SM's 49; story's 14
Versova (Mumbai slum) 135
viewpoint 30, 157: deliberator's 4; director's 26; localities' 27; SM's 67; tornadóros' 16; vantage 19; Western 66, 90
violence 111, 168, 171, 181, 202 (bibl.), 208 (bibl.): administrative 58; domestic 178; gang 58; social 57, 89, 95, 98; state 167; state-sponsored 103; structural 106; urban 58
Virgin Mary 65–66
vision 26, 31, 79, 94, 101, 134, 194 (bibl.), 205 (bibl.), 216 (bibl.), 229 (bibl.): aerial 105, 109, 153; alternative social 29; audio- 24, 193 (bibl.); camera-like 146; child's 82; cinematic 38; deep ecological 163; distorted 108; edu-tourist 151; fundamentalist 8; Ghandi's 122; God's 104; hallucinogenic 108; haptic 100; hero's 74; humorous 86; mechanical 14; moving 150; narrowing of 75; opposite 151; realist 63; statist 111; technologies of 75; technologised 152; utopian 110. *See also* aesthetics, synaesthesia, technology (-ies)
vision du monde 47: tragic 31
voyeurism 40, 155, 229 (bibl.); ethnographic 28
vulnerability 19, 63, 86, 169, 176, 184: human 62; Latika's 60; poor people's 162

Waka Waka (anthem) 122
wallah (-s) 62, 103–104, 106, 108, 169: chai 101
Walpole, Horace (politician, b. London, 1717 – d. London, 1797) 93
warlords 163
Way, Chris (Reality Tours co–founder) 144, 150, 151
Webber, Andrew Lloyd (composer, born Kensington, London, 1948) 50
Who Wants To Be A Millionaire? (British quiz show, 1998) 3, 14, 58, 59, 73, 75, 102, 109
Wien Westbahnhof Westbahn 126
woman 57, 63, 64, 77, 117, 207 (bibl.), 208 (bibl.), 229 (bibl.): brown 89;

de-hypostacised 67; Hindu, 111; Latika 59; light 119; raped 138
women 9, 12, 18, 89, 99, 100, 101, 109, 111, 119, 125, 159, 178, 179, 192 (bibl.), 208 (bbl.), 214 (bibl.), 218 (bibl.), 219 (bibl.), 222 (bibl.): cheap 97; destitute 50; European 171; learned 97; middle-class 64
work 5, 8, 9, 15, 32, 36, 40, 80, 89, 105, 132, 150, 152, 181, 183, 188 (bibl.), 204 (bibl.), 228 (bibl.): art- 7, 8, 11–16, 19, 27, 30, 34, 37, 39, 42, 44, 49, 50, 51, 61, 66, 70, 78, 89, 90, 92, 99, 106, 108, 116, 117, 121, 123, 126, 127, 133, 140, 145, 159, 162, 177, 183; Beaufoy's 44; Boyle's 55, 60; camera 16, 26, 41, 55, 56, 57, 58, 66, 74, 91; development 13, 177; dream 77, 86; ethnographic 157; Eurasian 8; memory 59, 72, 167, 167; music 26; philanthropic 173; sex 6
worldview 12, 37, 48, 69, 176,

Yadon Ki Barat (dir. Nasir Hussain, 1973) 68
You Tube 25, 89, 121, 125, 230 (bibl.)
Yuvvraaj (dir. Subhash Ghai 2008) 115

Zaidi, Hussein S. (author and journalist, b. Mumbai) 58
Zanjeer (dir. Prakash Mehra, 1973) 100
Zürich 126